DETROIT RED WINGS

Greatest Moments and Players

Stan Fischler

SPORTS PUBLISHING L.L.C.
www.SportsPublishingLLC.com

Director of Production: Susan M. Moyer
Book Design, Senior Project Manager: Jennifer L. Polson
Book Layout: Jennifer L. Polson, Jim Henehan, and Greg Hickman
Dust jacket design: Kenneth J. O'Brien
Developmental Editors: Joanna L. Wright and Noah Amstadter
Copy Editor: Cindy McNew

ISBN: 1-58261-271-4

SPORTS PUBLISHING L.L.C.
804 North Neil Street
Champaign, Illinois 61820

Visit our website at www.SportsPublishingLLC.com

*To my pal, Jimmy Devellano, who helped build
a dynasty on Long Island and then did a
wonderful encore in Detroit.*

*And to my coaching buddies, Scott Bowman,
Barry Smith and Dave Lewis.*

Contents

SECTION II

SECTION III

SECTION IV: THE FRONT OFFICE

ACKNOWLEDGMENTS

The rich and diverse history of the Detroit Red Wings is one that has been treated by many authors over the years. Most recently Brian McFarlane—as part of his "Original Six" series—covered some fascinating aspects of the Motor City sextet.

Other authors who have dealt with the Red Wings in one form or another include legendary Detroit writers Marshall Dann, Lew Walter, Bill Brennan and Joe Falls as well as contemporaries such as Mitch Albom, Terry Kulfan, Terry Foster, and Bob Wojnowski.

In addition, Colleen and Gordie Howe have covered many years—and stories—of Red Wings life in an assortment of books that they have produced in the past decade. Many correspondents for the Fischler Report contributed as well. Special thanks to Bob Matuszak in Dallas and Eric Reich in Buffalo, whose reporting helping immensely in the final draft. Both Bob and Eric were of special help in the research and writing of the contemporary Red Wings. Unending thanks to them as well as eminent hockey chroniclers like Dick Irvin, Scott Young, Bill Roche, Dick Beddoes, Russ Conway, David Cruise, Alison Griffiths, Gerry Eskenazi, Peter Gzowski, Bill Houston, Frank Orr and Charles Coleman took due notice of Detroit hockey heroics in their varied and informative works. Ditto for *Rinkside* magazine editor Keith Loria. Some material herewith originally appeared in *Rinkside.*

These and many others—too numerous to mention—provided insights and background for this publication. We acknowledge their contribution and appreciate their advancement of hockey history.

Without a doubt, this book would not have been possible without a hard-working staff of researchers including Jeff Klein, John Marino, Angela Panzarella, Justin Poitras, Eric Reich, Adam Rogowin, Michael Rudman, Joshua Samuelson, Brian Schiazza, Nicole Stern, Vanessa White, Adam Raider, Max Feinberg, and Joey Ruchinsky.

Thanks to that indomitable crew for their energetic efforts.

And of course, our enormous thanks to our friends at Sports Publishing L.L.C., especially Mike Pearson, Jenn Polson, and Joanna Wright for their patience and fortitude.

INTRODUCTION

When the Detroit Red Wings are singled out as a distinguished member of the National Hockey League's Original Six, the historical significance is twofold. On the one hand, Detroit's franchise dates back to the league's early expansion into the U.S. during the late 1920s. On the other hand, the Winged Wheel, which adorns the Red Wings' jersey, actually has its roots in the very origins of hockey.

It was the Montreal Athletic Association—otherwise known as the Winged Wheelers—which won the very first Stanley Cup. And it was the MAA's flying wheel logo that caught the eye of Detroit sportsman Jim Norris whose fortune put the Red Wings on the map. It was Norris who selected the name Red Wings for the hockey club after it had previously been known as the Cougars and the Falcons.

Few teams in any sport have been so steeped in history as the Motor City's hockey franchise. Nor have many been more successful.

Between Norris's leadership at the owner's level and Jack Adams's management genius, Detroit won two straight Cups in the mid-1930s and another in the midst of World War II.

But it wasn't until the post-WWII years that Adams's marvelous farm system paid its richest dividends. For a decade starting in the late 1940s, the Red Wings set a new standard of excellence, both in the regular season and in the playoffs. From 1948 to 1955, Detroit put together seven straight first-place teams. And beginning with a pulsating double overtime win in the seventh game of the 1950 finals, the Wings won four Stanley Cups in six years.

Such luminaries as Gordie Howe, Ted Lindsay, Terry Sawchuk and Sid Abel set a tradition that has been maintained in the past decade. Under the ownership of Mike and Marian Ilitch, the Red Wings have continued among the NHL's elite. When the Ilitches gave Jimmy Devellano the administrative reins in 1982, Jimmy D laid the foundation for Stanley Cups that would come in 1997 and 1998.

With Ken Holland as General Manager and living legend Scotty Bowman as coach, Detroit served notice into the new millenium that it is deservedly called Hockeytown, USA. Steve Yzerman, Chris Osgood, Sergei Fedorov, Brett Hull, Chris Chelios and Vladimir Konstantinov may have replaced the Howes, Lindsays and Delvecchios, but the luster of stardom shines at Joe Louis Arena as it once did at Olympia Stadium.

This book attempts to capture the feel of the Red Wings both past and present, acknowledging in detail the stars and their most memorable moments.

GORDIE HOWE

BORN: Floral, Saskatchewan, March 31, 1928
POSITION: Right Wing
NHL TEAMS: Detroit Red Wings, 1946-71; Hartford Whalers, 1979-80
AWARDS/HONORS: NHL First All-Star Team, 1951-1954, 1957, 1958, 1960,
1963, 1966, 1968-1970; NHL Second All-Star Team, 1949, 1950, 1956, 1959,
1961, 1962, 1964, 1965, 1967; Art Ross Trophy, 1951, 1952, 1953, 1954, 1957,
1958, 1960, 1963; Lester Patrick Trophy, 1967; NHL All-Star Game
1948-1955, 1957-1965, 1967-1971, 1980; Hockey Hall of Fame, 1972

He isn't called Mister Hockey for nothing. Gordie Howe has been called a number of other things as well. Like the greatest all-around hockey player who ever lived, certainly the most renowned stick handler ever to grace the city of Detroit and possibly the finest athlete ever to play pro in the state of Michigan.

No athlete in any sport has withstood the test of time as well as this Western Canadian, nor has any withstood physical punishment for so long and excelled at such a high level. In that sense, Howe clearly surpasses Wayne Gretzky.

Ironically, the beginning of Gordie Howe's Detroit saga coincided with the retirement of another Red Wing with the same surname. Syd Howe—no relation to Gordie—had been a splendid National Hockey League forward who retired at the close of World War II. It was precisely then that the new Howe arrived in the Motor City. Remarkably, the Howe named Gordie would remain a Red Wing from 1946 through 1971.

There have been many descriptions of Howe's artistry and strength from friend and foe alike. Perhaps the pithiest of all came from a New York Rangers right wing who played against Howe during the 1954-55 season.

In a moment of understated drollery, Aldo Guidolin, an opponent of Howe, once remarked,

"Gordie plays a funny kind of game; he doesn't let anyone else touch the puck!"

Howe was a right wing possessed of extraordinary strength in a body measuring six feet, one inch and 200 pounds, at a time when that was considered huge by league standards. Howe's armament was the most formidable the game has known. "His shot was uncanny," said goalie Glenn Hall, a Hall of Famer, "because it would come at the net in so many different ways."

Unique among superstars, Howe was an ambidextrous stick handler who would deliver a remarkably accurate shot with so fluid a motion that goalies frequently failed to see the puck leave Gordie's stick.

Howe's credentials said it all. He won the Hart Trophy as the NHL's most valuable player in 1952, 1953, 1957, 1958, 1960 and 1963. "He was not only the greatest hockey player I've ever seen," said defenseman Bill Gadsby, himself a Hall of Famer, "but also the greatest athlete."

Skating for the Red Wings, with whom he spent most of his professional career (1946-71), Gordie led the NHL in scoring in 1951, 1952, 1953, 1954, 1957 and 1963.

It has been said that hockey is a game of mistakes. And when one considers that players employ artificial feet (skates), artificial arms (sticks) and maneuver on

Gordie Howe

an artificial surface (ice), it is not surprising that errors are part of the game's fabric. Yet Howe was a flawless performer in a flawed and often brutal pastime.

Two episodes define the essential Howe. The first occurred on a night in March 1950, when a collision nearly ended his life at the age of 22. The Red Wings had taken on their bitter rivals, the Toronto Maple Leafs, in the opening round of the Stanley Cup playoffs.

Ted "Teeder" Kennedy, the Leafs' captain and center, was carrying the puck toward the Wings' zone when Howe swerved diagonally across the ice to intercept his foe. A split second before Gordie connected, Kennedy pulled up and, according to the Red Wings, fouled Howe with his stick. Gordie was catapulted into the wooden sideboards, and he crumpled to the ice with a fractured skull. Removed to a hospital, Gordie was considered a goner. His mother was summoned from distant Saskatchewan and, at best, it was presumed that if he did manage to survive, Howe would never again play professional hockey. A year later he was the league's scoring leader.

The second incident took place during a regular-season game between the Wings and the New York

Rangers. Howe had learned from the Kennedy affair that, for survival in the ice jungle, it was essential to hit first, keep the elbows high and ask questions later. "Gordie," explained Islanders' general manager Bill Torrey, "would simply psych out his enemies."

Rangers coach Phil Watson had assigned his big, rambunctious left wing Eddie Shack the dubious task of checking Howe. At one point the two collided behind the Rangers' net, whereupon Shack's teammate, Lou Fontinato, then regarded as the NHL's best fighter, pushed in and began flailing at Gordie. It was the worst move in Fontinato's career.

Referee Art Skov, who was only three feet away from the battlers, described the ensuing blows: "Howe began smashing him with lefts and rights and then fired an uppercut that broke Lou's nose. I just stood back and said, 'No way I'm going to break up this one.' Big George Hayes was the other linesman in the game, and he told me to stay out of it. Howe cleaned Fontinato like you'd never seen."

It was a measure of Howe's absolute superiority over all challengers that he not only outperformed but also outlasted the aces with whom he was most frequently compared. In the early 1950s the standard argument was: "Who's better, Gordie Howe or Maurice Richard?" Yet upon his retirement in 1960, Richard was the first to allow that Howe was the best of them all. "Gordie," said Richard, "could do everything."

Howe was already an NHL star when Bobby Orr was born in 1948. And Gordie was still in the majors when Orr retired as an NHL defenseman in 1979. Neither Richard nor Orr, nor any other skater for that matter, could compare with Howe when it came to surviving the test of time.

Ironically, as a youngster Gordie suffered severe doubts about his ability to make a career out of hockey, although from the moment of his NHL debut, he had winner written all over him. Even after he led all scorers in the 1949 playoffs, Gordie wondered how he rated against the Richards and Kennedys. "I still wasn't sure I was a star," Howe explained. "When I went home to Saskatchewan that summer, I started playing baseball again. One day, a kid came up for my autograph, and while I signed it, he said, 'Mister Howe, what do you do in the winter?'"

In 1971 Gordie played his last game for the Red Wings and accepted what he later, sadly, discovered was an innocuous front-office job. After two years of inac-

OPPOSITE: He's called Mr. Hockey for good reason. Nobody—not even Wayne Gretzky—could match Gordie Howe's total skills as a performer.

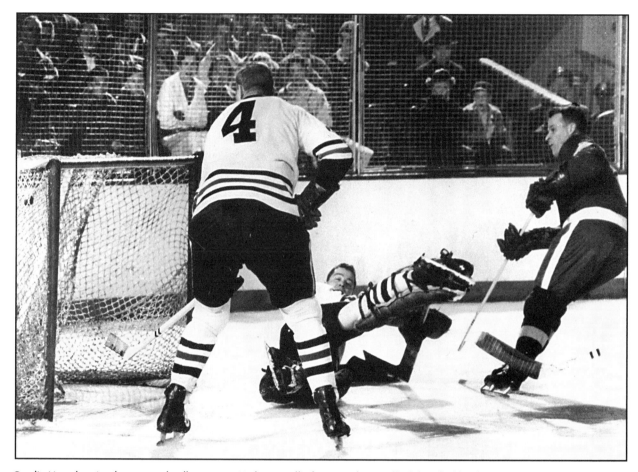

Gordie Howe's wrist shot was a deadly weapon. He beats Hall of Famer Glenn Hall of the Blackhawks in a game at Olympia Stadium.

tivity, Gordie executed one of the most astonishing comebacks in sports history. At age 45, he signed with the Houston Aeros of the World Hockey Association. Among his teammates were his sons Mark and Marty. Slower perhaps but no less superb, Gordie orchestrated the Aeros the way Leonard Bernstein conducted the New York Philharmonic. Houston won the AVCO World Cup and the WHA title. That done, Gordie was selected to play for Team Canada against the Soviet All-Star team. Having shown the Russians the tricks of his trade, Howe returned to Houston and led the Aeros to another AVCO Cup in 1975.

Gordon Howe was born March 31, 1928, in Floral, Saskatchewan, near the city of Saskatoon. Gordie was the fourth of nine children born to Catherine and Albert Howe. The Howes were a loving family, but like so many others living through the Great Depression, they were poor.

"The only equipment I had was skates," Howe remembered, "and a stick. I took magazines and mail order catalogs, stuck 'em in my socks and had shin pads. I tied 'em together with rubber bands made from inner tubes. We played with tennis balls instead of a puck. The ball would get so hard from the cold [often 30-40 degrees below zero, Fahrenheit], we'd have to get new ones all the time. A woman next door used to warm them up in an oven for us."

Despite the hardship, Gordie recalled his youthful hockey years with affection. Long after he had established himself as the game's greatest star, he acknowledged that his most fervent wish was to skate on a line with his eldest sons, Mark and Marty. That wish came true on February 17, 1971.

"It was," said Howe, "the game I'll never forget."

It was an exhibition charity match—the Detroit Red Wings against the Junior A Red Wings. Gordie skated alongside his kids, who then played for the Junior club. It was then that Gordie perceived what other hockey scouts later would realize—that Mark Howe possessed many of the same ice gifts as his dad.

No matter where Howe skated, his trademark—effortless excellence—made an impression on critics. "Gordie had the ability and the knack for making the difficult plays look easy, routine," said Chicago Blackhawks vice president Tommy Ivan, who had coached Howe in Detroit.

He was no less appreciated in Hartford, where he emigrated with his two boys in 1977 to play for the WHA Whalers. When Hartford was admitted to the NHL in 1979, Gordie returned to his former hunting grounds and drew capacity crowds as a Whaler. They wanted to see whether the 50-year-old grandfather could skate with young Turks like Bryan Trottier, Marcel Dionne and Wayne Gretzky.

"Gordie proved that he could," said Whalers president Howard Baldwin. "In our first year in the NHL, we were the only former WHA team to make the playoffs. We can thank Gordie for that."

Howe retired at the age of 51, but remained close to the game in various capacities for another two decades.

In 32 years, Gordie scored 975 goals, had 1,383 assists and tallied 2,358 points, totals exceeded only by Gretzky. But most of Howe's points were obtained when the value of a goal in a defense-oriented game was considerably more than it is today. He was an incredibly gifted forward, an accomplished defensive player, revered as a team man and the only player to have dominated three eras—the postwar NHL, the Golden Era of the 1960s and the Expansion Era.

"Hockey," Gordie liked to say, "is a man's game."

In that game, Gordie Howe was *the* man.

In his prime, Gordie Howe had the perfect build for a hockey player. He was one of the biggest and strongest skaters and rarely was knocked down in front of the net. Here, he beats Chicago's Glenn Hall while teammate Johnny Wilson watches the puck hit the twine.

2

Steve Yzerman

BORN: Cranbrook, British Columbia, May 9, 1965
POSITION: Center
NHL TEAMS: Detroit Red Wings, 1983–Present
AWARDS/HONORS: NHL All-Rookie Team, 1984;
Lester B. Pearson Award, 1989; Conn Smythe Trophy, 1998;
Frank J. Selke Trophy, 2000; NHL First All-Star Team, 2000;
NHL All-Star Game, 1984, 1988-1993, 1997, 2000

Throughout his illustrious career, Steve Yzerman has heard all the praise and accolades that the captain of a two-time Stanley Cup championship team rightfully receives. He has shown it all—determination, grit, perseverance, leadership and resiliency.

But one word best personifies this native of British Columbia: loyalty.

Playing in an era where hockey players quickly bolted teams for the almighty dollar, Yzerman never wavered from his undying spirit and loyalty for his one and only team, the Detroit Red Wings.

"I love playing in Detroit," said Yzerman. "I feel honored to play for an Original Six team that has so much tradition both on and off the ice. To play my whole career here is something that I want to do." And he did!

But were it not for the sweet-talking of then-Detroit general manager Jimmy Devellano, Yzerman might have played on Long Island. The Islanders were his favorite team while he was groing up outside of Ottawa in suburban Nepean.

As a youth, Yzerman idolized Islanders' Hall of Famer Bryan Trottier. Trottier could systematically read

a game, showing his offensive skills when need be, or playing a more controlled and disciplined game when times warranted.

"I grew up loving the Islanders ever since they first joined the league," said Yzerman. "Trottier was my hero growing up. That's who I patterned myself after. He's the reason why I wear No. 19."

Moments before the 1983 NHL Entry Draft, Yzerman almost got his wish to play on the Island. Detroit owner Mike Ilitch, who had purchased the club just a year earlier on June 22, 1982, nearly pulled the trigger on a deal that would have sent Yzerman to the defending Stanley Cup-champion Islanders.

The Red Wings had the fourth overall pick that year, thanks to their lackluster 57-point season. In addition, the club was in the midst of one of the most lackluster periods in its rich history. For 14 straight seasons, Detroit had ended the regular season with a record below .500. And not surprisingly, attendance lagged.

Determined to begin a new era, Ilitch wanted to select the offensively dynamic Pat LaFontaine, who was from nearby Waterford, Michigan. According to Ilitch, LaFontaine was just what the Red Wings needed at that time. He possessed great speed, an uncanny stick han-

OPPOSITE: Detroit captain Steve Yzerman has spent his entire career with the Detroit Red Wings.

Yzerman is considered one of the hardest working Red Wings.

dling ability, and more importantly from a marketing standpoint, good looks and charisma.

The Islanders, who were to draft one slot ahead of Detroit, had also planned to select LaFontaine. Ilitch talked to the New York brass about possibly swapping picks, enabling him to select his prized player. He was even prepared to pay the Islanders an extra $1 million bonus for the rights to LaFontaine.

But Devellano knew better. He quickly persuaded Ilitch to go with Yzerman, who was playing junior hockey for the Peterborough Petes of the Ontario Hockey League. Devellano argued that Yzerman might not have LaFontaine's scoring prowess but was the kind of player around whom the Red Wings could rebuild their struggling franchise.

Ilitch relented. Soon after Brian Lawton, Sylvain Turgeon and LaFontaine were selected, the Red Wings picked Yzerman.

"Well, if I did wind up with the Islanders," Yzerman would later say, "I wouldn't have been able to wear No. 19."

Yzerman's toughness as a hockey player has never been questioned. But "Captain Cup," as his adoring fans in Detroit call him, suffered through some horrible and downtrodden times while ascending to the summit.

"I don't think I'm unlucky," he said. "Things happen. Not just to me, but to all players. A lot of good things have happened to me."

But before the good came the not-so-good.

In the opening game of the 1984 Canada Cup Tournament, Yzerman crashed heavily into the boards at the old Montreal Forum. The collision resulted in a hip-pointer and knocked the youngster out of the game. After the contest, Yzerman was barely able to walk, and his status for the rest of the tournament was in jeopardy.

But showing the determination and fortitude that would become his trademark, Yzerman rebounded after missing just four games. He returned to the lineup to help Team Canada win the event, even though he accumulated no points in the four games that he played.

In March 1988, Yzerman tore ligaments in his right knee during the same game in which he scored his 50th goal of the season. He missed the final 15 games of the regular season as well as the first two playoff rounds.

On April 14, 1994, Yzerman sprained his right knee on the final night of the regular season, with just two minutes remaining in the contest. The Red Wings collected 100 points that season, but Yzerman's injury ruined the team's chances of hoisting the Stanley Cup.

He missed the first four games of Round 1 of the playoff series against San Jose, returning for Game 5, but was a nonfactor for the rest of the series. The Red Wings were upset by the upstart Sharks in seven games.

"Steve has always felt the need to carry the weight of the team on his shoulders," said assistant coach Dave Lewis

"Not only is he great in terms of how he has played, but he's been an inspiration to others because they see him playing in pain," said general manager Ken Holland. "There have been times when it was almost like he grabbed the team and said, 'I will find a way to lead you to victory,' and then he would do it."

"Steve works so hard, he deserves only the best in this game," said former teammate Bob Errey. "He's genuine; not a phony in a game full of them."

Steve Yzerman was born on May 9, 1965, in Cranbrook, British Columbia. His family moved to Nepean when he was young and instilled in Steve the values of a good attitude and hard work.

As a youngster, he always dreamed of hoisting the Stanley Cup. But as a professional, that dream was slowly evaporating, as the Red Wings improved during his early years but couldn't seem to get to the next level.

In 1993, the Red Wings hired Scotty Bowman to be their coach. He had already won the Stanley Cup six times when he was hired by Mike Ilitch. Bowman immediately instituted a defensive style of play, much to the chagrin of his captain, Yzerman.

Nonetheless, Bowman decided to change the way his captain played. He knew that Yzerman had the offensive skills, but for the team to succeed and take its game to another level, it required Yzerman to become an even smarter, more disciplined player.

"Steve made a conscious effort to change his style and play the way Scotty wanted," said teammate Brendan Shanahan. "But then he went back to doing some of the other things he could do offensively as well. I think sometimes one of the first things you do when you start playing Scotty's style is you err on the side of caution, and I think Stevie's come full circle. He knows his game, he knows his defensive game, and now he's going out and attacking, too."

During the lockout-shortened 1994-95 season, the Red Wings' Stanley Cup Finals opponent was the Eastern Conference's New Jersey Devils. Yzerman and his teammates were confident that they could beat Jacques Lemaire's trap and bring Detroit the silver mug. But New Jersey beat Detroit at every facet of the game, sweeping the Red Wings four games to none. It was an embarrassing loss, especially for the captain.

"The thing that I'm surprised about is getting swept and losing," a dejected Yzerman said afterward. "I didn't expect that. I thought we'd have more success against them. I thought eventually we'd be able to persevere and get through their defensive shell. Obviously, we couldn't do that.

"I think the key to the whole series was after Game 1. We not only lost that game, but we were outshot [28-17]. We were sort of bewildered. But I thought that if we came out in Game 2 and only recorded another 17 shots that we would need to change things up. We ended up managing 18 shots in Game 2, and that was pretty much it for us."

Undaunted, the Wings reached the Stanley Cup Finals for the second time in three years in 1997. Their opponent was the Eric Lindros–led Philadelphia Flyers. Before the series, pundits salivated over the matchup between Detroit's disciplined style and the physical style of the Flyers. But everyone knew who the key was for Detroit.

"Stevie is playing unbelievable hockey for us right now, killing penalties and playing on the power plays," said teammate Kris Draper. "You see the fire in his eyes, and that definitely rubs off on you."

Yzerman anxiously awaited the start of the series, wanting desperately to throw off the albatross of playoff failure.

"The last couple of years we'd play well defensively, and the strongest weapon we had was our explosiveness," he said before Game 1. "This year, we've been content with not being as explosive, and the players are more comfortable. It's going to be one of those games where we fight along the boards, dump it in and dump it out and wait for a scoring chance to happen. I think we're more able to wait than we have in the past because we don't have the explosiveness."

Before the series, and perhaps as a motivating ploy, coach Bowman paid his seasoned veteran the ultimate compliment.

"Steve doesn't take a second off," he said. "There are a select few players who show up for every game and every practice. That's why they get to where they are. [Wayne] Gretzky was like that. Bobby Orr was like that. [Guy] Lafleur was like that in Montreal.

"We try to encourage them to take time off, but they don't want it. You never have to push them. They push themselves."

His teammate and card-playing buddy Joey Kocur offered this analysis of Yzerman's questioned ability to lead a team to a Stanley Cup victory.

"Steve has always been more of a quiet leader," said Kocur. "This year he has stepped up more and he's

Yzerman celebrates winning hockey's ultimate prize.

saying his piece a little more. Before, he didn't know what to say or how to say it because a lot of players were older than him. He was a young captain. But if he sees something going on now, he's the first one to step in and straighten it out."

In the locker room after St. Louis had humiliated the Red Wings 4-0 in Game 4 of Round 1, Yzerman lashed out first and foremost at himself, then calmly but emphatically went on to explain to his teammates what the team's problem was. The silence in the room as the captain spoke was deafening. But his comrades got the message.

"He was putting a lot of pressure on himself, and us as well," said Shanahan as he described Yzerman's monologue. "When you say something like he did, the first thing you have to take care of is yourself. He went out and scored the first goal of the next game."

Detroit won Game 5 by a score of 5-2, aided by Yzerman's 80-foot slap shot, which staked the Red Wings to an early lead. His teammates soon followed, and the Red Wings qualified for the showdown with the Flyers in the Finals by winning 10 of their next 12 games.

The elusive ring was just four wins away.

"As you've been in the league a few years, you get to know more guys, and a lot of your friends have won Stanley Cup rings," Yzerman said. "Envy isn't the word, but you dream of the day you get a chance to win one. I'm excited to have another opportunity.

"But my approach is to have fun. My desire to win the Cup hasn't changed at all, but I'm not consumed by it now. I want to experience the celebration of winning the Cup, of getting to carry it around the ice. I've dreamed about it since I was a little kid."

And with those words, Steve Yzerman led his team to a four-game sweep of the Flyers, capturing Lord Stanley's Cup for Detroit for the first time since 1955.

Flyer general manager Bobby Clarke witnessed firsthand how his team was beaten with buzz-saw efficiency. "I don't think teams like Detroit happen by accident," said Clarke, who won two Stanley Cups himself as a player for the Flyers in the 1970s. "They're obviously well coached and obviously well led. Leadership comes from the captain of the club. Yzerman had a huge influence, both on the opposition and also on his own teammates."

But tragedy marred the victory as two team members incurred serious injuries in an automobile accident. Team masseur Sergei Mnatsakanov and defenseman Vladimir Konstantinov both suffered severe nerve damage in the wreck, leaving Konstantinov paralyzed and unable to play hockey again.

Yzerman and his team dedicated the following season to their fallen friends—and Detroit won its second straight Stanley Cup.

The challengers were the Washington Capitals. Again, Detroit trounced its opponent, four games to none.

Yzerman was brilliant during that run, leading all scorers with 24 points in 22 games. He won the Conn Smythe Trophy as Most Valuable Player in the playoffs.

"He was phenomenal," said teammate Darren McCarty about Yzerman's award-winning performance. "He's one of the hardest workers. It's motivation. You can't be on top of your game all the time, but seeing him out there doing all the little things; that's what the team is all about."

In Game 2, Yzerman scored two goals, including a third-period tally that sparked a Detroit comeback from a 3-1 deficit. The Red Wings eventually won the game in overtime, 5-4. But Yzerman's best decision of the playoffs was made in Game 4—on the bench. With two minutes to play, the Stanley Cup victory was well in hand. Yzerman began to think about the postgame Cup ceremony.

At first, he decided to give the prize to goaltender Chris Osgood, the often-maligned net minder who had vindicated himself of prior years' failures with a tremendous performance in the playoffs.

But then, Brendan Shanahan and Igor Larionov leaned over to their captain with a proposition. The two asked Yzerman if he could give the Cup to Konstantinov, who was actually at rink level in his wheelchair, waiting to be carted onto the ice for the postgame celebration.

"It was an automatic decision," said Yzerman. "At this time a year ago, we still weren't sure if either Vladdie or Sergei were going to survive, so to have him on the ice with us was pretty significant."

True to his word, Yzerman handed the mug to Konstantinov in one of the most emotional and touching moments ever witnessed at a championship celebration. And if the world didn't know what type of person Steve Yzerman was before that moment, it certainly did now.

During a six-year period, from 1987-88 through 1992-93, Yzerman posted numbers that were simply phenomenal—scoring 331 goals and registering 732

points, an average of 55 goals and 122 points per season.

Included was an electrifying 65-goal and 90-assist season in 1988-89 that earned him the Lester B. Pearson Award as the top performer in the league, as voted by his peers. Both marks are Red Wing franchise records. Besides Yzerman, only three other players ever topped the 150-point barrier—Wayne Gretzky, Phil Esposito and Mario Lemieux.

In addition, Yzerman recorded the top three single-season goal-scoring totals and the top two assist marks in the franchise's long history. He also holds the Red Wings' record for most goals (39) and most points (87) by a rookie, finished second to Tom Barrasso in the Calder Trophy voting for Rookie of the Year honors and was selected to the NHL All-Rookie team in 1984.

But of all the celebrated and dazzling goals that Yzerman has scored, perhaps his most dramatic was in the 1996 Stanley Cup playoffs against the St. Louis Blues. The Wings had forced a seventh game with a dramatic Game 6 victory in St. Louis. Thus the stage was set for a winner-take-all battle.

The game was played on May 16, 1996, at Joe Louis Arena in Detroit. The teams skated hard all night but could not put anything past net minders Grant Fuhr and Mike Vernon. Regulation time ended with the scoreboard showing goose eggs under both clubs' names.

The first overtime came and went, as again Fuhr and Vernon continued their mastery over the tiring skaters. But during the second overtime, Yzerman gathered the puck in the neutral zone and crossed the St. Louis blue line, galloping down the right side. Steve took two strides as he crossed the blue line and wound up to take a long slap shot.

As the puck left his stick, it elevated so quickly and dramatically that it startled everyone on the ice. Most important, the shot shocked Fuhr, and the net minder, known for his catlike reflexes, was unable to lift his shoulder in time to prevent the puck from going behind him. The Red Wings had won the game, 1-0.

"Yeah, there's a certain amount of gratification in having my name included on a trophy with so many great players," Yzerman said after winning the Conn Smythe. "When I first came into the league, I don't think there were many people who could correctly spell or pronounce my name. Winning this award along with the Stanley Cup definitely is a nice stamp on my career."

3

LEONARD PATRICK "RED" KELLY

BORN: Simcoe, Ontari,; July 9, 1927
POSITION: Defenseman
NHL TEAMS: Detroit Red Wings, 1947-59; Toronto Maple Leafs, 1959-67;
Coach, Los Angeles Kings, 1967-69; Pittsburgh Penguins, 1970-73;
Toronto Maple Leafs, 1973-77
AWARDS/HONORS: Norris Trophy, 1954;
Lady Byng Trophy, 1951, 1953, 1954, 1961; NHL First All-Star Team,
1951, 1952, 1953, 1954, 1955, 1957; NHL Second All-Star Team, 1950, 1956;
Hockey Hall of Fame, 1969

Leonard Patrick "Red" Kelly was the most deceptively versatile player ever to don the red-and-white Detroit Red Wings jersey.

So mild-mannered, neer uttering a curse word, Kelly nevertheless was one of the NHL's most feared fighters during those rare occasions when he engaged in fisticuffs. Likewise, he was a nonpareil defenseman, yet he could carry the puck on attack better than most of the foremost forwards. Half his career was spent as an All-Star backliner and the other half as a commanding center. An NHLer doesn't come more versatile than that.

One could also make a solid case that the redhead was the finest Detroit blueliner of the pre-expansion era and perhaps the best of them all. In a sense, Kelly was also a trailblazer.

Throughout the first half-century of hockey history, defensemen were expected to defend, and defend only. Goaltenders were paid to stop the puck, while forwards had a mission of their own—to score goals. Very few defensemen ever broke the tradition. One who did was Eddie Shore, the immortal Boston Bruins backliner who perfected the end-to-end rush during the late 1920s and 1930s.

Like Shore, Kelly was equally proficient at defending and rushing the puck. It was Kelly who was the first of the modern backliners to carry the rubber deep into the enemy zone. Kelly was every bit as smooth a rusher as Bobby Orr and a much better defender. What better proof than the fact that Red skated for eight championship squads and four Stanley Cup winners in Detroit? (By contrast, Orr played for only four first-place teams and two Cup winners.) Red won the Lady Byng Trophy for competence combined with gentlemanly play four times and was a First All-Star six times.

In 1959, after more than 12 seasons and four Stanley Cups as a Red Wing, Red fell into disfavor with Detroit hockey boss Jack Adams. At first the Red Wings' GM tried trading Red to the New York Rangers, but Kelly refused the move and "retired" instead. Finally, Kelly was dealt to the Toronto Maple Leafs. Adams figured that Red was washed up. The Leafs, on the other hand, were being rejuvenated by general manager

OPPOSITE: The first of the truly outstanding rushing defensemen of the post-World War II era, Red Kelly excelled on defense as well as on the attack.

Red Kelly (right) was one of the NHL's cleanest defensemen, but occasionally his stick rose above shoulder level. The victim in 1959 action is Red Sullivan of the Rangers.

George "Punch" Imlach. Punch didn't think Kelly was through, not by a long shot.

The turnabout and the events preceding it were most unusual for both Kelly and the NHL high command. During the 1959-60 season, Red appeared to be a fixture in the Motor City because of his unwavering competence and devotion to the team. But the Wings' aging and crusty manager had become angry with Red because of a contract dispute they had had the previous summer.

Adams stewed over the dispute, and midway into the season dealt Kelly and forward Billy McNeill to New York for defenseman Bill Gadsby and forward Eddie Shack. "When I heard about the trade," said Kelly, "it didn't take me long to make up my mind about what I was going to do. I decided to retire rather than go to New York. So did McNeill."

Kelly didn't know it at the time, but his stance was the predecessor of free agency in hockey. The NHL was rocked by his decision, and the Rangers, not surprisingly, cried foul. Adams had no choice but to call off the deal while Gadsby and Shack returned to the Rangers.

NHL President Clarence Campbell advised Kelly that he had five days to report back to Detroit or go on the retirement list. "If I went on the retirement list," said Kelly, "I couldn't become active again if even one NHL club objected."

Kelly returned home and mulled over the matter for three days. He finally decided—reluctantly—to quit the game and concentrate on his bowling alley and tobacco farm. Two days remained before Campbell's deadline took force when King Clancy, assistant coach of the Maple Leafs, phoned. "Punch (Imlach) wants you on his hockey club," snapped Clancy. "Come to Toronto and the three of us will talk about it."

Unlike most of his contemporaries, Imlach believed that older, experienced hockey players were more useful in building a championship team than youngsters. He pointed out to Kelly how important he would be to the Maple Leafs' future even though he had turned thirty-two. Kelly was persuaded and agreed to play in Toronto providing that a deal could be worked out with Adams. Imlach phoned Detroit and offered Marc Reaume, a younger defenseman who was believed to be a potential ace.

Adams approved the trade, but there was still the league to contend with, particularly Rangers general manager Muzz Patrick, who was furious over Kelly's snub of New York. The deal was ultimately approved, but not before Kelly phoned his nemesis Adams. "I had to tell him I was reporting back to the Wings," said Red, "so he could reinstate me and trade me to the Leafs."

Had the trade not been consummated, and had Kelly retired as threatened, Red would have been remembered for what he was: one of the game's premier defensemen. But the night of February 10, 1960, proved to be a milestone in Red's life and in the life of the Maple Leafs. He donned the royal blue and white Toronto jersey and was presented with the same No. 4 jersey he wore in Detroit.

Imlach the innovator was not certain precisely how he would exploit Kelly's talents, but he knew for sure that he would at least experiment with him at center, although Red had been a defenseman all his life. The Leafs' opponents that night were the Montreal Canadiens, already winners of four straight Stanley Cups and perhaps the greatest team of all time.

"I want you to go up against [Jean] Beliveau," said Imlach. The tall, majestic Beliveau was merely the best center in the league. Kelly skated to center ice, lined up opposite Beliveau and waited for the referee to drop the puck for the opening faceoff. "I was as nervous as a rookie," said Kelly. "I won the draw and sent the puck straight into the Montreal zone. The Canadiens' goalie, Jacques Plante, darted out to intercept the puck before I got there. I came right down like a shot and somehow got tangled up and went head over heels—into the net!"

Although the Leafs lost the game, 4-2, Imlach knew that his instincts were correct. Red would be more valuable to him as a center than as a defenseman. Never has the game known a more brilliant brainstorm. The next question was: With whom should Kelly play?

Imlach had a huge, brooding young left wing named Frank "The Big M" Mahovlich, who could skate like a zephyr and fire the puck with the fury of a howitzer. Somehow, the Big M's power had not yet been harnessed, no doubt for want of a competent center. The Leafs also had Bob Nevin, an unobtrusive right wing, but one who excelled at all of a forward's basic skills. Imlach decided to unite Kelly with Mahovlich and Nevin.

From that point on, the Maple Leafs' troubles were over. With Kelly ladling the passes to the Big M and Nevin, the Maple Leafs won four Stanley Cups in the seven and a half years that Red played in Toronto. (Bill Gadsby, for whom Kelly was traded, played 20 years in the NHL and never skated for a Stanley Cup champion.)

Even more astonishing is the fact that Kelly was able to maintain his standard of excellence on the ice in Toronto while serving a term as a member of Canada's Parliament.

Leonard Patrick Kelly was born July 9, 1927, in Simcoe, Ontario, and like so many youngsters determined to become professional hockey players, he enrolled at Toronto's St. Michael's College (a private high school by American standards), where he teamed with such future NHLers as Ted Lindsay and Jim Thomson.

"When I was ready to turn pro," Kelly recalled, "the scouts took a good look at me. The Leafs didn't want me because their scout said I wasn't good enough to last 20 games in the NHL. Detroit didn't see it that way, so the Red Wings signed me." Red was only 17 when he launched his major league career in Detroit.

Low-key throughout his hockey and political careers, Kelly to this day remains the most underrated superstar to come down the pike, yet his dossier cannot be disputed. He was the balance wheel of champions as a defenseman in Detroit, and as a center, he was the most decisive factor in creating a dynasty in Toronto more than a decade later.

No other hockey player can make that statement, which is why Red Kelly sits high in the annals of both the Red Wings and the Maple Leafs.

4

ROBERT BLAKE THEODORE "TED" LINDSAY

BORN: Renfrew, Ontario, July 29, 1925
POSITION: Left Wing
NHL TEAMS: Detroit Red Wings, 1944-57, 1964-65;
Chicago Black Hawks, 1957-60; General Manager,
Detroit Red Wings, 1977-80; Coach, Detroit Red Wings, 1980-81.
AWARDS/HONORS: Art Ross Trophy, 1950;
First All-Star Team, 1948, 1950-54, 1956-57; Second All-Star Team, 1949;
Hockey Hall Of Fame, 1966

Twenty-five years after retirement as a Detroit Red Wings forward in 1965, Ted Lindsay was still on skates roaming the left alley in old-timers' games—with nearly the same vim, vigor and vitality he had displayed during his prime. His aggressive style had not eroded with time. At age 56, Lindsay was so aggressive that some players urged that he not be invited back again.

Vigor could have been Lindsay's middle name, although opponents might have preferred the term *vicious* or *venal*. After all, he didn't get the nickname "Terrible Ted" because he was Mister Nice Guy.

Like Maurice "The Rocket" Richard, Lindsay played with a no-holds-barred intensity that often exceeded passion. So hated was his opponent that Ted considered it absolutely *verboten* to ever talk to the enemy off the ice, except in one mitigating circumstance: discussion of the formation of a National Hockey League Players' Association.

"By my definition," said Lindsay, "there's one helluva lot more to being a tough guy than getting in a few phony fights where no real punches are tossed. To me, being tough includes wanting to win so badly that you give it all you got every shift, going into corners without phoning ahead to see who's there, backing up your mates if they're in trouble, and stepping into guys even if they're bigger than you."

One of Lindsay's most devastating bouts included the Bruins' "Wild Bill" Ezinicki. The fight, at Olympia Stadium in Detroit, took place on January 25, 1951. When it was over, Ezinicki had lost a tooth and had acquired two black eyes, a broken nose and 19 stitches. Lindsay needed only five stitches above his eye, but he was treated for badly scarred and swollen knuckles on his right hand.

Apart from his labor-organizing activities, which immersed him in a cauldron of trouble away from the rink, Lindsay dedicated himself to fighting for the Red Wings and then—briefly—for the Chicago Blackhawks.

The results were impressive. He came to Detroit as a teenager toward the end of World War II and hung up his skates two decades later in the midst of the Cold War. In between he accomplished just about everything

OPPOSITE: He might look like a choirboy, but Ted Lindsay usually played like a Tasmanian devil. He was clearly the greatest left wing in Red Wings history.

"Terrible" Ted played 13 seasons in Detroit.

a professional hockey player could wish for—and then some.

It was Lindsay, Gordie Howe and Sid Abel who made up the famous "Production Line" for the Wings. Furthermore, during his 13 seasons with Detroit, Ted played on eight first-place teams, four of which were Stanley Cup champions.

Lindsay's blazing competitive spirit made him one of the toughest and most feared skaters in the NHL, although by today's standards, Ted was virtually miniscule. Stature notwithstanding, Lindsay was one of the best left wings of his generation and one of the meanest of all time.

More than that, Lindsay was a courageous rebel: He was one of the first organizers of the Players' Association. For this act, the lords of hockey duly punished him, and like fellow organizers Jim Thomson and Doug Harvey, he was traded to a mediocre team—in Lindsay's case, hapless Chicago. "The concept we had for the Players' Association," said Lindsay, "was not the household for all players in the NHL. What we were aiming for was to benefit the game of hockey, not just the players."

Rowdy and rambunctious, Lindsay accumulated over 760 stitches on his person, mementos from his various battles waged on the ice. The stitches earned him the moniker "Scarface," in addition to several other nicknames that attested to his aggressive style of play, such as "Terrible Ted" and "Tempestuous Ted."

At 5'8" and only 163 pounds, Ted resented players who thought they might take advantage of his small stature. He would not be intimidated. "Okay, so I was cocky," he admitted, reflecting on his career. "I had the idea that I had to beat up on everyone in the league, and I'm still not convinced it wasn't a good idea. Probably I'd do it the same way if I did it over again. That's the way I am."

Once during a game between the Red Wings and the Toronto Maple Leafs, Ted battled Gus Mortson all night. The peculiarity of this situation was that Gus had been Ted's friend since boyhood, a teammate at St. Michael's College and also a partner with Lindsay in a

In his last championship year with Detroit, captain Ted Lindsay backhands a shot at goalie Jacques Plante.

gold mine they owned near Kirkland Lake. "I don't know anybody when a hockey game starts," Ted explained.

In his 17-year career, Lindsay played in 1,068 games, scored 379 goals and added 472 assists for a total of 851 points. He also spent 1,808 minutes in the penalty box, ranking him high on the all-time penalty leaders list. In 133 playoff games, Ted scored 47 goals and 49 assists for 96 points and spent 194 minutes in the penalty box.

In 1949-50, while playing in 69 games, Ted scored 23 goals and registered 55 assists for 78 points, which garnered him the Art Ross Trophy as the league's leading scorer during the regular season. Lindsay was a league leader of another ilk in 1958-59 when he spent 184 minutes in the sin bin while playing for Chicago.

Lindsay also made the First All-Star Team eight times, first in the 1947-48 season, and then from 1949-50 to 1953-54. He repeated during 1955-56 and 1956-57 and was named to the Second-All Star Team in 1948-49.

Robert Blake Theodore Lindsay was born in Renfrew, Ontario, on July 29, 1925. The youngest of six brothers, Ted's large family also included three sisters. His dad, Bert, had been a fine hockey player a generation previous, in goal for the Renfrew Million-

aires of the National Hockey Association, then for the NHL's Montreal Wanderers in 1917-18 and the Toronto Arenas in 1918-19.

Ted tried goaltending in an attempt to follow in his dad's footsteps. "But I soon discovered I'd rather shoot than be shot at, so I gave up goaltending," he remarked.

By this time, World War II was in full force, and in 1940 the five older Lindsay boys joined the armed forces. With no more family practices to join, Ted tried out for—and made—the Holy Name Juveniles. He played with them for four years, during which time they won the Ontario championship.

By the 1943-44 season, Ted was considered an up-and-coming player. He accepted an invitation to join St. Michael's College and played well during the second half of the season after a poor start. St. Mike's was eliminated that year, but while on a trip to Hamilton in the spring of 1944, Carson Cooper, chief scout for the Detroit Red Wings, spotted him.

Jack Adams signed him at once. Lindsay was drafted as a wartime replacement by the Oshawa Generals to help them win the Memorial Cup. With Ted scoring several goals, Oshawa did win the Cup.

In the fall of 1944-45, Ted was invited to Detroit's training camp. Sixty-three rookies tried out; only two

Ted Lindsay always loved to score—and fight as well, particularly against the Toronto Maple Leafs. In this case, peacemaking linesman Doug Davies comes out the loser, as his bleeding face attests.

would make the club. Ted, despite being only 19 years old, was one of them.

Lindsay appeared in 45 games for the Red Wings and had 17 goals and six assists—a respectable rookie outing. But his sophomore stint was a disappointment, as he accumulated only seven goals and 10 assists in 47 games during the 1945-46 season.

As the 1946-47 season neared, Adams—then coaching the team—decided to take a risk with the young man from Renfrew. Adams placed him on a line with a farm boy from Saskatchewan—Gordie Howe—and the veteran center Sid Abel. Adams's daring risk proved to be the creation of what would become known as the "Production Line," one of the greatest in NHL history.

To illustrate how powerful a team they were, Detroit won the Prince of Wales Trophy from 1948-49 to 1954-55 and again in 1956-57. At that time the trophy was presented each year to the team finishing with the most points (the league championship) at the end of the regular season.

That superior Detroit club also entered the record books for amassing the longest winning record including playoff games. They won 15 straight games from February 27, 1955, to April 5, 1955—nine regular-season and six playoff games. Detroit also held a lock on first place for seven straight years (from 1948-49 to 1954-55). During that dynastic period, it won the Stanley Cup four times, in 1949-50, 1951-52, 1953-54 and 1954-55.

The Red Wings again finished first in 1956-57, and Ted produced his greatest season—85 points on 30 goals and 55 assists. But it was also the year that Adams—now GM—decided to break up the Red Wings' famous line. Adams traded Ted, with goaltender Glenn Hall and forward Forbes Kennedy, to Chicago for Johnny Wilson, goaltender Hank Bassen, Bill Preston and cash.

Lindsay was now reunited with Tommy Ivan, who had coached him 10 out of his 13 seasons with Detroit. But the Blackhawks were a pathetic team, occupying the basement of the league in each of the previous four seasons.

Ted scored 15 goals in his first season with Chicago, 22 the next, but only seven in 1959-60—when he chose to retire at the age of 34. "I guess my heart wasn't in it at Chicago," Ted revealed. "They treated me well, but my home and business were in Detroit. I'm a Detroit guy."

For the next four years, Lindsay spent most of his time tending his automotive plastics firm in Detroit, occasionally engaging in workouts with the Red Wings. Then, in 1964, Ted applied for the job of color commentator for Detroit, but the team's GM had another idea. Sid Abel asked Ted if he would like to join Detroit again—on the ice instead of in the broadcast booth. After careful thought, Ted decided to report to training camp and give it a shot. He made the team, and when the Red Wings opened their 1964-65 season (against Ted's most hated adversary, Toronto), Ted was at left wing. The Olympia fans gave him a standing ovation as he took the ice in his 1,000th NHL game.

Reunited with Howe, Ted helped the Wings finish in first place (after they had finished fourth the previous year). Ted scored 14 goals, had 14 assists and, proving that nothing had changed, spent 173 minutes in the penalty box. Even his longtime foe, league prexy Clarence Campbell, conceded that Lindsay's comeback after four years away from the game was " . . . one of the most amazing feats in professional sport."

Ted retired to the broadcast booth after that one season. When asked why he chose to play one final season, he answered, "I thought it would be nice to finish my career as a Red Wing."

In 1966, in honor of his illustrious career, Ted Lindsay was elected to hockey's Hall of Fame.

Lindsay was hired as color commentator for the NBC-TV network's "Game of the Week" in 1972 and never hesitated to speak out on controversial issues. Especially critical of the NHLPA and its director, Alan Eagleson, Lindsay said, "The Players' Association has encouraged familiarity among the players. They're one big, happy family now. The coaches have no way of pushing players. They can't send them to the minors; they can't fine them because the Players' Association will raise hell."

Lindsay's colorful comments lessened only slightly when he was named general manager of the ailing Detroit Red Wings in 1977 and later coached the team briefly, until he was dismissed in 1981.

Ted and his wife then retired to a 240-acre farm in Metamota, Michigan, where they raised horses. Ted, a physical fitness and nutrition buff, operated a vitamin business and was also involved with an energy conservation company.

"Old Scarface" had as many detractors as boosters. Some intimates swore by him; others cursed him to the core. But there was no disputing "Terrible" Ted Lindsay's essential talent and the contributions he made to a superior Red Wings club.

5

PETER ALEXANDER
"FATS" DELVECCHIO

BORN: Fort William, Ontario, December 4, 1931
POSITION: Center/Left Wing
NHL TEAMS: Detroit Red Wings, 1950-74
AWARDS/HONORS: NHL Second All-Star Team, 1953, 1959;
Lady Byng Trophy, 1959, 1966, 1969; Lester Patrick Trophy, 1974;
NHL All-Star Game, 1953-59, 1961-65, 1967; Hockey Hall of Fame, 1977

The eternal Red Wing.
One would think such a title would best fit Gordie Howe, or perhaps Ted Lindsay. Certainly, of the moderns, it has been worn well by Steve Yzerman.

But unlike Howe and Lindsay, who played on other National Hockey League teams in the twilight of their careers, Alex "Fats" Delvecchio was a Red Wing from the very start in 1950 to the very finish in 1974: two decades plus four years in red and white.

He was also one of the finest centers ever to skate down the pike and a member of three Stanley Cup–winning teams including the 1954-55 squad, the last Detroit sextet to win the championship before the expansion of 1967.

Everything about Delvecchio was likeable, from his gregarious personality to his delightfully clean play. If ever a major league hockey player could be called a gentleman, scholar and artist, Fats was that man.

Ironically, there was nothing fat about Alex except his cherubic face. He measured 6'0" and 195 pounds—big for his era—but moved around the rink with a lyrical style that sometimes suggested nonchalance.

How good was Delvecchio?

Perhaps the best way to put it is that he had an awfully tough act to follow in Detroit, and not only did he follow captain Sid Abel as top center, but he eventually outperformed his predecessor.

In the late 1940s and during the 1949-50 season, when the Red Wings beat the New York Rangers to win the Stanley Cup, Abel centered the famed Production Line with Ted Lindsay at left wing and Gordie Howe on the right. The trio's gears meshed so well together that most observers doubted another center could work as well with Lindsay and Howe. But when Abel left Detroit after the 1951-52 season to become player-coach of the Chicago Blackhawks, Delvecchio stepped in without missing a beat.

Less abrasive than Abel, Delvecchio nevertheless was a stylist in the clean, competent manner of such respected centermen as Syl Apps and Jean Beliveau. Delvecchio was a three-time winner of the Lady Byng Trophy (1959, 1966 and 1969) and was voted to the Second All-Star Team in 1953. He was also one of the few players to gain All-Star acclaim at two different positions, also being named to the All-Star squad as a left wing in 1959.

There was good reason why Fats never made the First Team during his 23-year National Hockey League career, as he played mostly in the shadows of such classic centers as Beliveau, Stan Mikita and Henri Richard. Nevertheless, Delvecchio's high-grade credentials are abundant. He played on three Stanley Cup champion

Alex Delvecchio spent his entire 24-year career in Red Wing red and white. In this 1955 action, he beats the Toronto defense, slipping the puck past goalie Harry Lumley.

teams and seven first-place clubs. He became captain of the Red Wings in 1961 and scored 20 or more goals in 13 of his campaigns.

In his 23 seasons with the Wings, Delvecchio was widely known as one of the classiest players around, polished both on and off the ice. "Respect, that's the word," said Canadian journalist Earl McRae. "It's not hard to respect Fats Delvecchio."

Also blessed with durability, Delvecchio missed only 43 games in 22 full seasons; from 1957 to 1964, Fats played in 490 consecutive games.

Bruce MacGregor, Delvecchio's Red Wings teammate during the late 1960s, also remembers big No. 10's easy, graceful approach to the game. "Alex was a natural athlete," MacGregor said. "His biggest assets were his skating and passing, a fluid skater with an effortless style. I remember him centering for big Frank Mahovolich. Frank had that big, sweeping stride, and it was tough for centers to judge where he'd be for a pass. But Alex would hit him almost every time—right on the money."

Because of his calm demeanor, Fats avoided controversy, although he was once inadvertently drawn into a brouhaha involving referee Red Storey. In his autobiography, *Red's Story,* the Hall of Fame referee detailed the Delvecchio episode, also involving Montreal's Hall of Fame defenseman Doug Harvey, which took place at old Olympia Stadium in February 1958.

"Delvecchio and Harvey were heading in my direction," related Storey, "both chasing the puck at top speed. I was next to the boards, but they were so intent that neither saw I was there. I realized I was about to get run over. . . and I wasn't going to let anyone belt me if I could help it. I yelled, 'Look out!' and they glanced up and veered off to miss me.

"There was a fan in a seat right there who was a friend of [Jack] Adams. He said to him: '. . . Storey is coaching the Canadiens. He told Doug Harvey to look out when Alex was going to hit him.' Adams then started this big to-do about . . . my 'directing the Montreal club during play.' Adams said I was doing it because I was from Montreal. The Detroit papers were full of it the next day.

"The league decided it had to have a hearing. They had the players in first, and Harvey told them, 'The only time Storey ever did anything for me was last summer in the referees' golf tournament, when he helped

me find a golf ball I lost.' . . . That stopped it right there and [NHL president] Campbell dismissed Adams's charge."

Born December 4, 1931, in Fort William, Ontario, Peter Alexander Delvecchio made the Red Wings varsity at the tender age of 19, contributing 15 goals in his rookie campaign as the Wings swept to the Stanley Cup championship. Alex went on to roll up impressive statistics—1,549 games, 1,281 points, and 825 assists. He also potted 456 goals.

His calm but firm demeanor eventually made Fats one of the most suitable candidates to take over the chores behind the bench of a struggling Red Wings team in 1973, and in November of that year, Delvecchio was officially named coach of the 2-9-1 club. His controlled discipline, laced with a healthy respect for his players as individuals, made Fats successful at his new craft, raising the comatose Detroiters to a level of respectability and at the same time making life pleasurable for his troops. He was not averse to picking up some cold cuts and beer after a game or taking the team out to dinner after a practice. But rather than taking advantage of his good nature, Delvecchio's entire team respected him, allowing his teammates to simply go out and do what they were paid to do: play hockey.

A man of skill, honor and respect, Alex Delvecchio was a realist as well. A poem that hung on the wall of his office during his term as Red Wings coach summarized the precarious nature of the NHL coach and player:

The Indispensable Man

Sometimes when you're feeling important
Sometimes when your ego's in bloom
Sometimes when you take it for granted
You're the best qualified in the room
Take a bucket and fill it with water
Put your hand in it up to the wrist
Pull it out and the hole that's remaining
Is a measure of how much you'll be missed.

But Alex Delvecchio, one of Detroit's finest skaters, purest centers and most diligent coaches, was definately missed after he left the NHL scene. Fats truly was one of a kind.

6

TERRANCE GORDON "TERRY" SAWCHUK

BORN: Winnipeg, Manitoba, December 28, 1929
DIED: May 31, 1970
POSITION: Goaltender
NHL TEAMS: Detroit Red Wings, 1950-55, 1957-64, 1968-69;
Boston Bruins, 1955-57; Toronto Maple Leafs, 1964-67;
Los Angeles Kings, 1967-68; New York Rangers, 1969-70
AWARDS/HONORS: Calder Trophy, 1951;
Vezina Trophy, 1952, 1953, 1955, 1965 (shared with J. Bower);
Lester Patrick Trophy, 1971; NHL First All-Star Team, 1951, 1952, 1953;
NHL Second All-Star Team, 1954, 1955, 1959, 1963; Hockey Hall of Fame, 1971.

One of the greatest and most tragic players ever to grace a major league hockey rink was Terry Sawchuk. Terry was one of the best goalies ever to strap on the tools of his trade, but he was also a moody, brooding figure who was a physical and mental wreck when he met his untimely death in 1970.

His 20-year career in big-league hockey included tours of duty with the Detroit Red Wings, Boston Bruins, Toronto Maple Leafs, Los Angeles Kings and New York Rangers. Terry broke into the majors with the Wings, making the First All-Star Team during his maiden season and copping the Calder Trophy as the NHL's rookie of the year.

Incredibly, his goals-against average never topped 2.00 during his first five years with Detroit, a stretch that saw him rack up 56 shutouts. He finished his up-and-down career with an amazing 103 career shutouts—nine more than an earlier paragon, George Hainsworth, and 19 more than his then-closest challenger, Glenn Hall. Sawchuk's early years were great ones, but he insisted that the finest moment of his career came with the 1966-67 Toronto Maple Leafs, when he dramatically guided the Leafs to an upset Stanley

Cup victory. As of 2001, the Leafs had not won another Cup.

It was said of Terry Sawchuk that he wasn't a whole man; rather, that he was stitched together—held in place by catgut and surgical tape. He suffered a painful shoulder injury early in his career that, for the rest of his playing days, prevented him from lifting his stick hand any higher than chest level. A full-page photo of Terry once appeared in a national magazine illustrating each stitch he had taken in his ruined face. The shocking picture could easily have passed for a horror-movie publicity shot.

An enigmatic, bitter man to the end, Terry would die in a New York hospital from injuries received in a somewhat mysterious scuffle with Rangers teammate Ron Stewart on the lawn of his Long Island home shortly after the 1969-70 season.

Creator of the "crouch style" of net minding, Sawchuk was named to the First All-Star Team in 1951, 1952 and 1953 and was a Second Team choice in 1954, 1955, 1959 and 1963. He played for four Stanley Cup winning teams and four first-place teams.

In Detroit, an exceptionally gifted crew including Gordie Howe, Ted Lindsay, Red Kelly, Marcel

At the very height of his career, goalie Terry Sawchuk is hoisted up by teammates Marcel Pronovost (left) and Glen Skov (right). The Red Wings had just finished first in the 1954-55 season.

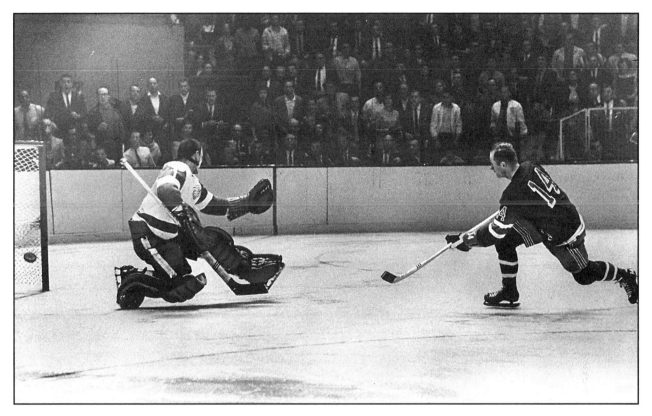

Terry Sawchuk is the victim of Val Fonteyne's first goal as a New York Ranger.

Pronovost and Alex Delvecchio fronted Sawchuk, but he was as responsible as any for the club's success. He was an innovator, and his ability to cope with screened shots by use of the crouch was considered a great advance in goaltending technique in its day.

Sawchuk was the product of the Red Wings' farm system, which developed a remarkable string of Hall of Famers, starting with Harry Lumley and also including Glenn Hall. In fact, Lumley starred on Detroit's 1950 Stanley Cup winning team, while Sawchuk waited in the wings, playing superbly on the Indianapolis farm team.

In a terrific gamble, Red Wings manager Jack Adams dealt Lumley to Chicago and elected Sawchuk as his No. 1 net minder. The results were obvious from the start. Lumley was quickly forgotten, and by springtime Sawchuk was the talk of the ice world. The Red Wings annexed the Stanley Cup in eight games, during which Terry allowed but five goals for an 0.62 goals-against average.

Nothing speaks more eloquently about Sawchuk's first five NHL seasons than his goals-against average, which never rose higher than 1.98. Yet despite the triumphs, there always was a shadow of gloom surrounding him. His right elbow, which had been dislocated in

a childhood football accident, continued to devil him, and he underwent operations in the summers of 1950 and 1951 for removal of pieces of bone that had chipped off in the elbow.

The operations were unsuccessful, and surgery was ordered again in 1952, whereupon the surgeon removed 60 pieces of bone. Sawchuk believed his troubles were over. For the first time in 10 years, he had almost complete movement in his right arm.

But the cumulative effect of all the hospitalization seemed to have a boomerang effect on Sawchuk, psychologically and physically. His weight, which had been consistantly around 205 pounds, dropped to 168 during the 1952-53 season. Sawchuk was given exhaustive medical tests.

Less than a month later, he was hospitalized for an appendectomy. Even Terry himself found humor in his woes. When a reporter asked him what he did during the off season, he chortled, "I spend my summers in the hospital."

He wasn't kidding. He returned to the hospital in 1954 after an auto accident resulted in severe chest injuries. Once again he recovered to play more than competently for the Red Wings, but now—irony of ironies—Sawchuk's threat was the Detroit farm system.

Jack Adams now had another whiz goalie in Indianapolis named Glenn Hall, who could not be kept in the minors.

Once again the Red Wings' boss packaged a major deal involving a goalkeeper, this time sending Sawchuk to the Boston Bruins. What few skeptics there were questioned Terry's ability to play superior goal for a relatively weak team like the Bruins, but his high standard of performance delighted Boston Garden fans, and for one season, at least, the deal looked good.

But his second year in Beantown was a disaster. He was stricken with infectious mononucleosis and spent 12 days in the hospital. When he returned to the ice—perhaps prematurely—he seemed a mere shade of the Sawchuk who once had starred for Detroit.

Sawchuk lost four of his next eight games, and the Boston press turned on him. His weight was now 166 pounds, and at age 27, he felt he had had it. To the astonishment of teammates and foes alike, he announced that he was retiring. "I told them I thought it best to quit since my nerves were really shot."

It was suggested that much more was being concealed than reached print. Sawchuk, some noted, never did take to the Boston scene and yearned for his old digs in Detroit.

Sawchuk's "retirement" lasted until the beginning of the next season, when Adams sweet-talked the Bruins into giving him the rights to Sawchuk "because he's too good a goalie to remain out of hockey." That done, Adams dealt Hall to Chicago, and Sawchuk played seven more years for the Red Wings, often displaying pre-illness form.

Following the 1963-64 season, the Red Wings' high command figured that Terry was washed up. Toronto Maple Leafs general manager Punch Imlach, always one to give a veteran a chance, signed Sawchuk, and Terry demonstrated emphatically that there was still some good goaltending left in him. In 1967 the Leafs won the Stanley Cup, defeating Chicago and Montreal, and Sawchuk was in the net for six of Toronto's eight playoff victories.

While one might have expected Terry to be a joyful man in Toronto, where he was receiving unanimous raves, he seemed to be unhappy. "He reminded you of a prisoner in a wartime concentration camp," said Toronto journalist Jim Hunt.

Nevertheless, the Toronto experience provided Sawchuk with a measure of inner peace and satisfaction, particularly the Cup-winning effort. "I'd like to leave hockey like that," said Sawchuk. "In style."

He didn't, of course. When the NHL expanded from six to 12 teams in 1967, Terry was obtained by the new Los Angeles Kings, played one season on the west coast, and then returned to the Red Wings in 1968-69. A year later he was signed by the Rangers, playing for Emile Francis, a former net minder who greatly admired Sawchuk.

It was always difficult for Terry to enjoy even the most intense moments of victory. One that should have brought him happiness was the Stanley Cup finale in 1967, when he and another veteran, Johnny Bower, guided the Leafs to the championship. While teammates exulted in the dressing room, sipping champagne, the goalies, as Jim Hunt observed, "sat in a corner by themselves, dragging deeply on cigarettes and grappling silently with the frayed nerves and many physical ailments that are an inescapable part of life for aging men."

He played his last professional game on April 9, 1970, against a mighty Boston Bruins team in the Stanley Cup playoffs. The Rangers were beaten 5-3 and were soon eliminated from the Cup round. It's conceivable, though, that Emile Francis might have invited Sawchuk back to the Rangers for the 1970-71 season as a goaltending coach and possible second goaltender. But three weeks after the Rangers were eliminated, Sawchuk, who shared a room in suburban Long Island with teammate Ron Stewart, had a row with his pal. The precise details have never been fully pieced together, but Sawchuk was taken to a local Long Island hospital for treatment of internal injuries.

At first it seemed just a matter of weeks until he would be released, but Terry's condition worsened dramatically, and finally he was moved to a more sophisticated Manhattan hospital, where emergency surgery was preformed.

It was all in vain. Sawchuk died of a pulmonary embolism on May 31, 1970. His was one of the most tragic of hockey careers, but also one of the most glorious. He was a greatly gifted but fatally flawed goaltender who enjoyed the best years of his career as a Detroit Red Wing.

Terry Sawchuk races out of his crease, beating Rangers forward Dean Prentice to the puck. Gordie Howe (right) helps out.

7

SERGEI FEDOROV

BORN: Pskov, Russia; December 13, 1969
POSITION: Center
NHL TEAMS: Detroit Red Wings, 1990-Present
AWARDS/HONORS: NHL All-Star Rookie Team, 1991;
Hart Trophy, 1994; Lester B. Pearson Award, 1994;
Frank J. Selke Trophy, 1994, 1996; NHL First All-Star Team, 1994

Rare is the athlete who can single-handedly change the way a game is played. But Sergei Fedorov not only changed what hockey became on the ice in the 1990s, he was also paramount in the transformation of the fiscal policies that governed it during that decade.

With his shiny white skates and the golden-brown hair flowing from his helmet, Sergei Fedorov, a native of Minsk, hit the NHL at high speed and instantly impressed both friend and foe alike.

"I've played with multitalented players such as Mario Lemieux, Jaromir Jagr and Eric Lindros in my career, but none of them has the explosive speed of Sergei Fedorov," said Philadelphia Flyers ace Mark Recchi. "Great players like that have the ability to paint a picture like Picasso. Sergei has proven his whole career that he can still paint on the ice, regardless of what anyone else thinks."

Fedorov's road to the NHL was paved with adventure. In fact, it was a story right out of a James Bond movie, with political ramifications and high drama.

Sergei was born on December 13, 1969, in Pskov, Russia. As a youngster, he was trained by his father, Viktor, a professional athlete himself. They lived in a poor country where indoor rinks were few and far be-

tween. Young Sergei would have to learn his hockey on outdoor rinks and rivers that would freeze during the long, harsh winters.

He would skate for seven hours on weekends and days when school would be canceled if it was too cold to study.

"Growing up, I owed all my vision and skills to my father," Sergei said.

By the time he was 16, Sergei was playing for Central Red Army, the highest-ranked club in the country, and soon was invited to Moscow. While there, he would be trained by the best coaches and teachers in the Soviet Union and play with the likes of future NHLers Alexander Mogilny and Pavel Bure.

"We were like kids playing together who had played together all our lives," said Fedorov. "We had that great feeling you get when you understand a teammate so well. I don't know if we realized how good we all were individually, but we knew how well we worked together. It was fun. Nobody was thinking about the NHL back then."

The three young Russians began dominating their competition, winning world championships for their club seemingly at will. In 1989, Sergei scored 19 goals and added 10 assists in 48 games while helping the

When it comes to dazzling with footwork and stick work, Sergei is in a class by himself.

Soviet Union win the gold medal in the World Championships.

But in 1990, at the age of 20, Sergei wanted more; specifically, he wanted to play in the National Hockey League. But in those days, a Russian player simply could not move to North America. To leap to the NHL, Fedorov would have to defect, as his teammate Mogilny had done before him.

In 1989, while the Russian Junior team was visiting Stockholm after winning the 1989 World Junior Tournament in Anchorage, Alaska, Mogilny had made the daring move. He simply left the hotel at which the team was staying and never returned.

"By the end I knew he was going," said Fedorov. "I didn't know the details, but I knew. I came back to the room to say goodbye. He asked me if I wanted to come, but I hadn't been drafted by an NHL club. Alex had been drafted by Buffalo. I had nowhere to go. I told him, 'What am I going to defect to?' He walked out the door and there was a car waiting. It was exciting, actually."

Mogilny's action changed everything. Before that, NHL clubs were hesitant to risk draft choices on Russian players. But the year after his defection, NHL teams drafted 18 Russian players. Sergei Fedorov was the first selected, taken in the fourth round of the 1989 draft by the Red Wings.

"At the time, Fedorov was one of the top five players in the world, but their [Russia's] political situation prevented him from being a high pick," said Craig Button, now Calgary Flames general manager. "You really have to give the Wings—and in particular Jim Lites—credit for taking the chance. They figured, 'Why not draft him? It can't hurt anything.' That was their theory."

Lites, who later became president of the Dallas Stars, was a member of the Red Wings high command at the time. The organization saw an opportunity not only to select Fedorov, but also to get him out of Russia.

"Prior to Mogilny defecting, we knew that Soviet players would never leave because they feared for their families' safety," Lites remembered. "That incident gave us the impression that the Russian players no longer were afraid for their families. Now was the time to start drafting them."

But getting them out of the Soviet Union was not that easy. While the Soviet government was beginning to loosen its rein, it did not want to freely release its great resource of hockey players.

"We had the ability at the time to make contact with Fedorov and Vladimir Konstantinov, whom we had also selected in the same 1989 draft," Lites continued. "Through this third party, we found out that both players were interested in coming to the NHL, but that Konstantinov would be unlikely to come due to his military rank and family concerns."

Fedorov, however, was extremely interested. Another meeting between the parties was arranged during the 1989-90 Super Series, which pitted NHL clubs against the Soviet Central Red Army team, of which Sergei was a member. The Central team was in Chicago for a game against the Blackhawks in early January 1990.

There, Fedorov, Lites and an interpreter met for almost three hours and discussed problems, answered each other's questions and got to know each other a little better.

"I tried to tell him that there was no time like the present," said Lites. "We could be in Detroit before they knew he was gone. But Sergei was smart. He knew he would have additional problems because his service duty in their army was not complete. He wanted to wait until the summer, when his hockey season was over and his service time was up."

Sergei's concerns stemmed from his fear that a person who left the Soviet army prematurely would be brought up on charges of desertion and perhaps even treason. Fedorov understandably disliked those possibilities.

The Wings waited until they finally got the word—Sergei was ready to move. In a matter of days, the final scheme was designed, carried out and completed.

"We actually got word that Fedorov was ready to defect in July at the 1990 Goodwill Games being played in Seattle," continued Lites. "Their team was playing an exhibition game prior to the actual Games in Portland. After their game that day, he wanted to return with us to Detroit."

Lites boarded the Red Wings' private jet and headed to the Pacific Northwest. Upon his arrival in Seattle, Lites had the plan in place. "We told him to pack his bags and place them on his hotel bed when he left that morning," said Lites. "As he was leaving, he came by our room and slipped his key under our door. We had his bags and a car ready to go."

The team assembled in a hotel banquet room for a pregame meal. Sergei soon excused himself, telling his teammates that he had forgotten his room key. But instead of going back to his room, Fedorov met Lites in the hallway.

"We met in the hall, simply nodded at one another, and he said, 'Jim, I'm ready to go.' We were almost out of the hotel when an elevator opens up and out walks his roommate. He stopped and said something to him in Russian and then we left.

"I asked him in the car what he had told him, and he said he just let him know that he was going to Detroit and was going to be in the NHL. He told him not to worry about what the officials back home might tell them; he would be safe. Of course, his roommate looked at him like he was pulling his leg."

"It was fun," said Fedorov afterwards. "Nobody was thinking about anything like the NHL back then."

But soon the NHL began thinking about him.

He broke into the league with fire in his eyes and jets in his skates. On October 4, 1990, Sergei Fedorov made his NHL debut in New Jersey. He promptly scored his first goal on a power play.

Everyone immediately began to take notice..

"We're putting the future of our game in the hands of people like Sergei Fedorov," said Wayne Gretzky. "He's a first-class guy, he loves the game and he cares about the game. He is great news for hockey."

Fedorov finished his rookie year with 31 goals and 48 assists and was selected to the NHL All-Star Rookie Team in 1991. He also finished second in the Calder Trophy voting for Rookie of the Year honors, losing out to Chicago goaltender Ed Belfour.

"I think he could be [as good as] Gretzky, he just doesn't realize it yet," said former Gretzky and Fedorov teammate Paul Coffey. "With a guy like Sergei, the sky's the limit. He could be the best player on the ice every night. He's got the ability, because of his skating, to pick up and say, 'OK, I'm going to get a goal' or 'I'm going to set up a goal.'"

As the Red Wings rose to the top of the league in the mid-'90s with the likes of captain Steve Yzerman and goaltender Mike Vernon, Fedorov continued his ascent to stardom.

In 1993-94, he had a magical season. Playing in all 82 games, Sergei scored 56 goals and added 64 assists, becoming only the fourth Red Wing ever to win the Hart Trophy as the NHL's Most Valuable Player. In addition, he won the Lester B. Pearson Award as MVP of the league, as voted by his peers, and the Frank J.

Selke Trophy as best defensive forward. He was also a First-Team NHL All-Star.

"Fedorov is a game-breaker," said teammate Thomas Holmstrom. "He's like a thoroughbred. He has breakaway speed and can play tough defense. He can beat you in more ways than any center in the game today. Playing with Sergei is like playing five-on-four all the time. When he has the puck, he opens up the ice for the rest of us. It's almost like the defense is hypnotized by his skill."

Fedorov began to forge his impeccable stick-handling skills and skating abilities at the age of 14 on the ice of a humble rink in what is now known as Belarus.

There, youngsters would swarm around Sergei, desperately scampering and falling in attempts to take the puck away from him.

"That's one of the memories that's still with me, skating with the kids," said Fedorov. "It was a big part of my hockey development. And it's very nice that I can have the ability to help kids out, because when I was a kid, nobody really helped me out except my family."

In 1997, Fedorov and the Red Wings entered the playoffs looking to end a 42-year Stanley Cup drought. Detroit began the playoffs as a slight underdog to win the championship.

The previous three seasons, Detroit had posted outstanding regular-season records, only to falter in the postseason. However, this year was going to be different, as the Wings actually finished the regular season just 12 games over .500.

During the latter part of the season, coach Scotty Bowman even began to experiment with Sergei, using him as a defenseman from time to time. Fedorov didn't seem to mind.

"I can do better things up front," he said, "but that's not where the team wants me. It's an honor for me to have the team say they need me on defense and I am not going to let them down. I'm a very responsible person. I've been responsible for myself since I was 13."

Proving his all-around worth, Sergei led the club in postseason points (20), assists (12) and game-winning goals (4) en route to helping Detroit win its first Stanley Cup since 1955. Teammate Mike Vernon won the Conn Smythe Trophy as Most Valuable Player in the playoffs that year, but many hockey insiders believe that Sergei deserved that honor.

During the summer of 1997, Sergei became a restricted free agent and was free to sign with any club in the league. The stipulation, however, was that his new club would have to surrender a maximum of five first-round draft picks to the Red Wings.

Negotiations were still deadlocked as the new season began. Fedorov was not in uniform as the Red Wings hung their Stanley Cup championship banner from the rafters of Joe Louis Arena. The two sides continued to stage what was to become an epic battle that would soon include a third party.

By 1998, Fedorov's agent, Mike Barnett and Red Wings general manager Ken Holland still could not hammer out a deal. In February, the NHL—for the first time ever—allowed its players to participate in the 1998 Winter Olympics in Nagano, Japan. Sergei Fedorov was invited to play for the Russian team.

Not having played in a game since Game 4 of the previous year's Stanley Cup Finals against the Philadelphia Flyers, Fedorov donned his skates for a practice and whipped around the ice as if he were a young kid again back home in Russia.

But as the Olympics began, the Sergei Fedorov saga took an unexpected turn.

On February 18, 1998, Carolina Hurricanes owner Peter Karmanos authorized his general manager, Jim Rutherford, to submit an offer sheet to the Fedorov camp that was of astronomical and seemingly insurmountable proportions. The offer was for a six-year contract worth $38 million.

Some say Karmanos made the offer out of spite. He and Red Wings owner Mike Ilitch had a long-running feud that dated to the days when Karmanos owned an Ontario Hockey League team that played in Ilitch's Joe Louis Arena. Ilitch ended that working agreement and hung Karmanos and his team out to dry.

But Karmanos denied that the offer was anything but a legitimate opportunity to improve his hockey club, which was having an awful time attracting customers.

"He called me at midnight and was very enthusiastic about the deal," Karmanos said about Fedorov. "He said he wanted an opportunity to go someplace where he could be the go-to guy."

Part of Fedorov's problem with the Red Wings during the holdout was his perception that he would see limited action on the club. He couldn't understand how one year (1994) he was the MVP of the league, then later (1997), he would be relegated to third- and

OPPOSITE: Sergei Fedorov celebrates yet another goal.

fourth-line status during the latter part of the season. Scotty Bowman's experiment that put Fedorov on defense during that same period also irked the Russian as he thought back over it.

The deal Carolina submitted to Fedorov included $26 million in bonus money—$14 million paid out for the 1997-98 season and $12 million to be prorated over four years. But if the Hurricanes made it to the Eastern Conference Finals, the $12 million would be paid in one lump sum. In addition, he would receive $2 million annually for the rest of the 1997-98 season and the next five years.

Since Fedorov was a restricted free agent, the Red Wings had seven days to match or exceed the offer. The problem was that the Wings had a much better chance of reaching the conference finals than Carolina did, a fact that was not overlooked by their front office.

"Certainly it's structured to try and deter the Red Wings from matching," said Holland about the offer.

"The offer sheet is very disappointing," Wings senior vice president Jimmy Devellano countered. "Fortunately, we've got seven days to consider things."

Meanwhile, Fedorov continued to play in the Olympics. His team would eventually win the silver medal, losing to the upstart Czech Republic in the gold-medal game. But international hockey was the last thing on Sergei's mind.

The sticking point to the offer was the conference finals bonus clause. The Wings felt that the clause was unfair to them and their attempt to match Carolina's bid for the superstar. They took their argument to an arbitrator, who quickly upheld the validity of the clause. The Wings now had only 56 hours to decide whether to match the offer.

But the decision was already made. The Red Wings would match the Hurricanes' offer, and Fedorov would be in a Detroit uniform for five more seasons.

"I believe in the adage, 'Time heals all wounds,'" said Holland. "I've heard [trade demands] many times before in this business, and players have gone back and found a way to make it work.

"We won the Stanley Cup last year, and he led us in playoff scoring and in scoring in the playoffs the last three seasons. I'm not going to forget how important and what a role he played in our playoff success over the course of the last three years. Without Sergei in our lineup, we're a good hockey club. With Sergei in our lineup, we're a much better hockey club."

Fedorov seemed relieved that the ordeal was over.

"It has been a roller coaster of emotions that we have been through," he said. "But now I am anxious to resume my career."

He did. On February 27, 1998, Sergei Fedorov played his first game of the season against the Florida Panthers. And to show his teammates that there were no hard feelings, he took them all out to dinner when the team arrived in Phoenix later that week.

But winning over the fans of Detroit wasn't easy. He was met with boos during his first few home games at Joe Louis Arena. But on April 1, he scored both goals in an emotion-filled 2-0 victory over archrival Colorado.

"It's nice to have fans all around the world, but the most important ones are the ones right here in Detroit," he said.

After a tumultuous season, the Red Wings and Fedorov were finally ready to defend their 1997 Stanley Cup championship. Playing in only 21 regular season games, Sergei looked stronger than ever as the Wings prepared for their first-round opponents, the Coyotes.

"He's fresh, and obviously it shows," said Bowman before the playoffs began. "It also shows the impact on our team, getting him back. We'd be in dire straits right now without him."

Fedorov took off like a rocket, as Detroit defeated Phoenix in the first round four games to two. He had five goals in the first five games of the series, and Coyotes coach Jim Schoenfeld called him the best Detroit player on the ice. He wasn't alone in that assessment.

"Sergei's getting better with each game," said Holland. "What he's shown is that he's one of the best players in the game. What he has now is the confidence to score goals. That's what we needed him to get during the 20 games or so he played in the regular season, and he did that."

"Everybody knows how he performs in the playoffs, with big goals and big plays at key times," added assistant coach Dave Lewis.

It was now on to Round 2, where Detroit would face the St. Louis Blues. And again, it was Fedorov who led the Red Wing charge, scoring three goals and adding four assists to help Detroit advance to the Western Conference Finals with a 4-2 series victory.

As the Red Wings prepared to face the Dallas Stars, all eyes were on Fedorov. Not only was he the best player thus far in the playoffs, but he also earned his bonus payment of $12 million. For Sergei, though, the money was the last thing on his mind.

"I don't consider that side of my hockey being in

my mind now," he said as the series opened in Dallas. "It is not motivating me to play hockey. The business is over and hockey starts. I don't need to think about that bonus clause to be happy to play."

But the Stars were able to contain Fedorov for the first five games of the series. He registered no goals and just one assist in those games. But leading three games to two, the Red Wings returned to Joe Louis Arena for a possible series-clinching Game 6. Much to the chagrin of the veteran-laden Stars, Fedorov was ready to answer the bell.

Detroit took a first-period lead on a goal by defenseman Larry Murphy, and then Fedorov was knocked silly by a bone-crushing check from Stars defenseman Richard Matvichuk. Fedorov lay facedown on the ice for several moments as the "The Joe" went silent. Rising slowly and wobblling, Sergei shook off the hit and skated toward his bench. Little did anyone realize it at the time, but that hit was the worst thing that any Dallas player could have done to him.

Fedorov regained his senses and began dominating the game with his crafty stick handling, pinpoint passing and relentless backchecking.

In the second period, he took a pass from Murphy and swept the puck past Belfour to give the Wings a 2-0 lead. It was Fedorov's first goal of the series. And it was lights out for the Stars, as the Wings held on for a 2-0 victory. For the second year in a row, Detroit advanced to the Stanley Cup Finals, where they would meet the Washington Capitals.

Detroit swept the Capitals in four games, thereby winning the Stanley Cup for the second straight year. Again showing why he will be remembered as one of the best playoff performers in the history of the NHL, Fedorov scored the game-winning goal in Game 3 and helped open the scoring in the deciding Game 4 after curling away from a would-be defender to whistle a perfect pass to Doug Brown, who lifted the puck into the net.

After missing 59 games due to his contract dispute, Fedorov had regained the respect of his teammates, coaches and fans.

Sergei Fedorov is a stickhandling master.

"I didn't work maybe physically those 60 games, but I worked so hard mentally," he said of his time off, "just to get back and play competitive hockey. I was really, really excited when [the contract] got worked out.

"Next step was winning fans back and proving to my teammates I was maybe a little bit better player and person. I've got to tell you, it was very, very hard."

Fedorov's time with Detroit may best be remembered by the contract dispute. However, there is no disputing that this Russian-born player not only helped liberate his peers back in the former Soviet Union, but that he also a earned a reputation as a clutch playoff performer.

Since then, Fedorov has remained among the elite.

8

RENÉ MARCEL PRONOVOST

BORN: Lac La Tortue, Quebec, June 15, 1930
POSITION: Defenseman
NHL TEAMS: Detroit Red Wings, 1950-65;
Toronto Maple Leafs, 1965-70
AWARDS/HONORS: NHL First All-StarTeam, 1960-61;
NHL Second All-StarTeam, 1958-59; Hockey Hall of Fame, 1978

Just as Lou Gehrig played in the shadow of Babe Ruth on the outstanding New York Yankee teams of the late 1920s and early 1930s, so did Marcel Pronovost—a remarkable defenseman—skate in the shadow of Red Kelly.

Both were splendid in their own end, giving their goaltenders enormous security. Likewise, both were superior puck carriers and excellent team players. They played on Stanley Cup champion teams. When still at the acmes of their respective careers, Pronovost and Kelly were traded to the Toronto Maple Leafs. There they continued to excel. But when analyzing Pronovost's career, one can only conclude that he was first and foremost a Red Wing.

Of all modern hockey players, Marcel Pronovost can lay claim to the unofficial award for the most frequently injured man in hockey. Episodes of Marcel's derring-do were legend around NHL rinks. He broke into big-league hockey with Detroit in the Stanley Cup playoffs of 1950 and was around to play a few games for the Toronto Maple Leafs in the 1969-70 season. In between, he collected hundreds of stitches and innumerable broken bones.

Once, in a game against the Chicago Blackhawks, Marcel sped across the blue line as two husky Chicago defensemen dug their skates into the ice, awaiting his arrival. They dared Pronovost to pass. "I decided there was only one move," said Marcel. "Bust through the middle." Even the most iron-fisted hockey players shudder at the thought of crashing a defense, but Pronovost wasn't thinking about getting hurt. He never did. He eyed the two-foot space between the Hawks, boldly pushed the puck ahead and leaped at the opening.

Too late. The crouched defensemen slammed the gate, hurling Pronovost head first over their shoulders. In that split second of imminent danger—when even the strongest of men would automatically have shut their eyes—Marcel looked down and saw the puck below him. He swiped at it, missed and had to settle for a three-point landing on his left eyebrow, nose and cheek.

A few minutes later the doctor was applying ice packs to Pronovost's forehead as he lay on the dressing-room table. Marcel's skull looked as if it had been the loser in a bout with a bulldozer. His nose was broken and listed heavily toward starboard. His eyebrow required 25 stitches. "And my cheekbones," Marcel re-

OPPOSITE: At times, Marcel Pronovost (center) was overshadowed by teammate Red Kelly, but Pronovost was a powerful force behind the blue line, here checking Toronto's George Armstrong off the puck. The Detroit goalie is Terry Sawchuk.

38

called in his deep tone, "felt as if they were pulverized." He was right: They were cracked like little pieces of china.

"What hurt most," said Pronovost, whose face became as craggy as an alpine peak, "was that I had to miss the next two games. As for the injuries, I didn't think twice about them." Marcel always regarded his misfortunes casually. "To me," he said, "accidents are as common as lacing on skates. One of the prizes of my collection of injuries is a break of the fourth dorsal vertebra."

In 1959, after Pronovost had broken his beak for the 13th time, he examined it with the air of a true connoisseur and said, "Frankly, I was disappointed. After a few towels were put on, I could see out of both eyes. The first time I broke my nose in a hockey game, my eyes were swollen shut for three days."

Pronovost's dubious distinction as hockey's most injured player makes his career accomplishments that much more remarkable. It is a rare athlete indeed who can suffer just about every injury in the medical dictionary and overcome each one to return to his previous level of excellence. But Marcel Pronovost took all that in stride.

Pronovost's 1950 NHL debut came when an injury to Gordie Howe forced the Wings to move defenseman Red Kelly to the forward line and bring up the youngster from the Omaha Knights to fill the gap on the back line. With the 19-year-old Pronovost playing the brand of hockey that earned him the U.S. League's Rookie of the Year honors, the Wings captured their first Cup since 1943, defeating the Rangers in a hotly contested final series. Pronovost, with less than a season of NHL experience behind him, played with the composure of a hardened veteran and became one of the youngest players to have his name inscribed on the Stanley Cup. He went on to play on seven championship teams in Detroit, including Cup-winning teams in 1952 and 1954.

When Marcel arrived in training camp in 1951, he fully expected to crash the Detroit varsity. Instead, he was blasted right out of the NHL. On a patented Pronovost rush, he tried bisecting the defense of iron men Leo Reise and Bob Goldham. When the three fell to the ice, Goldham's stick creased Marcel's face. His noble charge cost him a fractured cheekbone and a ticket to Indianapolis. But after 34 injury-free games in the minors, he was recalled, and from that time on he became a fixture on the Detroit blue line.

Stitches, bruises, fractures and separations all wracked Pronovost's 6'1", 175-pound body at one time

or another, but none defeated the determination that was his armor. No injury, it seemed, could discourage Pronovost from playing his position with anything short of reckless abandon.

Dancing with danger never fazed Pronovost, and he dismissed the perils of the rink as just another fact of life. "Making a dangerous play on the ice didn't make me any more nervous than crossing the street might make someone else," he said. "He doesn't worry about getting hit by a car, and I don't worry about getting hurt on the ice. If I did, I'd probably go crazy."

Pronovost's *kamikaze* approach to the game may not have taken its toll on his nerves, but it had a significant effect upon him physically. As a young horse in his early NHL days Pronovost was known as one of the finest rushing defensemen of his time and is sometimes compared to the likes of Ken Reardon before him and Bobby Orr after him. Those rink-long dashes were not only glorious, but grueling as well. As the injuries mounted, Marcel mellowed into a graceful puck carrier and a solid two-way defenseman.

Overshadowed by the brighter stars of the powerful Red Wings teams of the 1950s, Pronovost emerged as a bona fide star himself when Red Kelly was traded from Detroit to Toronto in 1959. Along with recognition by his team as the anchor of its blue line corps, Pronovost began to gain more notoriety league-wide and was named to the First-Team All-Stars in 1960 and 1961.

René Marcel Pronovost was born June 15, 1930, in Lac la Tortue, Quebec. At the age of 15, Marcel was "stolen" from the French-Canadian province by Detroit scout Marcel Cote, who first spotted the youngster playing juvenile hockey in Shawinigan Falls.

During his NHL career, from 1950 to 1970, Marcel Pronovost played in 1,206 games, netting 88 goals and adding 257 assists. He was also engaged in 134 playoff contests, scoring eight goals and 23 assists, and appeared in 11 All-Star games. His personal high for offensive production was 34 points in 1954-55.

Pronovost worked for the Detroit club for fifteen seasons until, at the age of thirty-four, he was traded to Toronto as part of an eight-player swap. Prior to the trade, Pronovost was second only to Gordie Howe in length of service with the Red Wings.

With the Maple Leafs, Pronovost played five more seasons and drank from the Stanley Cup one more time, in 1967, before retiring in 1970.

In the contemporary game, where players are motivated by incentive clauses, the likes of Pronovost's pure dedication to the game are simply nonexistent.

With goalie Terry Sawchuk down after making a save, defenseman Marcel Pronovost (left) clears the rubber. Detroit forward Jimmy Peters crosses in front of the crease to help his mate against the Rangers at Madison Square Garden.

One scenario which took place during the 1961 Stanley Cup Finals illustrates the intensity that typified Marcel Pronovost.

With the Red Wings matched against the Chicago Blackhawks, Pronovost played four games on a badly cracked ankle. He would arrive at the arena on crutches, play the game and then put his leg back in a cast. A teammate who watched him suffer through each torturous turn on the ice put it simply: "He played on guts alone, nothing else." He played for two decades, always underrated, but one of the most versatile defensemen of all time.

When hockey historians grasp for comparisons to Marcel Pronovost, they will be hard pressed to find any. Adding a new twist to an old cliché, it could be said that if they hadn't broken the mold after they made Pronovost, he'd probably have broken it himself. He did, after all, manage to break everything else.

9

NORMAN VICTOR
ALEXANDER ULLMAN

BORN: Provost, Alberta, December 26, 1935
POSITION: Center
NHL TEAMS: Detroit Red Wings, 1955-68;
Toronto Maple Leafs, 1968-75
AWARDS/HONORS: NHL First All-Star Team, 1965;
NHL Second All-Star Team, 1967;
NHL All-Star Game, 1955, 1960-65, 1967-69, 1974;
Hockey Hall of Fame, 1982

When discussions about the top Detroit centers of all time take place, names like Sid Abel, Alex Delvecchio and Steve Yzerman inevitably emerge.

But over the years, there has been another cadre of peerless pivots headed by Ullman, who served the Red Wings nobly for more than a decade, starting with the 1955-56 season.

Ullman's act was a difficult one to follow, to say the least. He was called upon to center Gordie Howe and Ted Lindsay, who were two-thirds of the original Production Line.

The center who originally set the standard was Sid Abel, who helped the Red Wings win the Stanley Cup in 1950. After Abel left Detroit in 1952, he was succeeded by Delvecchio.

When Red Wings general manager Jack Adams decided that Delvecchio would be more useful on another line, others auditioned with Howe and Lindsay. One of them was Earl "Dutch" Reibel, a prodigy who had been developed in the vast Red Wings farm system. Reibel fit in well at first, but his effectiveness diminished and Adams resumed his search. Norm Ullman came to the rescue.

Ullman had been skating for the Red Wings' farm team in Edmonton and was summoned to the big club in 1955. Once he got the feel of the NHL, Norm was placed between Howe and Lindsay and turned out to be as reliable as Abel and Delvecchio before him.

Nobody knew it at the time, but Ullman had begun what would become a distinguished 20-year career as a major leaguer, beginning as the Red Wings were in the midst of a 1950s dynasty.

Playing between Howe and Lindsay, Ullman became one of the most unobtrusive high scorers in NHL annals. In the 1964-65 season, Ullman scored 42 goals, topped only by Chicago's Golden Jet, Bobby Hull, and Norm's teammate, Mr. Hockey himself, Gordie Howe.

In the view of some observers, Ullman operated on the ice with computer-like efficiency—and this in a day preceding PCs! It was as if his manager-coach, Sid Abel, flipped a switch inside the 5'10", 182-pound center's jersey before each game and then Ullman went out and backchecked, forechecked and scored with perfection. "He had torsion-air suspension and automatic transmission," Adams said.

He might have added that Ullman also fulfilled his 10-year warranty. In his first decade with the Red Wings, Ullman amassed 237 goals and 324 assists for 561 points, putting him in a tie with Syd Howe for fourth place among all-time Detroit scorers. During that 10th season, 1964-65, he was the Red Wings' high-point (83) man and most valuable player, as well as the NHL's First Team All-Star center and runner-up for

The race is on between the Red Wings' Norm Ullman (7) and the Rangers' John McKenzie to see who can get the rebound left by Detroit goalie Roger Crozier. Defensemen Gary Bergman (next to McKenzie) and Doug Barkley (to the right of Bergman) also give chase.

the Hart Trophy. Not bad for a player who had the charisma of a sphinx.

Because he shunned publicity, avoided public appearances and gave the impression he'd rather play hockey in private, few people outside the highly provincial confines of the hockey world knew Norm Ullman existed. "I really didn't like the limelight," said Ullman, who spoke like a dulcet-voiced disc jockey. "I'm kind of quiet."

With Ullman, it was a pathological kind of quiet, so much a trademark that they made jokes about it around the league. "Normie never opened his mouth when I managed the Red Wings," said Jack Adams, "so I called him 'The Noisy One.' "

The Red Wings cautioned reporters on the trail of an Ullman story. "I'd be surprised if you'd get more than a few sentences out of him all year," Abel once said.

"Ullman anecdotes?" asked a member of the Detroit publicity department. "Are you kidding? He never talked."

When the Red Wings played the Blackhawks in the March 1964 Stanley Cup semifinals, Chicago coach

Billy Reay acknowledged that Ullman was the key to the Red Wing success. "Hawks' Reay Fears Ullman" blared the headline the following day. "With these words," a Detroit publicity man said, "Ullman gained more recognition than he'd gotten in his previous eight years in the league."

Ullman confirmed Reay's fears by scoring hat tricks (three goals in a game) in two of Detroit's victories over Chicago, tying a league record. Ullman's explanation of his clutch shooting: "It just worked out that way."

When Ullman did speak, it was slowly and calmly, with a complete absence of emotion. It was that way in the fall of 1955 when he was a rookie in the Detroit camp and was asked to pose for a photo with Gordie Howe and Ted Lindsay, the biggest stars on the team.

"What's up?" Ullman asked a member of the Red Wing staff.

He was told that the greatest of all possible things was about to happen to him. Norm Ullman, then a rookie, would be center for the deans of hockey, Lindsay and Howe. It was a time for a cheer, a cartwheel and champagne. But Ullman didn't even smile.

"That's nice," he said and posed for the photo.

"It was two years before you heard him say a complete sentence," said Howe. "His answers used to be 'yup' and 'nope.' But I think he was beginning to enjoy things more."

Maybe it was because at the time, more people were saying nice things about him and he was beginning to believe in himself. "He reminded me of Charlie Gehringer, the best second baseman who ever lived," said Adams. "That type of athlete did everything so gracefully, you tended to underestimate him." To which goalie Terry Sawchuk added, "He was hockey's most underrated player."

By the fans, perhaps, but not by the players. They'd seen too much of Ullman's skill to knock the product, especially the Blackhawks. They recalled April 11, 1965, very unpleasantly. At 17:35 of the second period in the fifth game of the Stanley Cup semifinals, Ullman whipped a 45-foot shot between defenseman Elmer Vasko's legs and past goalie Glenn Hall's right pad. Seconds later, he captured the face off from Bill Hay, took six strides and shot the puck past defenseman Matt Ravlich and Hall. The two goals, because they were scored in a span of five seconds, set a league record. Ullman scored a third goal in the last period, and Detroit won 4-2.

Ullman had been equally effective during the regular season. In it he scored the winning goal in 10 games and assisted on the winner in 10 others. "He got the big goals," said Howe. "And he skated miles and wrecked the other team's offense with his checking. The rest of us just tagged along."

NHL statistician Ron Andrews said, "Ullman had the most improved eye in the league that season. He took 38 more shots and scored 21 more goals than in the previous season, 1963-64. He also led in important goals, with 30 of his 42 falling in that category." (The NHL considered a goal "important" if it was the first goal of a game, a game-tying goal, a go-ahead goal, an insurance goal—putting a team two goals ahead, or a proximate goal, which moved the losing team within one goal of its opponent's score.)

Yet Ullman was hardly noticed even after he scored. One reason for this, perhaps, was that he was seldom involved in fights on the ice. But when he did throw a punch, it was usually at a large defenseman and under extreme provocation. Once, during a clash with Aut Erickson, then with Boston, Ullman beat him so badly with lefts and rights that the defenseman was left blood-smeared and in need of two stitches to close a gash over his right eye. Another time, Ullman pum-meled Kent Douglas of the Maple Leafs so vigorously that fellow defenseman Bobby Baun of the Leafs felt obliged to leap on Ullman's back in a humanitarian gesture to save Douglas.

"Mostly," said Ullman with typical modesty, "I was involved in draws."

There was no draw, however, in the voting for All-Star center. Ullman was elected over Chicago's future Hall of Famer Stan Mikita, 159-105, although Mikita had led the league in points. It was Ullman's first selection as an All-Star. In balloting for the Most Valuable Player, he was runner-up—103-96—to Bobby Hull. But in the second-half vote for the Hart Trophy, Ullman routed Hull, 74-15.

At the time, Jack Adams was quoted as saying, "If I was building a hockey club and had my choice of players in the league, my first choices would have been Ullman and Bob Pulford of the Leafs. I'd have put a $250,000 price tag on Normie."

Still, for all his recognized skills, Ullman remained largely ignored by fans and press. "He won hockey games," said one NHL veteran, "but he didn't sell tickets."

"I think Ullman's shyness had something to do with his hockey style," said Bobby Hull, who was never called shy. "It kept him from freewheeling and being noticed."

But Ullman was unconcerned about this lack of attention. "If you look around the league," he said, "you'll find that the better players were not the guys who fooled around and made all the noise. The better ones were the more serious types. To be very honest, I'd rather stay the way I am."

During the 1956-57 season, Ullman, Howe and Lindsay set a league point-scoring record for a line (226), but the line was broken up after that season, and Ullman was placed with lesser talents. "Both Normie and Gordie were puck carriers," explained Sid Abel, who was responsible for the move. "If Ullman was out with Howe, one of them would be left standing with little to do. Since Norm was such a hard worker, I often put him on a line with rookies, and he usually improved their play."

Ullman finished the 1963-64 season with 21 goals. The leap to 42 in 1964-65 indicated that Ullman must have been doing something right, but he was not sure exactly what it was, except possibly playing on a line with Floyd Smith, whose digging style blended well with Ullman's style.

Abel believed a change in style was at the root of Ullman's improvement. "Norm used to wheel after he got the puck over the enemy's blue line," said Abel. "Now he was driving in. He was getting the puck in deeper, getting more opportunity for plays, and he was taking more shots for himself. He always was a great team player, but he carried it to extremes. He was trying to wait and make his pass extra perfect. Now, he passed more quickly or took the shot himself. So we got two or three chances instead of just one, or maybe none."

If Ullman had a weakness, it was his shot, which lacked the speed of either Hull's or Howe's. But Hull said that Ullman penetrated so deeply behind enemy lines, he'd be able to score with a shot of just average velocity. "He got in close enough, then he shot for the corners," Hull said, "and often got them."

But Ullman was not a Hull and he knew it. "Bobby was stronger," Ullman conceded, "and had a much harder shot, and he got a lot more chances."

Ullman was born in Provost, Alberta, on December 26, 1935, and attended school in Edmonton with singer Robert Goulet. But Ullman quit high school at the age of 17 to devote himself to hockey.

"Looking back," he said, "I felt I was real foolish to give up my education. I was hoping all along that I could make it in pro hockey, but I was never sure that I could go all the way. If I hadn't made it in hockey, I don't know what I'd have done now. No doubt quitting school was the biggest gamble of my life."

But he won that gamble. In 1954, at the age of 19, he set a record for a 36-game schedule by scoring 101 points for the Edmonton Junior Oil Kings. The Red Wings promoted him to the Edmonton Flyers for the 1954-55 season and to Detroit the following season.

Ullman played 13 full seasons for the Red Wings, becoming a household name in the Motor City—although it was a name more whispered than shouted.

Then it happened.

Ullman was dealt to the Maple Leafs with Floyd Smith and Paul Henderson for Frank Mahovlich, Pete Stemkowski, Garry Unger and the rights to Carl Brewer on March 3, 1968. Ullman would go on to play seven full seasons for Toronto, often distinguishing himself as he had with the Red Wings—with massive efficiency and no fanfare.

Norm ended his playing days in Edmonton, his hometown, putting in two seasons for the Edmonton Oilers before calling it a career: one of the most laudable in hockey history.

10

SIDNEY GERALD
"SID" ABEL

BORN: Melville, Saskatchewa,; February 22, 1918
DIED: February 8, 2000
POSITION: Center
NHL TEAMS: Detroit Red Wings, 1938-43, 1945-52; Chicago Blackhawks, 1952-53;
Coach, Chicago Blackhawks, 1952-54; Detroit Red Wings, 1958-70;
St. Louis Blues, 1971; Kansas City, 1975-76; General Manager, Detroit Red Wings, 1962-71;
St. Louis Blues, 1971-73; Kansas City Scouts, 1974-76
AWARDS/HONORS: Hart Trophy, 1949; NHL First All-Star Team, 1949, 1950;
NHL Second All-Star Team, 1942, 1951; Hockey Hall of Fame, 1969

Ole Bootnose.
It sounds like a cowboy's favorite horse.
Hewas one of Detroit's favorite centers.
Sid Abel, whose proboscis looked like a boot, nonetheless looked like one of the best National Hockey League centers from the pre–World War II days to his retirement from the NHL as a player in 1953. Ole Bootnose-Sid Abel: one and the same.

Except for a final stint as player-coach of the Chicago Blackhawks during the 1952-53 campaign—he led the 'Hawks to an unlikely playoff berth that year—Abel was pure Detroit through and through, later to return to Motown where he successfully managed and coached for several years.

Most of all, Abel is remembered as the artful center on the most successful unit of three that Detroiters ever had the good fortune to watch. Skating between right wing Gordie Howe and left wing Ted Lindsay, Abel was the balance wheel of the Production Line. And what more apt name could anyone have conjured up for high-scoring forwards in the Motor City?

Although both Lindsay and Howe lasted considerably longer in the NHL, Abel helped them reach stardom, although when he discussed his role, he always minimized his achievements. Once during the 1948-

49 season, when he was the league's leading goal scorer and Detroit finished in first place, he told his wife, Gloria, to pinch him.

"I kept telling her that because I felt sure that I was going to wake up someday and find out that I had been having a wonderful dream." It was no dream; rather, it was the talent of Sid Abel that made everything happen.

He was as creative a center as he was abrasive. His passes were crisp and accurate and his body checks were lusty. His durability fooled those who thought he was over the hill.

In 1949 at the age of 31, he blasted a winning goal past Turk Broda of the Toronto Maple Leafs. After the game, Broda met Abel in the corridor and shook his head. "What's got into you?" Broda asked. "You found the fountain of youth?"

"I don't know," Abel grinned. "But, boy, this is living! Don't ask me what's happening. It just seems that every time I shoot, I score. And I love it!"

The Abel-Lindsay-Howe line developed into one of the finest units in hockey history. Abel had the savvy, and Howe and Lindsay had a mixture of style and aggressiveness that intimidated their opponents.

Sid was the backbone of the Red Wings. While

OPPOSITE: Because of his proboscis, Sid Abel was nicknamed Ole Boot Nose.

he played for Detroit, the powerful team won the Prince of Wales Trophy in 1942-43 and again for four straight years, from 1948-49 to 1951-52. (The trophy was then awarded to the team finishing with the most points in the regular season.)

In 1941-42, Sid was named to the second team All-Stars at left wing. In 1948-49 and 1949-50, he was named to the first team All-Stars at center. Again, in 1950-51, he was named to the second team All-Stars at center, sharing the honor with Ted Kennedy of the Toronto Maple Leafs. He thus became the first player ever to win an All-Star rating at two different positions.

In 1948-49, while playing in 69 games, Sid was the individual goal-scoring leader, scoring 28 goals. Most of his goals that year were tying or winning goals, and it was in 1949 that he won the Hart Trophy—emblematic of the player judged to be the most valuable to his team. *Sport* magazine also bestowed upon him the honor of "Hockey's Man of the Year."

With Sid playing for them, the Red Wings won the Stanley Cup in 1942-43, 1949-50 and 1951-52. They finished first five times, in 1942-43, 1948-49, 1949-50, 1950-51 and 1951-52.

In his 13 seasons of professional hockey, Sid played in 612 games, scoring 189 goals and registering 283 assists for a total of 472 points. In 97 playoff games, his statistics were 28 goals and 30 assists for a total of 58 points.

The Red Wings' intimidating Production Line was acclaimed as one of the all-time greatest lines of hockey, and it had the statistics to prove it. In 1948-49, its total of 66 goals ranked as the high mark for any line in the league.

During the 1949-50 season, Abel scored 33 goals (finishing third to Maurice Richard with 43 and Howe with 34), and the Production Line swept to new heights, finishing 1-2-3 in the scoring race. Lindsay won the championship with 78 points, Abel had 69, and Howe was third with 68.

Sid's career was filled with many highlights. One came in a game against the Boston Bruins. On November 2, 1949, Abel fired three pucks past goalie Jack Gelineau as the Wings beat the Bruins, 5-3. It was the first time he had ever scored a hat trick. "It took me 10 years to do it," he cracked, "but it was sure worth the wait."

Sid realized another one of his lifelong ambitions in the 1948-49 season, when he scored the100th goal of his NHL career. It was his 18th goal that year, and the goalie was Turk Broda in a game at the Maple Leaf Gardens. Shortly afterwards, at the age of 31, another of Sid's dreams came true when he had his first 20-goal season, scoring 28 goals. That same season, he had a total of 54 points, ranking him third in the league.

In the 1949-50 playoffs, the Red Wings had to recover from a 5-0 beating in the first game against Toronto and the loss of the injured Gordie Howe. Sid's leadership finally helped the Red Wings end the Toronto jinx and eliminate the three-time Stanley Cup winners.

It would be Sid's indomitable play that would prove to be the turning point in the 1950 championship series with the New York Rangers.

Sidney Gerald Abel was born in Melville, Saskatchewan, on February 22, 1918. Like most of the youngsters from around there, he played hockey every available moment, wherever there was ice to be found.

Fortunately for Sid, he became the "favorite son" of the postmaster, "Goldie" Smith, who was also a scout for the Red Wings and had helped discover other NHL stars, including Hall of Famer Eddie Shore.

Abel caught Smith's eye with his earnest approach to the game. Sid had drive and tenacity of purpose, all of which impressed Goldie so much that he invited Abel to visit the Red Wings' training camp in the fall of 1937.

When Abel reported to manager Jack Adams, the boss took one look at the slim 155-pound westerner and then at the intense practice session that was taking place out on the ice. Adams felt sure that this young man would never stand up under the battering of the pro game. Still, Adams was impressed. He suggested that Sid stay in Detroit and play in the Michigan-Ontario area. Abel graciously declined the offer, telling Adams that he would be going back to his home to play for the Flin Flon team and for Goldie Smith. With that, the young man turned and headed west.

Abel played left wing for the Flin Flon Bombers of Manitoba during the winter of 1937. They enjoyed a fine season and ended up as finalists in the Western Canada play-downs for the Allan Cup. Abel was thought to have been one of the best players on the team, but he felt his performance that year was only mediocre. Upon his return to Melville, he met a very excited Goldie Smith.

"We're in, Sid," Smith told Abel. "The Red Wings want to sign you to a contract." Abel was stunned. "Sign me—what for?" was his reply.

The two men eagerly examined the contract. It was true. But on June 25, 1938, only a few short weeks later, Sid was confronted with the shocking news that his friend Goldie had died. With Goldie gone, Abel suddenly felt alone. Sadly, Sid reported to the Wings' training camp. Goldie had discovered his last Detroit star.

In 1938, the Red Wings were rebuilding. There were almost 60 youngsters trying out, all with hopes that they could make the team. Sid was nervous until he happened to overhear Adams say, "If he can stand up to the rugged going, young Abel is our best bet for the future."

Sid was sent down to the Pittsburgh Hornets of the American League that season. He played under Larry Aurie (a former Red Wing star) and scored 21 goals, adding 24 assists for 45 points. Occasionally during the season, he would be called up to join the Red Wings.

Sid played the next season with the Red Wings. However, he began to think Adams's initial fears might become reality. He was injured, smashing into an opponent and breaking his shoulder. When he recovered from that injury, he was sent down to Detroit's Indianapolis farm team.

But Abel's tenacity on the ice soon had him back on the parent club, and Sid improved his playing ability at left wing and at center. In 1942-43, Abel's first year as captain, the Red Wings went on to beat the Bruins in four straight games to win the Stanley Cup.

World War II was blazing, and Sid saw many of his friends leaving to join the armed forces. At the end of the 1943 season, Sid joined the Royal Canadian Air Force, and in doing so, left a void on the Red Wings' club.

In February 1946, Sid returned to hockey. He was 28 and found it was difficult picking up where he had left off. The younger players were fresher than ever, and the game was now much faster due to the "red-line" pass, a wartime innovation.

In 1946-47, back at center ice, Sid installed several wing combinations, but mainly played with Lindsay and Pete Horeck. Abel had to force himself to keep up with the young men's pace. He practiced skating and strategy for long hours until he caught up with the new "modern" game.

Eventually, Sid again became the spark plug for Detroit. Ole Bootnose suddenly found himself, and in 1949-50 he moved between Ted and Gordie, passing and scoring as though he were a rookie. In 1950,

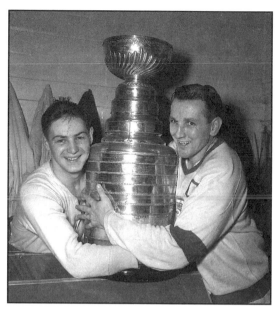

Sid Abel (right) and Terry Sawchuk embrace the Stanley Cup.

Captain Abel helped the Red Wings beat the Rangers and brought the Stanley Cup back to Olympia Stadium.

But by the early 1950s, Jack Adams got the impression that Sid was slowing down. And before the 1952-53 season, Abel was released by the Wings and became player-coach in Chicago. The Blackhawks were a pathetic team that had finished last in five of its six previous seasons. Coaching would be a big challenge for Sid.

What he performed was a miracle of sorts. Both playing and coaching, Sid turned the club around. His spirited play at center, along with the incredible goaltending of Al Rollins, helped Chicago into the playoffs. The 'Hawks almost beat the Canadiens in the semifinals, but lost the series in the seventh and final game.

Abel returned to Detroit, becoming the coach of the Red Wings in January 1958. He remained at that position until 1962-63, when he succeeded Jack Adams as Wings' general manager. Despite the fact that Abel and Adams were at odds with each other, Sid remained with Detroit in one capacity or another through part of the 1970-71 season.

In 1971-72, Sid signed to coach the St. Louis Blues, a move that proved to be a mistake from the beginning. He was named general manager of the Blues in October 1971 and stayed until April 17, 1973, when he was named general manager of the Kansas City Scouts. As a manager-coach, Sid never did enjoy the success he had achieved as a player. In 1976 he left hockey to become a broadcaster in Detroit.

Few centers have been more productive in the vital areas than Sid. He was a dogged and creative playmaker, the cog in the wheel with Howe and Lindsay. In 1969, Sid was elected to hockey's Hall of Fame in recognition of all he had accomplished during his career.

"Sid," said hockey historian Ed Fitkin, "will go down in the Red Wings' history as the greatest competitor and inspirational force the Red Wings ever had."

11

SYDNEY HARRIS HOWE

BORN: Ottawa, Ontario, September 28, 1911
DIED: May 20, 1976
POSITION: Forward
NHL TEAMS: Ottawa Senators, 1929-30, 1932-34;
Philadelphia Quakers, 1930-31; Toronto Maple Leafs, 1931-32;
St. Louis Eagles, 1934-35; Detroit Red Wings, 1935-46
AWARDS/HONORS: NHL Second All-Star Team, 1945;
Hockey Hall of Fame, 1965

Not one, but two Howes were superstars in Detroit at different times during half a century of Red Wings hockey.

Everyone knows Gordie Howe, but actually Syd Howe (no relation to Gordie) was the first outstanding Howe to skate in Olympia Stadium, located at Grand River and McGraw.

If Gordie Howe was the Babe Ruth of Detroit hockey, one could say that Syd Howe was the Joe DiMaggio.

Sydney Harris Howe was born September 28, 1911, in Ottawa, Ontario. He broke into the National Hockey League with his hometown NHL team, the Senators, during the 1929-30 season and a year later moved to the Philadelphia Quakers before returning to the Senators in 1932. He was transferred to the St. Louis Eagles in 1934 and came to Detroit in 1935 along with defenseman Ralph "Scotty" Bowman in a deal said to involve $50,000, which was big money in those days of the Great Depression. It was one of Detroit's best deals, for Howe emerged as a versatile forward who could play virtually any position, and play it well—although he was deployed primarily on the left wing and at center.

Howe was named to the Second All-Star Team as a left wing in 1945, but his most notable accomplishment had taken place a year earlier, on the night of February 3, 1944, to be exact. The Red Wings were at home against the New York Rangers on that night, and at 11:27 of the first period, Howe launched what was to become known as one of the most impressive individual performances in history.

Taking a pass from Don "The Count" Grosso, he beat Ken "Tubby" McAuley in the Rangers' net. Just 18 seconds later, Howe scored again. The score was 3-0 in favor of Detroit late in the second period when defenseman Cully Simon delivered a pass to Howe, who beat goalie McAuley at 17:52, giving him a hat trick. Exactly 62 seconds later, Grosso spotted a free Howe, dispatched the pass, and still another red light went on for Syd. It was 5-0 for the Red Wings, and Howe had four of the five goals.

For eight minutes of the third period, the Rangers stymied him, but then his linemates, Grosso and Modere "Mud" Bruneteau, moved rapidly into the Rangers' zone. Howe was in position and whipped the rubber home at 8:17.

By now, Detroit coach Jack Adams knew he had the game in the bag—it was 8-0 for the Red Wings—so he gave his top line as much ice as possible and, sure enough, less than a minute later, Bruneteau and Grosso collaborated once more and fed Howe. Just like that, he had *his sixth goal of the game.*

"They left me out there on the ice to try and get more goals," Howe remembered. "I had a good chance to break the all-time record (Joe Malone's seven goals for the Quebec Bulldogs in 1920), but I couldn't do it."

Over the years, Howe played down the importance of his six-goal game. "I got a lot more satisfaction out of two other nights," he said.

In one of them he set a league record for what then was the fastest overtime playoff goal: 25 seconds after the start of the extra period. It happened on March 19, 1940, against the New York Americans.

"The score was 0-0," Syd recalled, "and I was playing on a line with Bruneteau and [Carl] Liscombe. I went down the left side and sent a low shot into the corner. The other time I'll never forget is the 'Night' Detroit fans gave me toward the end of my career. I got a lot of gifts, including a piano.

"You know how it is when they give you a 'Night.' It usually turns out that the team gets beat and you can't come close to scoring. I was a lot luckier. We beat the Blackhawks, 2-0, and I scored both goals."

In terms of points, Syd's best season was 1943-44, when he scored 32 goals and added 28 assists for 60 points in 40 games. He played for three Stanley Cup-champion teams and three first-place teams.

It is noteworthy that Howe pinpointed the turnabout in hockey's attacking style as having taken place during the 1942 Stanley Cup Finals between the Red Wings and the Toronto Maple Leafs.

"Up until that time," Syd explained, "the attacks and counterattacks were more or less straight up and down, with the puck either carried or passed back and forth into the enemy zone. But in the 1942 series, Detroit started the 'new' way of *shooting* the puck into the opposition's zone and *chasing* after it."

Syd Howe completed his NHL career with Detroit in the 1945-46 season. He's forechecking against Rangers forward Ab DeMarco in a game at New York in November 1945.

Syd remained a Red Wing through the 1945-46 season and then retired just before Gordie Howe came on the scene. After retirement, Howe returned to his native Ottawa and would be reminded of his six-goal accomplishment whenever another NHLer came close to matching his feat. In the early 1960s, while Howe was attending a gathering at the home of friends in Ottawa, word got around that Bobby Rousseau had scored five goals. "The people at the party," said Howe, "were more worried than I was about Rousseau breaking the record."

In time Red Berenson, then of the St. Louis Blues, would equal Howe's six-goals-in-one-game mark, but it has never been surpassed. Interestingly, Gordie Howe made his Red Wings' debut as a rookie during the season following Syd's retirement.

Syd Howe was elected to the Hockey Hall of Fame in 1965, but by that time his record had been overshadowed by the *other* Howe, one of the greatest NHLers of all time.

12

BRENDAN SHANAHAN

BORN: Mimico, Ontario, January 23, 1969
POSITION: Left Wing
NHL TEAMS: New Jersey Devils, 1987-91; St. Louis, 1991-95;
Hartford Whalers, 1995-96; Detroit Red Wings, 1996-Present
AWARDS/HONORS: NHL First All-Star Team, 1994, 2000;
NHL All-Star Game, 1994, 1996-2000, 2002

Throughout the 1980s, the position of "power forward" began to evolve in importance. The likes of Clark Gillies and Cam Neely epitomized this type of player. They were big, strong, and agile and could crash the net on a nightly basis. Some of the first players to get the title included Rick Tocchet of the Flyers and Cam Neely of the Bruins. Brendan Shanahan joined the ranks of this rare breed.

Playing junior hockey in London, Ontario, Shanahan was not your prototypical power forward. Not blessed with a dominating physique, Shanahan was nonetheless a coach's dream. Not only could he score goals, but he could also play an aggressive and gritty style that few gifted players can.

After the Buffalo Sabres selected Pierre Turgeon with the first overall pick in the 1987 NHL entry draft, Brendan was chosen by the New Jersey Devils. Ironically, the draft was held in Detroit that summer, the city where Shanahan would eventually achieve all of his childhood dreams. The Devils' brass admired Shanahan's aggressive style. He was a perfect fit on a team on the verge of making a serious playoff run later that season. But Brendan immediately slumped under

the enormous pressure. His ice time soon diminished; his confidence wavered.

"The pressure on Shanny right in the beginning was that Turgeon was picked one ahead of him and he started off really fast and had a great rookie year for the Sabres," said Devils teammate Kirk Muller. "The problem was that Brendan stepped into a young team at the time, and we eventually went to the semifinals. His role was sort of limited for the first part of the season.

"He was a key guy when he played in junior, and now in the NHL his first year, everything's new to him and he's not playing much, so he had to adjust. He then decided to do some fighting until he progressed and got going his first year."

Shanahan began taking on all comers and finished his first season as a pro with 131 penalty minutes in 65 games. However, his six goals that season didn't exactly endear him to New Jersey's coaches.

He had always been considered a goal scorer first and a fighter second—before the NHL, that is. But as Shanahan's big-league career progressed, the two abilities appeared to be switching places in importance. The change took place after Shanahan signed as a free agent

OPPOSITE: Brendan Shanahan, one of the best of the contemporary Red Wings.

Brendan Shanahan slides past the goal post.

with St. Louis in July of 1991. Suddenly, the goal scorer appeared, as Brendan produced two seasons of 50-plus goals for the Blues.

It appeared, however, that Brendan was developing a bad reputation. He'd play a few seasons for a team, his goal production would slack off after a couple of seasons, and his team would begin dangling Shanahan as very seductive trade bait. The Blues traded him to Hartford (now Carolina) in the off season of 1995 for up-and-coming defenseman Chris Pronger. Brendan whipped up 46 goals for Hartford in 1996-97, then was traded again. This trade, however, would produce the perfect marriage between Shanahan's undisputed skills and the Red Wings' need for a talent to help produce a Stanley Cup for the first time since 1955. It

worked. Detroit won Cups in 1997 and 1998, with Brendan an integral part of the team.

But few people really knew the story behind Shanahan's hugely successful shot.

"The thing that may surprise people is that Shanny had just an awful shot when he first came up with Jersey," said Muller. "It was terrible! But the best thing that could have happened to him was when he went to St. Louis and learned how to shoot from the best."

The "best" happened to be Brett Hull, the most prolific goal scorer in the 1990s. Hull was coming off an amazing 86-goal season when Shanahan arrived in July of 1991.

"The thing with Shanny was that he had such a big tape knob at the top of his stick," recalled Hull.

"He just couldn't move and maneuver his wrists the way you need to in order to get a good and quick shot away. But the thing was, he was able to score goals even with that knob because he was so strong."

Shanahan took the advice of Hull and began to use smaller amounts of tape on the butt end of his stick. The positive results soon appeared, with 51 goals in 1992-93 and 52 in 1993-94.

In October 1996, the Red Wings acquired Shanahan and defenseman Brian Glynn from the Hartford Whalers in exchange for Keith Primeau, Paul Coffey and a first-round pick in the 1997 entry draft. Some felt the Red Wings paid too steep a price for Brendan. But the Mimico, Ontario, native soon changed the naysayers' opinions.

In Detroit, he exploded offensively during the 1996-97 season, tallying 46 goals and 41 assists for a team that dominated in the regular season on a consistent basis, but continually faltered in the playoffs. Brendan was exactly what the Detroit doctor had ordered.

The Wings had been somewhat low on grit and toughness. But with Brendan, the club soon realized its full potential. Shanahan's physical presence began to create open ice for freewheeling skaters such as Sergei Fedorov and Slava Kozlov. His aggressive style resulted in 131 penalty minutes that first year with the Wings. But he backed up his feistiness with some of the best offensive numbers of his career.

In 1996-97, he led the team in points, goals, power-play goals, game-winning goals and short-handed goals. He was also named NHL Player of the Month in February 1997 after leading all players with 21 points. He also recorded three hat tricks—two in back-to-back games.

After several seasons of early playoff exits or playing bridesmaid in the finals, the Red Wings swept the Philadelphia Flyers in the 1997 Stanley Cup Finals, four games to none. Shanahan was everything and everywhere on the ice during his team's playoff run. He led the team in goals and game-winning goals. And he drank from the silver chalice for the first time in his career.

As the 1997-98 season approached, Detroit coach Scotty Bowman had been pondering a scheme that would affect Shanahan. Bowman knew the road to repeating as Stanley Cup champions was going to be difficult, and he needed his best players to adapt to a style of play that would benefit the team.

During Bowman's tenure as coach, he had tweaked the styles of such offensive players as Steve Yzerman and Sergei Fedorov. Both players readily accepted the change from offensive to defensive philosophies, and the team in turn won the championship.

Now, in order to capture Cup No. 2, it was time for Bowman to alter Shanahan's offensive thinking. The days of Brendan being a 40-goal scorer appeared doomed. Shanahan soon learned that his role with the club was going to consist of hanging more often in the offensive zone. Gone were the days of crashing the net for goals. Gone were the days of setting up in the face-off circle for his lightning-quick and accurate one-timer. If Brendan didn't like it, he would soon be gone, just like former Red Wing Dino Ciccarelli, who could seemingly score goals with his eyes closed but who refused to adapt to Bowman's defensive ways.

"It's all about winning here," he said. "That's the reason all of us are here."

Bowman explained his decision.

"We have enough goals," he said. "We haven't been looking for anybody to have to score more than they have. I think a lot of it is the way the game is played now. Teams are keying on certain guys on our team, and we have our players kind of spread out."

Shanahan was certainly being "keyed on" by opponents as the 1997-98 season progressed. Sergei Fedorov was in the midst of a bitter contract squabble with the Red Wings organization, and Brendan was feeling the brunt of the feud between the two camps on the ice.

Not only was Brendan concentrating more on his defensive game, but other clubs began to focus their defensive game plan on stopping him. During the first 29 games of the season, Shanahan registered 14 goals. But as the season wound down, so did his production.

Shanahan ended the year with only 28 goals, failing to score 30 goals for the first time since 1990-91. Only 12 of his tallies came during even-strength situations, the fewest since his 1987-88 rookie season. Shanahan himself seemed frustrated as the playoffs approached.

"I'd be lying if I said I wasn't disappointed not to be up in the league leaders, where I feel I should be," he said. "I'm not having big nights as far as scoring a lot of goals in a game.

"You've got to feel like a sniper to be one, and that's confidence, and it comes from getting on a roll and having big nights."

Hull agreed with his former teammate's comments. However, he added that the style of play during that particular season had changed dramatically throughout the whole league.

"It's totally different from when we were lighting it up in St. Louis," Hull said. "It's a totally different game. I try to tell myself that all the time.

"I try to tell myself I'm still as good of a goal scorer as I always was. I haven't talked to Shanny about it, but I know I surely don't like to even think about it."

Yzerman corroborated Hull's reasoning for Brendan's offensive drop-off.

"It's no different from any other team," the captain said. "Their top scorers' points are down, too. Offense is down in the whole league.

"But Shanny's such a physically strong guy with a great shot in tight games. And in close games, when you need a quick chance and have to get a quick shot away, it makes a big difference."

A perfect case in point came in a late-season game against Chicago. The Red Wings and Blackhawks were tied at two apiece when the teams lined up for a face-off in the Chicago end with less than 10 seconds to play.

Yzerman quickly won the draw back to his defenseman Dmitri Mironov, while Shanahan drifted from his spot on the faceoff circle. As Mironov wound up and blasted the puck off Chicago goaltender Jeff Hackett's pads, Shanahan appeared seemingly out of nowhere and cranked the rebound past a sprawled Hackett with just 2.8 seconds left.

Shanahan rebounded with a vengeance during the 1998 Stanley Cup playoffs. In Game 6 of Detroit's first-round matchup with Phoenix, Brendan scored two power-play goals, including the series winner. Facing St. Louis in the second round, Shanahan again came up with a clutch performance, tallying two game-winning goals during the series, including the overtime winner in Game 3.

"Shanahan recognizes that the playoffs take an awful lot of energy," said Dallas Stars coach Ken Hitchcock. "And he knows exactly when to start really asserting himself."

Brendan and his Detroit teammates eliminated Hitchcock's Stars in the 1998 Western Conference Finals to secure their second straight berth in the Stanley Cup Finals. Their opponents were the Washington Capitals, led by goaltender Olaf Kolzig.

But the Caps were no contest against the determined group wearing red and white. With Detroit leading three games to none, Shanahan took his pregame nap before Game 4 and dreamt that he and his teammates were going to hoist the Cup for the second straight year later that evening. And after the Red Wings defeated the Capitals by a score of 4-1, Brendan's pregame fantasy became reality.

"It was the most unbelievable thing," Shanahan said about his sleep-induced premonition. "I only slept a half-hour, but it was a vivid dream. It was like a flash of clarity.

"I saw us all on the plane flying home partying. I could see it. I've never experienced anything quite like that."

In the dream, teammate Joey Kocur walked over to Shanahan and gave him a whack across his aching back. Eerily enough, Kocur did exactly that a few minutes before Game 4 in the MCI Center in Washington.

"I can't believe you just did that," Shanahan screamed. "I had a dream before the game that we won the Stanley Cup and you hit my back before the game and I threw a stick at you."

"Well, what are you waiting for?" replied Kocur. "Do it."

Shanahan launched a stick in the culprit's direction.

After the game, Kocur's skepticism about Shanahan's dream evaporated.

"I couldn't believe it when Shanny told me," he said. "I thought he was full of it at the time, but he said, 'No, no, I really had that dream.' So I told him to throw the stick. I'm not really that superstitious. He's the superstitious one. It was the weirdest thing."

Unfortunately, Brendan's dad was not around to see it. Born January 23, 1969, in Mimico, Ontario, Brendan had always been a happy-go-lucky kid who always enjoyed his time on the rink. The youngest of four boys, Shanahan was devastated when his father died of Alzheimer's disease in 1990.

"I think that all of us in the NHL are lucky to be doing what we're doing," he said. "Still, looks are deceiving. Everything looks all neat and tidy from the outside, but it's never that simple when you're the person."

Shanahan signed a four-year contract extension with the Red Wings right before the playoffs in 1999, after finishing the season with 40 or more goals for the fifth time in his career. The contract signaled Shanahan's desire to finish his career with the organization in which he has enjoyed his greatest success.

"He's arguably the best power forward in the game right now," said Muller. "He can score, plus he adds the toughness, which is one more ingredient. He's simply one of the toughest competitors that I have played with or against."

Well on his way to recording 500 goals and 1,000 points in a stellar career, Brendan Shanahan was the right pick for New Jersey as second overall in the 1987 draft—but it's the Detroit Red Wings who have reaped most of the benefits.

Brendan Shanahan demonstrates his backchecking ability.

13

ROBERT "BOB" GOLDHAM

BORN: Georgetown, Ontario, May 12, 1922
POSITION: Defenseman
NHL TEAMS: Toronto Maple Leafs, 1941-42, 1945-47;
Chicago Blackhawks, 1947-50; Detroit Red Wings, 1950-56
AWARDS/HONORS: NHL Second All-Star Team, 1955;
NHL All-Star Game, 1947, 1949, 1950, 1952, 1954, 1955

A case could be made for Bob Goldham as the most underrated defenseman in the annals of the National Hockey League.

Overshadowed by flashier types, Goldham was nevertheless a winner wherever he played. There's no better proof than the fact that he played on four Stanley Cup–winning teams, one the Toronto Maple Leafs and three the Detroit Red Wings.

Tall and powerful, Goldham was a deceptive type of player. He was faster than he appeared and considerably tougher than his outwardly passive nature suggested.

One could argue that the Georgetown, Ontario native was the quintessential defenseman, doing his job with a minimum of fuss and fanfare.

But there was one aspect of Goldham's technique that lifted him above the masses. Few—if any—backliners were as adept as puck blocking on a consistently effective basis.

Employing exquisite timing, Bob would dauntlessly throw his body in front of dangerous shots and invariably smother the rubber or deflect it out of harm's way.

"Goldham was as about as good as anyone at blocking shots," said Toronto teammate and Hall of Fame defenseman Red Kelly. "Bob may not have invented the puck-blocking technique, but he certainly took it to a new and more effective level."

The Red Wings' acquisition of Goldham was a fortuitous one after the youngster had launched his big-league career in Toronto (1941-42) before enlisting in the Canadian armed forces after the Japanese attack on Pearl Harbor.

He returned to the Maple Leafs after World War II, but was dealt to Chicago in a blockbuster deal. Toronto hockey boss Conn Smythe was determined to obtain center ice strength and traded five regulars—Gaye Stewart, Bud Poile, Gus Bodnar, Ernie Dickens and Goldham—to the Chicago Blackhawks for future Hall of Fame center Max Bentley.

After three seasons in the Windy City, Goldham was moved to Detroit in another huge deal. Along with Sugar Jim Henry, Gaye Stewart and Metro Prystai, Goldham went to the Red Wings for Harry Lumley, Jack Stewart, Al Dewsbury, Don Morrison and Pete Babando.

At the time of the exchange, Goldham was not considered the prime acquisition. Prystai was a star in the making—or so Detroit boss Jack Adams hoped—and Henry was supposed to supply goaltending insur-

OPPOSITE: Bob Goldham (center) listens to coach Tommy Ivan along with teammate Marty Pavelich.

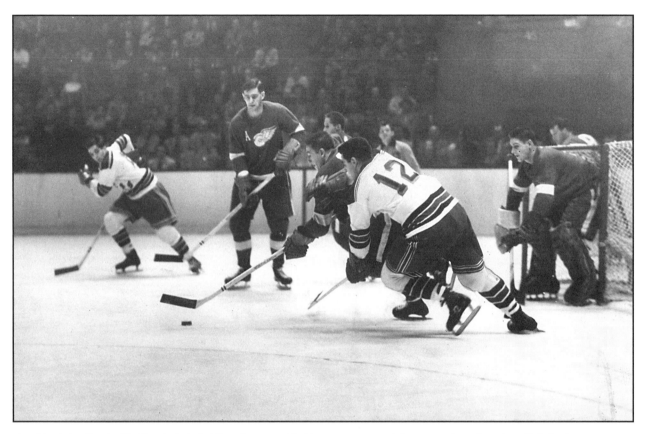

As a Maple Leaf and a Blackhawk, Bob Goldham (center, with A) was an average defenseman. But when the tall defender came to Detroit in 1950, he became one of the best puck blockers of all time and one of the top defensive defensemen. Here, he stands guard as teammate Marcel Pronovost clears the puck.

ance. As it happened, Goldham was the best acquisi-tion for either team. He meshed smoothly with the Red Wings' system, which resulted in several first-place fin-ishes and Stanley Cup championships in 1951-52, 1953-54 and 1954-55.

"Bob was like a rock on our blue line," said Adams. "It was no coincidence that we were a first-place team with him in the lineup."

Many students of The Game believe Goldham should have been inducted into the Hockey Hall of Fame along with such teammates as Gordie Howe, Ted Lindsay and Red Kelly. They cite his overall defensive effectiveness and the fact that the Red Wings won three Stanley Cups with him as balance-wheel defenseman.

But Bob—despite the fact that he perfected the puck-blocking technique—was continually overlooked. This could be explained—in part—by his absence from the league for three full seasons when he served in the Canadian armed forces during World War II.

When Goldham retired following the 1955-56 season, he had played a dozen years as a major leaguer. Considering that lesser defenseman made it into the Hall of Fame, he was conspicuous by his absence. It was yet another Hall of Fame injustice, but it should not for a moment detract from what was a brilliant—though unobtrusive—career as a defenseman.

After retirement, Goldham became a popular hockey commentator in Toronto in the 1960s, cam-paigning tirelessly for increased pension benefits for retired NHL players.

14

NICKLAS LIDSTROM

BORN: Vasteras, Sweden, April 28, 1970
POSITION: Defenseman
NHL TEAMS: Detroit, 1991–Present
AWARDS/HONORS: NHL All-Rookie Team, 1992; Norris Trophy, 2001;
NHL First All-Star Team, 1998, 1999, 2000, 2001
NHL All-Star Game, 1996, 1998-2002

How good is Nicklas Lidstrom? Red Wings captain Steve Yzerman summed it up best in 1999. "I'd hate to think how ordinary we would be without him," said Yzerman at the time.

Lidstrom was contemplating leaving the Red Wings and moving his family back to his native Sweden. Detroit had many irreplaceable or indispensable players on their roster. Lidstrom was both.

"Nick plays more quality minutes than anyone in the NHL," continued Yzerman. "He kills penalties, plays on our power play and he's always out there on defense against the opponents' best players."

General manager Ken Holland, who held the key to Lidstrom's return, said that "to lose a player of his quality, especially a defenseman who plays 30 minutes against the other team's best players and also scores, would be the kind of impact that is beyond any words I can come up with." Nobody could have anticipated such praise a decade ago, when Lidstrom came to Detroit.

He broke into the NHL as a shy rookie in the fall of 1991. After being selected by Detroit in the third round (53rd overall) of the 1989 draft, Lidstrom played in the Swedish Elite League for three seasons before heading to Michigan.

He registered the first two points of his career on October 5, 1991, against Toronto en route to tying Reed Larson's franchise record for most points by a rookie defenseman (60). That year, he also tied Marcel

Dionne's club mark for most assists by a rookie (49), was named to the NHL All-Rookie team, and finished second to Pavel Bure in the Calder Trophy voting for rookie of the year.

Not bad for a kid whose boyhood idol was the best Swedish defenseman ever to lace on a pair of skates, Borje Salming.

"Borje was my hero, my idol. He was the big guy back then," Lidstrom said of Salming. "I had the opportunity to play with him in the (1991) Canada Cup. He was my partner. It was a big thrill, with him being the legend he is, especially back in Sweden."

Lidstrom himself has become somewhat of a legend for younger Red Wings prospects hoping to make it to the NHL.

"In 1999 I was at my third training camp, and I still had not seen him get beat one-on-one," said prospect Jesse Wallin, who has the same 6'2", 190-pound frame as Lidstrom's.

With his lean physique, Lidstrom plays more of a mental game than a purely physical one. He positions himself perfectly on every play, keeping the opposition away from scoring chances. Offensively, Lidstrom skates effortlessly as he moves out of his zone, passing the puck at the precise moment with pinpoint accuracy. His intelligence helps him outmaneuver his opponents.

His overall style of play, however, is very unassuming, just like his personality.

"There's quiet, and then there's Nick," said

Nicklas Lidstrom won the Norris Trophy as the NHL's best defenseman in 2000-01 and again the following year.

Yzerman, describing his teammate's unobtrusive persona.

Friends contend that it is his humility that makes him such a special person, both on and off the ice.

"It's just as well as that I'm not a big, menacing type of player," Lidstrom explained. "I've used my size to my advantage. I worked a lot with [assistant coach] Dave Lewis, and he helped me improve on things like locking up the guy's stick when he gets into our zone. It's nothing that's going to bring people out of their seats."

But it helped bring the Detroit organization back-to-back Stanley Cups in 1997 and 1998.

Nicklas Lidstrom was born in Vasteras, Sweden, on April 28, 1970. As a youngster, he played hockey in the winter and soccer in the summer while studying to be an engineer. To this day, he thoroughly believes that the skills he learned as a young soccer player in his homeland helped him excel in the world's fastest sport.

"I got my hockey skills from playing soccer," he said when asked about his ability to successfully hold the puck in at the blue line. "I played a lot of soccer when I was growing up. It helps me now to stop the puck with my feet."

Growing up, Lidstrom never really dreamed of playing in the NHL until he was well into his teens. Until that point he figured he would play professionally in his native Sweden.

"When I first started out, I just wanted to play on the big team in my hometown," he said. "When I was 13 or 14, I wanted to play in the Elite league. It wasn't until I was about 16 that I started to think about the NHL. That's pretty much when everybody started talking about it. Then, when I got drafted, I knew I had a chance to play in the NHL."

But it wasn't until that 1991 Canada Cup tournament that he truly knew he had what it took to make it in the world's best pro league.

"That Canada Cup helped me a lot," he said. "We played head-to-head against Canada and the U.S. I realized then that I could play in the NHL. I thought that in that tournament, the game would be so much better in every aspect. But I could skate with them."

Nick learned a great deal from playing sports as a youngster in Sweden. What he didn't learn as a child, though, was his father's temper. Lidstrom rarely lets his emotions get the best of him—almost to the point of it becoming quite uncomfortable to those around him.

Asked when he last lost his temper, Nicklas said, "I really can't remember. That's the way I've always been. My mom's like that. My dad's quite the opposite. He has a temper. He can get mad."

Swedish reporter Bengt Eriksson, for one, has tried feverishly to find out why Lidstrom never gets unnerved.

"We used to ask his father, back when Nick was in Sweden, how do we get him mad?" Eriksson said. "And we'd tease Annika, his wife, and say to her, 'What can we do to get Nick in an ugly mood before the game so he'll play mad?' And she'd say, 'I don't know, he's always so calm.'"

But what Lidstrom lacks in outward intensity, he compensates for with a willingness to do whatever it takes to win a hockey game.

One such instance came in the Western Conference Finals in 1997. The Red Wings were facing their archrivals from Colorado in Game 2 on March 17. The Avalanche had already defeated Detroit in Game 1 by a score of 2-1. Another Colorado win in Game 2 would certainly harm the Red Wings' chances of making it to the Stanley Cup finals for the second time in three years.

With Detroit up 3-2 in the game, Colorado forward Eric Lacroix was the recipient of a rebound left by Detroit goaltender Mike Vernon. Vernon made a sprawling save on the initial shot, but was out of position when Lacroix teed up the puck and stared into an empty net.

Enter Lidstrom. The defenseman with the accountant's attitude calmly saw what was happening and slid across the crease to stop Lacroix's point-blank shot. As play continued, no one in the building could believe his eyes.

But replays soon confirmed what everyone had witnessed firsthand. Lidstrom made the save of the game and quite possibly the series. Darren McCarty scored a minute later, icing the victory for Detroit. But afterwards, all accolades were sent in the direction of Lidstrom.

"Once I saw their guy free, I thought, 'Oh, no,'" Yzerman recalled.

"What an unbelievable play," assistant coach Dave Lewis said. "The biggest play of the series, right there. Yzerman scored a tremendous goal, but Nick robbed them of a sure goal. It was an empty net and the guy put it right on Nick's stick and Nick made an unbelievable play.

"I didn't even realize what had happened, because the play kept going. Then, after the replay, we realized what had happened. We almost fell down. I was watching the video and I almost fell down."

But it was all in a day's work for the modest Lidstrom.

"It was my guy from the faceoff, so I had to make up for letting him go along the boards," he explained.

"Just instinct. Just try to get in the way. Just try to get the puck out of there.

"I just reacted. I didn't really have time to think. Vernie kicked the puck out, and I just tried to get in front of the net. I just tried to get my stick in the way."

McCarty witnessed the larceny from behind the net.

"I was standing back in that position," he said. "You can't get there. You're too far away. You're just watching it. Then Nick just dives across, and it hits his stick. That was definitely the break we needed."

The following year, Detroit faced St. Louis in the second round of the playoffs. The Blues were a high-flying offensive team that led the league in goals during the 1997-98 season. Paced by the most prolific goal scorer of the 1990s, Brett Hull, St. Louis was ready for the challenge of facing the defending Stanley Cup champions.

But the Blues dropped three of their first five games and faced elimination in Game 6. In the closing seconds of the first period, Blues forward Geoff Courtnall slashed Lidstrom in the back of his right knee. He fell to the ice as the Detroit bench watched in horror.

He tried to get up, but his first attempt failed miserably. It was then that Lidstrom began to break a sweat.

"The leg just went numb," he later said.

Calm, cool and composed, Lidstrom soon returned to the game, and Detroit defeated St. Louis to advance to the Western Conference Finals for the fourth straight year. For all the offensive might the Blues had, Lidstrom was an integral part in shutting down Hull and Co. In fact, Hull scored only one goal in the entire series.

"Every time I stepped onto the ice, [Lidstrom] and [Larry] Murphy were out there," a frustrated Hull said. "I rarely saw any room to operate. Both are tremendous position defensemen.

"I wish he was bigger and more inclined to go after you. That way it would be easier to make a move on him or to get him to bite. You just can't rattle him into making mistakes."

Other Lidstrom opponents agree.

"He's always there, always around you, not letting you do what you want," said Keith Tkachuk.

Flying home from a game in Boston in the winter of 1997, the Dallas Stars were discussing the just-completed first quarter of the 1997-98 season. The players decided to write down on a piece of paper who the leading contenders for the major postseason awards were at this juncture.

"A number of our guys picked [Lidstrom] as the best defenseman and also for the Hart Trophy (MVP) winner," said Stars coach Ken Hitchcock. "That's how highly he is regarded."

After a spectacular rookie year, Lidstrom struggled during his sophomore season. He slumped to seven goals and 41 points in 1992-93. It was his lowest goal and point total in his career.

"I didn't play as well my second year," he said. "Dave Lewis really helped me get through that. We looked at tapes of what I was doing my first year compared to my second year. He had been a defenseman for many years in the league. He worked with me and helped me get out of that slump in the second half of the season."

Part of the problem that year was adjusting to his new defensive partner, future Hall of Famer Paul Coffey. The smooth-skating Coffey relieved some of Lidstrom's offensive load while relaying his expertise to the young defenseman.

"Having Paul helped develop my game even more," Lidstrom said.

Bouncing back in 1995-96, Lidstrom played in his first All-Star Game. That year, he posted what were then career highs in goals (17) and points (67). And it was during that season that he developed his powerful one-time shot.

"I started working on it more and more after I came over here," he said. "I wasn't shooting the puck as much when I played in Sweden. I was setting other guys up for shots or down-low plays. Over here, my shots got better and better. We've been using it a little more, too. I've been kind of the guy; the puck gets to me and I shoot it. That developed after I got here.

"The big thing is to have the goalie moving. When the puck is coming and he's moving—there might be guys in front of him, he might not see the puck—he has to react, get over there and stop. The quicker it goes, the tougher it is for the goalie."

Perhaps Lidstrom's most amazing feat throughout his career has been the lack of time spent in the penalty box. He has never accumulated over 30 minutes in penalties in one season. And in 1999, he was the runner-up for the Lady Byng Trophy, given to the most sportsmanlike player in the league. Lidstrom was also a three-time nominee for the James Norris Trophy (1998, 1999, 2000) until finally winning it in 2001.

Former Red Wing ace Red Kelly was the last defenseman to win the award back in 1954. But the comparisons between the two don't stop there.

When Detroit won the Stanley Cup in 1955, Kelly spearheaded the blue line. The next time they won it, in 1997, it was Lidstrom who anchored the rear guard. They each had 15 goals during their championship seasons, with Kelly finishing with 30 penalty minutes. Lidstrom, however, stopped at 28 PIMS.

In 1997-98, Lidstrom made the NHL's First All-Star Team for the first time in his career. He finished the season with 59 points, which led all defensemen in the league. But it was in that year's playoffs that Nick shone. Lidstrom finished the 1998 postseason by setting a Detroit record for most points (19) and most assists (13) by a defenseman as the Red Wings won their second consecutive Stanley Cup.

As his career prospered and Hall of Fame possibilities beckoned, Lidstrom was ready to throw it all away. Late in the 1998-99 season, he pondered returning to his native Sweden. Not because he was sick of playing hockey for the Red Wings. Not because he thought he had accomplished everything that there was in The Game. But simply because he wanted his family, especially his two young sons, to grow up in Sweden.

"The issue has to do with what is best for our kids," he said in the spring of 1999 after finishing second for the second straight year in voting for the Norris Trophy.

As his contract expired in the summer of 1999, Lidstrom's threats of leaving became very real and very frightening for the Red Wings' high command.

"Nick leaving would be a loss you can't even put into words," general manager Ken Holland said.

To make matters worse for the Wings, Lidstrom received a contract offer from Vasteras, a Swedish Elite team that offered him $550,000, prime real estate for a home, business opportunities for him and his wife and private education for his sons.

Finally, in June of 1999, Lidstrom instructed his agent, Don Meehan, to begin negotiations with Holland. Lidstrom had earned $2 million the previous season and was looking for a raise that would bring him into the $6-$7 million range.

Negotiations dragged through the first two weeks of training camp. Frustrated, Lidstrom walked into Holland's office one day and asked him one simple question: Is the Detroit organization committed to being and staying competitive?

Holland assured his superstar it was. Lidstrom repeated the question more than once. He received the same answer. Shortly thereafter, the two sides agreed on a three-year contract worth close to $22 million.

"I want to get back to winning the Stanley Cup," Lidstrom said. "We all remember those two years we won it, how good you feel about yourself and how good the city feels about the team. That's what I want to get back to."

With the new contract under his belt, Nicklas went on to enjoy the best season of his career in 1999-2000. He recorded career highs in goals (20), assists (53) and points (73).

But the statistics meant nothing to him without a Stanley Cup ring.

"I've always looked at the Norris [Trophy] as being a bonus if you have a chance to win it all," he said. "I think the ultimate goal is to win the Stanley Cup. That's the way I felt when I was the runner-up in '98."

As Lidstrom's career continues, so does recognition of his quiet accomplishments.

"He makes things look easy," said Red Wings broadcaster Mickey Redmond. "If you don't watch him closely, you won't notice a lot of the good things he does. He's so smart. He knows how to read the play so well and how to read the individual opponents. He plays like a superstar. And he does it without taking penalties."

But Lidstrom's calm demeanor on the ice could ultimately be his undoing when critics reflect on this warrior's career.

"That's the one thing that may keep Nick from super-stardom," said Hakan Andersson, Detroit's European scout. "He's such a laid-back kind of guy. If he had the same kind of drive, the same mentality as Chris Chelios or Ray Bourque, who knows how good he would be? If he had that drive, that he wanted to be a No. 1 star, who knows how good he'd be?"

But teammates and those close to Nick disagree.

"He's always overlooked," said Darren McCarty. "That's the story of his career. He's one of the most underrated players in the league. He does it all. He plays great defensively. He's got a heck of a shot. He's a great offensive player. He plays 35 minutes a game.

"He doesn't get the respect, but we know how good he is, and that's what counts. When your teammates appreciate you, that's all that matters."

Lidstrom's quiet excellence on Detroit's blueline was finally recognized in June 2001. Nick became the first European to win the James Norris Trophy as the "defenseman demonstrating the greatest all-round ability in the position." After three seasons of being runner-up, Lidstrom was at the top. And he stayed there through 2001-02.

15

WILLIAM ALEXANDER
"BILL" GADSBY

BORN: Calgary, Alberta, August 8, 1927
POSITION: Defenseman
NHL TEAMS: Chicago Blackhawks, 1946-55;
New York Rangers, 1955-61; Detroit Red Wings, 1961-66
AWARDS/HONORS: NHL Second All-Star Team, 1953, 1954, 1957, 1965;
NHL First All-Star Team, 1956, 1958, 1959; NHL All-Star Game, 1953, 1954,
1956-60, 1965; Hockey Hall of Fame, 1970

No NHL player has ever contributed more in terms of blood, sweat and tears without collecting a Stanley Cup than defenseman Bill Gadsby. His major league stint spanned two decades, but ultimately, Gadsby's NHL career could be defined with that old carny lament, "Close . . . but no cigar."

Early in his career, Gadsby was a blue line ace for the Chicago Blackhawks (1946-55) and then the New York Rangers (1955-61). But it was not until he was traded to Detroit in June 1961 for Les Hunt that Gadsby achieved the level of excellence that eventually earned him entrance into the Hockey Hall of Fame.

Gadsby was equally adept at both shot blocking and puck carrying. He worked especially well with Gordie Howe and Alex Delvecchio on a club that appeared destined to win the Stanley Cup during the 1964 playoffs with Toronto.

After the Red Wings had dispatched Chicago 4-3, in the semifinals, they took on the defending-champion Maple Leafs in the finals. With Gadsby playing the best defense of his life, the Red Wings moved into a three-games-to-two lead.

Game 6 was at Olympia Stadium in Detroit and the Motown fans were primed for the knockout blow. Late in the second period, Gadsby appeared to supply that fateful punch, with a pass enabling Gordie Howe to put Detroit ahead, 3-2. But Toronto rallied to tie the count at three, sending the game into sudden-death overtime.

Still, Detroit appeared to be in command, because Toronto's solid defenseman Bob Baun had broken an ankle stopping a shot late in regulation time. Nevertheless, when the first overtime began, Baun reappeared on the Toronto defense, his ankle shot up with painkiller. As luck would have it, it was not Gadsby but Baun who scored the game-winning goal, setting up Toronto to take the next game and recapture the Stanley Cup. It was the closest Gadsby ever came to sipping champagne from Lord Stanley's silver.

Gadsby broke in with the Blackhawks during the 1946-47 season and remained in the big time until 1965-66, when he retired as a member of the Red Wings. During that span, he was a three-time (1956, 1958 and 1959) member of the NHL First All-Star Team and was equally comfortable as a defensive or offensive defenseman. Gadsby played for Chicago until the 1954-55 season, when he was traded to the Rangers a day before Thanksgiving, along with Pete Conacher, for Al Stanley and Nick Mickoski.

He worked especially well with Gordie Howe and Alex Delvecchio on a club that appeared destined to win the Stanley Cup during the 1964 playoffs with Toronto. With Gadsby playing the best defense of his life, the Red Wings moved into a three-games-to-two lead. As luck would have it, the Red Wings lost Game Six in overtime and Toronto went on to win the Cup. It was the closest Gadsby ever came to sipping champagne from Lord Stanley's silver.

Bill Gadsby

16

VLADIMIR KONSTANTINOV

BORN: Murmansk, Russia, March 19, 1967
POSITION: Defenseman
NHL TEAMS: Detroit Red Wings, 1991-97
AWARDS/HONORS: NHL Second All-Star Team, 1996

If ever there was a heart and soul on the modern Red Wings—or a last line of defense on their 1997 Stanley Cup team—it was Vladimir Konstantinov. Vladdie, or "The Vladinator," as his teammates called him, was one of the best, if not the most devastating, open-ice hitters in league history. He would physically punish his opponents with an aggressive, hard-hitting style that became a trademark of his six-year Red Wings career.

Konstantinov joined the Wings with little fanfare in 1991 but quickly established himself as a tremendous physical force on the blue line. Even though he was only 5'11" and 190 pounds, he was—pound for pound—one of the toughest players in the NHL.

A native of Murmansk, Russia, Konstantinov shone brightly as he became a major contributor to a Detroit franchise that began to dominate the league in the mid-'90s. But tragedy awaited on a June night in 1997.

On the evening of Friday, June 13, just six days after the Red Wings had defeated the Philadelphia Flyers to win their first Stanley Cup in 42 years, 17 players attended a celebratory golf outing and dinner. Among them was Konstantinov. Shortly before 9 p.m., Konstantinov, along with fellow Russian teammate Viacheslav Fetisov and team masseur Sergei Mnatsakanov, climbed into a limousine driven by Richard Gnida. Unbeknownst to the trio, Gnida was unlicensed.

At approximately 9:15 p.m., in suburban Birmingham, Michigan, Gnida lost control of the vehicle and struck a tree. Gnida escaped unscathed, saved by the front-seat air bag. Fetisov, Konstantinov and Mnatsakanov did not.

The three were not wearing seatbelts and were consequently thrown around the back of the limo. Fetisov suffered chest contusions. Konstantinov and Mnatsakanov weren't so lucky. Both men incurred massive head injuries that nearly cost them their lives.

"The long-term prognosis for this is impossible to tell," Dr. James Robbins, a trauma surgeon at William Beaumont Hospital, said about Konstantinov after the accident. "The next few days are going to be very important to determine which way he is going to go."

Word of the tragedy soon spread throughout the Detroit organization and NHL headquarters. "Our organization is devastated," said Wings captain Steve Yzerman. "I hope and I ask for everyone's prayers. Do whatever you do in difficult times that helps make things work out better."

OPPOSITE: An elated Vladimir Konstantinov hoists the Stanley Cup in 1997.

NHL spokesman Arthur Pincus conveyed the league's thoughts the next day, saying, "Our prayers are with them."

Birmingham police released a statement later that evening, saying that the limousine was moving from the right lane to the far left lane when it continued moving left, onto the median, and struck a tree.

"There were no other vehicles involved in this accident," said Sgt. John VanGorder. "Witnesses said the roadway was clear in front of the limousine to move into the median."

Ironically, the accident occurred just 15 miles down the same road on which the Red Wings' victory parade had taken place three days earlier, before more than a million people.

"This Cup is for you, for Detroit, for Michigan," Konstantinov had told the throng that day.

Following the accident, a group of fans kept a vigil outside the hospital where Konstantinov was being kept alive with the aid of a ventilator. Other well-wishers went to the tree the limo had struck, leaving flowers and bouquets out of respect and hope. A stuffed octopus and several brooms symbolizing the Red Wings' sweep of the Flyers were also left, as well as a sign reading, "Our Hearts and Prayers Are With You All."

For the next 39 days, Konstantinov remained in a coma. He finally emerged on June 23, 1997. At a press conference, doctors spoke encouragingly about the prospects of Konstantinov being transferred out of intensive care within a few days to a special rehabilitation unit for brain-trauma victims.

Though Vladimir was not fully conscious and unable to communicate, spirits were high for the first time in over a month. Both Konstantinov and Mnatsakanov were now breathing on their own without the assistance of a ventilator.

"[Vladimir] is awake and significantly more alert and responding to friends and family . . . showing significant signs of improvement," said Dr. Karol Zabalik, a neurosurgeon specializing in brain trauma.

"In the next couple of days, both [Konstantinov and Mnatsakanov] will be transferred in the rehabilitation unit," said Dr. Sherry Viola, head of the Beaumont Hospital's inpatient rehab program.

Given the upbeat news, reporters asked if there was any hope that the Russians would fully recover. But with one single word, Konstantinov's ride as a professional hockey player abruptly ended. Stepping up to the microphone in the hospital pressroom, Dr. Zakalik solemnly said, "No." Thus a promising career, which had begun in a different land, had ended.

Vladimir Konstantinov was born on March 19, 1967, in the Soviet Union. At the age of 17, he made the Soviet Red Army team, where he played for the next seven years.

Konstantinov was one of a rare breed, playing for Red Army coach Viktor Tikhonov. The legendary bench jockey preached a puck-handling and swift-skating system dominated by finesse. Physical play was certainly a part of the game, but was not encouraged by either the Russians or the rest of Europe.

But Konstantinov developed into a rock-solid defenseman, learning how to position his body properly to take his opposition out of the play. This intelligent positioning helped him adapt to the more rugged style of the NHL when he made his debut with Detroit in 1991.

Originally selected by the Red Wings with their 12th pick (221st overall) in the 1989 NHL entry draft, Konstantinov made an immediate impact on the blue line. In his freshman year, Vladdie registered 34 points and 172 penalty minutes in helping the Wings to a 22-point improvement over their 1990-91 point total.

Over the next three years, Konstantinov became known for his bone-crushing hits and intimidating presence as a rear guard. He frustrated his opponents with his relentless drive, passion and competitive fire. Typical of many blueliners who were hard open-ice hitters, Konstantinov was sometimes labeled "dirty" and "cheap."

But whether he was praised as a tough player or reviled as one who displayed questionable actions to get the job done, everyone in and around The Game had respect for him.

"He really gets guys off their game," said teammate Brendan Shanahan. "I used to really dislike him when I played against him. Playing with him, I really appreciate how he does it game after game."

"He's so competitive," continued defense partner Nicklas Lidstrom. "He gets in every aspect of the game, he's not afraid of anybody."

Fellow Russian Slava Fetisov first knew he was witnessing a special player when he and Konstantinov played together for the Soviet Red Army team.

"I know him since he was 16," Fetisov said. "Everybody called him 'Grandpa' because he was so serious when he played, even when so young. He is very competitive when he plays the game. He doesn't take stupid penalties. He would hit his brother; he is never soft on anyone. But everybody respects him."

In 1995-96, Konstantinov definitively emerged as one of the league's elite defensemen. He won the

Vladimir Konstantinov crashing the St. Louis Blues' goal crease.

NHL's plus-minus competition, finishing the regular season with a plus-60 rating—the best mark since Wayne Gretzky finished plus-70 in 1986-87. He was also named an NHL second team All-Star that season.

The following year (1996-97), Konstantinov finished with a plus-38 rating while collecting a career-high 38 points before the Red Wings embarked on their Stanley Cup voyage in the spring of '97. He was also runner-up to New York Ranger defenseman Brian Leetch in the voting for the Norris Trophy, given to the best defenseman in hockey.

During the 1997 Western Conference Finals against Colorado, Konstantinov was at his agitating best. Through the first three games of the series, Avalanche forwards Joe Sakic and Peter Forsberg were being neu-

tralized by Konstantinov's physicality, much to the dismay of Colorado head coach Marc Crawford.

Down two games to one, Crawford needed to find some kind of an edge for his club heading into Game 4. Looking for an advantage, he decided to vent his frustrations to the media regarding Konstantinov's constant clutching and grabbing that nullified the Avalanche's speed.

"It's a great skill, but it's also a penalty," Crawford said in hopes of attracting the referees' attention.

Konstantinov, however, welcomed the verbal war with Crawford.

"The ref pays attention to me all the time for the last six years," he said. "I know what to do. I just need to control my emotions a little, try to skate away when they hit from behind after the whistle.

"We have a lot of guys who can run players. We can be in their face. It's very important to do the dirty job like that so the skill players can score goals."

Crawford's plan backfired, as the Wings notched a resounding 6-0 victory that propelled them to the Stanley Cup Finals against Philadelphia.

As the matchup between the Red Wings and the Flyers approached, many looked forward to the battle that would be waged between Konstantinov and Philadelphia's mammoth center, Eric Lindros. Lindros was a hockey freak of nature, combining size (6'4" inches, 236 pounds) with grace and enormous scoring ability (93 points in 71 games in 1996-97). In fact, Lindros was one of the few players to knock Konstantinov out of a game with a crushing hit. During a regular-season game in January 1997, Lindros hit Konstantinov so hard into the glass that Konstantinov received a two-inch cut to the back of his head.

Game 1 was uneventful between the two warriors, as the Red Wings defeated the Flyers, 4-2. Lindros, however, did receive a two-minute penalty for roughing when he ran Konstantinov into the boards with less than two minutes to play. But the message Lindros attempted to send Konstantinov and the Wings was never received, as Detroit swept the Flyers in four games.

The victory was a culmination of all the hard work that Konstantinov and his teammates had displayed over the previous three seasons. But it was also meant to be the foundation from which Vladimir Konstantinov would be recognized year in and year out as one of the most dominating defensemen of all time to play the game of hockey.

The foundation crumbled on June 13, 1997. After the tragic limousine accident, Lindros talked about his rival Konstantinov.

"It's horrible," he said. "You're talking about a person's life here. It goes a lot deeper than hockey, and we all send him our best. There's affection everywhere for him."

Though Lindros and Konstantinov delivered the punishing hits against one another during the finals, Lindros allowed that what epitomized Konstantinov's style of play was a devastating check he delivered to Flyers center Dale Hawerchuk during Game 3.

"It was the funniest thing," Lindros said. "Dale came back to the bench, and I asked him if he was OK. He said, 'Yeah, I'll be OK. But you know, I saw him coming, too.' I told him 'It was a good thing you saw him, otherwise [you'd] still be lying there.' "

The summer of 1997 was a somber one for the entire Detroit Red Wings family. Though they had ac-complished something that no hockey team in Detroit had done in 42 years by winning the Stanley Cup, everyone involved with the team had his fallen comrades, Konstantinov and Mnatsakanov, on his mind.

On the cusp of the 1997-98 season, Red Wing scout Mark Howe finally took it upon himself to say what many Detroit players could not bring themselves to admit: Vladimir Konstantinov would never play hockey again.

"It's a situation where you hope and pray that by some force of nature, something good will happen," Howe said. "My feeling is that I never, ever expect him to pull on a pair of skates. I'm just hoping and praying that he'll be able to have a normal life with his family again soon.

"If he can, it would be a real blessing. In most of those cases, it doesn't work out that way. Vladdie's such a great guy, one of my best buddies. Somehow, his [teammates] have to overcome this and get back to playing hockey."

With those words, the Red Wings began the season determined to win their second consecutive Stanley Cup for Konstantinov and Mnatsakanov. Wearing patches all season on their right shoulders with their friends' initials and the word "believe" in English and Russian, Detroit captured the Cup in another four-game sweep, this time over the Washington Capitals.

One of the most dramatic and emotional events ever witnessed in an arena occurred during the post-game presentation. After the teams had exchanged handshakes, Konstantinov, who watched the game from a private box in the MCI Center in Washington, was wheeled onto the ice wearing his No. 16 Red Wing jersey.

After NHL commissioner Gary Bettman presented the silver chalice to Detroit center Steve Yzerman, the captain immediately skated over to Vladdie and put the cherished trophy on his lap. From there, his teammates formed a circle around him and soon whisked their inspirational defenseman around the rink in a victory lap, as not only thousands of MCI Center patrons cheered, but also people across the world watching on television.

"That was one of the greatest moments I've ever had," said Brendan Shanahan. "Not too often does a moment in hockey transcend sports, but that was one of them. That's a greater victory than winning the Stanley Cup."

Konstantinov, meanwhile, feebly raised two fingers in recognition of Detroit's second straight Stanley Cup victory.

"I told him I was getting him out of the wheel-chair," said Slava Fetisov. "I said, 'Vladimir, you are going to walk soon.'"

The moment was not lost on losing Capitals coach Ron Wilson either.

"I think that was outstanding," he said in reference to the celebration with Konstantinov. "That's outstanding what they did. That was a very emotional, professional thing that they did, and you'd only see that in hockey."

In the Detroit locker room, seemingly every player acknowledged that the past year was unlike any other, an emotional roller coaster of huge magnitude. The Wings had overcome the contract holdout that kept Sergei Fedorov out of the first 59 games of the year and the trading of 1997 Conn Smythe Trophy winner Mike Vernon. Through it all, they were all motivated and inspired to succeed for the Vladinator.

"We built this season around trying to repeat, but also winning it for Vladdie and Sergei," said Joey Kocur. "It was a tough time when it happened. It is something we will never forget, and to win it in the fashion we did and to have him here and to see that smile on his face and the improvements he has made in his life since the accident, it's something you can't explain."

Konstantinov spent over 30 minutes in the joyous locker room that evening, sipping champagne and holding a cigar for all to see. Although he couldn't speak, his gleaming smile ensured everyone that he comprehended exactly what was happening.

One by one, his teammates made their way to the corner of the dressing room where Konstantinov sat. Forward Igor Larionov leaned over and spoke to him in Russian for several seconds. Forward Kris Draper and goaltender Chris Osgood tipped the Cup slightly toward his mouth after asking him if he wanted a sip of champagne.

All of this came barely a year after Konstantinov had been in a suburban Detroit hospital, kept alive with the help of a ventilator.

Two days later, a crowd of more than 1.2 million jammed the downtown streets of Detroit to celebrate the club's second straight championship. It was a joyous occasion, as the fans cheered wildly for their heroes. But the loudest cheers were saved for Konstantinov and Mnatsakanov.

Fans began yelling "Vlad-die! Vlad-die! Vlad-die!" as Konstantinov and Mnatsakanov rode together in the motorcade, and again when the two were wheeled on to the main stage, where members of the Red Wings organization addressed the crowd.

"I know they played a major role in us winning the Stanley Cup and being back here," general manager Ken Holland told the enthusiastic crowd about Konstantinov and Mnatsakanov. "I know that you all and we all pray that they can lead a normal life. But they're special, special people."

Then suddenly, as if delivering a board-rattling hit against an opponent, Konstantinov sent the crowd into a frenzy when, balanced by Slava Fetisov and trainer John Wharton, he got out of his wheelchair and walked a few feet across the stage. It was the first time that he had walked in public.

According to Red Wings trainer John Wharton, we will someday be able to witness Vladimir Konstantinov defeat his most imposing opponent right now, the wheelchair.

"I don't think anyone has to be reminded where this group of guys was one year ago today," said Wharton at the 1998 Stanley Cup celebration. "A team that's used to sharing a dressing room and sharing good times was sharing a waiting room at Beaumont Hospital.

"And while we shared that waiting room, we shared with you in belief, the faith and our hope that our two friends Sergei and Vladdie would recover.

"And because of you and your faith and your belief, this team found the strength to do the same. And because of everything that you believed in, Vladdie and Sergei can be here today.

"And make no mistake about it, you did see Vladimir Konstantinov walk on this stage today. And next year, because we will all still believe, Vladdie will walk across this stage himself."

Sadly, it was not to be, as the Red Wings were eliminated in the conference semifinals in both 1999 and 2000, and the conference quarterfinals in 2001.

But when Detroit won the Cup again in 2002, Konstantinov was there to share in the joy. He will never play hockey again but he will always be remembered for his contributions to the Red Wings.

17

HARRY "APPLE CHEEKS" LUMLEY

BORN: Owen Sound, Ontario, November 11, 1926
DIED: September 13, 1998
POSITION: Goaltender
NHL TEAMS: Detroit Red Wings, 1943-44, 1945-50;
New York Rangers, 1944; Chicago Blackhawks, 1950-52;
Toronto Maple Leafs, 1952-56; Boston Bruins, 1957-60
AWARDS/HONORS: NHL First All-Star Team, 1954, 1955; Vezina Trophy, 1954;
NHL All-Star Game, 1951, 1954, 1955; Hockey Hall of Fame, 1980

When it comes to evaluating the best Detroit goaltenders of all time, the names Terry Sawchuk, Dominik Hasek and Glenn Hall invariably come to mind. But there was an earlier Red Wings puck stopper who ranks in the pantheon of first-class net minders.

Harry Lumley was unique.

The native of Owen Sound, Ontario, had only reached the age of 17 when he went between the pipes for the first time as a Red Wing. It was during the 1943-44 season, at the very height of World War II, when many stars had joined the armed forces, including Detroit's Johnny Mowers.

The teenaged Lumley was not ready for the big time, and it showed. His two-game trial was a disaster, as he allowed 13 goals for a 6.50 goals-against average, which is about as bad as it gets.

But if nothing else, Lumley was a fighter—in more ways than one—and a year later, he returned to Detroit, where he eventually became the club's top guardian of the crease.

Tall for his time, Lumley earned several nicknames—among them, "Apple Cheeks." The label was handed down when he still was a youth, but as his belligerent style became notorious throughout the National Hockey League, the names bestowed on Harry were less generous. Denizens of the balcony at New York's Madison Square Garden liked to call him Horseface Harry.

"It all started when I was a rookie," recalled Lumley. "I was pretty rosy-cheeked at the time and people noticed it. The funny thing is that if I was playing a good game, the fans would call me 'Apple Cheeks.' But if I was bad on any given night, they'd call me 'Redneck.'"

Lumley's natural goaltending ability was garnished with spice. He was short-tempered and thought nothing of whacking any foe who happened to invade his crease, accidentally or otherwise. Once during a particularly vicious playoff game between Detroit and Toronto, Lumley and his Maple Leafs counterpart, Turk Broda, wound up throwing punches at center ice.

OPPOSITE: Harry Lumley was a 17-year-old wonder when he was imported by the Red Wings for the 1943-44 season. The logos on each arm are World War II slogans. Lumley would enjoy a Hall of Fame career, including a 1950 Stanley Cup win with Detroit.

"At that time, the league didn't have a rule, as it does now, forbidding goalies from skating past the blue line," Lumley recalled. "The whole thing began with a brawl between both teams. It seemed that everyone from the Leafs and the Red Wings was involved. The whole thing happened at the end of the period, which is why everyone was on the ice. Remember, I was quite young at the time and just felt the urge to get in the act. You could say that I was the aggressor. I just shoved Turk around a bit, not much more than that, since no punches were thrown. It's pretty tough to throw punches with all that equipment on."

Under general manager Jack Adams, Lumley became the centerpiece of a powerful postwar Detroit dynasty in the making. Featuring such stalwarts as Red Kelly, Marcel Pronovost and Leo Reise Jr. on defense and the likes of Gordie Howe, Ted Lindsay and Sid Abel up front, the Red Wings finished first in both the 1948-49 and 1949-50 seasons.

"There's no doubt," Lumley asserted, "that Howe was the best all-around player I have ever seen. The thing about Howe that always made it difficult for a goalie was the fact that he was ambidextrous. He was always switching from his forehand to his backhand, and a goalie continually had to change angles on him. Then there was Rocket Richard, who was fantastic from the blue line to the goal. He could bring a crowd to its feet like nobody else."

During the Spring of 1949, Lumley was outgoaled by Broda as Toronto swept Detroit in four straight games of the Stanley Cup finals. But a year later, the Red Wings exacted revenge. With Lumley in goal, the Red Wings defeated the Maple Leafs in a bitter seven-game semifinal series and then won the Stanley Cup by edging the New York Rangers in another seven-game set.

Just when Lumley thought he had it made in Detroit—the fans loved his combative style—Adams pulled the rug right out from under him.

On July 13, 1950, Adams pulled off one of the biggest trades in NHL history. He dealt Lumley, along with Jack Stewart, Al Dewsbury, Don Morrison and Pete Babando, to the Chicago Blackhawks for Sugar Jim Henry (also a goalie), Bob Goldham, Gaye Stewart and Metro Prystai. Adams was able to engineer the move because his farm system had cultivated yet another young goaltending ace: Terry Sawchuk, who was able to fill the breach now that Lumley was gone.

Interestingly, Detroit was unable to successfully defend its Stanley Cup in the first year of Lumley's absence, although some experts believe that had Harry been a Red Wing in 1950-51, another Cup would have been ensconced at Olympia Stadium. Whatever the case, Lumley had established his credentials as a premier puck stopper.

In Chicago his goals-against average and his blood pressure climbed to alarming heights. Fortunately for Harry, he was rescued by Toronto Maple Leafs manager Conn Smythe in 1952 and eventually played some of his best hockey for the tight-checking Leafs. He led the NHL in shutouts for two consecutive seasons and won the Vezina Trophy in 1953-54 with a tidy 1.85 goals-against average in 69 games out of a 70-game schedule.

The Leafs traded Lumley to Boston before the 1957-58 season, and though a more than a 10-year NHL veteran, he played more than adequate goal. A year later, goaling only on a part-time basis, he helped Boston to a second-place finish. His NHL career was completed—16 years after it had started—with Boston in 1959-60, when he played 42 games, produced two shutouts and emerged with a 3.50 goals-against average. When he finally retired, old Apple Cheeks turned to his hobby, harness racing, and remained active in sports.

"You don't find 16-year-old kids jumping into the NHL the way I did," said Lumley. "Of course, the war was a factor. World War II had taken a lot of good players away from the NHL, and there was a need for replacements. I was one of them, and it turned out to be a good break for me. Whether I was mature enough to accept the responsibility is something that my bosses would have to comment on, but whatever the case, it was quite a jump for a lad out of Owen Sound, Ontario.

"Fortunately, most of my older teammates took me under their wings. Old-timers such as Flash Hollett and Earl Siebert treated me as if they were my father and I was their son. If you look back you'll see that I wasn't the only kid to come into the NHL real early. Bep Guidolin did it with the Boston Bruins a little later. Gordie Howe did it with the Red Wings.

"The entire big-time scene was a thrill to me. I practically lived at Olympia Stadium. I wanted to practice every day, and when I wasn't practicing, I was at the Olympia watching one event or another. In a way, I was like a rink rat."

Lumley matured with the Red Wings. In 1947-48 he produced seven shutouts and repeated the feat in 1949-50, a thrilling year to be a hockey player in Detroit. Facing Toronto in the opening playoff round, Lumley and the Red Wings were pushed to the limit by the Maple Leafs. Toronto actually led the series, three

Harry Lumley makes a kick save for the Red Wings against the Rangers in 1950 action at Madison Square Garden.

games to two, but Detroit won Game 6 at Maple Leaf Gardens when Lumley registered a 4-0 shutout. That tied the series at three games apiece and sent the clubs back to Olympia for the decisive seventh encounter.

Incredibly, Lumley and his Toronto counterpart, Turk Broda, each had a shutout at the end of regulation, sending the match into sudden death. In Game 4 of the series, the clubs had played sudden death after ending regulation in a 1-1 tie. Defenseman Leo Reise of Detroit won that game with a goal at :38 of the second overtime period. This time both Broda and Lumley stoutly guarded their respective nets through more than eight minutes of overtime before Reise received the puck inside the Toronto blue line and fired the puck past Broda at 8:34 of sudden death. The score ended Toronto's three-year hold on the Stanley Cup and catapulted the Red Wings into the finals against the New York Rangers. This time, Lumley was pitted against another superb goaltender, Chuck Rayner of the Broadway Blueshirts.

Although Lumley produced the series' only shutout (4-0 in Game 2), the Rangers surprised Detroit and took a three-games-to-two series lead on a pair of sudden-death goals by Rangers center Don "Bones" Raleigh. But the doughty Red Wings followed the same pattern as they had in the Toronto series and won Game 6 to tie the final at three games apiece. The decisive seventh game went into overtime, tied 3-3.

Both Rayner and Lumley played remarkably in the first sudden death and neither team scored. The second sudden death seemed to be headed in the same scoreless direction until just past the eight-minute mark, when the Red Wings won a faceoff deep in the Ranger zone. The puck came back to Pete Babando, a native of Braeburn, Pennsylvania, the only American on either team. Babando's shot beat Rayner through a scramble, and Lumley sipped his first champagne from the Stanley Cup. "That," said Lumley, "was the high point in my career up until then."

18

FRANCIS WILLIAM (FRANK) "THE BIG M" MAHOVLICH

BORN: Timmins, Ontario, January 10, 1938
POSITION: Left Wing
NHL TEAMS: Toronto Maple Leafs, 1956-68;
Detroit Red Wings, 1968-71; Montreal Canadiens, 1971-74
AWARDS/HONORS: Calder Memorial Trophy, 1958;
NHL First All-Star Team, 1961, 1963, 1973;
NHL Second All-Star Team, 1962, 1964-66, 1969, 1970;
NHL All-Star Game, 1959-65, 1967-74; Hockey Hall of Fame, 1981

A superstar whose career was star-crossed: that's the best way to describe the hockey life of Frank Mahovlich, alias the Big M.

He excelled for Toronto, Detroit and Montreal, but while a Red Wing, that star shone more brightly than ever. Mahovlich in Detroit was as much a headliner as Gordie Howe or Alex Delvecchio.

But to reach that point, the tall left wing with the long strides had to tread an often tortuous path that began in 1956 at Maple Leaf Gardens, where the young forward was considered a can't-miss prospect.

Playing under tyrannical general manager-coach Punch Imlach, Mahovlich achieved stardom during the 1960-61 campaign when he almost maintained a goal-a-game pace. His target was Maurice "Rocket" Richard's record of 50 goals in a regular season.

Skating on a line with veteran center Red Kelly and workmanlike right wing Bob Nevin, the diffident Mahovlich emerged as the most exciting shooter of his day and was chased by newsmen in the manner of Roger Maris at the time that the New York Yankees outfielder was challenging Babe Ruth's 60 home-run record.

Unlike Maris, Mahovlich never did break the record, although he ultimately did quite well by himself and his assorted teams. He won the Calder Trophy as Rookie of the Year in 1958 and was a first All-Star left wing in 1961, 1963 and 1973. He made the second team in 1962, 1964, 1965, 1966, 1969 and 1970. Frank played on no fewer than five Stanley Cup champion teams, four with the Maple Leafs and one with the Montreal Canadiens.

The statistics suggest that Mahovlich luxuriated through a lengthy career sprinkled with laughs and coated with dollars. In fact, Mahovlich was plagued with trauma and tribulation beginning in 1960-61.

"Life was never the same after that," Frank smiled. "I wound up with 48 goals that year, so everybody figured that next year I would do better. And the season after that would be greater than the other two."

Mahovlich can afford to laugh now, having been knighted by hockey's Hall of Fame, but the scars remain.

Like Hall of Famer Jean Beliveau before him, Mahovlich was truly superb, but never superb enough.

OPPOSITE: Frank (The Big M) Mahovlich in his golden year as a Red Wing.

"They expected too much from me," he said. "The year of the 48 goals, I had scored 38 in 35 games. I was on a roll, heading for the Rocket's record, but that was expecting too much.

"We didn't have depth on that club. All of a sudden four of our guys got injured and our balance was gone. So the opposition began zeroing in on me, and I was neutralized."

Unfortunately for Frank, neither Toronto fans nor general manager-coach Punch Imlach were neutralized.

The abrasive Punch had his own way with hockey players and he nettled the Big M. He deliberately mispronounced his name, calling him Mahallovich, and he would often treat Frank—and others—as if they were invisible.

One of the favorite tortures in the Imlach camp was inflicted after a losing weekend of hockey for the Leafs. They would often play at home on Saturday night and travel as far as Chicago or Boston for a Sunday-night game. Explained Mahovlich:

"We'd catch a plane back to Toronto on Monday morning, and then he would take us directly from the airport to the rink for a practice. If that were the case, why didn't he practice us on the ice right after the game?

"After a while I began to wonder how long I could take this kind of thing. A day off from hockey does a man a lot of good, but we never seemed to get a day off with Imlach."

Then there were the demands from the supposedly sophisticated Toronto fans. If Frank had scored 48 goals when he was 23 years old, they reasoned, he should score at least 50 goals a year later. On top of that, Chicago owner Jim Norris had allegedly offered $1 million for Mahovlich, but the Leafs had turned him down. When Frank slipped to 33 goals in 1961-62, a few local purists in Maple Leaf Gardens began what was to be a chronic chorus of boos whenever the Big M played a mediocre game. Soon the hoots began grating on his nerves, not to mention those of other stars around the league.

Mahovlich couldn't conceal his anxiety. He became introverted and distant. "I played with Frank for 11 years," said teammate Bob Baun, "and didn't say 22 words to the guy."

Eventually, Mahovlich began to feel hounded by some of the reporters, and he burrowed even deeper into his shell. By November 12, 1964, doctors privately said he was suffering from "deep depression and tension," but the exact diagnosis wasn't made public at the time.

While Toronto fans indulged in the usual wild speculation about the Big M's condition, Frank remained in seclusion for a couple of weeks before returning to the Leafs' lineup. He remained secretive about his ailment and became confidential about his interviews with reporters.

A season later, reporter Paul Rimstead asked to talk with him. "Okay," said Frank, "but not on the team bus. I'll see you later sometime."

They eventually held their rendezvous at a Montreal hotel, where Mahovlich allowed that his relationship with Imlach was worsening. The Big M pointed out that his doctor advised him to ignore Punch whenever possible. "He told me to pull an imaginary curtain around myself whenever Punch was around," Frank said. "I've been doing it, and feel a lot better."

But the boos from the crowds became more frequent and more annoying. In the middle of the 1967-68 season, Mahovlich played superbly as the Leafs routed the Montreal Canadiens, 5-0, at Maple Leaf Gardens. Frank scored a goal and had two important assists. Even his harshest critic, Imlach, described Frank's game as "outstanding."

Mahovlich was named the second of three stars picked after every home game by broadcaster Foster Hewitt. Normally a "star" is greeted with cheers or, at worst, mild applause when he skates out on the ice to acknowledge the selection. When Frank planted his blades on the ice, he heard some applause, but there was no mistaking the boos that were uttered by some spectators.

Mahovlich completed the home-game ritual and returned to the dressing room. He showered, changed into street clothes, and later headed for the team's sleeping car, which would carry the Leafs to Detroit for their next game. The Big M boarded the sleeper and prepared to go to bed, but somehow he couldn't shake the memory of the catcalls, and he couldn't get to sleep.

Torn by his anxiety, Mahovlich finally walked off the sleeper at about 4:00 a.m. He contacted a club doctor and was escorted to a hospital. This time his ailment was no secret. Dr. Hugh Smythe disclosed that the Big M was suffering from "deep depression and tension" and was in the care of Dr. Allen Walters, a psychiatrist.

The Maple Leafs' brass had begun thinking about dealing Frank to another team, but they couldn't make a move until he returned to the lineup and proved to the satisfaction of prospective buyers that he was capable of playing big-league hockey again. The sabbatical proved beneficial to both Mahovlich and the Leafs, and he once again rejoined the club after a few weeks' rest.

Early in March 1968, Imlach finally concluded a

deal with Detroit. The Leafs would receive Norm Ullman, Floyd Smith and Paul Henderson in return for Mahovlich, Peter Stemkowski and Garry Unger, all forwards. In addition, the Leafs would receive the right to obtain ace defenseman Carl Brewer, who had quit pro hockey.

The deal was one of the most spectacular trades ever negotiated in the NHL. Mahovlich, of course, was delighted to be free of Imlach's shackles. For years the Red Wings were renowned as a relaxed team with an obvious *joie de vivre*. During playoff time, manager Sid Abel would take his men to the racetrack rather than seclude them in some distant hideaway. Frank was aware of this, but he wasn't quite sure how the Detroit players would react to him.

The Big M was restored to life in Detroit. "Detroit," said Frank's younger brother, Peter, "is a different hockey city. Frank will be treated differently by the Red Wings."

He was, and it showed immediately. Within a month, Frank scored seven goals and closed the season with the clear suggestion that better things were to come. "I'll be tickled," said Detroit coach Bill Gadsby, "if Frank scored 35 goals in his first full season with us."

Mahovlich obliged with 49 goals, the most he had ever scored in 12 NHL seasons. It was the most goals for a Red Wings' player since Gordie Howe had scored the same number in 1952-53. Frank was also voted the No. 1 star in the 1969 All-Star Game in Montreal.

Skating on a line with Howe and Alex "Fats" Delvecchio, Mahovlich was a new man. With 118 goals, the line broke the record of 105 set in 1943-44 by the famed Montreal Punch Line of Maurice Richard, Toe Blake and Elmer Lach. The line's 264 points smashed the 223-point mark set in 1956-57 by Detroit's Production Line of Gordie Howe, Ted Lindsay and Norm Ullman.

The grand game once expected of Mahovlich was now on magnificent display at Detroit's Olympia Stadium. In the 1969-70 season Frank scored 38 goals and 32 assists for 70 points and was a prime catalyst in pushing the Red Wings into a playoff berth for the first time in four years.

Still, there was a gray cloud hanging over Mahovlich's future in Detroit. His kid brother, Peter, an equally big and enormously gifted center, had fallen into disfavor with the Red Wings' front office and was traded to Montreal. In addition, Detroit now had a new coach, Ned Harkness, who had new ideas.

As it happened, Harkness failed as coach, but was elevated to management. Meanwhile, Frank played as if he were skating in mud. A trade was inevitable, and on January 13, 1971, Mahovlich was dealt to the Canadiens in exchange for Mickey Redmond, Guy Charron and Bill Collins.

For the fourth time in his big-league career, Frank was being asked to make a major comeback, and he produced as well as he had in Detroit.

Canadiens fans immediately took Frank to their collective hearts and he responded by helping Montreal win the 1971 Stanley Cup as he broke the playoff goal-scoring record with 14 big red lights. Manager Sam Pollock acknowledged Frank's leadership qualities by naming him an alternate captain. Mahovlich was touched by the honor. "It's the first time I've ever been chosen for anything," he said. "Canadiens management showed that they respected me. It's a nice feeling."

In 1971-72, his first full year in Montreal, he scored 96 points in 76 games and followed that with 93 points in 78 contests during 1972-73. Once again he was a tower of power, as Montreal marched to the Prince of Wales Trophy and the Stanley Cup in 1973.

It was a remarkable accomplishment for a misunderstood athlete who had thrice been written off—even though he was a superstar. Nothing underscores the value of Frank Mahovlich more than his ability, which enabled him to surpass the 500-goal mark and finish the 1972-73 campaign with an all-time goal total of 502.

In his final NHL season, Mahovlich scored 31 goals and 49 assists to lift his all-time NHL totals to 1,182 games played, 533 goals, 570 assists, 1,103 points and 1,052 penalty minutes. He jumped from the Canadiens to the WHA's Toronto Toros during the off season and was named team captain. In his first WHA game, Mahovlich scored a hat trick and went on to a respectable 82-point season. Mahovlich followed the Toros when they moved south to Birmingham, Alabama, ending his playing career with the Bulls in 1978.

Although his tenure in Detroit was relatively brief, it was also most meaningful.

In Mahovlich's case, the figures don't lie.

19

GLENN HENRY
"MR. GOALIE" HALL

BORN: Humboldt, Saskatchewan, October 3, 1931
POSITION: Goaltender
NHL TEAMS: Detroit Red Wings, 1952-53, 1954-57;
Chicago Blackhawks, 1957-67; St. Louis Blues, 1967-71
AWARDS/HONORS: Calder Memorial Trophy, 1956; NHL First All-Star Team, 1957, 1958,
1960, 1963, 1964, 1966, 1969; Vezina Trophy, 1963, 1967 (shared with Denis Dejordy);
Conn Smythe Trophy, 1968; NHL All-Star Game, 1955-1958, 1960-1965, 1967-1969;
Hockey Hall of Fame, 1975

Among the more poignant episodes of Detroit Red Wings mismanagement, the case of Glenn Hall ranks at the top.

A goaltender extraordinaire, Hall would one day earn the title of Mr. Goalie throughout the hockey world. No other puck stopper who ever played in the bigs can make that statement.

Unfortunately for Motown fans, by the time Hall had become renowned as Mr. Goalie, he was playing somewhere else: Chicago, of all places.

But that's getting ahead of the story.

It all began with Red Wings general manager Jack Adams in the early 1940s.

Jolly Jawn, as he was known, had become obsessed with producing high-quality net minders on his developmental teams. In fact, the goalies grew so well and so fast on Detroit's farms that Adams had a surplus.

Johnny Mowers won a Stanley Cup for Adams in 1942-43, but he was soon crowded out of the crease by another Red Wings up-and-comer named Harry Lumley.

When Lumley took Detroit to another Cup in 1949-50, he seemed set in goal for at least a decade.

But the goalie crop continued to flourish. Adams's scouts raved about Terry Sawchuk, a prodigy who was starring at Indianapolis. There was only one thing to do: trade Lumley and promote Sawchuk, which is precisely what the general manager did.

With Sawchuk between the pipes, Detroit won Stanley Cups in 1952, 1954 and 1955. Like Lumley before him, Sawchuk appeared to have a mortgage on the goaltending job, but Adams couldn't help himself. Once again, a goaltending ace in the making was developed on the farm.

Glenn Hall was so good that Adams invited him to play two games during the 1954-55 season despite the presence of Sawchuk. Hall allowed only one goal in the pair of matches, and his play suggested that he had more ability than the great Sawchuk.

Adams got the message and, following the 1955 Stanley Cup triumph, dealt Sawchuk to Boston. Glenn Hall had become *the* Red Wings goaltender for the start of the 1955-56 season.

Hall won the Calder Trophy as Rookie of the Year and appeared to be a fixture in Detroit until a game between the Red Wings and Boston Bruins in the semi-final round of the 1957 playoffs. Minding the net for Detroit, Hall found himself the target of a straight-on rush by Boston's Vic Stasiuk who roared in on the young goalie and shot a bullet that caught Hall on his unprotected face. Glenn dropped to the ice, out cold, blood flowing from his mouth. The crowd buzzed, and one writer noted that Hall, lying in a heap in his goal crease, "looked dead."

Taken from the ice on a stretcher, Hall regained consciousness in the trainer's room. Hardly impressed by the severity of his injury, his first words upon awakening were, "C'mon, doc, let's get this thing over with." The physician proceeded to weave 23 stitches into Hall's upper lip and mouth, which the puck had ripped open.

A half-hour later, Hall emerged, skating onto the ice, his eyes black and his face swollen and covered with bandages. As he took up his position in front of the goal, a Bruins player remarked, "I don't believe it. How do you stop this guy?" By that time, the answer was clear: You didn't.

Jack Adams produced a never-ending supply of top goalies during the decades of the 1930s, 1940s, and 1950s. One of the best by far was a man who became known as Mister Goalie, Glenn Hall. He is seen here after a save against Dean Prentice of the Rangers.

Nevertheless, Jack Adams became skeptical of Hall's play after the injury and soon believed that Glenn was puck-shy. Thus after two campaigns in Detroit, Hall was traded to Chicago, where he captured the Vezina Trophy in 1963 and 1967 (shared with Denis DeJordy). In 1961, Hall led the Blackhawks to their first Stanley Cup since 1938, performing spectacularly as Chicago eliminated, ironically, the Red Wings in the final round. With the coming of expansion, Hall was drafted by the St. Louis Blues, with whom he won his third Vezina in 1969 (shared with Jacques Plante), and the Conn Smythe Trophy in 1968. Hall also was an 11-time All-Star, his seven first-team berths a record for NHL goaltenders.

Starting with his Detroit days, Hall was an innovator. He is credited with originating the "butterfly" style of goaltending—fanning out his pads toward the goalposts while dropping to his knees to block shots. Hall's technique, originally scoffed at as a perversion of the traditional stand-up goaltending style, eventually became the standard for goalkeepers from the late 1960s to the present.

A native of Humboldt, Saskatchewan, Glenn Hall was born in 1931, the son of a railroad engineer. As a boy, he played center and captained his public school hockey team. When he was 10, the club's goalie quit. "I picked someone to replace him but he refused," Hall said. "So did the next 10 guys. As captain, I had no choice but to put on the pads myself. After a few years, I actually got to like it."

So treacherous did Hall find his work that he became unique in his pregame preparations. "Before every game, and sometimes between periods, I'd get sick to my stomach; I'd have to throw up. Sometimes it happened during a game, and I'd have to fight it off until the whistle blew. I tried drinking tea between periods and that seemed to help. But I didn't worry about it. Nervousness was part of the game. It helped keep me sharp."

Despite taking scores of painful stitches to his face, Hall did not don a goalie mask until the twilight of his 18-year big-league career, claiming it restricted his vision when the puck was at his feet. Hall was named to the Hockey Hall of Fame in June 1975.

20

HUBERT GEORGE "BILL" QUACKENBUSH

BORN: Toronto, Ontario, March 2, 1922
DIED: September 12, 1999
POSITION: Defenseman
NHL TEAMS: Detroit Red Wings, 1942-49; Boston Bruins, 1949-56
AWARDS/HONORS: NHL Second All-Star Team, 1947, 1953;
NHL First All-Star Team, 1948, 1949, 1951; Lady Byng Trophy, 1949;
NHL All-Star Game, 1947-54; Hockey Hall of Fame, 1976

One of the stupidest trades ever made for the most inane reason resulted in the Detroit Red Wings losing a Hall of Fame defenseman in the prime of his career.

The defenseman was Hubert George "Bill" Quackenbush, and the reason he was traded was that he won the Lady Byng Trophy for good sportsmanship and high-quality play. Macho-minded Red Wings general manager Jack Adams considered the Lady Byng award a badge of dishonor and supposedly said, "Any player who wins the Lady Byng doesn't belong on my club."

Apparently Adams meant it, because he promptly dispatched Quackenbush to Boston—along with Pete Horeck—for Pete Babando, Clare Martin, Lloyd Durham and Jim Peters. Quackenbush never won another Lady Byng Trophy, but spent the second half of his career with Boston playing as splendidly as he had the first half with Detroit.

Although he made his debut during the 1942-43 NHL season, it wasn't until 1943-44 that Bill established himself as a regular in the Motor City.

Although the temptation to join the brawlers always existed, Quackenbush resisted the lure and played a pure defense. In so doing, he made a greater impact on the game than some of his more violent colleagues.

More than anything, Quackenbush was an extraordinary practitioner of his art. He was named to the National Hockey League's First All-Star Team in 1948, 1949 and 1951, during an era when the NHL was oozing with top-notch backliners. Bill made the Second Team in 1947 and 1953.

It is a measure of the influence of Quackenbush that some hockey writers have, over the years, suggested that the NHL name a trophy to be given to the league's best defensive defenseman: The Quackenbush Trophy.

Along with winning the Lady Byng trophy in 1949, quite an accomplishment for a defenseman, he once went a span of 137 games (over three different seasons) without taking a penalty.

Quackenbush played with some of the all-time greats of the sport, and he was a regular when a kid by the name of Gordie Howe came to Detroit.

Said Quackenbush: "Gordie came in when he was

OPPOSITE: Wearing a V (for victory) symbol on his left shoulder during the 1942-43 season, Bill Quackenbush launched a prosperous career, first with Detroit, later on with the Bruins. The V was worn by all Red Wing players during World War II to bolster the war effort.

17, and anyone looking at him could tell he had talent. It was just a matter of time before he became the kind of hockey player he was. He was one of the best all-around hockey players I ever played with."

Hubert George Quackenbush was born March 2, 1922, in Toronto, Ontario. He played his hockey on the city's innumerable outdoor rinks during the Great Depression and was ready for the big time shortly after the outbreak of World War II.

Quackenbush played on the Red Wings' 1943 Stanley Cup–winning team and played on two first-place teams. When the Red Wings finished first in 1948-49, there was no hint Bill would be traded. But Adams stunned the hockey world by dealing Bill to the Boston Bruins.

For Quackenbush, it was a comedown in more ways than one. Not that life in Detroit was all glamor. Adams ran a spartan ship at Olympia Stadium, but conditions in Boston Garden were even worse. Still, Bill became a stalwart on the Bruins' back line.

In the spring of 1952, the Boston Bruins took on the powerhouse Montreal Canadiens in the Stanley Cup semifinals. Quackenbush, normally known for his sturdy, inconspicuous, mistake-free play, was involved in one of the most famous episodes in Stanley Cup history.

The series had gone seven games, with Montreal winning the first three games and Boston winning the next three. Early in the seventh game, Maurice Richard of the Canadiens was knocked flying by a vicious check from burly Leo Labine. As the Rocket lay on the ice, motionless, speculation was that he was through for the series, if not longer, but eventually Richard returned. The game was tied late in the third period, 1-1. The Bruins, with Quackenbush at his defense position, had just killed off four minutes of penalties.

All of a sudden, the Rocket was on the ice and the puck was on his stick. With a quick motion, he dug his blades into the ice and turned toward Quackenbush's side of the ice. Bill remembered, "I was on the left side just then—normally I played the right side—when the Rocket started coming down towards me. I chased him into a corner, and I thought I'd closed him off, but he made a quick turn and was moving out in front of our net.

"My partner on defense was a rookie, and from lack of experience, he neglected to come out and cut off the Rocket, who swiftly put the puck behind Sugar Jim Henry. That made it 2-1; eventually we lost 3-1 on an open-net goal."

The play is one of the all-time greats in hockey lore, and though Quackenbush boasts, "It's the only time in 14 years the Rocket beat me," Richard made this type of play a common element in his arsenal against rival teams and shell-shocked goalies.

At the conclusion of the 1955-56 season, Quackenbush hung up his skates for good, opting to return to school. For seven years he attended Northeastern University in Massachusetts at night while working as a manufacturing agent during the day. He also raised three sons after retiring from the NHL, while earning an associate's degree in engineering.

"After about 12 years out of hockey I decided I'd like to get back into it, so I talked to Herb Gallager at Northeastern and went to work there as assistant coach," he said.

In the mid 1960s, Princeton was looking for a quality coach for its men's ice hockey team. Quackenbush applied and was accepted. For six years he coached the team, lending his vast knowledge and great understanding of the game to the young men of the Princeton University hockey team. When after his sixth year the team began faltering, Quackenbush stepped down as coach, but was soon back coaching a different kind of ice hockey.

"Eventually they got a girls' team here and they needed a coach. They asked me to volunteer. I felt that anything I could do to help them learn the game would be a pleasure for me. The girls were very receptive—they really wanted to learn. When I told them things, they thanked me. It was a lot of fun."

Aside from coaching the women's hockey team, Quackenbush also coached the varsity golf team. Always, he remained the same gentleman and scholar he was when he originally signed a contract with crusty Adams in 1942.

There have been better defensemen than Quackenbush, but none were classier, on or off the ice. Furthermore, Bill's unusual penalty-free career on the NHL blue line proved that nice guys could not only survive, but thrive, in the on-ice war games—even though Jack Adams obviously felt otherwise.

21

DOUG BARKLEY

BORN: Lethbridge, Alberta, January 6, 1937
POSITION: Defenseman
NHL TEAMS: Chicago Blackhawks, 1957-58, 1959-60;
Detroit Red Wings, 1962-66

Some critics might suggest it is illogical to place a player among the elite in franchise history if he only played four seasons for the Detroit Red Wings, but Doug Barkley deserves to be an exception.

Tall, tough and tenacious, Barkley was a Larry Robinson before the latter arrived on the scene to redefine defensemen's play for the Montreal Canadiens a decade after Doug was forced to retire because of an eye injury.

A gifted defenseman during the National Hockey League's six-team era, the native of Lethbridge, Alberta, was buried in the minors during some of the best playing years of his life. The Chicago Blackhawks owned him from 1957 through 1960 but only brought Barkley up to the bigs for a cup of coffee. Doug finally got a break when the Red Wings signed him in 1962.

Handling offense as well as defense with consummate ease, Barkley was quickly touted as the find of the year. During an era when defensemen played defense, Barkley led all NHL backliners in scoring (with 11 goals) during the 1963-64 season. As Doug's play improved, so did the Red Wings'. In 1964-65, Detroit finished on top of the NHL for the first time in eight years and loomed as a playoff contender as long as Barkley patrolled the defense.

But tragedy struck on the night of January 30, 1966, during a game against the Blackhawks. In a collision with Doug Mohns of the Blackhawks, Barkley was struck in the right eye by the blade of the Chicago left wing's stick. Intensive medical care failed to restore the sight in his injured eye, and Barkley was forced to retire as an active player. Not surprisingly, the Red Wings missed the playoffs for the next three consecutive seasons.

Doug eventually returned to Detroit to coach the Red Wings—twice—first during the 1971-72 season and then in 1975-76. His second stewardship with the Wings was short-lived, and Barkley was eventually transferred to the scouting sphere and later became a broadcaster.

Barkley was born in Lethbridge, Alberta, on January 6, 1937, and got his first pair of skates at age five. "The skates were hand-me-downs from my older brother," he said. "A year after I got 'em, I started playing organized hockey. Nowadays it may be hard to believe, but when I was six years old, I already was property of the New York Rangers. In those days, NHL clubs sponsored junior clubs all over Canada. In Lethbridge, the Rangers sponsored the Native Sons. So, before I was in second grade, I belonged to a professional team, so to speak."

In those days, the early '50s, a hockey prodigy generally moved slowly up several rungs on the ladder to the pros. It started with junior hockey and then followed with the senior level, which could be either senior A (the best) or senior B, followed by any one of

Until he suffered a career-ending eye injury, Doug Barkley was a towering force on the Detroit defense.

several minor professional leagues in either Canada or the United States. Ultimately, Barkley made it to the Calgary Stampeders of the fast Western (professional) Hockey League. Although he had suffered serious injuries to both knees, Barkley was invited by the Chicago Blackhawks to their training camp in St. Catharines, Ontario.

For Doug, cracking the Chicago lineup would be a formidable task. The Hawks oozed with offensive talent, including such aces as Pierre Pilote, Elmer "Moose" Vasko, Al Arbour, Jack Evans and Dollard St. Laurent. As low man, Barkley was sent back to Calgary, where he honed his game to sharpness. Doug was shuffled between Calgary and Buffalo, of the fast American Hockey League. "I was having some good years in the minors—I set a scoring record in the Western League and was on a league champion with Buffalo—but I couldn't wait to get called up to the NHL," he said.

The break finally came in June 1962 when Chicago traded Barkley to Detroit in exchange for Len Lunde and John McKenzie. "It was like a dream come true. I was a 25-five-year-old, but I wasn't quite sure

whether I had lost anything during all those years in the minors. Next thing I know, I'm playing alongside stars such as Marcel Pronovost, Bill Gadsby and Gordie Howe. And getting a regular shift, to boot."

Right from the start, Barkley and Howe became friends. The Wings took time out after a scrimmage to play golf, and the rookie Barkley found himself without a set of clubs. Howe not only provided the clubs but gave Doug his golf shoes. "The Red Wings of that era were just super people. And still are."

From his very first game as a big leaguer, Barkley proved that the Red Wings were wise in signing him. "My football training was a big help to me," he explained. "I had good timing and I could hit. I had a knack of bolstering our forwards. The other teams knew that I could hit, and if anyone on our club got into trouble, the opposition knew that I would back up our guys."

Barkley scored three goals and 24 assists for 27 points in his rookie NHL season and played in all 70 regular-season games. "I played four years in Detroit, and in three of those years, we made it to the Stanley

Cup finals. One of those seasons we finished fourth and knocked off Chicago in the semifinals but lost to Toronto in the finals. We shouldn't have gotten that far in the first place. The next year we won our division and figured we had a great chance to win the Stanley Cup. We were actually leading Toronto three games to two in the finals, but they wound up tying the series in an unbelievable game. Leaf defenseman Bobby Baun scored the winner in sudden death, bouncing a shot off Bill Gadsby's leg. We ran out of steam in the seventh game and Toronto beat us, 4-0. It was the low point of my major-league career, until I got hurt."

The 1965-66 season appeared to be another equally bright one for Barkley until he skated against the Hawks in what ordinarily would have been a routine game. "I was at the Chicago blue line, just taking a shot on goal, when Doug Mohns came up behind me and tried what we call a 'pitchfork' with his stick. At the moment I shot, his stick came directly up and hit me in the eye. That was it.

"Instantly, I knew I was seriously hurt; I just didn't know how bad it was. They took me off the ice and ordered me taken to a hospital. On the way to the hospital, I sat up, which I wasn't supposed to do, and when I got there had surgery on the eye. After the first operation, they said they didn't think there would be any problems, that they got everything out. But four days later, they found out that the retina had been detached, so they sent me to Boston for two more operations.

"After the first two operations in Boston, I began to regain my vision, and it looked like it could be pretty good, but then the doctors told me I had a giant retinal tear. You have to have about 360 degrees of retina in the eye, and they thought that about 275 were torn off. It was very doubtful that they could do anything to save the eye. After the third operation, I lost vision again and they told me that that was it."

Barkley had several options at this point—he could have quit hockey altogether, or he could have remained in the background as an assistant or returned in an administrative capacity, working full-time for the Red Wings. Everything hinged on the attitude of the club toward the permanently injured star.

The deciding vote would be cast by Bruce Norris, multimillionaire owner of the Red Wings. "After the playoffs, he called me into his office and said not to worry, to take a rest and then come back to Detroit," Barkley said. He promised me a job in the organization. As far as I was concerned, Bruce was the greatest owner in the NHL. He did everything to help the team

and the players, and he certainly helped me. So did Sid Abel, who was our general manager at the time, and Baz Bastien, who was Sid's assistant. Baz had been a goaltender himself in pro hockey until he had lost an eye. Baz was a tremendous help in my rehabilitation. So were the players. They treated me like I was one of them again, and that certainly helped."

Abel offered Barkley a job as a scout with the Red Wings at a time when the NHL was undergoing the first of several phases of expansion. The Detroit high command liked what they saw of Barkley off the ice and soon named him general manager and coach of their Fort Worth, Texas, affiliate in the Central Hockey League. "I was flattered that Sid gave the whole operation to me. The thing I liked most was the coaching, working with the kids. I was a one-man gang down there, making all the decisions, handling season tickets, the travel arrangements. It was a great way to learn the hockey business from the ground up."

Although Doug didn't realize it at the time, he was laying the groundwork for his own NHL coaching career. He looked back at his own NHL experiences and applied the same principles of hard work that had been such an asset to him. Sometimes it paid off for Barkley the coach, and other times it didn't.

"I was more of a disciplinarian than most coaches," he remembered. "My theory was that if the kids had good training from me, it would help them later in their careers. I know they thought I was too hard on them, but I sincerely believed I was doing the right thing. What was happening, of course, was that, with expansion, more jobs were open to the kids and there was a feeling that the discipline of the past wasn't as necessary as it had been when I was playing."

After a year of coaching and managing in Fort Worth, Barkley was named head coach of the Detroit Red Wings. "The move up to the NHL at that time was the biggest mistake I ever made. I didn't have that much experience and I was taking over a team with most of the same personnel who were once my teammates. Besides, now I was younger than a lot of the players I was coaching. They knew I lacked coaching experience and I knew it, too. Except I wasn't willing to admit it at the time."

Barkley did get another coaching chance with Detroit, but like his first attempt, it ended in failure.

The second firing by the Red Wings ended Barkley's NHL coaching career. But he is fondly remembered for his stint as one of the best defensemen ever to wear the Red Wings' uniform.

22

John Sherratt
"Black Jack" Stewart

BORN: Pilot Mound, Manitoba; May 6, 1917
DIED: May 25, 1983
POSITION: Defenseman
NHL TEAMS: Detroit Red Wings, 1938-50, Chicago Blackhawks, 1950-52
AWARDS/HONORS: NHL First All-Star Team, 1943, 1948, 1949;
NHL Second All-Star Team, 1946, 1947;
NHL All-Star Game, 1947-50; Hockey Hall of Fame, 1964

When veteran hockey writers hark back to "old-time defensemen" who played the frontier-style game, John Stewart is the prototype they have in mind.

In fact, his nickname says it all—Black Jack, as in Black Jack Pershing, commanding general of the U.S. Army in France during World War I, and Black Jack Stewart, as in the roughest, toughest backliner the Red Wings ever owned. Opponents both hated and respected him at the same time.

"He wasn't dirty," Hall of Fame defenseman King Clancy once explained, "but Black Jack Stewart was the roughest son of a gun you ever would want to meet."

A Detroit Red Wing for most of his career, Stewart played on two Stanley Cup winning teams and three first-place clubs. Along the way, he accumulated 50 scars and 220 stitches, but never missed a minute because of it during his first 10 years in the bigs. "Sew fast, Doc," Stewart would tell the medics who were repairing his injuries. "I'm due back on the ice."

Stewart was as brave as any pro and once played an entire season with a broken hand. A special device attached to his stick and wrist enabled him to firm up his grip. Red Wings manager Jack Adams called him

"one of the strongest guys I've ever seen in a hockey uniform."

Like the Rangers' legendary Ching Johnson, Stewart took a joyous delight in bodychecking. "He was a mean individual," said ex-Wing Ted Lindsay, "but when he was mean, he had a big smile on his face. When he had that smile, it was time for the opposition to look out.

"Once, Gordie Howe and I decided we'd take this old guy into the corner during practice and rough him up. Jack took his left arm and pinned me across the chest against the screen and then he lifted Howe off the ice by the shirt. Then, he just smiled at both of us."

One of Stewart's toughest battles was with Johnny Mariucci, the brawling Chicago defenseman. They once battled for 15 minutes on the ice and then continued brawling in the penalty box. At the very worst, it was a draw. Stewart rarely lost a fight.

Any forward who attempted to penetrate the Detroit defense of Stewart and his heavily bearded sidekick, Jimmy Orlando, took his life in his hands. Red Wings manager Jack Adams, who paired them, boasted one of the most muscular one-two combinations on any blue line.

OPPOSITE: Black Jack Stewart was the prototype of the "old-time" defenseman.

Stewart's style of play earned him over 200 stitches in his career.

Apart from being a rough hombre, Stewart (unlike Orlando) was a highly polished defenseman who was named to the first All-Star Team in 1943, 1948 and 1949. He made the second team in 1947.

A stickler for conditioning, Stewart would spend the summer on his Manitoba farm and then report to training camp ready for the season to start, "He would be tougher than a pine knot," recalled *Toronto Star* columnist Milt Dunnell, "dour, dedicated, and full of pride. He was fast for a defenseman. In the routine practice races around the rink, few of the forwards could outskate him."

John Sherratt Stewart was born May 6, 1917, in Pilot Mound, Manitoba. He was discovered by Gene Houghton, who worked in the grain exchange at Winnipeg and was friendly with the Red Wings' owner,

Jim Norris Sr., who happened to be a grain tycoon as well.

Stewart was as fine a sportsman as he was a hockey player. Hockey historian Ed Fitkin, who once was the publicist for the Toronto Maple Leafs, recalled how Stewart could perceive the worth of the opposition even in defeat.

"Jack was always one of the first to congratulate the victors after the Wings participated in a lost cause. Once when Turk Broda of Toronto won the Vezina Trophy in the last game of the schedule at Olympia Stadium in Detroit, Jack heartily threw his arms around the Turk.

"The two game veterans skated off the ice arm in arm. Thousands in Detroit stood up to give them thunderous tribute," noted Fitkin.

Although Stewart's checks were often described as thunderous, Black Jack the man was quiet to a fault, except on special occasions. One such occasion was the seventh game of the 1950 Stanley Cup finals against the New York Rangers.

"At our pregame meeting," said Jack Adams, "I warned our forwards they weren't hitting anybody. Rangers had been making them look silly. I tried to tell them they should do some bumping.

"Suddenly, Black Jack jumped up. I don't think he ever opened his mouth at a club meeting before—unless he was asked a question. This time, he said: 'You bums get out there and hit somebody. If you don't, I'll be hitting you.' That night we got some bodychecking."

And with Stewart providing airtight defense, the Red Wings won the Cup in the second sudden-death overtime on Pete Babando's screened shot.

As much as he revered Stewart, Adams realized by the start of the 1950s that his thumping warrior was approaching the end of his career. Less than five months after the defeat of the Rangers, Adams included Stewart, along with goalie Harry Lumley, defenseman Al Dewsbury and forwards Babando and Don Morrison, in a blockbuster deal with the Chicago Blackhawks. The Red Wings received goalie Jim Henry, forwards Metro Prystai and Gaye Stewart and defenseman Bob Goldham in return.

Black Jack was playing capably for Chicago when he suffered a ruptured spinal disc. Doctors wrote him off as a hockey player. He was 34, and medics said he should be grateful if he could walk again without a cane or a crutch.

Stewart listened to their advice, applied some of his own willpower and returned to the lineup. He did, after all, have a job to do. Unfortunately, the fickle finger of fate was working against him. During a game against the Rangers, Stewart and Clare Martin were paired on defense. They liked to line up an onrushing forward and put him in a human vise as the enemy tried to split their defense. On this night, the eel-like Edgar Laprade was moving into the Chicago zone. Stewart and Martin figured Laprade was coming through and closed the trap. But the little Ranger fooled them, and Martin rammed his partner to the ice, as one observer noted, "colder than a mackerel."

Black Jack was hospitalized and required 21 stitches to close his wounds. After spending two weeks in the hospital, he announced his retirement. Then, to the amazement of all, he returned to the ice and played two more games for Chicago.

He concluded his career after the 1951-52 season and 566 regular-season games. Stewart then went into coaching, starting with Chatham in the Ontario Hockey Association's Senior League. He then coached two years at the junior level with Kitchener before moving up to the high pro ranks with Pittsburgh of the American League. Stewart gave up coaching for good in 1963 but remained active as a horse trainer and often appeared at race meetings.

23

LARRY
"LITTLE DEMPSEY" AURIE

BORN: Sudbury, Ontario, February 8, 1905
Died: December 11, 1952
POSITION: Right Wing
NHL TEAMS: Detroit Red Wings, 1928-39
AWARDS/HONORS: NHL First All-Star Team, 1937;
AHL Second All-Star Team, 1939; NHL All-Star Game, 1934

His full name was Harry Lawrence Aurie, but soon after he came to Detroit in 1927, the skillful right wing was nicknamed "Little Dempsey," after heavyweight champ Jack Dempsey.

Larry Aurie was hardly a heavyweight, but he was a champion. And by the mid-1930s, he had become one of the most popular Red Wings. A native of Sudbury, Ontario, Aurie stood 5'6" and weighed 148 pounds. But his grit weighed a ton.

As the Red Wings developed a powerhouse in the mid-1930s, coach Jack Adams fortuitously teamed Aurie with center Marty Barry and left wing Herbie Lewis.

As a unit, the Aurie-Lewis-Barry trio became the first great line in Red Wing history. It might have been Detroit's greatest ever were it not for the advent of the Production Line of Gordie Howe, Ted Lindsay and Sid Abel 15 years later.

At a time when low scoring was the norm, Aurie excelled in the 1934-35 season, scoring 17 goals and adding 29 assists for a career-high 46 points in a 48-game season.

But it was a year later that Aurie and his two pals put Detroit on the hockey map. The Red Wings not only finished first in the American Division, but established their supremacy by sweeping the Montreal Maroons in the Stanley Cup semifinal round, three games to nothing. They then whipped Toronto, three games to one, to win the Motor City's first Stanley Cup on April 11, 1936.

The next season, Aurie made headlines by leading the NHL in scoring with 23 red lights in 45 games. By today's standards, that's not an impressive number, but it was then. Aurie's scoring streak earned him a place on the first NHL All-Star team.

Again, the Aurie-Lewis-Barry line would prove decisive, as Detroit would motor on to its second consecutive Stanley Cup, making the Red Wings the first NHL team to finish first and win the Cup in two straight seasons.

Aurie, however had reached the end of his hockey rope, and the Red Wings sagged terribly in subsequent seasons. Detroit manager Jack Adams always regretted not trading Aurie after the 1936-37 season. "Instead of standing pat," said Adams, "I should have traded. I'd never hesitate to bust up a champion team again."

Larry "Little Dempsey" Aurie had nonetheless been an integral part of the Detroit Red Wings' early glory years.

Larry Aurie, along with Marty Barry and Herbie Lewis, starred on one of the top Red Wings forward lines during the Great Depression. He played a dozen seasons in the Motor City.

24

MARTIN A. "MARTY" BARRY

BORN: St. Gabriel, Quebec, December 8, 1905
DIED: August 20, 1969
POSITION: Center
NHL TEAMS: New York Americans, 1928; Boston Bruins, 1930-35;
Detroit Red Wings, 1936-39; Montreal Canadiens, 1940-41
AWARDS/HONORS: Lady Byng Trophy, 1937; NHL First All-Star Team, 1937;
Hockey Hall of Fame, 1965

What Tinker to Evers to Chance was to baseball, Marty Barry to Larry Aurie to Herb Lewis was to hockey in the mid-1930s. The Detroit Red Wings' best forward combination—the Barry-Aurie-Lewis line—led the Wings to the top of the American Division of the NHL in the 1935-36 campaign, after Marty was traded to Detroit in June of 1935 with Art Giroux for Cooney Weiland and Walt Buswell.

Just why Boston manager Art Ross wanted to unload Barry remains a mystery to this day. Marty had been one of the most productive Bruins since his first regular season in Beantown, 1929-30. He remained productive for the Bruins through 1934-35, scoring 20 or more goals in each of those five seasons.

Until that 1935-36 season, Detroit had never won an NHL championship. But that all changed when Barry left Beantown and lined up with right wing Larry Aurie and Herbie Lewis, who had been with Detroit since 1928-29.

How the deal came about is a story in itself. It began with Jack Adams, who had become the coach and GM of the Red Wings during the Great Depression. During the 1935 playoffs, Adams and his Boston counterpart, Frank Patrick, talked trade.

"If I had Cooney Weiland," Patrick said, mentioning Detroit's crack center, "Boston would be in this final."

To which Adams shot back, "If I had Marty Barry, Detroit would win the Stanley Cup."

A few minutes later the exchange was made. Weiland became the center between Dutch Gainor and Dit Clapper on Boston's Dynamite Line. Barry was placed between Larry Aurie and Herbie Lewis to form a set of forwards that would heavily influence the Red Wings' destiny.

The Lewis-Aurie-Barry line paced Detroit to a first-place finish in the American Division in 1935-36, although the trio had formidable reinforcements. Johnny Sorrell and Ebbie Goodfellow were splendid second-liners, and as one observer aptly put it, "Ebbie Goodfellow was Gordie Howe before Gordie Howe became a Red Wing."

In the spring of 1936, the Red Wings took a serious run at the Stanley Cup and began by dispatching the Montreal Maroons in the opening round. The highlight, by far, was the longest hockey match ever played in the NHL: Exactly 116 minutes and 30 seconds of sudden-death overtime was required—almost two ad-

OPPOSITE: After five productive seasons in Detroit, Marty Barry helped the Red Wings win back-to-back Stanley Cups in 1936 and 1937.

The Barry-Aurie-Lewis line was hockey's answer to baseball's Tinker to Evers to Chance.

ditional full games. The winning goal was scored by Modere "Mud" Bruneteau of Detroit at 16:30 of the sixth overtime.

The goaltending of Norm Smith and the defensive work from Bucko McDonald and Doug Young were instrumental in the victory and set the stage for the triumphant drive to the finals. Adams coached Detroit to a three-games-to-one victory to annex the silver mug.

Winning two consecutive championships was considered a virtual impossibility in the highly competitive NHL of the mid-1930s. No less daunting to the Red Wings during the 1936-37 season was an unusual spate of injuries. Captain Doug Young suffered a broken leg and was lost for the season. Orville Roulston soon followed him to the sidelines, also with a broken leg.

When the Red Wings' leading scorer and Barry's linemate, Larry Aurie, broke his ankle early in March 1937, Adams wondered if and when the bad luck would ever end.

Despite the injuries, the Red Wings finished first in the American Division for the second consecutive year, winning 25 games, losing 14, and tying nine, for 59 points, once again tops in both divisions. The Red Wings' superiority extended into the playoffs, where they first disposed of the pesky Montreal Canadiens,

three games to two. The fifth game was another sudden-death classic, lasting until 12:45 a.m., when Hec Kilrea of Detroit beat Habs goalie Wilf Cude after 51 minutes and 49 seconds of overtime.

Although the defending champions should have been favorites to defeat the New York Rangers in the 1937 Stanley Cup finals, an injury to goalie Norm Smith in the first game at Madison Square Garden left Detroit in the underdog role. New York won the opener, 5-1, forcing the Red Wings to start substitute goalie Earl Robertson in Game 2.

Robertson beat the Rangers 4-2 in the second game, lost 1-0 in the third, but then blanked the Rangers 1-0 to tie the series at two games apiece. Responding nobly to the pressure, Robertson hit new heights in the finale on April 15, 1937, at Olympia Stadium.

It was at this point that Barry delivered his finest clutch performance. He scored two goals in a 3-0 victory over the Rangers. Thus Detroit became the first team to finish first and win the Stanley Cup in consecutive seasons.

Marty skated for the Wings through the 1938-39 season before signing with the Montreal Canadiens as a free agent. He concluded his playing career with Montreal after the 1940-41 season, but his best years were with Detroit.

25

IGOR LARIONOV

BORN: Voskresensk, Russia, December 3, 1960
POSITION: Center
NHL TEAMS: Vancouver Canucks, 1989-92; San Jose Sharks, 1993-95;
Detroit Red Wings, 1995-Present; Florida Panthers, 2000
Detroit Red Wings, 2000-Present
AWARDS/HONORS: NHL All-Star Game, 1998

His teammates call him "The Professor," not only for his bespectacled look, but more important, for his wizardry with the puck. With his 5'11", 170-pound frame, Igor Larionov indeed looks more like a college professor than a hockey player. But the lessons he taught on the ice throughout his career certainly proved otherwise.

Larionov was born on December 3, 1960, in a place called Voskresensk, a grimy industrial city of 80,000 about an hour away from Moscow.

Larionov honed his skills as a 17-year-old with Khimik, a local team within his hometown. It was there that he began to display his undying commitment toward the sport of hockey, improving all facets of his game on a daily basis.

In 1981, he began his tenure with the Central Red Army team, where he soon centered one of the greatest forward lines in history. During the 1980s, Larionov was the pivot man of the famous KLM line, flanked by wingers Vladimir Krutov and Sergei Makarov.

The world had never seen a triumvirate like this before. Appearing to keep the puck on a string between them, the trio became instant heroes in their homeland and drew rave reviews from players, coaches and scouts across the globe.

Larionov earned Soviet Player of the Year honors in 1987-88 and was named to five All-Star teams with

the Central Red Army squad. In addition, he captured gold medals at the 1984 and 1988 Winter Olympics and a gold medal at the 1983 World Championships.

But Larionov never wanted to play his entire career with the Red Army team. He originally wanted to just fulfill his mandatory two-year term in the army and return home to rejoin Khimik. But Red Army coach Viktor Tikhonov did not allow the anchor of his most gifted line to leave, forcing Larionov to stay against his will. He ended up playing eight seasons under Tikhonov, collecting 165 goals and 361 points in 334 league games.

The names of the most gifted Soviet hockey players had begun showing up in the annual NHL entry draft. But teams would draft these untouchable Soviet players in the late rounds, knowing that as long as the Soviet Union existed, Russian players would not be allowed west of the Iron Curtain. Larionov, in fact, was drafted by Vancouver in 1985—214th in the draft, the Canucks' 11th pick.

In 1989, however, the Iron Curtain began to rust and crack, as gifted players like Sergei Fedorov and Alexander Mogilny defected to North America. But Larionov did not want to defect; instead he waged a self-imposed war with Soviet authorities to secure his freedom from their iron fist.

Finally, after years of negotiating, the Soviet hockey regime relented, and Larionov was able to go to

99

Igor Larionov, alias "The Professor."

Vancouver to play with the Canucks, making his NHL debut on October 5, 1989, against the Edmonton Oilers.

"Larionov is the most important athlete in the history of Soviet sport, leading the campaign for Soviet athletes to play abroad without defecting," said Robert Edelman, the author of the definitive study *Serious Fun: A History of Spectator Sports in the U.S.S.R.*

Though he was thousands of miles from Moscow, Larionov played as if he were toiling in the Soviet Union. His dazzling puck movement and ability to complete passes blindly immediately endeared him to the Vancouver faithful—not to mention hockey fans across the country, who were amazed at the Russian's grace and finesse.

"The first thing you notice," said Vancouver play-by-play announcer Jim Robson, "is the effortless way he skates. His skate blade isn't even on the ice.

"You also see how small he is. He looks so small and frail compared to others. But then so does [Wayne] Gretzky."

The comparisons between the two playmakers began immediately. Like Gretzky, Larionov was not the fleetest of foot. But he captivated those in and around the game with his ability to thread passes through a maze of sticks and skates to a waiting teammate.

"I'm impressed with the way he sees the whole ice," said Vancouver teammate Barry Pederson. "You can see that he's played hockey at a very high-paced tempo. He's a world-class player. The only guy I've seen better at using the whole ice is Gretzky."

Larionov played three seasons with the Canucks, registering 51 goals and 92 assists in 210 games. But in 1991, he decided to play for a team in Switzerland after the Russian government demanded compensation from Vancouver for signing what they considered their "property."

Rather than have the Canucks make transfer payments to a government he now despised, Larionov regretfully bolted. The Canucks consequently put him on waivers, and the San Jose Sharks ultimately selected him on October 4, 1992.

But before putting on a Shark uniform, he played one season in Switzerland (1992-93) before heading to the Bay area, where he was reunited with former Red Army linemate Sergei Makarov.

"It isn't every day you could pick up a No. 1 center on the waiver wire," recalled Sharks executive vice president and director of player personnel Chuck Grillo. "It was probably the only good player move we did that year. Everything else was pretty much a disaster. The coaches that year would have liked to have had him on the ice."

As he did in Vancouver, Larionov made an immediate impact on his newest club. Although many considered the 32-year-old to be a fading offensive player, Larionov collected 56 points in 60 games with the Sharks that season. He also was an integral part of that team's most defining moment—the shocking first-round playoff upset of prohibitive favorite Detroit.

"From my point of view, me and Makarov played together for so many years, we've got a winning spirit, because we played on the winning team," Larionov said upon arriving at his first Sharks camp. "Our goal now is to try to develop some skills and put some winning spirit on this team, because after last year, it's very important to get some fans excited during the season. I don't want to be just [an average] player, I also want to be a team leader."

Larionov led the Sharks in scoring (18 points in 14 games) during that emotional 1994 playoff season, one that featured two seven-game series against the Red Wings and Toronto. It's surely no coincidence that the Sharks, in only their third year of existence, also set an NHL record in 1993-94 for the largest single-season turnaround (a 58-point improvement).

Larionov played one more season with San Jose before Dean Lombardi began to purge his lineup of older players. The Russian was subsequently traded to Detroit on October 24, 1995, in exchange for Red Wing forward Ray Sheppard. At the time, Larionov expressed a certain amount of bitterness towards the Sharks organization, since it let not only him go, but also his old pal Makarov.

"The chemistry was gone," he said. "For the last year and a half, I have not been happy with the way the team is going. The last thing was Sergei Makarov being

released. He was part of the team, he was a veteran player."

But one team's loss is another one's gain, and both Red Wings general manager Ken Holland and coach Scotty Bowman were delighted in obtaining the talented center.

"He brings the total package," Bowman said of Larionov. "We saw the effect he can have in games. He's single-handedly won games for that team. He's a complete player."

The acquisition also allowed the Hall of Fame coach to put together one of the most exciting units on the ice. Bowman's Wings had one of the more Russian-dominated lineups in the league during the mid-'90s, and the addition of Larionov inspired Bowman. He soon put together a five-man, all-Russian unit, which consisted of forwards Larionov, Sergei Fedorov and Vyacheslav Kozlov and defensemen Slava Fetisov and Vladimir Konstantinov.

Rather than mixing forward lines with different sets of defensemen, Bowman decided to play these five individuals together every time they went on the ice. The five soon began to skate and weave just as Tikhonov had taught them in the Soviet Union. It was a daring but highly successful experiment that in 1997 brought Detroit to the cusp of its first Stanley Cup championship since 1955.

By this time the Red Wings had been dubbed "Moscow in Motown," a nickname of which Larionov was not particularly fond. "I don't like it at all," he said on the eve of Game 1 of the 1997 Stanley Cup finals between Detroit and the Philadelphia Flyers. "There are no Russians, no Canadians, no Swedes. It is one team, one family, and we all represent the Red Wings.

"Everybody is the same. Everybody tries their best, and not only Russian guys. There's Steve Yzerman, Brendan Shanahan, Joey Kocur, Mike Vernon . . . not just Russians. You would think that people would get over that."

Larionov's first Stanley Cup final was bittersweet for both himself and Fetisov. The two countrymen had a history together that went back 20 years; they shared memories not only of the highs, but also of the lows.

"We have gone through so much—Olympics, Canada Cup, World Cup, world championships, so this is very special for me," said the 36-year-old Larionov. "We have been friends for 25 years, and it would be nice to finish our career with a Stanley Cup."

Fetisov also wanted nothing less than to win a Cup with a teammate who shared in the same struggles for freedom against the Communist-led regime in the Soviet Union.

Igor Larionov, seconds after scoring.

"We've played almost 18 years together and we went through a lot," Fetisov said, referring to Larionov. "He is an honest guy and a great player. We have lots of memories, lots of good stuff."

True to their wishes, Larionov and Fetisov drank from the silver chalice after the Wings swept the Flyers in four games.

In the summer of 1997, Larionov, Fetisov and Kozlov brought the world's most famous trophy to their homeland. The trio spent five days in Russia sharing the Cup with masses of fans and posing for pictures on Red Square. Larionov and Kozlov also made an emotional trip back to their hometown of Voskresensk, lugging the Cup to the Khimik hockey school, where they had perfected their craft as youngsters.

"Even playing far from the motherland, we could feel your support," Larionov told the throngs of family and friends who choked back tears while watching their native sons raise the coveted trophy. "Now you can see what it was all about. Now you can see the Cup. Thirty years ago, I could never have imagined that I'd be standing here one day with the Stanley Cup. It's a dream come true."

Larionov finished the 1997 playoffs fourth on the team in scoring, with four goals and 12 points in 20 games.

The following season, Larionov won his second Stanley Cup championship with Detroit, and the 37-year-old appeared to defy his age with his remarkable skills as the 1998-99 season began.

"I think he's more like 31 or 32," said assistant coach Dave Lewis. "I think he lied on his birth certificate the other way. He's an amazing man. We were watching him do stuff the other day and it was just incredible in a scrimmage. Just handling the puck, making plays and doing stuff that nobody in the rink sees but him.

"Igor has such tremendous vision. He sees everything on the ice."

Detroit linemate Martin Lapointe agreed.

"Just skate around and get open," said Lapointe. "Igor will find you. The way he plays, Igor could play until he's 50. He makes it so easy."

To demonstrate Larionov's confidence, Lapointe talked about a situation that took place during the 1999-2000 season in which the Wings found themselves on a power play. Coach Scotty Bowman liked to put Lapointe on the ice when Detroit had the man advantage because of his willingness to go to the front of the net and take a pounding from the opposition's defensemen, which in turn created space for skill players such as Larionov and Sergei Fedorov.

"Igor said, 'Go there and I will find you,'" recalled Lapointe. "I said, 'I don't know if Scotty Bowman would want me to go there. He likes me in front of the net.' Igor said, 'Just do it one time.' Sure enough, I did. And I scored."

In the 2000 playoffs, the Red Wings faced the Colorado Avalanche for the second straight year. Down two games to none, the Wings were in dire straits as the series moved to Detroit for Game 3.

Larionov was having a poor playoff up to that point, having registered just one assist. But when the team needed him the most, the Russian reached into

his bag of tricks and, for one night, answered all of the questions that surrounded him regarding his fading skills.

Less than 10 minutes into the game, Larionov swatted a puck in midair and got it past Avalanche goaltender Patrick Roy, staking Detroit to an early lead that it never relinquished. But it wasn't just the act of hitting the puck like a baseball that impressed his teammates.

"What Igor did on that shot was like trying to hit a knuckleball—with two guys on each side of you hitting you with bats," said teammate Brendan Shanahan. "That's a real tough shot."

By the 2000-01 season, Larionov was with the Florida Panthers, thinking he could help Pavel Bure. By the end of the campaign, however, he was back in Detroit, the oldest player in the NHL but still sharp. Although he came to Detroit at the end of his illustrious career and didn't quite play five complete seasons with the Red Wings, Larionov is ranked among the top 50 all-time-leading scorers in Detroit history (with 282 points) and collected his 500th career NHL point in 2000.

"He's probably one of the smartest players in the National Hockey League," said Red Wings GM Ken Holland, who orchestrated the trade with San Jose that brought Larionov to Detroit in 1995. "He lets the puck and his mind do a lot of work. Some guys have to skate six times as far to do one-quarter of the work he does. He thinks the game so well."

26

WILLIAM (BILL) "FLASH" HOLLETT

BORN: North Sydney, Nova Scotia, April 13, 1912
DIED: April 20, 1999
POSITION: Defenseman/Left Wing
NHL TEAMS: Toronto Maple Leafs, 1933, 1934-36; Ottawa Senators, 1934;
Boston Bruins, 1935-44; Detroit Red Wings, 1944-46
AWARDS/HONORS: NHL Second All-Star Team, 1943;
NHL First All-Star Team, 1945

He started his NHL career with Toronto, then played the lion's share of it with the Boston Bruins. But it was as a Detroit Red Wing, late in his career, that William "Flash" Hollett etched his name in NHL history books.

A native of Sydney, Nova Scotia, Hollett showed up at the Toronto Maple Leafs' Kingston, Ontario, training camp in 1933, looking for a spot on the Toronto defense. He impressed everyone with one destructive body check that sent King Clancy to the ice. "If they don't sign you to this team," Clancy told the kid later in the dressing room, "look me up, and I'll see that you're placed somewhere in the NHL."

Flash was sent to Buffalo in the minors, only to be recalled after the notorious Eddie Shore-Ace Bailey affair, when Leafs defenseman Red Horner was suspended. Upon Horner's return, Hollett was traded to Ottawa, but he returned to the Maple Leafs the next season (1934-35). He scored 10 goals and 16 assists for 26 points, best among NHL defensemen.

But manager Conn Smythe was unimpressed by Flash and dropped him back to Syracuse the next fall. Hollett played for two weeks, but succeeded only in

persuading Smythe that he was dispensable. A week later Hollett was sold to the minor-league Boston Cubs for a paltry $16,000. But from there he graduated to the Bruins, playing seven splendid seasons for the Beantowners. Appropriately, Flash applied the *coup de grace* to the Maple Leafs in April 1939, when he scored the goal that crushed Toronto and won the Stanley Cup for Boston.

During the 1938-39 season, Hollett became a full-fledged star. He scored 10 goals—remarkable for a defenseman during those low-scoring years—and 17 assists. On the Bruins' excursion to the Stanley Cup, he added a goal and three assists in a dozen playoff games.

It was a delightful state of affairs for Flash—also nicknamed "Busher," "Headline" and "Laughing Bill"—except for one thing. He mostly wanted to play defense with a capital D.

"I finally insisted that Art Ross keep me exclusively on the blue line," Hollett remembered. "Moving around so much certainly wasn't getting me anywhere and wasn't paying off for the team as much as it could if I stuck to defense."

OPPOSITE: Bill "Flash" Hollett, one of the NHL's finest rushing defensemen.

Hollett finally put his foot down during the 1940-41 season when Boston went 23 games without a defeat, an NHL record at the time. Two seasons later he topped all rear guards in points by collecting 19 goals and 25 assists to erase the record (41 points) held by Tommy "Cowboy" Anderson.

Asked to recall his biggest thrill, Hollett remembered the Boston-Toronto best-of-seven semifinals of 1938-39. Boston led the series, three games to one, with Game 5 at Boston Garden.

"We needed the one victory to eliminate Toronto, and we were grimly hanging on to our 2-1 lead with three minutes to go in the game," said Hollett. "Just then, Eddie Shore got a penalty and we were worried because we felt we had to win this game. We didn't want to return to Maple Leaf Gardens for any more games.

"Many of the Bruins had remembered in a previous season when Boston had a 4-0 lead in the first period before Charlie Conacher led them to a comeback when the same Eddie Shore had been penalized. Because of that, nobody wanted to take any chances this time."

Ross dispatched Hollett and Milt Schmidt to the ice for penalty-killing purposes. They captured the puck and sent it back to their own end of the rink.

Hollett: "We then began moving forward and finally got the puck into Toronto's area. Milt passed to me and I faked a long shot. All the Leaf players, with the exception of Gordie Drillon, went behind the net to retrieve the puck. Except that I still had it. Drillon dropped to his knees to block my shot.

"But I faked their goalie, Turk Broda, and drew him about 10 feet out of the net. Then, I got so excited I could hardly put the puck in the goal. But I did, and that gave us the win, 3-1, and the Stanley Cup. I kept the photos that showed how I managed my two fakes."

In 1943-44, the Bruins began slipping, and on January 5, 1944, Boston coach and manager Art Ross dealt Hollett to Detroit for Pat Egan, a younger, hard-hitting defenseman. It was one of Ross's worst moves, as the Bruins missed the playoffs while Detroit finished second.

At first, Hollett was crushed by the deal. "Boston was like home to me," he declared.

Nevertheless, he reported to the Red Wings, and in 1944-45, Flash showed why Ross had erred. Hollett tallied 20 goals and 21 assists for 41 points during the regular season, followed by three goals and four assists in 14 playoff games leading to the Cup Finals.

During the 1945 Finals, Hollett firmly endeared himself to Detroit fans. The Red Wings trailed in the series, three games to none, when Hollett led a stirring three-win comeback by opening Game 4 with a goal. Flash later set up the insurance tally.

Flash then scored the winning goal in Game 5. Inspired by Hollett, Detroit won Game 6 to tie the series at three matches apiece.

In the decisive seventh game, Toronto took a 1-0 lead in the first period and held on well into the third frame. Just past the eight-minute mark, Hollett fed Murray Armstrong, who tied the count at 1-1. But Toronto went on to win, 2-1, on a late power-play goal by Babe Pratt.

A year later, Flash suffered pleurisy plus groin and knee injuries. The medical problems hurt his game and caused Red Wings general manager Jack Adams to trade Hollett to the New York Rangers. Flash refused to report.

"When I got traded," said Hollett, "I was pretty mad. When I didn't go to the Rangers, they suspended me. There were a lot of factors involved. I had a young family, and the prospect of apartment living in Manhattan didn't appeal to me or my wife.

"But from a hockey standpoint, I should have gone. Frank Boucher was running the Rangers and he was a great fellow, plus the Rangers played my kind of game. I could have fit in with them because I was a playmaker and they were a passing team."

Sadly, Flash Hollett never played big-league hockey again. He eventually drifted to senior-level hockey in Ontario, playing for the Kitchener Dutchmen and the Toronto Marlboros. He ended his playing career in 1950 and retired to the Toronto area. Hollett died in 1999, always remembered as a Detroit hero in the 1945 playoffs and one of the best offensive defensemen of his time.

27

ANTHONY JOSEPH "TONY" LESWICK

BORN: Humboldt, Saskatchewan; March 17, 1923
POSITION: Left Wing/Right Wing
NHL TEAMS: New York Rangers, 1945-51; Detroit Red Wings, 1951-55, 1957-58;
Chicago Blackhawks, 1955-56
AWARDS/HONORS: NHL Second All-Star Team, 1950

Tony Leswick came to Detroit in one of Jack Adams's least discussed but most important deals. It happened in 1951 and would directly result in a Red Wings' Stanley Cup triumph.

But before Leswick became a Red Wing, he already had established himself as one of New York's most popular stick handlers.

In 1946, it was clear to Frank Boucher, who had taken over the helm of the Rangers, that new blood was needed to replace the prewar heroes, who had lost their spark and their style. One of the first of the finds was Leswick, a small, bulldog-type forward. Within two years, "Tough Tony," as he was known on Broadway, became the team's leading scorer.

The turnabout for the Rangers from chronic losers to consistent winners didn't happen overnight, but Leswick went a long way to pumping fighting blood into the postwar team. He not only led it in scoring during the 1946-47 campaign, but he was just as useful as the supreme needler of the opposition and shadower of its leading scorers until he was traded to Detroit in 1951-52.

More than anyone else, the fabulous Maurice "Rocket" Richard of the Montreal Canadiens had the life annoyed out of him by Leswick. Once, at the Montreal Forum, Leswick needled the Rocket, and Richard swung his stick at Leswick. The referee sent Richard to the penalty box with a two-minute minor. Leswick didn't stop there—he pestered the Rocket throughout

the match. With just a minute remaining, Richard blew up again, and again the referee sent him to the penalty box.

At game's end, Richard bolted from the penalty box and charged Leswick, whereupon the two of them brawled for several minutes while teammates and officials attempted to separate the pair. The Richard-Leswick feud continued for several years.

Of course, Richard wasn't Leswick's only target. Once, in a playoff game against the Red Wings, he was given a two-minute penalty, followed closely by a two-minute penalty to teammate Nick Mickoski. The timekeeper, whose duty it was to wave inmates back onto the ice when their penalty time had expired, became Leswick's target.

"Tony chattered and argued about the time he was to return to the ice," said Rangers' publicist Stan Saplin, "and so confused the timekeeper that he was allowed back in the game long before his penalty time was up."

Leswick could also score. During an era of low scoring, "Mighty Mouse" recorded 27- and 24-goal seasons, which put him in the high echelon of attackers.

After starring on the minor league level during the World War II years, Leswick made his major league debut during the 1945-46 season with the Rangers.

"Tony was a combative little bugger," said Boucher, general manager of the Broadway Blueshirts. "He played a lot bigger than his size."

Red Wings GM Jack Adams made many good deals in the 1950s, but none better than the acquisition of right wing Tony Leswick (right), who scored the Stanley Cup winner in 1954. Here, he battles ex-Detroiter Bill Quackenbush.

At 5'7" and only 160 pounds, Leswick was a lightweight playing against much bigger foes. But he had an indomitable spirit, and it showed in his first five years in New York, where he played on a line with Edgar Laprade and Grant "Knobby" Warwick as well as Ed Slowinski.

During the 1949-50 playoffs, Leswick keyed the Rangers' upset of the Montreal Canadiens in the opening round. Tony also was an offensive force when New York took the eventual Stanley Cup-champion Detroit Red Wings to seven games—and double overtime in the finale—before losing on a screened shot.

The playoff was also a scouting opportunity for Jack Adams, who liked what he had seen of Leswick. Adams made a mental note to keep tabs on the winger, and on June 8, 1951, the scouting report paid off for Detroit. In one of the best unheralded deals in fran-

chise history, Adams shipped forward Gaye Stewart to New York for Leswick.

A one-time Calder Trophy winner, Stewart was a complete bust with the Rangers. Playing barely two seasons in New York, Stewart would go on to flop yet again in Montreal. By contrast, Leswick emerged as one of the most valuable skaters in the Motor City. It was no coincidence that during Leswick's tenure in Detroit, from 1952 through 1955, the Red Wings won three Stanley Cups. The most memorable of all, from Tony's viewpoint, were the 1953-54 finals between Detroit and Montreal.

The teams went down to a seventh and final game played at Olympia Stadium. The date, April 16, 1954, will always live in infamy for Canadiens fans—in fame for Detroiters, and Leswick, in particular.

With the score tied 1-1 after regulation, the Wings

Gordie Howe (left, on the ice) completes a thrust at Toronto goalie Turk Broda in the Red Wings first All-Star game. Howe's teammate Tony Leswick is on the right.

looked to top scorers such as Gordie Howe and Ted Lindsay for the big goal. But at the four-minute mark of the first extra session, coach Tommy Ivan dispatched a checking unit to the ice that featured Leswick and Glen Skov.

As they completed their turn, Skov dished the puck to Leswick, who shot a soft drive at Canadiens goalie Gerry McNeil. It should have been an easy shot for the Montreal net minder to handle, but All-Star defenseman Doug Harvey was fronting for McNeil.

Ironically, Harvey was a talented baseball player in the off season and was attempting a baseball play on the rink as Leswick's shot approached the goal. Harvey reached up either to glove the puck or deflect it harmlessly into the corner. For some strange reason, the rubber ricocheted off the index finger of Harvey's glove and flew over the defenseman and the crouched McNeil.

Tony Leswick's most meaningful shot sailed into the Montreal net at exactly 4:29 of the overtime and won another Stanley Cup for the Red Wings.

A year later, Tony again played on a Detroit Cup–winning team, although his contribution was only one goal—not the championship shot that it had been a year earlier.

Manager Adams apparently believed that Leswick had had it after the 1955 championship year. On May 28, 1955, Tony was traded with Skov, Johnny Wilson and Benny Woit to Chicago for Jerry Toppazzini, John McCormack, Dave Creighton and Gord Hollingworth. However, Adams relented and reacquired Leswick on September 1, 1956, from Chicago for cash alone.

Tony's last NHL season was 1957-58, when he scored one goal and two assists in 22 games. He finished his pro career in the minors with the Edmonton Flyers, concluding in 1959-60 with the Western League's Vancouver Canucks.

Never a Hall of Famer, Tony Leswick nonetheless will always be a well-remembered Red Wing for his hustle and the 1954 blooper that turned into a Cup victory.

28

MICKEY REDMOND

BORN: Kirkland Lake, Ontario, December 27, 1947
POSITION: Right Wing
NHL TEAMS: Montreal Canadiens, 1967-71; Detroit Red Wings, 1971-76
AWARDS/HONORS: NHL First All-Star Team, 1973;
NHL Second All-Star Team, 1974; NHL All-Star Game, 1974

The sky once was the limit for Mickey Redmond. Then the roof fell in. A two-time 50-goal scorer, Mickey was forced into retirement at the tender hockey age of 28 because of a back injury that permanently damaged a nerve affecting his right leg. Yet in September 1979 he tried a comeback with the Detroit Red Wings. Redmond cannot recall the particular check or fall that caused the injury, ending a nine-year career of terrorizing net minders with his missile-like shot.

The Kirkland Lake, Ontario, native, who spent his National Hockey League tenure with the Montreal Canadiens and the Red Wings, was given his first taste of major league action with the mighty Habs in 1967. Mickey spent most of four years on the Montreal bench observing such stars as teammates Henri Richard, Jean Beliveau and Claude Provost. After proving his scoring ability during the 1969-70 season by tallying 27 goals in 75 games, Redmond was traded to Detroit, along with Guy Charron and Bill Collins, for Frank Mahovlich in 1971. The following year, the young right wing blossomed into a prolific scorer, blasting in 42 goals for the Wings. A season later, he surpassed the legendary Gordie Howe with 52 goals, a single-year record for a Detroit player, and was selected as a first-

team All-Star. Redmond was voted to the second team in 1974, this time after a 51-goal performance.

Although he never reached the playoffs during his great scoring years with Detroit, Redmond put his most important goal past Ed Johnston on April 13, 1969. His overtime tally against the Boston Bruins gave the Montreal Canadiens a 2-0 lead in their best-of-seven semifinal playoff series en route to yet another Stanley Cup championship.

It was during the 1974-75 season that the pain in Redmond's back began. There were months when he could not sleep, stand or walk properly. He scored 15 goals in 29 games that season, and only 11 goals in 37 games during the 1976 season, his last in hockey.

Redmond had major back surgery for a ruptured disc in 1975 and was confident he could return to play at 100 percent of his normal capabilities. The pain did not go away the following season, so Mickey went to see doctors at the Mayo Clinic, where he learned he had suffered permanent nerve damage.

"It's scary, frustrating, to think you'll never be healthy again," Redmond said when he heard the news. "I don't know anything but hockey; it's been my life, 24 hours a day."

OPPOSITE: More recently a Red Wings broadcaster, Mickey Redmond was one of the top sharpshooters of the 1970s.

Mickey Redmond

As a youngster in Kirkland Lake, Mickey began his devotion to hockey in the cellar of his home. He and brother Dick, the younger of the hockey-playing Redmonds, would set up glass bottles as targets and shoot at them for hours. The targets were provided by their mother on the condition that the boys cleaned up afterward, though Mickey admitted, "I guess she cleaned up a few tons of broken glass."

"What I remember best," he added, "was laying a cardboard box on its side and then putting a bottle right at the back of it. Dick and I would have a contest to see who could break it first. It was quite a trick to drive the puck into the box hard enough, and at the same time, there wouldn't be any fragments to clean up because it would all be in the box."

Along with the constant practice, Eddie Redmond, Mickey and Dick's dad, influenced the development of his sons' hard shots. He had honed his own skills for several years playing professionally in the minor leagues.

No one could have guessed in those days that Mickey would be selling steel for automotive parts as an employee of the Lafayette Steel Company in Detroit when he reached the age of 30. He appeared to be on the road to stardom as a 14-year-old playing junior hockey with the Peterborough Petes. When he was 18, he quit school while in the 12th grade to sign his first pro contract with the Montreal Canadiens, joining the cream of the major leagues after just 15 games with

Houston of the Central Professional Hockey League in 1967-68.

"Before I had time to think, I was there," Redmond said. "It wasn't even like a dream because it all happened so fast. It was more like I didn't know where I was. After all, I was 18 years old and playing on a team with Henri Richard and Jean Beliveau."

Mickey never played regularly with the Canadiens, a team that was overflowing with talent. He spent a lot of time researching his teammates, and his surprising favorite was Claude Provost, a player known for his defensive ability. "I'd watch him carry the puck," Redmond said, "and whenever he'd lose it, he'd turn around, put his head down, and skate back into his zone as hard as he could. That's the way hockey should be played, because if you're playing well defensively, the goals will come."

The goals did not come at an above-average rate until Sam Pollock reluctantly traded Redmond to Detroit for the Big M. It was not easy for Redmond to leave Montreal after being a part of two Stanley Cup championship squads in his first two NHL seasons, but the Habs were floundering for the first time in years and changes were inevitable. The move to the Motor City seemed like a giant step backward to Mickey at the time, because the Red Wings' playoff years had faded to a distant memory. Redmond soon realized that the trade "was probably the best thing for me." Finally given a regular shift, Mickey began scoring goals with alarming regularity.

Mickey joined the exclusive 50-goal club in 1972, pulling the trigger and letting the puck fly with his incredibly strong arms and wrists at "900 miles per hour," according to former Red Wing and then-Detroit broadcaster Sid Abel. He began his muscle-building program by shooting a heavy metal puck in the corridors of the Peterborough junior team's arena. "It was too heavy to slap," he said. "You had to push it with a wrist shot, but when I'd get out onto the ice with a real rubber puck, it used to feel like I was shooting a 25-cent piece."

Although the Red Wings possessed stars such as Redmond, Marcel Dionne and Danny Grant, the club constantly finished out of Stanley Cup contention. Individually, however, Redmond was closing in on superstar status, scoring 42, 52 and 51 goals in his first three seasons with Detroit. He was rewarded with a $1 million, five-year contract when the club feared he might follow Red Wing Hall of Famer Gordie Howe as a defector to the World Hockey Association.

Mickey was not satisfied with just personal scoring records as his club failed yearly and he recalled his Montreal upbringing. His own game was lacking an important dimension too, according to former Red Wings coach Johnny Wilson. "Mickey could easily score 75 goals a year," Wilson said, "if he could only develop a little finesse. He thinks he can blast that shot through anything. Well, that's pretty near true, but if he'd use a little deception once in a while, he'd score a lot more. Once he learns the knack of being a little tricky, he'll break all the records."

After Mickey scored 51 goals in 1974, the second year of his lucrative contract, his back began aching in October or November of the following season. It kept getting worse until doctors discovered that Redmond had a ruptured disc. Surgery was prescribed.

"I wasn't worried because I knew a lot of players who had back surgery and came back," Redmond recalled, "such as Rod Gilbert and Jean Ratelle."

During the early going of 1976, Redmond complained of constant aching in his back and right leg. After 37 games, Mickey entered the Mayo Clinic in Rochester, Minnesota, with permission from the Wings brass, who thought it would be a good idea for their high-priced winger to "sort out his problems."

It was then that Mickey's problems really began. The agonizing news was delivered: He had suffered neurological or nerve damage to his right leg, and although he would be able to play, he would never reach 100 percent of his playing ability. The doctors left him with three alternatives: He could retire, continue playing with discomfort and pain, or stop playing temporarily and begin an intensive physical therapy program in an attempt to return to his previous level of play.

Redmond chose to return to Ontario, work with his leg and try to overcome the problem, as one of his neurosurgeons had suggested. When Mickey had missed 10 games, Detroit manager Alex Delvecchio decided Redmond was AWOL and announced that he was suspending his high-scoring wing and placing him on waivers for any team that could hand over a mere $30,000. Delvecchio had nothing nice to say about his former teammate. "He doesn't want to play in Detroit. Otherwise, he'd be here," Delvecchio said. "We've gone long enough without him. He's no good to us. I'm tired of hearing players' excuses for mediocre work. I don't want to have such disruptive influences on my team."

Redmond was shocked and hurt. "All I hoped to do was get back and help the Red Wings, but I saw that Mr. Delvecchio didn't want me," he said.

"It put me in a tough position because I hurt my back playing for them. I thought I got along with Delvecchio. I played with the man, and he was a big figure in my scoring 50 goals the first time. My only interest was to get back and help the Wings. I was, and still am, interested in my health. That's the No. 1 thing."

National Hockey League president Clarence Campbell intervened immediately and stopped Detroit from completing waivers on Redmond. "They were out of bounds," said Redmond. "Whatever their reasons were, they weren't legal, and they were told so. Everything I did was straight above the board and legal. I can't control what he said, but I'm sure he had his reasons."

Mickey remained Red Wing property but never played again. He worked for four months in Toronto, all the time hopeful that his leg would respond. Redmond went to see his doctors in Detroit and was told to try to skate as he normally would if the leg were 100 percent.

"I got fully dressed and went out, but it was like a dead wing. I couldn't skate," Redmond said. "My foot was numb and I kept falling. After skating, I had to face the decision I had been putting off for six months."

At twenty-eight, Redmond suddenly had no future in hockey. He and agent Alan Eagleson negotiated a settlement from his Red Wings contract and Mickey was thrust into the real world.

"I wasn't prepared for it," Mickey said of his forced retirement. "I didn't do anything. I just went back up to my farm in Ontario and sat around and didn't do anything. I wanted to get back into hockey, but I couldn't think about that then."

Eventually, Redmond got a job at Lafayette Steel and worked on a deal to buy a bar restaurant with some friends in Boston, coincidentally the town where his brother, Dick, played defense wearing the Bruin black, white and gold.

In time, Mickey became a popular TV color analyst for the Red Wings, a position he held for many years. He gained valuable experience as a broadcaster, as his résumé includes work with Fox Sports, ESPN and CBC's Hockey Night in Canada.

29

DANNY GRANT

BORN: Fredericton, New Brunswick, February 21, 1946
POSITION: Right Wing
NHL TEAMS: Montreal Canadiens, 1965-66, 1967-68;
Minnesota North Stars, 1968-74; Detroit Red Wings, 1974-78;
Los Angeles Kings, 1978-79
AWARDS/HONORS: Calder Memorial Trophy, 1969;
NHL All-Star Game, 1969-71

For a brief yet meaningful period of time, Danny Grant owned one of the hottest shooting sticks in the National Hockey League. Because of that, he deserves mention among Detroit's all-time sharpshooters.

It was the 1974-75 season in which Grant joined a select group of athletes by scoring 50 goals for the Red Wings. But more important to Danny was the recognition he received—finally—as an excellent all-around stick handler.

Criticized throughout his seven-year NHL career to that point as a one-way, offensive-only forward, Danny enjoyed his greatest season in 1974-75 with the 50 goals and 37 assists as a Detroiter. His defensive performance, however, was a special source of pride to the left winger.

"How many one-way players kill penalties?" he asked in answering his critics. "I was never asked to do it before I came to Detroit, but I think I kill penalties pretty well. I also enjoy it."

Likewise, the Red Wings enjoyed having Danny around. The NHL's Rookie of the Year in 1968-69 when he registered 34 goals and 31 assists for the Minnesota North Stars, Grant proved a valuable addition to Detroit's roster. The Wings picked him up in exchange for Henry Boucha in what many observers termed an incredible heist. Minus Mickey Redmond for most of the 1974-75 season, the Wings figured to lose much of

their scoring punch, but Danny combined with Marcel Dionne to register more than 200 points.

Dionne was then dealt to Los Angeles the following year, and potential detractors watched Grant's adjustments closely. Some said Danny would be lost without Dionne. Others insisted he would be an even better skater. In fact, some even thought that Grant's best season would come in 1975-76, with Dionne gone, because of the extra ice time he was going to get and the added responsibility of being one of Detroit's—and one of the NHL's—best all-around performers.

"Sure I missed Marcel," Grant said. "He was the most unselfish guy and best center anyone could ever have wanted to play with. But there was no reason I couldn't do things on my own. I did them in Minnesota without him, didn't I?"

Dionne had deep respect for his former linemate. "The best left winger I ever played with," Dionne said of Grant. "He was always working, had a great shot and was always near the net."

Once near the net, Danny was not about to be displanted. A sturdy skater with a solid physique, Grant frequently was on the ice for more than half a game. The extra duty on the power play and as a penalty killer didn't bother him a bit.

"I felt as strong at the end of a season as at the beginning," Danny contended. "Besides, I didn't mind all that work at all."

Danny Grant unleashes a wrist shot against the St. Louis Blues while Alex Delvecchio (center) moves in for the rebound.

Had Grant continued to perform at the pace he established over his first eight NHL seasons, he surely would have surpassed the 300-lifetime-goals plateau, but it was not to be. In 1975-76, the Wings' captain suffered a torn right thigh muscle requiring surgery on December 29, 1975. The injury ended his NHL iron-man streak at 556 games, as he finished that campaign with only 10 goals and 13 assists over 39 games.

It was the beginning of the end for Grant as a big leaguer. He played only 13 games for Detroit in 1977-78 before being dealt to the Los Angeles Kings. Two more dismal years with the Kings marked the end of his major league career.

Injuries notwithstanding, Grant's numbers were impressive. He finished with 263 goals and 273 assists for a total of 536 points in only 736 games played.

The pity is that Danny's Detroit years were all too brief, ending just as he appeared to be reaching his peak. But 50 goals in 80 games is a singular accomplishment. For that Danny Grant will be remembered as a short-term, but notable, Red Wings captain and ace.

30

GARY BERGMAN

BORN: Kenora, Ontario; October 7, 1938
DIED: December 8, 2000
POSITION: Defenseman/Left Wing
NHL TEAMS: Detroit Red Wings, 1964-73, 1975;
Minnesota North Stars, 1974-75; Kansas City Scouts, 1975-76
AWARDS/HONORS: NHL All-Star Game, 1973

During some of the most depressing Detroit hockey seasons from 1964 through 1974, one of the most rewarding sights for Red Wings fans, game in and game out, was the indefatigable play of defenseman Gary Bergman.

Standing 5'11" and weighing 185 pounds, Bergman was not an imposing sight. But a combination of guts and savvy enabled him to compete on even terms with the very best.

Beginning in 1964, Bergman played nine straight seasons for the Red Wings, and for two straight years (1970-71 and 1971-72) he was voted the Red Wings' best defensemen by local hockey writers and awarded the Air Canada trophy at the team's annual night.

One of the high points of Bergman's career was in 1972 when he was invited to join the NHL's best players in the now-legendary Team Canada vs. Soviet series. Bergman was not only one of the best performers but also one of the toughest skaters in the eight-game series won by the North Americans in the final match.

Gary came to Detroit in 1964 via the NHL draft. As a minor leaguer with Winnipeg, Buffalo, Cleveland and Springfield, Bergman originally was the property

of the Montreal Canadiens. But on June 10, 1964, he was left unprotected and claimed by the Red Wings.

Bergman attracted attention during the 1965-66 season as a Red Wing after Detroit finished fourth and then upset Chicago, four games to two, in the semifinal round. In the finals, it appeared that the Motor City sextet would pull a huge upset and win the Stanley Cup. The Wings stunned the favored Habs, winning the first two games in Montreal, 3-2 and 5-2. But Detroit couldn't sustain the momentum, and Montreal won the next three games.

In Game 6, Bergman helped rally the Red Wings from a one-goal deficit midway through the third period, sending the game into overtime.

Many believed momentum had swung back to Detroit and that a Red Wing goal was inevitable. But soon Bergman would be the centerpiece of a strange episode that forever would be remembered by Olympia Stadium fans. Just past the two-minute mark, Detroit suffered the cruelest of fates, and Gary was an integral part of the moment.

Habs winger John Ferguson recalled the play: "Our coach, Toe Blake, sent the Pocket Rocket [Maurice

OPPOSITE: Although he was victimized on Montreal's Cup-winning goal in the 1966 playoffs, Gary Bergman was a stalwart on the Red Wings' blue line through the late 1960s and early 1970s.

116

Gary Bergman

Richard's younger brother, Henri], Dave Balon and Jim Roberts out for a shift. We won the puck in their end and it went to Balon. He tried to get it to Henri, but Richard was pulled down by Gary Bergman as he was heading for the net.

"Meanwhile, the puck was at the Pocket's skates as he kept sliding and sliding and *sliding* at [Detroit goalie] Crozier, until he slid right into the net—with the puck and Crozier! The goal judge had no choice but to hit the red light, because the puck had crossed the line.

"Our coach, Toe Blake, was watching. The minute he saw the light flash, he yelled, 'Get out on the ice! Get out on the ice!' So we tumbled off the bench and headed for Richard as if we'd won the Stanley Cup.

"The goal probably should have been disallowed by referee Frank Udvari, because Richard must have slid 15 yards down the ice and into the net with it. And if he'd disallowed it, we wouldn't have had a gripe. But Toe figured that if we all jumped over the boards and acted like it was legit, maybe Udvari would swallow his whistle.

"Toe was right. Udvari seemed stunned by the whole business and did nothing in the way of waving off the goal. By now, we knew it had counted and began to celebrate in earnest."

That bitter event aside, Bergman was, throughout his NHL career, a polished defenseman with a wealth of hockey knowledge. Even more rare, Gary universally was considered one of the truly honest performers in The Game. In 1967-68, he enjoyed his finest offensive season—a career-best 13 red lights and 28 assists for 41 points.

"Bergie was a strong skater with fine playmaking ability and a booming shot," said teammate and Hall of Famer Gordie Howe. "He could play a tough, rugged brand of defense, using the body check or poke check equally well."

Bergman remained a Red Wing until November 9, 1973, when he was traded to Minnesota for Ted Harris. He was traded back to the Motor City in 1974-75 and finished his NHL career in 1975-76 with Kansas City.

Never the perennial All-Star, Gary Bergman nevertheless was as honest and reliable a defenseman as ever graced the blue line of Olympia Stadium ice. After a long illness, Bergman died early on December 8, 2000.

31

ROGER ALLAN CROZIER

BORN: Bracebridge, Ontario, March 16, 1942
DIED: January 11, 1996
POSITION: Goaltender
NHL TEAMS: Detroit Red Wings, 1963-70; Buffalo Sabres, 1970-76;
Washington Capitals, 1977
AWARDS/HONORS: NHL First All-Star Team, 1965,
Calder Memorial Trophy, 1965; Conn Smythe Trophy, 1966

If Glenn Hall was the first goaltender to popularize the "butterfly" style of puck stopping, Roger Crozier was the first puck stopper to take that form to the next level.

Roger Crozier is never mentioned in the same breath as Glenn Hall when it comes to the all-time top goaltenders. But had constant ill health not bedeviled Crozier, there is every possibility he would have been ranked with the likes of Hall, Terry Sawchuk and Jacques Plante of the pre-expansion era.

A compulsive worrier, Crozier developed an ulcer at age 17. Many times he could not eat before a game or afterwards. But despite the many troubles that faced Roger—illness, nervousness and the plight of often being forced to backstop for mediocre clubs—he was nonetheless one of The Game's premier puck stoppers during his career, several seasons of which were spent with the Detroit Red Wings.

Crozier followed a line of great Detroit goaltenders, beginning with Johnny Mowers, Harry Lumley and Terry Sawchuk, and he rose to the occasion.

Initially, however, many scouts and critics weren't fans of Crozier, who was small at 5'8" and 155 pounds. Although Roger would ultimately perfect and refine the emerging butterfly style, initially minor league coaches tried to rid him of his sprawling style, thinking it would never succeed in the NHL. Crozier spent most of the 1963-64 season with Pittsburgh in the minors,

but unlike the youngster's detractors, Detroit coach Sid Abel had faith in him.

Roger broke into the National Hockey League in 1964-65 at the tender age of 21. "The Dodger" played extremely well, winning the Calder Trophy as the league's best rookie and helping the Wings finish first with a remarkable 40 wins. Crozier's rookie performance also justifiably earned him a slot in goal for the First All-Star Team in 1965.

The following season, in the 1966 Stanley Cup finals, Roger won the Conn Smythe Trophy as the MVP for his team in the playoffs, even though Detroit lost in the finals to the Montreal Canadiens after leading the series two games to none.

But for the first two games of the finals, Montreal was being beaten by Roger Crozier. Jacques Laperriere, the fine Canadien defenseman, remembered it like this: "We were just as good, maybe better. What won those first two games for them was their goalie, Roger Crozier. He was making all the saves, and it looked like we could never get the puck past him."

Montreal took the next two games from Detroit on the Red Wings' home ice and then won the fifth game at Montreal. Leading three games to two in the series, Montreal went back to Detroit to try to wrap it up.

The Canadiens got started when Jean Beliveau scored a goal in the first period. In the second, Montreal's Leon Rochefort put the puck past Roger,

Once Glenn Hall was traded, GM Jack Adams came up with another ace goalie, this one Roger Crozier. He juggles the puck as teammate Bill Gadsby moves to help out.

and Norm Ullman scored for Detroit to make it 2-1 in favor of the Habs. Floyd Smith tied it in the third period, and the game went into overtime.

Two minutes into sudden death, Montreal mounted a rush toward the Detroit goal, with Henri Richard heading for the slot. Just as Henri tried to get his stick on the puck, Detroit defenseman Gary Bergman knocked him to the ice.

Laperriere said, "Richard fell to the ice on his stomach and I remembered him sliding—I don't know how many feet—toward the goal, the puck against his arm or his body. Crozier was hugging the post as Richard slid toward him. It looked like he had it covered. But somehow the puck slid with Richard, and as he went past the post, the puck slid past Crozier—there couldn't

have been more than four inches of opening—and across the goal line. There it stopped."

With this unusual ending, Montreal had won the Stanley Cup. The most valuable player? Roger Crozier, whose play had been sparkling as he first held off the Chicago Blackhawks and almost duplicated the feat against Montreal.

After developing the ulcer while playing junior league in St. Catherines, Crozier was never again 100 percent healthy, and years of NHL-level hockey would only make him more nervous. Early one morning- before the start of his second NHL season, Roger woke up with a massive pain in his stomach. Rushed to the hospital, Crozier was diagnosed with pancreatitis and given only a 50-50 chance of survival. For four days

Roger hovered near death as he was treated with drugs and fed intravenously. Crozier recovered, but reported to training camp for the 1965-66 season having dropped 20 pounds, his skin tinted a yellowish hue. Remarkably, though, Crozier would go on to win the Conn Smythe Trophy.

Traded to Buffalo in 1970, Roger played several seasons but missed many games due to his chronic pancreas problem. Even when able to play, he was still not in the best of health. On a bad day, he felt weak and nauseated; on the "good" days, he still didn't feel well, saying, "I never feel 100 percent, and I never will again. I just have to accept it."

At one point, five pancreatic flare-ups put him in the hospital for over nine months. When Crozier came back to Buffalo after almost a year of illness, he was scheduled to start against Toronto. During warmups, he was hit on the right side of his neck, just above the collarbone, by a drive from the stick of defenseman Jerry Korab, in virtually the only spot on a goaltender's body not protected by a pad or a mask. The powerful shot knocked Crozier out cold. Sometimes, the goalie thought, it simply looked as though there were a conspiracy to keep him out of the net!

Born March 16, 1942, in Bracebridge, Ontario, Roger Allan Crozier was one of 14 children. After starting his ice career in goal at six years of age, by the time Roger was 14, he was playing goal on an intermediate team with men twice his age. It was then that Bob Wilson, the scout who discovered Bobby Hull, spotted Roger. The difference was that while Wilson knew immediately that Hull would be a star, with Crozier he figured the youngster was too small ever to make it to the National Hockey League. Still, the Blackhawks were in desperate need of a goalie for their junior team in St. Catherines, so Wilson signed Crozier.

Next up was St. Louis of the Central Pro League for the 1962-63 season, where Roger figured he would remain. "I never even thought about the NHL then," he said later.

Little did Crozier know what lay in his hockey future. The antics of defenseman Howie Young were grating the Detroit Red Wings, so they decided to unload him—for any offer. They sent Young to Chicago for Crozier and a minor-league defenseman. Roger then spent the 1963-64 season playing for Pittsburgh in the minors, doing such a good job that Abel decided he belonged in the NHL.

Crozier justified Abel's faith in 1964-65 becoming the only goaltender in the NHL to play all of his team's games (70). The young rookie allowed only 2.42 goals per game and led the NHL in shutouts that year with six. The Wings' first-place showing was due in large part to the excellent goaltending of Crozier.

Roger went home with $9,000 of bonus money, proof that he belonged in the National Hockey League. Although his self-confidence should have been growing by now, Crozier instead found himself worrying more than ever. "The only time I really forget my problems is after a game we've won," Roger said. "But by the next morning, I'll be worrying again."

The world-class fretter once recollected life as a National Hockey League goaltender. "I like everything about hockey—the traveling, the friends I've met, the interviews. Everything but the games. They're pure torture."

Acquired by the expansion Buffalo Sabres in 1970-71, Crozier helped lead Buffalo to the Stanley Cup finals in 1974-75, where the Sabres succumbed to Philadelphia in a memorable six-game series. Then, traded for cash to Washington on March 3, 1977, Crozier would finally hang up his pads after only three games, finishing with a respectable lifetime goals-against average of 3.04 and recording 30 shutouts. Crozier remained with the Capitals' organization as assistant general manager until a major club shakeup in 1982. Roger Crozier died on January 11, 1996.

32

MARCEL "LITTLE BEAVER" DIONNE

BORN: Drummondville, Quebec, August 3, 1951
POSITION: Center
NHL TEAMS: Detroit Red Wings, 1971-75;
Los Angeles Kings, 1975-87; New York Rangers, 1987-89
AWARDS/HONORS: Lady Byng Trophy, 1975, 1977;
NHL First All-Star Team, 1977, 1980; NHL Second All-Star Team,
1979, 1981; Lester B. Pearson Award, 1979, 1980; Art Ross Trophy, 1980;
NHL All-Star Game, 1975-78, 1980, 1981, 1983, 1985; Hockey Hall of Fame, 1992

At one point during the early 1970s, it appeared as if Marcel Dionne was on the threshold of having as long and dedicated a Detroit career as Steve Yzerman later would enjoy as both captain and top scorer. Despite a diminutive physique that some believed would hamper his survival in the rugged National Hockey League, Dionne exploited his speed and savvy to the point where size really didn't matter.

In his rookie year with the Red Wings, the right-handed center scored 77 points in 78 games. That total was significant because Dionne's freshman year marked the last season in more than a decade in which the tiny French-Canadian would fail to average at least a point a game or more.

By Dionne's sophomore season, he had lifted his scoring to 90 points in 77 games, and he topped the century mark two years later. Playing a full 80 games, Marcel set what were then career highs of 47 goals and 74 assists for 121 points. He recorded only 14 penalty minutes, which—all things considered—gave him every right to the Lady Byng Trophy for superior ability combined with clean play. It would be the first of two

sportsmanship-artistry awards he would win as a big leaguer.

With marks such as those, one might have expected Dionne to remain the cornerstone of the Red Wings' offense, but this was not to be. For one thing, Detroit missed the playoffs in each of Dionne's seasons, and for another, he had become a free agent before the 1975-76 season, and soon was gone.

Just why Marcel failed to remain a Red Wing has been debated for decades. Some claim that a series of incompetent coaches failed to correctly utilize the gifted scorer. Others suggest that management simply blew it when it decided that Dionne should leave Detroit.

Marcel completed his rookie season with 28 goals and 49 assists for 77 points, a new NHL record for points in a season by a rookie. Thus it was hardly surprising that he was given a veteran's responsibility.

Inexplicably, Dionne finished a distant third in the voting for the Calder Trophy, given to the NHL's outstanding rookie. Marcel placed behind Buffalo's Richard Martin, who scored 44 goals, and Montreal's goalie-lawyer, Ken Dryden. The rejection of Dionne provoked a hail of protest, especially in Detroit.

OPPOSITE: Long retired, Marcel Dionne often appears in old-timers' games with the NHL Heroes.

In his second season, Dionne enjoyed an outstanding offensive year, garnering 40 goals and 50 assists for 90 points. In Marcel's third season the irascible Ted Garvin took over as head coach, and instantly there was a personality clash. Garvin accused the young center of loafing, and Dionne responded by demanding to be traded. By now, the troubles were having a telling effect. Dionne slumped to a disappointing 24-goal year.

The 1974-75 season, Dionne's fourth in the majors, brought yet another head coach, this time former Detroit superstar Alex Delvecchio. But more important, it was Marcel's option year. By not signing a new contract, Dionne would be free to go to the team of his choice at the end of the campaign. Knowing this, the Red Wings attempted to make Marcel happy by giving him more responsibility. In a shocking move, Dionne was named team captain.

Playing like the Dionne of old, Marcel enjoyed his finest season in Detroit, amassing 47 goals and 74 assists for 121 points, placing him behind only Phil Esposito and Bobby Orr in the NHL scoring race.

But his productive campaign failed to erase the scars of bygone years, and once the season ended, Marcel's agent, Alan Eagleson, informed Delvecchio that Dionne would be taking his services elsewhere.

"We offered him a four-year contract for a million—$250,000 per year," said Delvecchio, "but he thinks he can get more money somewhere else. He said he didn't want to play in Detroit anymore. He said 'the name of the game is money' and he thinks he can get more money somewhere else. Personally, I think Dionne is a pretty selfish individual. Now it looks as though what he did for the Red Wings last year was all for himself." And so came the big question: Who would sign Marcel for 1975-76?

The Los Angeles Kings won the bidding war and surrendered veteran defenseman Terry Harper and rugged forward Dan Maloney to Detroit. Cooke signed Marcel to a five year, $1.5 million pact.

Although Dionne and Cooke danced cartwheels of joy, Kings coach Bob Pulford unhappily muttered that the deal was not in the best interest of the club. Under Pulford's disciplined defensive style, the Kings had previously enjoyed an extremely successful season. Los Angeles had the fourth-best win-loss record in the league, and only the Stanley Cup–champion Philadelphia Flyers allowed fewer goals. Terry Harper had been the captain of the squad and the leader on defense. Maloney, a muscular winger, could score goals and tend to checking. In Dionne, the Kings were adding a freewheeling player whose style appeared conspicuously out of place in the Kings' system. Coach Pulford worried

that Dionne might disrupt his previously sound club, both on and off the ice.

Marcel Elphege Dionne was born August 3, 1951, in Drummondvile, Quebec. He needed only two years before he was able to skate on a makeshift rink in his backyard. His parents encouraged young Marcel to play hockey, aware that if he didn't make a career of hockey, he would inevitably spend his life working in the steel mills like his father.

As a result, the Dionnes saw to it that their son's hockey thirst was always quenched.

When Marcel was 15, he had established himself as a professional prospect who had outgrown Drummondville. It was time for him to move on to the big time and play for the Montreal Junior Canadiens, one of the strongest amateur teams in all of Canada.

The move to Montreal also was part of the price of making it in the pros. Dionne played spectacularly for his new club, and after his rookie season, he received an invitation to play for the St. Catherines Ontario Jr. A team, a club that had developed such stars as Bobby Hull and Stan Mikita and sent them to the NHL. Dionne accepted the offer, although St. Catherines was in Ontario, where only English was spoken. Since Marcel could speak only French, he had catapulted himself into a very awkward situation.

During his three-year pro apprenticeship at St. Catherines, Marcel established an Ontario Hockey Association career scoring record of 375 points. He attracted attention throughout Canada, and NHL clubs scouted the mighty little scoring machine as if they had found a gold mine of goals. In fact, Dionne was so highly regarded that the Detroit Red Wings selected him second in the 1971 NHL amateur draft; only Guy Lafleur of the Canadiens was chosen before Dionne.

Desperate for help, the Red Wings expected instant miracles from Marcel. Detroit general manager Ned Harkness sought a replacement for the legendary Gordie Howe, who had quit the Wings following the 1970-71 season. Dionne hired attorney Eagleson to negotiate his contract, and the result was a pact that Eagleson labeled "the best I've ever negotiated for a rookie . . . better even than the original one I negotiated for Bobby Orr with the Boston Bruins."

Along with big money, Dionne received unprecedented attention from the Detroit press and the fans, who expected the kind of results that a six-figure contract suggested at the time. Consequently, Dionne found himself in a pressure-cooker atmosphere before he even put on a Red Wings' uniform.

"When you were 18 years old and playing junior hockey," Dionne said, "you did not think of pressure;

the game was fun. Then all of a sudden you were drafted by an NHL team, and everything changed."

During his first NHL exhibition season, Dionne scored a paltry two goals, and immediately the press was on his case. From savior to goat before he'd played his first game!

"It was more difficult in the NHL than I imagined," Dionne said. "There was such a big difference in the style of play; it's so much faster in the majors. I had scoring chances as a rookie, but I just couldn't connect. My teammates told me not to miss on those kind of chances in this league. They are just so much quicker and the checking is quicker, and then there is the pressure because you are playing for money—big money."

Red Wings coach Doug Barkley defended and shielded his prize 20-year-old rookie. "I'm not disappointed with Marcel," Barkley said at the time. "He's improving with each game. He can skate. He can shoot. He has all the moves. But he must learn the difference between the NHL and junior hockey. And mark my words, he will!"

But Dionne would suffer under six coaches in half a dozen years while searching in vain for a playoff combination. It wasn't that Marcel played bad hockey. In 1971-72, his 77 points as a rookie set a mark for NHL freshmen, and the next season he upped his total to 90, with 40 goals and 50 assists. In 1973-74, his 78 points (24 goals and 54 assists) led the team.

The problem was that Dionne and the Red Wings became entangled in the totally disorganized Ned Harkness regime in Detroit, as did "Mister Hockey" himself, Gordie Howe, who quit the Wings and signed with the WHA's Houston Aeros in 1973-74.

Dionne's dilemma began midway through the 1972-73 campaign, when Johnny Wilson was the Red Wings' coach. Before the dispute was over, Marcel and Harkness were to have their falling out. The boiling point was reached when Harkness accused the 5'8", 175-pound Dionne of not giving "the old 100 percent" in practice.

"I'm not going to give 100 percent in practice," snapped Dionne. "I don't believe practice makes perfect. I think it can only hurt a player if he skates his very best in practice." This sentiment put him on a collision course with Wilson, and a suspension followed.

But Wilson soon was fired by Harkness, and into the maelstrom stepped Ted Garvin, a tough old-school coach who strictly policed facial hair and shaggy heads and ran his practices with heavy emphasis on fundamentals. Only days after Garvin took over, a major clash erupted between Garvin and Dionne. Before November 1973 was gone, so was Garvin, fired by Harkness, who replaced him with the easygoing Alex Delvecchio. Even with Delvecchio piloting the club, Dionne was in trouble. General manager Harkness felt Dionne symbolized the pampered young hockey player.

Harkness got his walking papers late in the 1973-74 season, and into the breach stepped Delvecchio, a sophisticated, *laissez-faire* operator who became both coach and general manager. In a dramatic departure from Garvin's authoritarianism, Delvecchio took a soft-sell attitude toward his skaters. In 1974-75, Dionne responded with 47 goals and 74 assists for 121 points. Still unhappy, Marcel became a free agent in June 1975 and was obtained by the Kings.

In the end, Marcel's numbers were among the best in NHL history. Dionne had the fastest 500 goals and 1,000 assists in league history. He had six 50-goal seasons and five straight 100-point seasons. At the conclusion of the 1982-83 season, he again led the Kings with 56 goals, 51 assists and 107 points. "It's very impressive," said an NHL scout who remembered Dionne as a rookie. "But it would have been even more impressive if he had managed to skate for a champion."

Dionne completed his career in 1988-89 with the New York Rangers and went on to become a successful businessman. He will always be remembered, however, as a Red Wings ace who had the credentials of a superstar, but who never drank from the Stanley Cup.

33

VYACHESLAV
"SLAVA" KOZLOV

BORN: Voskresensk, Russia, May 3, 1972
POSITION: Left Wing
NHL TEAMS: Detroit Red Wings, 1991-2001; Buffalo Sabres, 2001-Present

Quiet and unassuming, Vyacheslav "Slava" Kozlov played left wing for the Detroit Red Wings with a blend of style and finesse. A relatively small player (5'10", 195 pounds), Kozlov excelled with quick hands, manipulating the puck like a magician.

During the Red Wings' dominant period of the 1990s, Kozlov scored some of the biggest playoff goals in club history, helping propel Detroit to back-to-back Stanley Cup championships in 1997 and 1998. Swift and deceptive, Kozlov became known more for finishing a play rather than starting one.

Many hockey people compared the native Russian to one of the most prolific scorers in NHL history, Brett Hull. Kozlov did not possess Hull's cannon nor his shooting quickness. But Kozlov and Hull were alike in their stealth. Slava found open space with his radar-like ability to read a play. He would cruise through the neutral zone like a shark eyeing his prey, as teammates such as Igor Larionov and Steve Yzerman brought the puck into the offensive zone. Kozlov then used a sudden, explosive burst of speed to find an opening, positioning himself not only to receive a pass, but also to take a deadly accurate wrist shot on net.

That darting style made him almost impossible for defenders to cover stride for stride. Often, opponents were left shaking their heads as they watched Kozlov put another puck into the net after suddenly showing up at the right place at the right time.

Vyacheslav Kozlov was born on May 3, 1972, in the Russian industrial town of Voskresensk. This modest municipality, just 50 miles outside of Moscow, was the home of several other players who would one day become NHLers, such as Igor Larionov, Valeri Kamensky and Valeri Zelepukin.

It was where Kozlov honed his stick handling and scoring skills. As a kid, Slava had two hockey heroes: Sergei Makarov was his Russian idol, while Wayne Gretzky stood tall as a Canadian role model. But it would be from his father that Kozlov would learn the game of hockey. Dad was a professional coach and Slava was a mere five years old at the time.

The two would spend countless hours in the backyard of their home, as the elder Kozlov taught Slava how to maneuver deftly on his skates, a skill Kozlov displayed as soon as he began to play in organized leagues as a teenager. In 1987, Kozlov began playing junior hockey for Khimik in the Soviet Elite League as a 15-year-old phenom.

OPPOSITE: Slava Kozlov gets crosschecked into Kings goalie Felix Potvin.

Slava Kozlov uses his speed to intercept the puck.

"When I play junior, I was the best player for my age," he said. "When I was 16, 17 years old, I won the Rookie of the Year award in Russia. I was the best player on the junior team. I was very young when I start playing for the Elite League."

Kozlov himself admitted that he was somewhat of a rebel while growing up—a self-confessed smart aleck. "I was like a big star," he said. "Not in hockey but, for example, I was like a wild kid. I didn't listen to my parents. My dad, he told me something; I said, 'I know everything.'

"I was a little bit fancy, you know. I didn't listen to the coach for Khimik in my hometown. That's why I went to CSKA. Because CSKA featured discipline."

CSKA was the Russian Red Army team, a formidable squad that included the likes of Sergei Fedorov, Alexander Mogilny and Vladimir Konstantinov. The squad was coached then by Viktor Tikhonov, who demanded that players be under strict control every second on and off the ice. As a soldier in the Red Army in 1991, Kozlov learned right from wrong, maturing as an individual.

"Not anymore," he said when asked if he was still the same "brat" who left Voskresensk. "Because I did lots of mistakes. And I don't want to do mistakes now."

But Kozlov participated in only 11 games for the Red Army in 1991. The reason? A fatal car accident that forever changed his life. A bus smashed into Kozlov's Russian-built car one day near Voskresensk. A passenger with him in the car was killed, while Kozlov's head was badly injured.

"I was in a coma for four hours," he said. "Three months in hospital."

Kozlov had been selected by the Detroit Red Wings in the second round of the 1990 NHL entry draft (45th overall). The Wings were aware of Kozlov's accident and soon sent front-office aide Nick Polano to Russia. Polano had been a coach for Detroit, but now was working for the team as one of its special emissaries involved in luring Russian players to Detroit.

"He came to Moscow and invited me to the United States to get treatment," Kozlov remembered. "I said OK."

But before Slava settled across the ocean, Red Army officials tried to stop the journey. Claiming the Red Wings had abducted Kozlov, they soon sued the club. The Wings eventually won the case and did not have to pay the Russians for grooming their soon-to-be ace.

"Before, when [CSKA general manager Valerie] Gushin came to Detroit, Detroit say, 'It's OK, we can pay money for Kozlov.'" Kozlov said. "But Gushin said, 'No, no, no. We don't need money. We need Kozlov. Send him back.'"

The Red Wings, however, held on to their prize possession and watched the youngster grow into an integral cog of a machine that was just starting to get revved up in 1992.

Kozlov made his NHL debut on March 12, 1992 against St. Louis and made an immediate impact. He recorded two assists that night, his first coming on his initial shift, when he set up fellow Russian Sergei Fedorov. It was certainly a sign of things to come, although Kozlov would spend most of the 1992-93 campaign with Detroit's minor-league affiliate in Adirondack, lighting up the American Hockey League with 59 points in 45 games.

In 1993-94, Kozlov, along with Darren McCarty, Kris Draper and Chris Osgood, joined the parent club in Detroit. The four had become part of a team that was on the verge of winning championships.

Under head coach Scotty Bowman, Detroit recorded 100-plus points for the second straight season, while Kozlov enjoyed one of his best years as a professional, netting 34 goals among a career-high 73 points. He also set a career mark between November 20 and December 3, when he recorded a point in eight straight games.

The following year, the Wings notched 70 points in a lockout-shortened season that consisted of just 48 games. Heading into the playoffs, Detroit was favored to win the Stanley Cup.

Kozlov amassed 33 points in 46 games that year, but broke out as one of the elite players in the league during the playoffs. He tied a team playoff record with four game-winning goals in the postseason, including a dramatic tally in double overtime of Game 5 against Chicago that clinched the Western Conference title for Detroit.

Facing New Jersey in the Stanley Cup finals, the Red Wings were ground to a halt by the Devils' tight checking and aggressive forechecking. The upstart Devils defeated the Red Wings in a surprising four-game sweep. But Kozlov proved his mettle during the physical series. Many experts were fond of Kozlov's natural abilities but said that he wouldn't be able to handle the North American style of hockey, which featured hard-hitting and close checking. But Kozlov proved them wrong throughout the postseason, constantly picking himself up after being on the receiving end of an opponents elbow or shoulder.

New Jersey Devils defenseman Scott Stevens leveled Kozlov as the Russian came dashing across the blue line with his head down. In a spectacular collision, Stevens knocked Kozlov to the ice, where he remained for close to five minutes. Woozy, Slava skated to the dressing room, where teammate Slava Fetisov waved a dollar bill in front of his eyes. When Kozlov recognized the money, Fetisov knew his comrade was all right. Kozlov returned to the contest, proving his toughness to the hockey world.

"He gets a lot and takes a lot," said assistant coach Barry Smith about Slava. "This kid is tough. You're not going to stop that kid."

In 1995-96, Kozlov tied for second on the Red Wings in goals (36), was fourth in points (73), and was the only member of the team to participate in all 82 games.

However, it was during the 1997 postseason that Kozlov proved just how important he was to the success of the Red Wings. In the first round of the playoffs, the Wings struggled with their opponent, the St. Louis Blues. The series was deadlocked at two games apiece before the Wings defeated the Blues in the next two games. Part of the reason for Detroit's brush with elimination was an ineffective Kozlov.

"I'm not a playmaker," he said. "I'm not a guy who can check well like Darren McCarty. If I don't score goals, I am very upset."

Slava finished the 1996-97 regular season with 23 goals (third on the team) and 45 points, the lowest point output of his career (excluding the 1995 shortened season). But late in the series against St. Louis, Scotty Bowman reunited the Russian Five, a unit he had introduced to the world in 1995.

Playing with forwards Igor Larionov and Sergei Fedorov along with defensemen Slava Fetisov and Vladimir Konstantinov, Kozlov seemed at home again, coming through with two meaningful goals to help clinch the Blues series for Detroit.

"I'll play with the Russian Five, and they pay attention to Igor and Sergei," Kozlov said of the opposition. "That's why I have so much room to skate. They can't cover five players."

Kozlov simply took off in the next round. He scored a game-winning triple-overtime goal against Anaheim in Game 2. In Game 3, Slava finished what he started, scoring the first and last goals of the contest. He also added an assist for good measure in the 5-3 Wings victory.

"It was big when Kozie scored the first goal on the power play," defenseman Slava Fetisov said. "When he scored that, then we had the confidence that we could win. There were a lot of complaints in the regular season that we couldn't compete and come back. Now you can see how the guys are focused."

The Wings finished off the Mighty Ducks in a four-game sweep then followed that with a six-game series win against arch rival Colorado. For the second time in three years, Detroit was heading to the Stanley Cup finals for a date with the Philadelphia Flyers.

But it was no contest for the Eric Lindros–led Flyers as the Wings captured their first Stanley Cup since 1955.

After the victory, Kozlov, along with teammates Larionov and Fedorov, took the silver mug to their Russian homeland. In Voskresensk, Kozlov was overjoyed as he displayed the Stanley Cup proudly to people showing the strains of a depressed economy.

"Right now, I am the happiest man in the world," he told the enthusiastic crowd gathered at the local rink.

34

HERBIE "THE DUKE OF DULUTH" LEWIS

BORN: Calgary, Alberta, April 17, 1907
DIED: January 20, 1991
POSITION: Left Wing
NHL TEAMS: Detroit Red Wings, 1928-39
AWARDS/HONORS: NHL All-Star Game, 1934; Hockey Hall of Fame, 1989

A pure Red Wing, Herbie Lewis spent his entire career wearing the Winged Wheel with distinction.

He came to Detroit in 1928 and left a little more than a decade later. In that time, Lewis skated on two Stanley Cup champion teams and helped propel the Detroit sextet from anonymity to a position of eminence in the hockey world.

One-third of the best pre–World War II Detroit line of Lewis-Larry Aurie-Marty Barry, Herbie was a native of Calgary who first cut his hockey teeth as a pro in Minnesota. Beginning in the 1924-25 season, Lewis became one of the finest products of the American Hockey Association and soon earned the nickname "The Duke of Duluth." He spent four seasons in the AHA before finally winning promotion to Detroit.

Once the left wing was aligned with Barry and Aurie, the Red Wings took off and in the spring of 1936 defeated Toronto, three games to one, to bring the Stanley Cup to Michigan for the first time. In the final match at Maple Leaf Gardens in Toronto on April 11, 1936, Lewis showed his mettle in the 3-2 Detroit victory. He assisted on both the second and the game-winning scores.

A year later, the Red Wings repeated as champs, this time beating the Rangers three games to two in a best-of-five series. Lewis finished in a tie for most goals scored with linemate Barry—each had four—and he also was the second leading scorer.

A member of the Hockey Hall of Fame, Lewis was best known as a fast skater, a creative passer and a regular candidate for the Lady Byng Trophy.

In addition to Barry and Aurie, his linemates also included Ebbie Goodfellow and Cooney Weiland, each playing with Aurie and Lewis.

Lewis completed his NHL career in 1938-39, finishing with career totals of 148 goals, 161 assists and 309 points in 483 games played.

OPPOSITE: One of the first Red Wing superstars, Herbie Lewis became a Red Wing in the 1928-29 season and lasted a decade in Detroit. He starred on two Stanley Cup winners—1935-36 and 1936-37.

35

HARRY CARLYLE "CARL" LISCOMBE

BORN: Perth, Ontario, May 17, 1915
POSITION: Left Wing
NHL TEAMS: Detroit Red Wings, 1937-46

Before Gordie Howe became a household word in Detroit, skater Carl Liscombe was right up near the top among Motor City hockey heroes.

A left wing from Perth, Ontario, Liscombe came to Detroit from the Hamilton, Ontario, Tigers and became a regular in the 1937-38 season. The Red Wings were in a rebuilding mode at the time, and Liscombe emerged as a primary forward. However, it wasn't until the start of the 1940s that Carl hit his stride as a major scoring threat.

During the 1941 playoffs, he averaged almost a point a game (eight games, 4-3-7) and did even better the following spring. Liscombe almost single-handedly delivered a Stanley Cup to Detroit in 1942, scoring what appeared to be the Cup winner at 4:18 of the third period to put Detroit ahead 3-2 in Game 4. The Wings then led the finals, three games to none. In a huge upset, however, Toronto went on to win that game, and eventually the Leafs won the Cup. Still, in a dozen playoff games, Liscombe had scored a half a dozen goals—second best in the playoffs—and six assists for 12 points in as many games.

In the 1943 Stanley Cup round, Carl was the leading goal scorer and point maker (6, 14) as the Red Wings won the Stanley Cup. In Game 2, for example, Liscombe put Detroit ahead of the Boston Bruins to stay, on a pass from Sid Abel at 6:21 of the third period. In the next match, Liscombe set up Don Grosso with the insurance goal in a 4-0 rout. To cap a remarkable postseason, Carl tallied the insurance goal again, at 2:45 of the second period, as Detroit captured the Cup.

In terms of individual performances, Liscombe entered the NHL record book on March 13, 1938, skating against the Chicago Blackhawks at Olympia Stadium. On that night Carl scored three goals in one minute and 52 seconds against the team that eventually would win the Stanley Cup. Thus, Liscombe entered the record book for "Fastest Three Goals" and remained there until displaced by Bill Mosienko—ironically of the Blackhawks—who scored three in 21 seconds in 1951-52.

Liscombe's high-water mark as a scorer was reached in 1943-44, when he tallied 36 goals and 37 assists for 73 points in 50 games. But by the conclusion of World War II, his skills had diminished. His final NHL season was 1945-46, during which he played in 44 games but only tallied 21 points (12, 9).

OPPOSITE: Carl Liscombe was a Detroit hero in the early 1940s

36

DOMINIK HASEK

BORN: Pardubice, Czechoslavakia, January 29, 1965
POSITION: Goaltender
NHL TEAMS: Chicago Blackhawks, 1990-92; Buffalo Sabres, 1992-2001;
Detroit Red Wings, 2001-Present
AWARDS/HONORS: NHL All-Rookie Team, 1992; Hart Trophy, 1997, 1998;
Lester B. Pearson Award, 1997, 1998; Vezina Trophy, 1994, 1995, 1997-99, 2001;
NHL First All-Star Team, 1994, 1995, 1997-99; William M. Jennings Trophy,
1994, 2001; NHL All-Star Game, 1996-99, 2001-02

Glenn Hall, Terry Sawchuk, Jacques Plante, Vladislav Tretiak. These are a few of the greatest goaltenders of all time. Now that his career is over, Dominik Hasek ranks alongside them as one of the best puck stoppers the world has ever known. It has been there for all to see, beginning in Chicago where ironically he was a backup to Ed Belfour. The career of the Czech-born goaltender blossomed in Buffalo following one of the most lopsided trades The Game has ever known. His philosophy was simple: "I love to play hockey. I love to win and that is why I play."

Detroit was fortunate to obtain Hasek while still in his prime. He was signed as a free agent by the Red Wings during the summer of 2001 and maintained the standard of excellence that he displayed in his early years.

It is hard to believe that Hasek's career began with little fanfare—at all levels. Born in Pardubice, Czechoslovakia, Hasek became a goaltender virtually by accident. "They held a tryout for six-year-old boys and my father took me there," Hasek remembers. "I didn't even have real skates. I had those blades that you screwed onto the soles of your shoes, but I was tall, and the

nine-year-olds didn't have a goalie, so they put me in with them."

Hasek developed goaltending instincts with unbelievable reflexes and flexibility that allowed him to make saves other young goaltenders didn't—or couldn't—execute. "I watched the other goalies to see what they were doing," he said. "They would stay deep in the net and hope the puck would hit them. I wanted to do more."

While growing up in what was then Czechoslovakia, Hasek did not have a goaltending coach, instead relying on his own ingenuity and cleverness to improvise a unique, almost wild style that brought curious visitors from around the world.

"I went to see Hasek play when he was still in the Czech Republic," remembered Eddie Johnston, the Penguins' assistant general manager and a former goalie himself. "He played about 80 percent of the game without his goal stick. He'd drop it and use his blocker glove to cover up the puck or punch the shots to the corner. I couldn't believe what I was seeing, but he stopped everything."

Hasek climbed the ranks of the Czechoslovakian junior hockey system and was initially drafted by the

OPPOSITE: Dominik Hasek jumps over Edmonton's Jochen Hecht to get back to his goal crease.

Chicago Blackhawks in the tenth round in 1983. Instead, he turned down the chance to play in the National Hockey League, electing to live and play in his native country where he was the top national team goaltender from 1986 to 1990. Hasek finally arrived in the NHL as a 25-year-old in 1990, but the Blackhawks had perennial All-Star Ed Belfour between the pipes. Mike Keenan, then coach of the Blackhawks, was unsure about Hasek's style. Would it work in the NHL? Keenan elected to keep young Jimmy Waite as Belfour's backup. Hasek was sent to the Indianapolis Ice of the International Hockey League where he remained unhappily for two seasons until he asked Keenan for his release and the ability to return and play in his homeland.

"I told him, 'Look, come on, I am too old for the NHL,'" Hasek recalled. "I am not a good goalie. Let me go back to Europe."

Keenan refused, and in August of 1992, Hasek was dealt in what then was considered an insignificant trade from Chicago to Buffalo for goaltender Stephane Beauregard and a draft pick that would become Eric Daze. Hasek worried about facing a similar set of circumstances. When he arrived in Buffalo, Dominik was relegated to a backup role behind the legendary but aging Grant Fuhr. When Hasek did play, his unusual antics made Buffalo coaches nervous. Sabres management was unimpressed and made the goalie available during the expansion draft, protecting Fuhr and Tom Draper. Both Anaheim and Florida passed on Hasek.

"Yes, we were dumb for not taking him," said Bobby Clarke, who then was general manager of the Panthers during their inaugural season, "but the Sabres were dumber for making him available." Hasek was again upset, but he did not make his feelings known. "The situation helped me become a strong person," he recalled. "I was about to give up. [Fuhr] had been on five Stanley Cup champions. I had been on none. I didn't think I'd ever be a No. 1 goalie in the NHL. But we say in Czech that 'Everything bad is good for something.' I remembered what happened in Chicago and I said, 'Now I am down and something good will happen.'"

Sure enough, during the 1993-94 season, Fuhr injured his knee and Hasek was thrust into a starting role. He showed the world a new type of goaltending. Soon, NHL highlight reels became filled with unbelievable Hasek stops, shocking opponents, fans and teammates alike.

"He was unbelievable," said teammate Pat LaFontaine. "I've seen some great goalies, but Dom kept us in every single game and gave us a chance to win, and I can't say that about many goalies."

In the first round of the playoffs that season, Buffalo faced the New Jersey Devils. Dominik Hasek turned in one of the most memorable goaltending performances of postseason play.

With New Jersey leading the series, 3-2, Game 6 was played in Buffalo's Memorial Auditorium. At the end of regulation, no team had scored. In the overtime that followed, Hasek and New Jersey's Martin Brodeur held shooters at bay for another three periods. Hasek and Brodeur matched one another with one spectacular save after another. While other players slowed with fatigue, Hasek seemed to grow stronger as the game progressed. At one point in the overtime, the Devils stormed into the Buffalo end on an odd-man rush. Hasek dove across the goal crease to foil the New Jersey shooter—with his elbow.

Buffalo's Dave Hannan finally ended the scoreless marathon more than five minutes into the fourth overtime at 1:52 a.m. the following morning. Hasek made 70 saves, including 39 in overtime. "He could have stopped 100 shots tonight," remarked Hannan.

Following the game, an exhausted Devils forward Bobby Carpenter simply said, "That was the best performance from a goaltender that I have ever seen."

Although Buffalo would go on to lose the decisive Game 7, Hasek's stellar play in the series was only the beginning of playoff heroics to come.

At the conclusion of the 1993-94 season, Hasek was named a First Team All-Star. He was also awarded his first Vezina and Jennings Trophies, along with becoming the first goaltender since Bernie Parent 20 years earlier to register a goals-against average below 2.00.

In the years to come, Hasek, with his arms and legs flailing around NHL goal creases, earned the nickname "The Dominator" for his ability to determine the outcome of games by himself. Before long, Fuhr was traded, and a new era in goaltending had begun.

Still, Hasek's style received mixed reviews. "We couldn't accept, as a hockey society, some of the things he was doing out there," recalled Darcy Regier, Buffalo's current general manager, who back then was a member of the Islanders' front office. "He was diving, flopping around, not standing up and not doing the things goaltenders are supposed to do."

"He is definitely creative when it comes to style. He has some moves that I wouldn't attempt in practice," said Curtis Joseph, the Toronto goalie.

"Hasek," joked Chris Chelios, "has no style; he just stops the puck."

Hasek came to the Red Wings after making his mark with the Buffalo Sabres.

However, Hasek remained undeterred, refusing to change his style and actually becoming more unpredictable—and as a result, more difficult to solve—with each game. "I don't want to say my style is best," he said, "but my style is best for me. The media and the coaches and the people in the league didn't believe my style was good. They say I am unorthodox and I flop around the ice like some kind of fish. Who cares as long as I stop the puck?"

Hasek captured another Vezina trophy in 1995 and in 1997 he became the first goaltender in 35 years to win the Hart Trophy, along with the Lester Pearson Award and another Vezina. In 1998, he equaled the accomplishment with another triple crown, winning all three awards yet again. However, it was in the 1998 Nagano Olympic Games that Hasek's play would become truly legendary.

With NHL players competing on the Olympic stage for the first time, Hasek stole the show. He led the Czech Republic in a dramatic semifinal match against Canada. Tied at the end of regulation, Hasek turned away each of the five Canadian snipers in a shootout en route to the gold medal game.

After such an astonishing goaltending display in the Canada game, Hasek intimidated the Russian team even before the gold medal game had begun. When Russian forward Sergei Fedorov was asked to predict the outcome, he replied with a coy smile, "I don't bet and I don't go to Las Vegas, but Dominik Hasek is the greatest goaltender in the world."

Hasek would prove Fedorov right, blanking the Russian team and recording his second shutout of the tournament. Hasek allowed only six total goals in six games against some of the best hockey teams ever assembled. "Hasek is the best," Jaromir Jagr said after clinching the gold. "He is a gift to us and he won games by himself."

Upon the team's return to the Czech Republic, Hasek and his teammates were mobbed in Prague's public square, feted by President Vaclav Havel and more than 150,000 Czech citizens.

After the Olympics, Hasek's unorthodox play was finally accepted as true genius. "He became so good that people didn't care about his style," said Rangers goalie Mike Richter. His techniques, which emphasize anticipation, quick reflexes and amazing flexibility, began to set new standards for the position. On occasion, players could find Hasek racing to the blue line to meet an unsuspecting offensive player or clearing a puck from his crease by using his stick like a baseball bat.

He set a new goaltending trend by intentionally stopping the puck with his helmet. Sometimes he would actually ask teammates to shoot at his head during practice. "I try to do it sometimes in practice, not every day, but once in a while," Hasek explained. "Sometimes when shots come at my head, it's an easier save to make (rather than using the glove). It is my job to stop the puck and I am not afraid to stop the puck with my head. I'll make a save with my head if I have to."

Hasek's trademark became the ability to miraculously recover position when a goal seemed inevitable. While other goaltenders are vulnerable when lying on the ice or when losing their goal stick, in those situations Hasek is at his best.

"Hasek has truly crafted his own game," said broadcaster and former goaltender John Davidson. "No one has done it like him."

While Hasek is blessed with incredible talent, much of his success can be attributed to his insatiable work ethic. "I have never seen a goalie work like him," Davidson added.

In addition to regular training, Hasek rigorously rides a stationary bicycle daily and does some stretching exercises that would break a normal man.

Prior to taking the ice, Hasek will stretch by sitting on the floor with his legs in a V-shape and touch the floor—with his stomach. "I am very, very flexible," allowed Hasek. "It helps me to reach farther than the other goalies. It's a very, very important part of my style."

When on the ice, Hasek is relentless in games and in training. "He has always hated getting beat in practice," said defenseman Petr Svoboda, a teammate of Dominik's in junior hockey in Czechoslovakia and later with Buffalo.

During one memorable practice late in his Buffalo career, Sabres defenseman Jason Woolley beat Hasek on three shots in a row. "He wouldn't let me go off the ice until we had a little competition," Woolley recalled. "He told me to shoot five pucks as hard as I could from 15 feet out. I would win if I scored once. I didn't score. He made saves that left me shaking my head."

One of Hasek's best known admirers is Ken Dryden, Hall of Fame goaltender and general manager of the Toronto Maple Leafs. After spending a few seasons watching Hasek closely, Dryden gave this analysis: "Dominik knows his job. The goaltender's job is to stop pucks and it doesn't matter how you do it or what part of you does it. There are lots of people who play goal very stylistically and do everything technically correct who don't stop shots."

Hasek's unconventional approach to goaltending makes him almost impossible for teams to scout and impossible to read for opposing shooters. "He doesn't have a weakness," said Wayne Gretzky. "There is no precedent, no book on him. You never know what he will do. I could usually look at a goalie and say where I wanted to shoot, but with Hasek it was a bit different."

During the 1998-99 season, Hasek would post a career-best goals-against average of 1.87 and lead Buffalo to the Stanley Cup finals. Dallas was unsure about beating the Dominator. "When he's in the net, his pads seem to cover post-to-post better than any goalie I've seen," Brett Hull said. "He doesn't give you anything to shoot at."

The series culminated in Game 6 with another multi-overtime marathon that saw some of Hasek's usual heroics. Hull, however, would have the last laugh, as it was his controversial goal that defeated Hasek and the Sabres in the third overtime.

Sabres coach Lindy Ruff reflected on his goaltender: "I don't know if you can even put into words my appreciation for the way he plays. He is the best that I have ever seen, the best that I have ever been around. Dom spoils you every night."

Unfortunately for Ruff, Hasek stunned the hockey world a few weeks later when he announced that the 1999-2000 season would be his last. However, in the first month of what would have been his farewell year, Hasek seriously injured his groin, forcing him to miss half of the season and reconsider his retirement. At the conclusion of the season, Hasek had won another Vezina, and he had his sights set on a new home and new challenges.

After all the accolades and all the individual awards, the only thing missing from the Dominator's *resumé* was a Stanley Cup. Finally, in the summer of 2001, Hasek asked Buffalo general manager Darcy Regier to trade him to a team that had the tools to win

Hasek came to the Detroit hoping to add the Stanley Cup to his resume.

hockey's ultimate prize. Regier complied, and Hasek was soon sent to the Detroit Red Wings for winger Slava Kozlov, a first-round draft pick, and considerations that depend on the length of Hasek's career in Detroit.

When he left Buffalo, Hasek held the Sabres' records in virtually all goaltending categories and joined Gilbert Perreault and Pat LaFontaine as the greatest players in the history of the Buffalo franchise. "People will reflect back on the time that Dom was in Buffalo and come to really appreciate his greatness," said Regier.

Not only did Hasek thrill Sabres fans with his play for nine years, but he was a fixture in the community as well. He gave much of his time to western New York charities and donated $1 million to build a youth hockey rink in downtown Buffalo.

Mike Keenan offered this post-mortem on the trade that sent Hasek to Buffalo: "I knew Hasek was a good goaltender when I brought him to Chicago. If I had known he was going to develop this way, I would have asked for Pat LaFontaine instead of Stephane

Beauregard. I know one thing: I'd like to have him back now."

The Red Wings welcomed Dominik with open arms. "It was a deal that we just could not pass up," Red Wings general manager Ken Holland said at the news conference announcing the signing of the five-time First Team All-Star. "Dominik is coming off another Vezina Trophy-winning season and we're all thrilled that he will be suiting up as a Red Wing."

With the addition of Hasek, Detroit added a goaltender who still intimidated shooters with his reputation alone. "Hasek," said Washington Capitals coach Ron Wilson, "can psych out players before they even go on the ice."

Hasek's season in Detroit reinvigorated his career and made The Dominator revaluate and rethink his retirement timeline. "I don't know how many years that I am going to play," he said. "Maybe more than one. Maybe more than two.

"I am here to win the Cup. Nothing else. Nothing less."

37

CHRIS CHELIOS

BORN: Chicago, Illinois, January 25, 1962
POSITION: Defenseman
NHL TEAMS: Montreal Canadiens, 1983-90; Chicago Blackhawks, 1990-99;
Detroit Red Wings, 1999-Present
AWARDS/HONORS: James Norris Memorial Trophy, 1989, 1993, 1996;
NHL All-Rookie Team, 1985; NHL First All-Star Team, 1989, 1993, 1995-96;
NHL Second All-Star Team, 1991, 1997;
NHL All-Star Game, 1985, 1990-94, 1996-98, 2000

For more than a decade of his National Hockey League career, Chris Chelios was one of the most disliked players to visit Joe Louis Arena.

First as a member of the Montreal Canadiens and later the Chicago Blackhawks, Chelios was reviled by the Motor City faithful because of the irreverent manner in which he manhandled skaters in the red and white uniforms.

But if you asked Detroit fans if they would like to have Chris on their team, the answer invariably was in the affirmative.

Unfortunately, the wait for Chelios to wear the winged wheel would be a long one.

A native of Chicago, Chelios starred for the University of Wisconsin before becoming a starting defenseman on the 1984 U.S. Olympic team. His coach, Lou Vairo, admired Chris both for his iconoclastic behavior as well as his skill.

"Chris was one of a kind," said Vairo. "He skated to his own drummer, but brother, could he ever skate. And hit. And lead his teammates."

Following the Winter Olympic Games at Sarajevo, Chelios moved directly to the Canadiens lineup, al-though not with consummate ease. During his first game at Nassau Veterans Memorial Coliseum against the defending Stanley Cup champion New York Islanders, the young defender seemed awkward and out of place.

"He was eager," said a press box observer, "but Chelios showed nothing that indicated that he would make a mark in the league."

However, those familiar with Chelios' tenacity and will to succeed realized that it would only be a matter of time before he reached the top. Actually, it took only five years, and in 1989, he won the Norris Trophy as the NHL's best defenseman for the first of three times.

It was only one of several awards bestowed upon Chelios before he ever dreamed of being traded to Detroit. And, as a young Chicagoan, the Red Wings were low on his rooting pole.

"I saw my first NHL game when I was five years-old at old Chicago Stadium," Chelios recalled. "My father took me along and Bobby Hull scored a hat trick. It turned out to be his 50th goal of the season. It was so exciting, and soon after that I started playing."

Chris' father, Gus, had emigrated to Chicago from

OPPOSITE: Detroit Red Wings defenseman Chris Chelios celebrates an open net goal by teammate Nicklas Lidstrom in a victory over the Colorado Avalanche.

Greece in 1951 and owned several small restaurants in the Windy City. Chris attended Chicago's Catholic Mount Carmel High School for two years and played hockey at the school. But his dad moved to San Diego so Chris finished high school in California before going to the University of Wisconsin.

In 1983, he led the Badgers to the NCAA championship and then moved on to the U.S. National Team which soon became the Olympians. Once the games were over in Sarajevo, Chelios played a dozen games for the Habs who were led by veterans Larry Robinson and Bob Gainey. Just two years after joining the Canadiens, they won a Stanley Cup (1985-86) and he seemed a fixture on Ste. Catherine Street Ouest's Forum as long as he chose to play for the bleu, blanc et rouge.

But the Canadiens of that era always preferred to have Quebec natives to lead the team, and when Chicago's crack forward Denis Savard became available, the Habs traded Chelios and a 1991 second-round draft choice to the Blackhawks in June 1991.

"I felt very fortunate to have been traded to my hometown," said Chris. "I liked the organization and in all the years I spent there, the organization was good to me."

Not surprisingly, Chelios became one of Chicago's favorite athletes. He anchored the defense in front of goalie Ed Belfour and helped the team to the Stanley Cup finals in 1991-92 before the Blackhawks were eliminated by the Pittsburgh Penguins. Prior to the Finals, the Hawks had amassed an 11-game winning streak.

As a Blackhawk, Chelios won two more Norris Trophies (1993 and 1996) and played in six All-Star Games.

A highlight of his career occurred in September 1996 when he was an integral part of the Team USA squad that defeated Team Canada in two straight games to win its first World Cup.

Chelios not only became a fixture in his hometown but opened a restaurant—Cheli's Chili—not far from the United Center. While Chris was on the ice, his dad, Gus, took care of business.

"Chris had so many friends from the Blackhawks, high school and the neighborhood," Gus remembered

with a laugh, "it seemed that the only people who paid in the place were the ones who got caught!"

As it happened, Chelios was not the fixture that some thought he would be at United Center. On March 23, 1999, he was dealt to the Red Wings for Anders Ericksson and Detroit's first-round choices in 1999 (Steve McCarthy) and 2001 (Adam Munro) Entry Drafts.

Chris played only 10 regular-season games and 10 more playoff games that season but managed 81 regular-season matches the following year along with nine playoff contests.

Knee injuries limited his play to 24 games and just five playoff matches in 2000-2001. A broken thumb further complicated matters and there were some who suggested that Chelios might be washed up, but Number 24 had other ideas.

He returned to Detroit for the 2001-2002 season in mint condition and also was named —by coach Herb Brooks—to lead the U.S. Olympic Team at Salt Lake City.

"I told Chris right at the start," said Brooks, "that he would be the man to lead us."

Uncle Sam finished with a silver medal and Chelios was every bit the player that Brooks had hoped he would be—and then some. Ditto for Detroit coach Scott Bowman and the Red Wings general staff which gleefully watched Chris romp through the 2001-02 campaign.

"Chelios was our 'Comeback Player of the Year,'" said Wings executive vice president Jimmy Devellano. "He played strong as a horse and had one of the best plus-minus records in the whole league."

With Chelios and Nicklas Lidstrom on defense— not to mention Dominik Hasek in goal—the Red Wings boasted one of the best blue line corps in the NHL.

"There's no question," added Devellano, "that our success during the regular season (2001-02) had a lot to do with Chelios's play on defense and his leadership in the locker room. He's been to us everything we hoped he would be."

Whatever Chris Chelios has been, one thing is certain—he will eventually become a member of Hockey's Hall of Fame.

Chris Chelios brings the puck up the ice during a game against the Buffalo Sabres.

38

BRETT HULL

BORN: Belleville, Ontario, August 9, 1964
POSITION: Right Wing
NHL TEAMS: Calgary Flames, 1986-88; St. Louis Blues, 1988-98;
Dallas Stars, 1998-2001; Detroit Red Wings, 2001-Present
AWARDS/HONORS: Stanley Cup, 1999; Hart Trophy, 1991; Lester B. Pearson Award, 1991;
Lady Byng Trophy, 1990; NHL All-Star First Team, 1990, 1991, 1992;
NHL All-Star Game, 1989, 1990, 1992, 1993, 1994, 1996, 1997, 2001

When the Chicago Blackhawks won their last Stanley Cup in 1961, Bobby Hull was the club's leading goal scorer, known far and wide as "The Golden Jet."

Four decades later, his son Brett emerged as an equally prolific scorer with an appropriate nickname, "The Golden Brett."

A chip off the old block if ever there was one in hockey, Brett's trademark is his dynamic shot, as well as his charismatic ability to capture both the fans' and the media's affection. Both father and son love to talk. Also, each played on one Stanley Cup-winning team.

But Hull didn't enter the NHL with trumpets blaring. He was a sixth-round pick in 1984 by the Calgary Flames, hardly high enough for the son of an NHL legend. In time, his natural goal scoring ability would shine brightly.

After two years of college hockey with Minnesota-Duluth, Brett made his debut with Calgary in Game 3 of the 1986 Stanley Cup Finals against the eventual champion Montreal Canadiens. He did not become an NHL regular, however, until the 1987-88 season.

He racked up 26 goals in his first 52 games, but his run-and-gun style incensed Flames management.

In a move that would prove shocking in hindsight, the brash young Hull was dealt in March of 1988 with Steve Bozek to the St. Louis Blues for goaltender Rick Wamsley and defenseman Rob Ramage.

Hull flourished in St. Louis. Under the tutelage of coach Brian Sutter, Brett began to score goals with such regularity and consistency that the rest of the league took notice. And when the Blues acquired center Adam Oates before the 1989 season, Sutter immediately paired the playmaking center with the natural scorer.

Hull had exploded with 41 goals in his first full season in Missouri, but a challenge from coach Sutter and an ice-kinship with Oates's Gretzkyesque passes kindled a 72-goal masterpiece in 1989-90, setting a record for right wingers. He also finished fifth in scoring and won the Lady Byng Trophy for sportsmanship—all in just his third full NHL season.

But it was during the 1990-91 season that Hull began to chase down a record that many thought no one would come close to reaching, let alone break. The record was Wayne Gretzky's 92 goals in a season, and Hull and Oates were on a mission to eclipse the mark.

In the process, Brett shattered his own record of goals for a right wing and scored a goal against every team in the league that year. Finishing the season with

OPPOSITE: Brett Hull, eyeing a teammate for a pass.

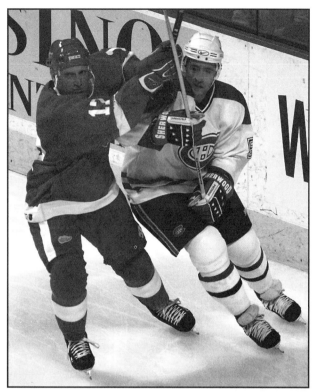

Hull duels with Montreal's Stephane Robidas.

86 goals, Hull legitimized himself as one of the best snipers in the game, capping that notion with a Hart Trophy nod in 1991.

Only Hull and Gretzky have enjoyed consecutive seasons of 50 goals in less than 50 games, and both players are the only ones to have three straight seasons of 70 or more goals.

Hull, in a very short time, had announced himself as a force in the NHL. Though he had come to terms with the comparisons to his dad, Hull succeeded in carving his own stone in the NHL, separate from that of his famous father.

Brett, as he detailed in his autobiography *Brett: Shootin' and Smilin'* with Kevin Allen, offered, "Dad wasn't one to get on the ice and teach his kids the game. His idea of teaching was telling us to watch him. We don't play the same style, yet I know that subconsciously, I learned to become a goal scorer by watching him fly up the ice. It was fascinating to watch him glide up the left wing and snap the puck in one fluid motion."

By 1993-94, he had become the Blues' all-time leading scorer with 353 goals. But as the years passed, and Hull piled up his points each season, he never came close to his 86-goal, 131-point performance of 1990-91; his numbers actually decreased over time in line with changes in coaches and personnel.

There was no change in the Blues' playoff failures; the team hadn't been successful since the 1970

Stanley Cup final sweep versus the Bobby Orr-led Boston Bruins, despite investments in the brand new Kiel Center and tons of players.

Hull scored plenty, but his loose attitude and frank manner began to irk many fans and teammates.

By the time Brett became an unrestricted free agent in 1998, Blues general manager Ron Caron decided to let Hull walk away from the franchise to which he brought national attention with his heroic scoring exploits.

Meanwhile, a high-quality team in Dallas was just pieces away from championship caliber.

After ignoring sentimental choice Chicago where his father played, Brett signed with the Stars in July 1998 because he felt the Stars were on the cusp of a Stanley Cup—an honor that had eluded him. He would be placed on the top line with two-way superstar Mike Modano and reunited with former Calgary teammate Joe Nieuwendyk, who knew what the Stars were getting.

"There are guys who play this game to score, and there are guys who play this game not to make a mistake," said Nieuwendyk. "Brett has always been one of those guys who, every time he's on the ice, wants to score a goal."

But his pedigree in goal-scoring was soon to be tested by defensive mastermind Ken Hitchcock, who coached the Stars to a second consecutive President's Trophy that season. Hitchcock demanded that Hull become a complete player and buy into his suffocating defensive system if their team was to win it all. Offensive creativity, which Brett thrived on, was to take a back seat to a system of play.

After some initial disagreements, Hull and Hitchcock whittled their philosophies down to the bottom line of winning. By the time the 1999 Stanley Cup playoffs rolled around, Hull was ready to do his part.

"You know you always heard the rumblings about, 'He's a one-dimensional player, all he does is score goals,'" Hull said. "Well, I've taken to that challenge." After showing up St. Louis in round one, the Stars, led by a surge of complete play from Hull, came back from a three-games-to-two deficit to the powerful Colorado Avalanche in the Western Conference Finals to win that round and advance to the Stanley Cup finals against the over achieving Buffalo Sabres.

For the first time, Hull found himself in the thick of hockey's greatest scenario with a great team. "I came here because this is a great organization," reflected Hull. "Obviously I knew there was great potential. It's an unbelievable feeling. It's wonderful to be a part of this."

After scoring a late game-winning goal in Game 2 to tie the series, Hull missed most of Game 3 and all of Game 4 with a torn groin muscle.

But he returned to help the Stars win Game 5, setting the stage for the most magical, and most controversial, moment in Brett's career.

With the young Sabres pressing the veteran Dallas team, Hull kicked into extra gear.

Game 6 in Buffalo's Marine Midland Arena went into a third overtime, with Hull hobbling all over the ice on his bad legs. But his quick shifts would reward the valiant Stars.

As he stepped onto the ice, linemate Mike Modano told him to go to the net. As play moved into the Buffalo zone, Modano dug the puck out and dished it to Hull who stood, as discussed, on Sabres goalie Dominik Hasek's doorstep.

With a few whacks, the unchecked Hull made hockey history and sent the puck behind Hasek for Dallas's first-ever Stanley Cup win. The circle of a great player's career complete, Hull celebrated with his Dallas teammates as Buffalo argued over the dreaded rule stipulating (that season) that a player's skate couldn't be in the crease for a goal to count. Hull's skate was clearly in the crease, but in any other year, that is as golden a goal that can be scored.

"You can have all the other goals," he said. "This is the biggest to me. It's unbelievable. It's just so emotional. I've dreamt about it, but it's unbelievable. This team's gone through so much together, and there was a lot of pressure on a lot of guys. But we really kept sticking to our guns."

In the press conference after the game, coach Ken Hitchcock talked at length about his superstar.

"He [Hull] played on one leg and no groins for his last three shifts," he said. "He might be rehabbed enough to be ready for next season. He has a grade three, full-blown torn MCL. He has a torn groin. And he came back and played."

And he's played well enough to score over 600 goals in the NHL.

"It's such an honor to now be classified with the likes of Wayne Gretzky, Mario Lemieux, Phil Esposito and of course, my dad," said Hull. "I'd be lying if I said I didn't dream about being ranked up there one day with those guys. I mean, those guys were my heroes."

Brett Hull always did it his way. But it was a long time in coming.

"Look, I've spent 34 years trying to become Brett Hull instead of Bobby Hull's son," he said. "I only have to answer to my own actions. And that's how I've always wanted it to be."

One cannot deny the fact that Brett and Bobby are the only father-son combination to record 600 goals in their respective careers—with Brett's count still rising after a vintage 39-goal campaign in 2000-01.

"He is the most natural goal scorer I have ever seen," said his father, Bobby. "We played two different styles in two different eras. But there's also a lot that's the same in his shot as in mine. And when I watch him in warmups, it's like looking in the mirror. He warms up for games exactly the way I used to warm up."

Again a restricted free agent in the summer of 2001, Hull signed with the Red Wings as the final signing of a busy summer aimed at a Stanley Cup-winning spring in 2002.

He joined fellow 600-goal scorers Luc Robitaille and Steve Yzerman for a formidable offense, as well as the great Dominik Hasek, who, ironically, Hull beat for his most memorable goal.

With Scotty Bowman, Brett continues his string of playing for intense coaches who have pushed their star players to maximum performance. They includ Sutter, Hitchcock, Terry Crisp, Mike Keenan and Bob Berry.

But only Hitchcock and Keenan have won Stanley Cups, each once. Bowman's masterminding of nine Stanley Cup winning teams lures players of Hull's caliber, and the Wings' record pace in 2001-02 proves all participants are on the same page.

Detroit's stable of superstars has throttled to the front of the NHL in the Olympic season, with Hull on pace for yet another 30 goals at the very least.

And at Salt Lake, the Golden Brett delivered a dramatic game-tying goal late in the third period of Team USA's intense 2-2 tie with Russia in the preliminary round: a sign of the grand expectations Detroit envisioned when signing their sniper, which is easily the operative word of Hull's legacy.

"I score goals, I love to play, I love to practice and I love to win," declares Hull in *Brett: Shootin' and Smilin'*. "How can you not want a guy like me around?"

As the third fastest scorer of 600 goals (behind Gretzky and Lemieux) and the National Hockey League's active leader in hat tricks, who could argue?

Hull's former boss in St. Louis, Ron Caron, mused appropriately, "Scoring is like a drug to the great scorers." And Brett Hull will undoubtedly go down as one of the greatest goal scorers in the history of the NHL.

39

BOB PROBERT

BORN: Windsor, Ontario, June 5, 1965
POSITION: Left Wing
NHL TEAMS: Detroit Red Wings, 1985-94; Chicago Blackhawks, 1995-Present
AWARDS/HONORS: NHL All-Star Game, 1988

Mention Bob Probert to the average hockey fan and the name conjures up the image of brawling and assorted other forms of intimidation that go with the violent side of hockey.

And for good reason. For a period of at least a decade—ranging from 1985-86 to 1994-95—Probert ranked as the heavyweight champion of the NHL. Period.

His IQ, as in Intimidation Quotient, ranked among the NHL's highest. But any opposition goaltender from that era will confirm that Probert was a major offensive threat, and he proved it in 1987-88 when he tallied 29 goals and 33 assists to go along with 398 penalty minutes, all career highs. Not only was Probert capable of those numbers, but he could also produce them when it mattered most: in the playoffs. That same year, Probert scored 21 points (8 goals, 13 assists) in only 16 playoff games to go along with 51 penalty minutes. Pretty impressive for an NHL bad boy.

No matter how impressive the numbers and goals and assists, the numbers of punches Probert has thrown over the years—particularly as a Red Wing—are what remain among his most impressive stats. And if Probert is remembered for any of his legendary fights, it would be those with longtime nemesis Tie Domi.

The bouts in question both took place in 1992, the first on February 9, and the second on December 2. In the first fight, Domi left Probert black-and-blue with a bloody nose. Probert didn't lose that fight, but the pugnacious Ranger at that time emerged from the fisticuffs pretending he was the NHL's heavyweight champion. Domi's histrionics tickled the fancy of bloodthirsty New York Ranger fans, but did not sit well with league officials or many of Tie's peers, who believed he was denigrating the ways of a true enforcer.

Domi was suitably abetted by a hypocritical media which, on the one hand, criticized hockey's violence, but on the other, wasted no time playing up the Domi-Probert rivalry for all it was worth.

No single piece of journalism did more to magnify the December 2 Domi-Probert bout than a column by *Toronto Sun* sports editor Scott Morrison. In the piece, Morrison liberally quoted a pumped-up Domi, who orated, "You know how much I've been looking forward to this one? I knew before the start of the season what day the game was."

Significantly, Morrison pointed out that Domi-Probert was as much of a news story as Mario Lemieux's scoring exploits. "The hockey world and Don Cherry have been waiting for this championship bout since

OPPOSITE: Bob Probert maintained a high Intimidation Quotient during his years with Detroit.

early last February when Domi and the Red Wings' thumper Bob Probert engaged in a memorable Sunday night punch up at the Garden," wrote Morrison. "That night, Domi declared himself champion, strapping on an imaginary belt, urging cheers from the crowd. He looked more boor than [Riddick] Bowe, but still packed a mean wallop."

Domi's "mistake," if it can be called that, was his natural candor. He couldn't help speaking his mind, and what was on his mind was another encounter with Probert. "I knew before the season that our first meeting was December 2," said Domi. "I know one thing—there'll be no instigator in this fight."

Domi uttered a few other gems that created a mountain of publicity. The *Detroit News*, for example, carried a "Tale of the Tape," with oversized caricatures of the two warriors. Finally, NHL president Gil Stein was questioned about the propriety of Domi's pop-offs. "I believe people have the right to defy the law if they wish, as long as they understand that they will pay a penalty for doing it," Stein said.

Throughout the furor, Probert characteristically ducked comment, but on the eve of the meeting, he exploded at reporters. "You media people blew the whole thing out of proportion," said Probert. Whether they did or not, there was no doubt that a fight of major proportions was going to erupt. Less than a minute into the game, the fight was on.

At the 30-second mark, Probert stepped on the ice, whereupon Ranger coach Roger Neilson sent out Domi, who skated right up to his foe for the face off. A split second after the puck was dropped, Probert twice crosschecked Domi, and the fists began flying faster than an out-of-control windmill. Probert went on the offensive, throwing the first eight punches out of a total of 47. In orderly retreat, Domi tossed 23 blows, but clearly lost the bout on points.

Hockey Night in Canada commentator Don Cherry, the ubiquitous critic of hockey fights, consid-

ered the 48-second tussle a world-class event. "It was a definite decision for Probert," said Cherry. "But I think it was a strong showing by Tie. It was no pushover, which is what made it even better. It was a good battle and the officials let it go. I knew they were going to let it go."

Many observers believe that the most devastating blow of all was one that never landed, a roundhouse Probert punch that just missed his foe. "If he had connected, Probie might have ended up in jail or Tie would be in the hospital," said Cherry, who watched the game on TV at his home. "It looked like Probert wanted this one, he was psyched. I didn't think he could ever match the [Troy] Crowder ones, but he did."

As for the principals, they had varying comments.

Domi: "A fight's a fight. You win some, you lose some. I'm just very happy that we won the game."

Probert: "It's just another day at the office. I just don't have anything to say."

The massive attention focused on the matchup left the NHL with a public-relations black eye. It was clear that the league would never again tolerate a premeditated fight. Many critics blamed Rangers coach Roger Neilson as much as Domi, since the home-team Rangers had the right to match any line Detroit put on the ice. Neilson guaranteed that Domi would face Probert.

Interestingly, Domi saw little ice in the weeks after the fight and eventually was traded to Winnipeg. Neilson was soon fired as Rangers coach.

In retrospect, it was an incredible fight, but one not likely to brew up (and be blown up) again. As for Probert, his Detroit career ended in 1994, whereupon he was signed as a free agent by Chicago.

Although he had lost some of his speed, Probert remained an effective enforcer with the Blackhawks through the 2001-2002 season.

But whenever Probie's name is mentioned in hockey history, it always will be as a Red Wing.

40

LUC ROBITAILLE

BORN: February 17, 1966, Montreal, Quebec
POSITION: Left Wing
NHL TEAMS: Los Angeles Kings, 1986-94, 1997-2001; Pittsburgh Penguins, 1994-95,
New York Rangers, 1995-97; Detroit Red Wings, 2001-Present
AWARDS/HONORS: Canadian Major Junior Player of the Year, 1986;
NHL All-Rookie Team, 1987; Calder Trophy, 1987; NHL All-Star Game,
1988-93, 1999, 2001; NHL First All-Star Team, 1988-91, 1993;
NHL Second All-Star Team, 1987, 1992, 2001

There have not been very many cases of a player drafted so low yet accomplishing as much over a 16-year career as Luc Robitaille.

Considered too slow and unskilled by a legion of scouts, the French Canadian from Montreal was plucked 171st in the talent-laden 1984 annual entry draft by the Los Angeles Kings. No one could have dreamed that he would become a Hall of Famer in the making.

In that year, the top five selections were Mario Lemieux, Kirk Muller, Ed Olczyk, Al Lafrate and Petr Svoboda, followed later by the likes of Patrick Roy, Brett Hull, Gary Roberts, Shayne Corson and Gary Suter.

Nobody gave Robitaille a tumble until the ninth round, which is as low as one could get. Such a subterranean selection, yet what a winner!

His initial junior year with the Hull Olympiques of the Quebec Major Junior League hardly commanded headlines, when he had 85 points in 70 games in a scorer's league. But the Kings' bird dogs figured that Luc was worth a low-level gamble. The response was arresting, to say the least.

As a reward for the Kings' faith in drafting him, Luc piled up 340 points over his last two junior sea-sons at Hull (remember that word) and won the Canadian Junior Player of the Year award.

He gained a regular National Hockey league berth in the 1986-87 season and proceeded to make an im-print as one of the most consistent and accurate goal-scorers of the 1990s and into the new century.

Luc was an instant hit in glitzy Los Angeles, scor-ing in his NHL debut on his first shift, first shot. Im-mediately, he earned a nickname that would eventually fit him to a T—"Lucky."

"Dave 'Tiger' Williams gave it to me," said Robitaille. "I was a rookie; I was living with Marcel Dionne, out star player. Marcel had the biggest house, and he would drive me to practice in his Mercedes. During our first game, we came into the dressing room and Tiger Williams called me 'Lucky.'

"Someone asked why he called me Lucky Luc and he said, 'Look at Luc. He lives in that big house, rides a Mercedes to work, and scored on his first shot. "What's not lucky about that?'"

That shot led him into a 45-goal, 84-point sea-son. Luc netted the Calder Trophy as the NHL's top rookie, as well as the everlasting adoration of Califor-nians. His popularity has remained solid to this day in L.A.

The landmark trade for Wayne Gretzky in 1988 only amplified the Kings' firepower which also featured Robitaille and Bernie Nicholls. With the Los Angeles hockey market in full bloom, Luc's career thrived.

He proceeded to score 40-plus goals in each of his first eight NHL seasons, cracking the 100-point mark four times before the age of 30. By that time, Luc had become a fixture on the NHL first-and second-team All-Stars for seven straight years.

In just five seasons, Robitaille had surpassed another longtime fan favorite, Charlie Simmer, to become the Kings' all-time leading goal scorer among left wingers. Furthermore, no other player other than the great Dionne scored more goals as a member of the Kings than Robitaille.

In L.A.'s magical season of 1992-93, Luc's 63 goals and 125 points set NHL single-season records for left wingers as he captained the team while Gretzky was injured. The Kings electrified the Great Western Forum with an incredible playoff charge led by coach Barry Melrose and stormed into the Stanley Cup finals. There, Luc became the team's all-time leading playoff goal scorer with 34 tallies.

Despite the cast of Robitaille, Gretzky, Marty McSorley, Jari Kurri and Rob Blake, Los Angeles only made one appearance in the finals. They lost in five games to the gritty Montreal Canadiens of 1992-93, with the turning point of the series coming on a controversial "illegal stick" penalty called on McSorley.

The loss was devastating. The Kings spiraled out of the playoffs the following season, and despite contributing 86 points to the club, Luc became a casualty.

Upon being dealt to the Pittsburgh Penguins for Rick Tocchet in the lockout summer of 1994, he ran into a string of unproductive seasons.

After Pittsburgh came back from a 3-1 deficit in the first round of the 1995 playoffs to defeat the Washington Capitals, an unstoppable New Jersey Devils team discarded the superstar Pens in a five-game set en route to their first Stanley Cup.

Later that summer, when the New York Rangers offered Petr Nedved and Sergei Zubov to the Pens for Robitaille and Ulf Samuelsson, Pittsburgh jumped at the deal with the idea of infusing youth into the former championship team.

Again, Luc was on the move just two years removed from being a major player for a Stanley Cup finalist.

Neither Steeltown nor Broadway, unfortunately, proved a good fit for Robitaille, as injuries and inconsistency plagued his game, some excellent playoff performances notwithstanding.

As a Ranger, Robitaille would help the team reach the 1997 Eastern Conference finals against Philadelphia, but the physical Flyers would pound the Blueshirts in five games. That lack of a physical element on the New York squad would prompt Luc's movement again, despite finishing sixth in scoring on a team that featured both Gretzky and Mark Messier, as well as Brian Leetch and Adam Graves.

In 1997, for the third summer out of his last four, Robitaille found himself being dealt again, only this time it was back to Tinseltown, with the Rangers receiving banger Kevin Stevens in return.

After scoring no less than 44 goals per season, Robitaille had only tallied as high as 24 goals between 1994 and 1996, three consecutive seasons of un-"Lucky" numbers. Had he lost his touch?

"Everybody thought I was done," Robitaille recalled. "When I went back to Los Angeles (in 1997), people thought I had nothing left, but I had had a groin injury that kept me out (for 25 games). After that, I worked hard during the off season and I tried to get a little bit stronger and quicker. It's really changed my game ever since."

Consistent scoring again became his trademark, as Luc battled back into the 35-goal plateau for Los Angeles. After he was limited to 57 games in his first season back, Ol' Reliable Robitaille recorded two straight 74-point seasons from 1998-2000.

He delivered an 88-point season in 2000-01 as a 35-year old, the most he had totaled since 1992-93.

What's more, his rejuvenation was accomplished without the presence of a superstar such as Gretzky, Messier, Mario Lemieux or Jaromir Jagr, each of whom helped contribute to Robitaille's earlier achievements.

"Some have suggested he's not a complete player," says Hall of Famer Gordie Howe, "but Robitaille has taken a beating to score all of those goals, and anyone who believes he doesn't have the credentials to be listed among the top players in league history isn't watching the game very closely."

Of his critics, Luc replied, "It doesn't bother me. I know what I've accomplished. People are always going to try and find something. Every player has to face it sometime in his career."

Kevin Stevens added, "Luc is one of those players said to be too slow, not able to skate well enough, but

OPPOSITE: Luc Robitaille joins Steve Yzerman and Brett Hull on the NHL's first-ever 600-goal line.

Robitaille celebrates his new team's success.

helped eliminate from the playoffs. The Red Wings were reloading for another run by signing goaltender Dominik Hasek and free agent sniper Brett Hull.

"Detroit is the place I wanted to be," said Luc. "As soon as they acquired Hasek, I told my wife, 'This is the team to beat.' I want to win a Stanley Cup. This is a team capable of doing it. Playing with centers like [Steve] Yzerman and [Sergei] Fedorov—you're talking about two of the best in the game. That's going to be a lot of fun. Then you have a coach like Scotty Bowman, and everything he has accomplished."

Complementing the cavalcade of superstars in Motor City will be just fine for Robitaille, an unheralded star, who has attained impressive individual credentials, but remains not "Lucky" enough to have sipped sweet victory from the Stanley Cup.

"I love the fact that I came in here and everybody says, 'We're not here to make the playoffs, we're here to win the Stanley Cup, nothing else is good,'" he said. "I personally love that kind of challenge. I think it's a lot of fun to be part of that. Then there's Scotty—the man has won so many Cups."

Marching to a record pace, Detroit has been the stage for another milestone for Lucky as he has eclipsed Bobby Hull as the NHL's all-time leading goal-scorer among left-wingers (611 and counting).

Even more amazing is the fact that Luc could really punctuate his mark when playing with two other 600-goal scorers in center man Yzerman and right-winger Brett Hull on the same line. The trio, along with Messier and Lemieux, firmly occupy the sixth through 10th spots on the NHL's all-time goals scored list, and now comprise the first-ever 600-goal line.

It doesn't seem that long ago that Robitaille was a young stallion on a star-studded Los Angeles Kings team. Now, he's a 16-year veteran sniper on a team sprinkled with veterans.

Of his own record, Robitaille stated, "I was more shocked to pass Rocket Richard (544 goals). I don't know how long it will last with all of the great left wingers today. But for the time being it is certainly something that I can look back on and kind of look at in disbelief. It's pretty special. Bobby Hull is one of the all-time great players. To be named with him is certainly something pretty unique. And to have his son on my team makes it even more special."

When asked about the goal that tied his fantastic father's mark, Brett Hull presented his teammate in purest fashion.

"Typical Luc Robitaille goal. He was in the right place at the right time and he capitalized."

Lucky indeed!

he's been able to get 600 goals in this league, and if you're slow you're not supposed to get 600 goals in this league."

Luc's eight consecutive 40-goal campaigns is the third longest string in league history, behind only goal scoring wizard Mike Bossy (9) and the Great One (12) himself.

"He deserves as much consideration as anybody else with the stats he's put up," continued Stevens, "It's pretty amazing. He is a Hall of Famer."

Excitement unexpectedly returned to Robitaille's L.A. stomping grounds in 2001, with the brand new Staples Center echoing the Great Western Forum's chants of "Luuuuuuuc!!! Luuuuuuuuc!!!"

Fresh from tying for 10th in the scoring race, Luc led his Kings in a six-game upset of heavily favored Detroit after being down 2-0 in round one of the Stanley Cup playoffs, and they nearly repeated the feat against Colorado, the eventual champs.

Though Luc scored key goals during that improbable playoff drive, his status as an unrestricted free agent helped him weigh other options.

Lucky decided to fully exercise his free agent's rights and looked to the juggernaut team he had just

41

LEO CHARLES REISE, JR.

BORN: Stony Creek, Ontario, June 7, 1922
POSITION: Defenseman
NHL TEAMS: Chicago Blackhawks, 1945-47; Detroit Red Wings, 1947-52;
New York Rangers, 1952-54
AWARDS/HONORS: NHL All-Star Game, 1950-53

There are not many chips-off-the-old-block so identical in style and ability than the Leo Reises, Senior and Junior. The younger Reise was a defenseman, like his dad, and a much-feared one at that.

Although Leo, Jr., broke in with the Blackhawks in 1945-46, he was dealt to Detroit the next year and played his best hockey for the Red Wings through the 1951-52 season. In 1952-53 he became a Ranger and like his dad, he finished his big-league tenure on Broadway (1953-54). Although Gordie Howe, Ted Lindsay, and Red Kelly received most of the Motor City ink, it often was Leo Reise, Jr., who performed the unheralded spade work for the champion Red Wing teams in 1950 and 1951 when they won the Prince of Wales Trophy.

Reise the Younger came to Detroit from the Windy City in December 1946 with Pete Horeck in exchange for Adam Brown and Ray Powell. Although overshadowed by glitzier defensemen such as Leonard "Red" Kelly, Reise emerged as a thudding body checker who played his position like a general operating on the battlefield. His lack of speed rarely was a problem because of that excellent positioning.

As the Red Wings rolled to juggernaut status in the late 1940s, Reise was acclaimed as the linchpin of the splendid Motor City defense. And he could fight. Ironically, though, it was as a clutch goal scorer that

Reise would go down in the annals of the Red Wings.

By far, Reise's most outstanding moment occurred during the 1949-50 semifinal playoffs between the Maple Leafs and Red Wings. Toronto had won an unprecedented three straight Stanley Cups and looked good enough to make it four in a row, particularly since the Leafs had swept Detroit four games to none in the 1949 playoffs.

The series was bloody from the outset. NHL president Clarence Campbell was forced to warn the players to calm down. After three games, Toronto held a two-games-to-one lead in the series.

Detroit tied the series with a 2-1 victory in the fourth game on Reise's overtime goal at 38 seconds of the second extra session. Then the Leafs went ahead again, blanking the Wings 2-0. Though their ace, Gordie Howe, was lost to them for the playoffs due to an injury, the Red Wings defeated the Leafs 4-0 at Toronto in the sixth game, carrying the semifinal series to a seventh and deciding game at Detroit.

In the final game the teams battled through three periods of regulation time without a goal. Checking remained close through the opening eight minutes of the sudden-death overtime.

Then coach Tommy Ivan sent out a line of George Gee, Steve Black and Joe Carveth against Toronto's Max Bentley, Fleming Mackell and Vic Lynn. The Leafs had Bill Juzda and Bill Barilko on defense; Detroit defend-

Leo Reise, Jr. spent his NHL career in Chicago, Detroit, and New York.

ers were Jack Stewart and Leo Reise, Jr. The last person on the ice that one would expect to score was Reise. Finally Gee captured the puck and slid it across the ice to Reise, who was standing near the blue line 60 feet from the goal.

His shot went straight to the net, where goaltender Turk Broda appeared to have the short side blocked with his skate, pad, and stick. But the puck bounced over Broda's stick at 8:34 of the first overtime and hit the back of the net. Detroit won 1-0, nabbing the Stanley Cup for the first time in seven years.

Reise would still be with Detroit as the team annexed Lord Stanley's silver again in 1952, although Leo, Jr.'s record in that postseason would be for most penalty minutes in the playoffs, with 27.

42

GARRY DOUGLAS
"IRON MAN" UNGER

BORN: Calgary, Alberta, December 7, 1947
POSITION: Center
NHL TEAMS: Toronto Maple Leafs, 1967-68; Detroit Red Wings, 1968-71;
St. Louis Blues, 1971-79; Atlanta Flames, 1979-80; Los Angeles Kings, 1980-81;
Edmonton Oilers, 1981-83
AWARDS/HONORS: NHL All-Star Game, 1972-78

It was to have been a glorious career for Garry Unger in Detroit. In some ways, he could have been an early-day Brendan Shanahan. All the ingredients were there—speed, radar shot, smarts and drive.

As it happened, his career in the Motor City was short-lived. Nevertheless, Unger demonstrated the ingredients that eventually would enable him to play starry hockey for 16 NHL seasons.

Unger's arrival in Detroit was a surprise in itself. He had already been earmarked as a future Toronto Maple Leafs ace during his teenage years and made his National Hockey League debut with Toronto in 1967-68. No doubt he would have remained a Leaf had the Red Wings not made an offer that the Leafs' high command could not refuse. On March 3, 1968, Toronto obtained Norm Ullman, Paul Henderson and Floyd Smith from Detroit. For that package, the Leafs relinquished Unger along with Frank Mahovlich, Pete Stemkowski and the rights to defenseman Carl Brewer.

Leafs boss Punch Imlach later claimed that he had been trying to swing an Ullman-Mahovlich even-up trade for several years. Unger, it developed, proved to be the catalyst. "No Unger, no deal," Sid Abel (the Red Wings' general manager) had said.

While pleased with a change of scenery, Unger was uncertain whether he would be relegated to one of Detroit's farm teams or remain in the bigs. "At the time I thought I was a throw-in, because of names like Ullman, Mahovlich and Stemkowski. I found out later that I was more influential in the trade than I'd thought. But it seemed then as if nobody knew me in Detroit. The team didn't even know who I was when I got there."

When the three new Red Wings reported to the team's stopping place in Manhattan, the Hotel Roosevelt, the first Detroit hockey official they encountered was assistant general manager Baz Bastien. "He came over and shook hands with Mahovlich and Stemkowski, calling them Pete and Frank," said Unger. "Then he said, 'And how are you . . . Norm, isn't it?' That broke everybody up. He didn't even know my name."

If Bastien didn't know the kid with the blonde hair, Abel certainly did. "We were so high on Garry," said Abel, "that even the Red Wings' owner, Bruce Norris, personally scouted him. He'd seen him play in junior hockey and with the Leafs and was very impressed. So was I."

But when Unger learned that coach Bill Gadsby was placing him on a line with Gordie Howe at right wing and Alex Delvecchio at center, nobody was more impressed than Garry himself. Howe not only had been

Upon his arrival in Detroit, young Garry Unger was placed on a line with future Hall of Famers Gordie Howe and Alex Delvecchio.

a childhood idol but also the chief protagonist in an eminently forgettable episode involving the two when Unger was a 17-year-old living in Calgary. Howe had come to a promotion at Eaton's Department Store and Garry ventured downtown to see the great star. But he couldn't summon the courage to approach him for an autograph.

Though Howe welcomed Garry as a full-blown professional, working on a line with the gifted Howe was not always easy because of Gordie's many talents. Superior centers were driven to distraction trying to orchestrate plays for Howe because *Howe* was the one who did the conducting. But for new center Unger it was less than a disaster.

"I remember the first time I played with Gordie. They put me on his line and right away we got a two-on-one breakaway. I kind of pulled the defenseman to one side and flipped the puck to Gordie. It wasn't a very good pass. In fact, it was a pretty bad one. But he leaned back and got it and—wham!—the puck was in the net for a goal. I remember thinking to myself as I skated behind the net, 'God, I'm going to get 900 assists this season.'"

It wasn't that easy, however. Garry played 13 games for Detroit in the latter portion of the 1967-68 season and had all the credentials of a whiz-bang center. He scored five goals as well as ten assists for an average that was better than a point-per-game. These figures, however, proved deceptive as they mistakenly inspired some impetuous writers to compare Unger with Howe.

"It didn't turn out to be a good thing for Garry," said Joe Falls, sports editor of the *Detroit Free Press*. "The problem came when Unger began to believe it all."

Coach Sid Abel watched in disgust as Garry began frittering away the 1968-69 campaign, his first full year with the Red Wings. Instead of averaging a point-per-game, Unger was hard pressed to produce 44 points in 76 contests. "The press built him up," said Abel, "and Garry figured he could get by without working, that he was a star already. The kid was good, but he wasn't Gordie Howe."

"As Unger's hat size went up, his goal production went down," Falls added. "Abel finally put him on the bench and that seemed to shake some sense into him."

The Unger syndrome is not unfamiliar to young athletes. The question was whether Garry could learn from his sophomoric failings, reform and contribute up to the Red Wings expectations.

The answer was apparent at the end of the 1969-70 season. Unger had established himself as one of hockey's brightest stars, scoring 42 goals, just one less

than league leader Phil Esposito, and this in only his second full NHL season. "I'm pretty lucky," he admitted that year. "I've never had too much trouble putting the puck in the net. I don't know what it is but it just is. I look at other guys, how they have to sweat and slave to get the job done, but scoring has always come easy to me."

If there was one minus among all the positives for Unger it was the fact that he collected only 24 assists to go with his 42 goals. His explanation: "I think some centers pass too much. They're passing the puck when they should be shooting it. Me, when I've got a shot, I take it."

Others took some shots too, but at Garry's lifestyle. The era of the flamboyant hockey star had not yet been popularized by Derek Sanderson of the Boston Bruins, so when Unger spoke joyfully about spending his summer in either "Europe, Japan or maybe I'll go to South America," Joe Falls remarked that he sounded "like a kid on the last day of school."

The kid drove a Corvette Stingray, rode a motorcycle, played the guitar, roped calves, climbed mountains, and bought clothes that according to one observer "would make a peacock blush." He also made headlines of sorts by dating then Miss America Pam Eldred.

Unger set a style for himself as a very special athlete, even down to taping his hockey sticks. Instead of using the conventional black tape employed by his colleagues, Garry preferred the thin white adhesive tape usually reserved for dressing wounds.

"I did this when I was a kid," he explained. "I used to make my Mom mad. I'd get the Johnson & Johnson tape out of the medicine chest and wrap it around my sticks. I didn't like the black tape because it looked dirty."

Ironically it was appearances that inadvertently but ultimately paved the way for Garry's downfall at Olympia Stadium. The root cause of the problem was a major shakeup in the Red Wings' front office during the spring of 1970. The focal character in Detroit's hockey upheaval was Nevin D. "Ned" Harkness, who had built one of the finest coaching records in United States collegiate hockey. During the 1969-70 season Harkness coached Cornell University to an unprecedented perfect record of 29 victories in as many games and the team won the Ivy League, the Eastern College Athletic Conference, and the NCAA titles. Then Ned came to Detroit.

CAN A COLLEGE COACH SUCCEED IN RUGGED NHL? asked *The Sporting News*. The answer would eventually be supplied by the likes of Garry

Unger, Gordie Howe, and other key members of the Detroit hockey organization. The mood in the Red Wings' dressing room was one of watchful waiting.

The first words Unger heard from his new bench boss were delivered at Harkness's press debut. When asked to compare college and pro hockey, Harkness said: "Hockey is hockey and the name of the game is to win. The pressure in the NHL is dollars and cents. But that's more on a management level. It doesn't come down to the ice level where I will be operating with the players. Down there the pressure is winning.

"Don't let anyone tell you it's tougher handling pros than college youngsters. The real motivation is pride. In college hockey if you find one player isn't skating, you can't bring so-and-so up from the farm at Fort Worth. You have to live and die with the men on your club. The age factor doesn't enter into it either. On the Wings we have young guys like Garry Unger who is the same age as players I had in college."

True. But Garry Unger had not been to college. Nor did he need a degree to recognize that in no time at all, Coach Harkness was destroying the Red Wings' club which had finished in third place during the 1969-70 season and comported itself commendably in the playoffs. "We had a lot of good scorers," said Unger, "and what looked to me like the makings of a great team. Then Harkness came along."

To say that Harkness the Detroit coach was a disaster would be a critical understatement. After 38 games, he had managed to amass but 12 wins while losing 22 and tying another 4. The Red Wings rested unhappily in sixth place in the NHL's seven-team East Division, and there were widespread cries up and down the state of Michigan for Harkness's scalp.

The problem was easy enough to understand: Harkness was simply unable to apply the techniques he had used so successfully at Cornell with the hard-bitten pros of the NHL. Colleen Howe, Gordie's wife, studied Harkness carefully and had to say, "Ned was so intense he had a difficult time relating to people. He was a person who listened hard and never heard what you said. He would go into a losing locker room and wish he could put his fist through the wall. He used the famous four-letter word so often in the locker room talks, Gordie complained, that he couldn't concentrate on what Ned was saying. He just found himself counting the number of times he said *that* word.

"But no one ever tried harder. He became so unpopular with the fans, his family had to stop coming to the games. Finally, the players held a private meeting to try to have him fired."

On January 8, 1971, Harkness *was* fired as coach; but instead of being released by Red Wings' owner Bruce Norris, he was elevated to the managership of the Detroit club. "If I fail to do the job," said Harkness, "Mr. Norris will not have to fire me, I will quit."

Unger then learned that his new coach was Doug Barkley, a former Red Wings defenseman who had coached Detroit's Central League club at Fort Worth. Unger also learned that Harkness, at least superficially, placed great faith in Unger's future.

"Garry," said Harkness, "is on top of our untouchable list. There is no way he will be traded. As far as I'm concerned he's our Gordie Howe of the future. He's the young leader type we want, and he is a leader. He is the guy we're going to build this team around." Harkness reiterated these points about Unger because "there have been numerous reports that we are willing to trade him. I mention Unger because of the reports."

Neither Unger nor his teammates seemed particularly impressed with any of the Harkness changes. Roommates Peter Stemkowski and Unger were both indicted by Harkness for their mod lifestyles and long hair. "Unger's hair was longer than Stemmer's," said defenseman Gerry Hart. "But Ned was on them both."

Unger was often badgered about his appearance. "He was treating us like 17-year-olds away from home for the first time," said Garry. "He told a veteran like Alex Delvecchio not to smoke cigars. He told me I couldn't wear a leather coat or mod suits."

If that wasn't depressing enough, Unger was further horrified by the manager's treatment of his close friend, Hart. More often than seemed necessary, Harkness would ridicule Hart. Once, the manager asserted: "I believe Gerry Hart is too small to play in this league regularly." When Hart ripped his shoulder early in the 1971-72 season, the Red Wings appeared to forget him. Later he was remembered, and this time Harkness ripped the sweater off the defenseman. "They decided they had a new prodigy (Serge Lajuenesse)," said Hart. "They decided I wasn't going to play at all. What could I do? The only thing I could do was hope to get out before it did permanent damage."

Harkness's treatment of Unger's buddy had a direct bearing on Garry himself, who came to loathe his manager. Fortunately, Gordie Howe was still around to provide a pleasant counterpoint. "Gordie would lend Gerry and me his car and his skis and let us use his cabin up in the mountains.

"Every so often Gordie and I would go skiing together, ride motorcycles together or go out in his boat. He's the type of guy who can do anything, and he's just as crazy as I am. Once we were out in his boat, pushing it as fast as it would go. The waves were about 15 feet high, and we were flying around. He likes that sort of thing, like a big kid, and that's what I liked about him. And he always made sure that a new guy on the team would feel welcome. He'd go right over to him, talk to him and put him at ease."

Perhaps if the patriarchal Howe had had more influence with Harkness the deteriorating situation between Garry and Ned might have been improved by his positive intervention. But a Harkness-Unger *détente* was never achieved. By far the most outstanding issue was hair. Unger flatly rejected Harkness's specifications for thatches. "Once," said Garry, "he even drew a sketch illustrating how he wanted my hair. I balked at that. I'm just not the kind of person who could submit to that type of regimentation."

By the middle of the 1970-71 season, Harkness was quite willing to forget that he had once placed an "untouchable" tag on his blonde center. "Unger," said Harkness, "has not been doing anything to help this club. He's been more downhill than uphill."

The time had come for Garry to reverse the trend. Ironically, it was his nemesis, Ned Harkness, who would catapult Unger back into the galaxy of stars.

Whether Garry Unger ever believed that he could outlast Ned Harkness as a member of the Red Wings hockey family is a moot question. But he did make certain moves that suggest he was comfortable in the Motor City, despite his collisions with the club's manager. For one thing, he bought 11 prime acres outside Detroit on which to raise quarter horses. Then there was his close relationship with Gordie Howe.

But it had become clear to Unger and almost everyone close to the team that Howe was rapidly becoming disillusioned with the club and its front-office decisions. "Actually," said Colleen Howe, "the franchise had been in decline since 1967. The team had reached the playoffs only once during that time." A disgusted Howe would eventually take his family and move to Houston, there to resume his playing career and star for the World Hockey Association club.

For reasons best known to Bruce Norris, the Red Wings' owner chose to place his complete support behind Harkness. The growing anti-Harkness bloc among the Detroit players sensed that they would sink or swim—or be traded—with Harkness.

Unger owns the second-longest consecutive games streak in NHL history (914).

"I was depressed," Unger admitted. "By February 1971 I had only 13 goals in 51 games and I was really starting to doubt myself. I began to wonder whether I could make it in this game after all."

The wondering, as far as Detroit fans were concerned, ended that same month when Unger was dispatched to St. Louis along with Wayne Connelly for Red Berenson and Tim Ecclestone. There he was told he could let his hair grow down to his ankles, if he wanted, as long as he scored goals. He did score goals, although not at record-breaking levels. But it was there under the Gateway Arch that Unger became the "Iron Man" of hockey.

Unger broke Andy Hebenton's then-record of 630 consecutive NHL games played during the 1975-76 season, and stretched his "iron man" streak to 914 games before injuries forced him out of the lineup in December, 1979. His streak remains the second longest in league history, behind the 964 games played by Doug Jarvis a few seasons later.

After departing the NHL in 1983, Unger played four years in Great Britain before retiring in 1987. Had he played under a coach other than Ned Harkness in the prime of his career, it's possible that Garry Unger would have been a much more popular Detroit sports hero.

43

MIKE VERNON

BORN: Calgary, Alberta, February 24, 1963
POSITION: Goaltender
NHL TEAMS: Calgary Flames, 1982-94, 2000-Present; Detroit Red Wings, 1994-97;
San Jose Sharks, 1997-2000; Florida, 2000
AWARDS/HONORS: NHL Second All-Star Team, 1989;
William M. Jennings Trophy (shared with Chris Osgood), 1996;
Conn Smythe Trophy, 1997; NHL All-Star Game, 1988-91, 1993

To some experts, Mike Vernon was too small to be a championship goaltender. In an age when the likes of Ollie Kolzig, Martin Brodeur, and Dominik Hasek were demonstrating that size is a major asset between the pipes, Vernon managed to excel—first with the Calgary Flames, and subsequently and most importantly with the Detroit Red Wings.

After all, it was the Calgary native who won the Stanley Cup not only for Calgary in 1988, but also for the Red Wings in 1997. To the Motor City faithful, the fact that Vernon helped break the 42-year playoff hex dating back to 1955 was significant enough. Vernon arrived in Detroit a June 1994 trade for defenseman Steve Chisson.

Scott Bowman wanted Vernon for both his clutch performances and for the fact that Mike could help his understudy, Chris Osgood, learn the game. It proved to be a wise decision.

Not that it was totally joyful in Detroit for Vernon. After helping the Red Wings to the Stanley Cup finals in 1995, the boys in red and white proceeded to lose four straight to the New Jersey Devils. Many critics noted that the veteran Vernon was outplayed by the younger Martin Brodeur. Others contend that Mike got a bum rap.

"Mike was never fully appreciated," said Detroit columnist Terry Foster. "He was unfairly blamed for the 1995 Stanley Cup finals loss to New Jersey, even thought the Red Wings combined for a total team no-effort. Vernon got little respect."

Redemption in Detroit would come only after the Red Wings won a Stanley Cup. It had been a long wait for Detroiters, but when the playoffs began in the 1996-97 season, the Red Wings were a determined outfit, and nobody was more focused than Mike himself.

The first round immediately proved to be a bit of a challenge, however, as they faced a talented St. Louis Blues club that included Brett Hull, Pierre Turgeon, Al MacInnis and the battle-tested Grant Fuhr in net. Detroit dropped the first game of the series, and right away people talked about a possible upset, almost anticipating another Red Wings collapse.

It would not happen this time, though, as Detroit got superb goaltending from Vernon in a critical Game 2 victory by the narrowest of margins, 2-1. Lifted by Vernon's performance, Detroit would go into St. Louis, and once again their veteran goalie would be the difference in a 3-2 triumph.

But this series was far from over. In Game 4, Vernon was chased from the net in what would turn

OPPOSITE: During his time in Detroit, Mike Vernon shared netminding duties with young Chris Osgood.

Mike Vernon sprawls to make a save.

In Game 4, the frustration mounted when the Avalanche were buried by Detroit in a 6-0 rout in front of a sold-out Motor City crowd that loved every minute of it. This was Detroit's biggest rival and bitter nemesis, revenge was on everyone's mind.

Colorado roared back to return the favor with a 6-0 victory of their own to stave off elimination and chase Vernon from the net in the process. But Vernon and the Wings finally exacted their revenge by eliminating Colorado, 3-1, in Detroit. As the series came to an end, one thing was certain—for this year at least—Mike Vernon was the better goalie, having outplayed Patrick Roy for most of the series.

In the Stanley Cup finals against the Philadelphia Flyers, Vernon nullified Eric Lindros and his vaunted legion of doom, and in no time at all the Red Wings had swept Philadelphia in four straight games.

Why was Vernon so important to Detroit's win? Former NHL goaltender Glen "Chico" Resch—now an analyst for New Jersey Devils telecasts—explained it this way:

"The one factor that cannot be disputed is the instinct. Mike had been around the crease long enough to instinctively know when to do what. Oh, yes, he has a nice butterfly, an excellent glove, and he does come out to challenge intelligently, but so much of his success is based on instinct.

"Mike Vernon's impact on the Detroit Red Wings' Stanley Cup win was as much psychological as it was physical. Let's remember, going into the playoffs everyone recognized the Wings confidence was extremely fragile. A questionable goal at a critical time could send them and their fans into an 'Oh no, here we go again,' mindset! Vernon refused to let that happen. Under every kind of pressure and tension, Mike never wavered

out to be the Wings' low point of the playoffs—a 4-0 defeat that knotted the series at two.

With their reputation on the line, Vernon and his teammates responded by taking Games 5 and 6 convincingly, moving them to a second-round, four-game conquest of the Mighty Ducks of Anaheim. Ironically enough, every game against Anaheim was close, with three of the four games decided by one goal. Mike Vernon was once again the difference.

With two rounds complete, Detroit was halfway to a Stanley Cup. But in the backs of everyone's minds—including the Red Wings players—was the reminder that when they had achieved the Final Four in the previous two years, they had come up short. To make matters worse, Detroit would be facing an all too familiar opponent: The defending 1996 Stanley Cup Champion Colorado Avalanche, in the Western Conference finals.

After Colorado got a vintage performance from Patrick Roy, outdueling Vernon 2-1 in Game 1, the Red Wings responded by taking the next three games. Games 2 and 3 saw Vernon deliver a spectacular performance in both contests, seemingly getting into the heads of the Avs' snipers.

or gave up a sloppy goal. Mike's winning of the Conn Smythe trophy was as much about his unwavering consistency as brilliant saves."

Winning the Conn Smythe trophy was the topper for Vernon. It culminated a career that began on his neighborhood rinks in southwest Calgary.

"As soon as I took him to the rink," Mike's father, Martin, once recalled, "he was about two or three years old at the time, he always stayed beside the goaltender."

Mike's mother, Lorraine Vernon, added, "In the dressing room, he'd try on the goalie's equipment and he'd drag it around with him. Even today he says he doesn't play hockey—he's a goalie. He always played goal. I don't remember him wanting to do anything else but play goal."

Martin Vernon added, "Mike was always a good skater and he still is. If he took his goalie equipment off, he'd skate as well as half the guys."

Vernon played well enough as a youngster in Calgary to attract scouts by the time he had become a teenager. When he was 15 he was invited to the Billings Bighorns camp, but he returned home and eventually starred for the Calgary (Junior) Wranglers. He was their starter from day one and twice was named the Western Canada Junior League's most valuable player.

Lorraine Vernon remembered, "He'd bring home those trophies and awards and he'd just put them in a corner and forget them. He was looking to the future, starting to really think he could get to the NHL."

That he did, and he succeeded beyond most expectations. Ironically, however, Vernon would go from winning the Stanley Cup to being traded to San Jose in the off season—mostly because Vernon had also performed his other role, guiding Osgood to the confidence and maturity he needed to assume the top slot in Detroit's goal. Management's decision would prove to be correct, as the Red Wings went on to a repeat Cup victory in 1997-98 with Osgood in goal.

As for Vernon, nearing the end of an illustrious career, he took over the No. 1 role during the regular season again, playing 62 games for San Jose in 1997-98 and 49 in 1998-99. Vernon was dealt to Florida on December 30, 1999, and then was part of a complicated trade series in the 2000 expansion draft, whereupon he ended up back in his first NHL team's net with the Calgary Flames. Vernon shared net minding duties with yet another up-and-coming youngster, Freddie Brathwaite, for the Flames in 2000-2001 with Roman Turek the following season.

Mike Vernon's career began, and may well end, in Calgary. But certainly his three years with the Red Wings, bringing Detroit its first Stanley Cup since 1955 and being awarded the Conn Smythe Trophy as Playoff MVP for 1997, were remarkable enough.

The bottom line is this: Over a substantial period of time, Mike Vernon has been better than most at keeping the puck from going over the Red Goal Line, even though he's a little guy in a big man's game.

Nobody has put it better than Vernon himself.

"It's no different how big or small you are. It's how good a goalie you are and if you're on your game or not. I've seen some great short goaltenders and some great tall goaltenders. It just doesn't matter."

44

CHRIS OSGOOD

BORN: Peace River, Alberta, November 26, 1972
POSITION: Goaltender
NHL TEAMS: Detroit Red Wings, 1993-2001, New York Islanders, 2001-Present
AWARDS/HONORS: NHL Second All-Star Team, 1996;
William M. Jennings Trophy (shared with Mike Vernon), 1996;
NHL All-Star Game, 1996-98

For his entire Red Wings career, Chris Osgood almost always was fighting for respect as a top-drawer goaltender. At times he was brilliant and at other times he would be the target of coach Scott Bowman's ire.

On the smallish side for goaltenders, Chris Osgood loomed large in the nets as the Red Wings began their climb to the top in the mid-1990s. But before backstopping the Wings to their second straight Stanley Cup victory in 1998, the 5'11", 180-pound native of Peace River, Alberta, had to endure four years of barbs from those who questioned his ability.

On the evening of April 30, 1994, the then-21-year old rookie skated between the pipes for Game 7 of the 1994 Stanley Cup quarterfinal matchup between Detroit and the underdog San Jose Sharks. Virtually every single one of the over 19,000 Joe Louis Arena faithful in attendance were certain the Wings would defeat the third-year Sharks and advance to the second round of the playoffs.

Displaying the maturity of a veteran throughout the 1993-94 season, Osgood had accumulated a 23-8-5 freshman record and was named Rookie of the Month in February 1994. More impressive, the diminutive Osgood blanked San Jose in Game 1 of the series—the

first Detroit rookie to record a shutout in a playoff game since the great Terry Sawchuk in 1951.

But as the teams battled into the third stanza of the decisive final game, the scoreboard showed each team with two goals, and the crowd's confidence turned to anxiety. When the puck went into the left corner of the Detroit zone with just under seven minutes to play in regulation time, anxious eyes watched as Osgood came out of his cage to play the loose rubber.

As the Sharks forwards made their way into the Detroit zone, Osgood inexplicably lost his focus and experienced an uncommon lapse in judgment. Normally cool under pressure, the rookie's self-awareness seemed to waver with every lumbering stride as he tried to fetch the puck. His decision to chase after the loose disc quickly became a prescription for disaster. The encroaching San Jose Sharks goaded Osgood into doing something that would hound him for the next four years. The net minder, whose best traits are his mental toughness and resolve, retrieved the puck and blindly shoveled it around the boards in an attempt to clear the zone.

The circling Sharks were ready. San Jose center Jamie Baker intercepted the errant Osgood clearing attempt and discovered a wide-open net staring him in

Chris Osgood eyes the rubber.

members his father, John Osgood. "We absolutely could never get him to eat. He'd look right at us and dump it on the floor. You could never coax him into anything."

Born November 26, 1972 in the prairies of Alberta, Canada, Osgood convinced his parents to purchase $1,000 worth of equipment when he decided to be a goaltender at the age of 10. Shortly thereafter Chris suffered a minor injury in an early game, and when he got home that night, he mentioned to his folks that goaltending might not be his cup of tea after all.

"I just said, 'Over my dead body. I just spent a thousand dollars on you; you're playing goal,' " said Chris's dad, John. "But Chris went out as a forward and scored seven goals."

Despite that offensively explosive episode, the elder Osgood convinced his son he was a better goalkeeper than forward. Young

the face. Osgood scrambled hopelessly to get back into the vicinity of the crease, but Baker rifled a shot into the yawning net with 6:35 left in the contest, winning the game and series for the underdog Sharks.

Suddenly the rookie net minder became suspect. The kid who had calmly recorded his first two career shutouts—in succession—earlier in the season, who had displayed such strong and mature goaltending during the regular season, was now the goalie Detroit fans loved to mistrust.

For the next four seasons these critics would hound Osgood, questioning his every move and seeming to delight in seeing the young man falter. Those who knew him most intimately were hardly surprised by the turn of events. Even as an a youth, Osgood displayed a certain stubbornness, earning himself the nickname, "The Littlest Rebel," before he reached the age of one. "Even when he was a baby, he was very, very stubborn," re-

Chris eventually found himself playing for the local junior team in Medicine Hat, Alberta.

As his son began to make his mark in juniors, particularly for his consistent play, John Osgood remembered talking to Wayne Simpson, then an NHL scout. Dad expected Simpson to tell him that Chris would make it as an NHL net minder based on his natural abilities. Instead, Simpson said that Chris's mental strength was what would make him an NHL star.

Osgood would be plucked by the Red Wings in the third round (54th overall) of the 1991 NHL entry draft. Wings scouting director Ken Holland—later GM—picked Osgood in the hopes of reversing a string of suspect goaltenders with whom Detroit suffered in the late 1980s and early 1990s. Holland was so absolutely certain of Osgood's potential that even after the Game 7 fiasco against San Jose he continued to be Chris' staunchest supporter.

However, knowing it had placed undue pressure on the 21-year-old, Detroit management traded for veteran goaler Mike Vernon in June 1994, to help take not only some of the physical load off Osgood, but some of the mental baggage as well. For the next three seasons the two net minders would forge a close bond rather than sinking into the strained relationship (aging superstar crowded by rising young talent) that many expected to develop.

"Before Mike got here, I worried about what everybody said," Osgood confessed. "I used to wonder, 'what's this person saying, what's that person saying?' He taught me that if there's something in the paper today, it doesn't mean anything the next day. You can't dwell on what happened. That's the biggest thing I learned from him—if you have a bad game, let go of it and go out there and play."

Coach Scotty Bowman soon began flip-flopping the two goaltenders—Vernon led the Wings to the Stanley Cup Final in 1995, where they eventually lost to the New Jersey Devils, while Osgood took over the reins the following season, leading the Wings to the Western Conference Finals before being ousted by Colorado. The seemingly daily swing from being the No. 1, only to be relegated to the bench the next day did not affect the mentor/protégé relationship.

"[Vernon] pushed me to play every day," said Osgood. "When I was playing in the playoffs in '96, instead of him being upset and not even talking to me, he pushed me and wanted me to play better and win the Cup. That was really when we grew close. Mike was always supporting me. That meant a lot, because sometimes there are not that many people pulling for you. He was always in my corner."

The tight knit duo shared the William M. Jennings Trophy for allowing fewest goals in the NHL during the 1995-96 season. However, one person who wasn't always in Osgood's corner was coach Bowman.

The legendary bench jockey was nonplussed with Osgood's inconsistencies early in Chris's career. Bowman's eyes would watch uncomfortably each time a player would launch a shot from outside the blue line, then close momentarily in quiet horror whenever Chris failed to play the puck cleanly.

"He does different things to motivate players," Osgood said about Bowman. "He hardly ever talks to me. That must be how he motivates me, through the paper."

During the 1996-97 season, Bowman utilized Osgood for the majority of the season but named Vernon his starting goaltender for the playoffs, putting a dagger through Osgood's confidence. But as the veteran Vernon led the Wings to their first Stanley Cup victory since 1955 and became the Conn Smythe Trophy winner as MVP of the playoffs, young Osgood watched and learned, hoping that someday he would be called upon to duplicate his mentor's feat.

He didn't have to wait long for that opportunity. A year later GM Holland decided that Osgood was the team's future, and further, the future was now. Holland shopped Vernon to San Jose in the summer of 1997.

Suddenly Osgood became a major focal point on the Wings, and the Doubting Thomases began crawling out of the woodwork. Few predicted the quiet net minder could lead the Wings to a second straight Stanley Cup victory, especially because he had done virtually nothing in postseason play to redeem himself since that fateful error in the 1994 playoffs.

But through all the controversy and concern stirred by the Vernon deal, Holland stood by his decision. "We wouldn't have traded Mike if we didn't think Chris Osgood was capable of giving us the net minding," Holland said.

Osgood shrugged off all who doubted he could carry the team after receiving the torch from Vernon, saying, "I think I've proven I can play. I'm not a rookie who's never played before. I'm 24, and I've learned a lot playing here for the last four years. I'm excited to be on my own. I'm not afraid. I think it's time for me to be on my own."

It can be argued that Osgood's regular season success was a by-product of the overall team prosperity enjoyed by the Red Wings in the mid-to-late '90s. But his teammates never bought that assessment. In fact, most believed that Osgood was a key factor in catapulting the team to all it had achieved in recent postseason play.

"He gave us an opportunity to win every night," said teammate Darren McCarty, who began playing with Osgood in 1992 at Adirondack of the American Hockey League. "He's one of the most underrated goalies in the league. Chris doesn't get as much credit as he deserves. But if you look at his record and his consistency, he's one of the best."

Osgood was named to the All-Star team in the 1995-96 season—his best career year to date. During that campaign, he tied in the NHL for best GAA (2.17), and led the league in victories (39). He also rattled off a 21-game unbeaten streak (19-0-2), setting a new club record. Included in that stretch was a 13-game winning streak, which broke Terry Sawchuk's club record of nine. Heading into the 2000-01 season, Osgood possessed the second best winning percentage in league history.

Osgood won two Stanley Cups during his tenure with Detroit.

But back to the 1998 playoffs: Osgood had yet to prove himself to the hockey world outside of the Detroit metropolitan area. "Most people that talk don't really know what I've done," Osgood said, rebutting his doubters on the eve of the postseason. "They're just judging by the last game that I've played . . . I don't think there are many 25-year-old goalies who have played in the conference finals and gone three rounds in the playoffs.

"So to say I have no experience in the playoffs is kind of unfair to me. But I know, geez, I still have to prove myself in the playoffs and play well, and I know I'm going to play well in the playoffs."

Former teammate Vernon also took offense at those who wondered if Osgood was good enough to lead a hockey team to a Stanley Cup victory. "Now the focus is on Chris, and I'm sure he'll get himself in the zone and play very well," said the reigning playoff MVP. "This is an exciting time for Chris, and I'm sure he'll rise to the occasion. I think he's a great goaltender.

"This is a time when you're depended upon. Goaltending can win you games and win you a series. And on the other side, it might not work out that well. You're either a star, or you're the goat. That's your position, and that's how you have to deal with it. It's all part of goaltending."

Before the 1998 playoffs, Osgood had 25 postseason matches under his pads, recording a quite-respectable 2.16 GAA. And as the Red Wings began their quest for back-to-back titles, Osgood could hardly wait to put on his pads, doubters be damned.

"I look back on it, and geez, I've had a really good five years here, and played in a lot of games and a lot of different situations," he said. "I'm just going to go out there and play, and I'm not going to let anybody ruin the time of my life.

"I'm going to have a good time; that's what it's all about. Why should I let people ruin what I'm doing right now, when this is probably the best time of my life?"

Detroit opened its Stanley Cup defense on April 22, 1998 at Joe Louis Arena, facing off against first-round foe, the Phoenix Coyotes, led by All-Star types like Jeremy Roenick, Keith Tkachuk and Rick Tocchet. The Coyotes were a formidable group, relying on a fierce forecheck to manufacture a majority of their goals. Many thought the Coyotes had a realistic chance of upsetting the favored Wings, if only because of the "Osgood Factor."

But Detroit cruised to an easy 6-2 victory that evening, with Osgood playing his best—out of the crease, challenging shooters, aggressively chasing dump-ins, and starting quick breakouts for his club. After the opening victory, Detroit was deemed too strong for the upstart Coyotes, and visions of a four-game sweep enthused Red Wing fans everywhere.

That pipe dream was rapidly burst in a wild Game 2, as Phoenix defeated Detroit by a score of 7-4. Complicating matters for the Wings was Osgood's shaky play, which included letting in a Roenick slap shot from just outside the blueline. Suddenly the pundits recalled that Chris had exhibited in years past a penchant for allowing long-range missiles to get past him. Roenick's goal not only solidified that rap, but gave critics the opportunity to again bleat a chorus of "I told you so's" about Osgood not being the man one really wanted between the pipes in crucial situations.

Things went from bad to worse for the defending champs. Before a sellout crowd decked out in all-white at America West Arena, the Coyotes defeated the Wings, 3-2, taking a two games to one lead in the series.

Many began asking, "Could it be? Could the upstart team from the desert bring an end to Hockeytown's dominance?"

Chris Osgood resoundingly answered that question in Game 4.

After spotting Phoenix an early 1-0 lead, Osgood shut down the Coyote attack and silenced the crowd as the Wings scored a 4-2 come-from-behind victory. It was this contest which proved to Ken Holland that he had made the correct choice by trading Vernon and putting all his marbles in Chris Osgood's mitt.

"I thought the whole turning point for him was Game 4 against Phoenix," Holland later said. "We're down 1-0, late in the first period, and he stoned Tkachuk on a breakaway and stopped Norm MacIver cold, and we go on and win that game. From that point on he felt good about himself and felt confident he could do the job, and he hasn't looked back since."

The Wings used the Game 4 victory as a catalyst, winning the next two contests and taking the series four games to two.

Next up for the Wings were the St. Louis Blues and legendary goaltender Grant Fuhr. In Game 1, Fuhr outshone Osgood, as the Blues pulled off a stunning 4-2 victory. Criticism flared again afterwards, but the Wings rebounded by winning Game 2.

Seemingly on their way to a victory in Game 3, Detroit was again purring like a well-oiled machine. That is, until Blues defenseman Al MacInnis let go with an 85-foot cannon with less than a minute to play in regulation—a blast that Osgood misplayed and allowed to get by him. MacInnis' long-range bomb tied the game and sent it into overtime.

Detroit ended up winning the game in sudden death on a goal by Brendan Shanahan to take a 2-1 series lead, but again Osgood drew the wrath of the media in the locker room. His penchant and reputation for allowing long goals seemed to grow with each series.

But Holland again stood by his man after Shanahan's overtime goal lifted the Wings to victory. "He seems to have the ability not to worry about it," said Holland about Osgood's attitude after allowing bad goals. "He gave up the long shot to MacInnis, but he did not carry it with him. He was able to shake it off."

The Wings soon shook off the Blues, defeating them in six games. The Game 6 clincher was spectacular, with Osgood allowing only a single goal on 31 St. Louis shots. Now it was on to Dallas and the Western Conference Finals. Osgood would face his toughest challenge against the Stars. The veteran team from Texas seemed determined to break Osgood's resolve, and their game plan was to fire shots at him from all angles and lengths.

But Dallas's guns were full of blanks in Game 1, as Osgood recorded his first shutout of the 1998 postseason by stopping all 14 shots headed his way. The Stars rebounded in Game 2, however, defeating the Motor City sextet by a score of 3-1, tying the series at one game apiece as the teams headed north to Detroit.

The Red Wings, spurred on by the fans chanting "Oz-zie! Oz-zie! Oz-zie!" swept the next two games at Joe Louis Arena, and thoughts of clinching the Western Conference crown for a second straight trip to the Stanley Cup finals danced in their heads on the plane back to Dallas for Game 5.

Reunion Arena was filled to the rafters as the Stars and Wings took the ice for the pivotal fifth game. The two teams traded first-period goals before Red Wing forward Igor Larionov slipped the puck past Stars goaltender Ed Belfour to give the Wings a 2-1 lead heading into the third stanza.

In the third, Dallas threw everything at Osgood,

peppering the net minder with 15 shots in the period. Chris stopped every single one, except for Guy Carbonneau's wrist shot that eluded him gently on his pads, reminding him that the club desperately needed him to regain his focus not only for the next period, but the remainder of the playoffs.

"He appears like this soft, shy kind of kid," Yzerman said about Osgood. "But he's tough, and he's confident. He knows when he makes a mistake. We don't have to say anything to him."

The teams skated fast and furious as overtime began. After 40 seconds, the Wings dumped the puck into Dallas's end in order to get a line change. Mike Modano of the Stars retrieved the puck and quickly passed to his teammate, Jere Lehtinen. Lehtinen barely held on to the puck before he delivered it to right winger Jamie Langenbrunner's stick. Langenbrunner caught the puck between his blue line and the center red line, took three strides, and launched a slap shot from the center ice faceoff slot.

En route to Osgood, the puck seemed to skip and gain speed on the freshly resurfaced Reunion Arena ice. Osgood tentatively began to move, first slightly down, then back up. And as the disc flew towards him, one could see that the shot was about to handcuff the netminder.

And it did. The puck hit Osgood's stick and caromed into the net, giving the Stars a 3-2 overtime victory. But even after he had allowed yet another long-range goal, the Dallas squad—to a man—was singing the praises of the Detroit net minder. They had just fired 36 shots on Osgood during the game, and many thought they were seeing the second coming of Jacques Plante. For the third consecutive game, Osgood had faced more than 30 Dallas shots.

Back in Detroit for Game 6, Osgood and the Wings could hardly wait for the opening faceoff. They all knew that Dallas was 2-17-2 at "The Joe" since moving to Texas from Minnesota in 1993.

True to form, the Wings won the game behind Osgood's second shutout, 2-0. The net minder blocked all 26 Dallas shots as Detroit headed to the Stanley Cup finals for the second straight year.

"I couldn't wait to play the game," Osgood said. "I got sick of talking to you guys (media) for the last two days. I just want to play hard and not talk about long shots.

"The two goals (in Game 5) were tough, but I forget about them as soon as they go in. The fans are always behind me and always have been. That's prob-

ably the one thing that means more to me than anything."

Detroit forward Martin Lapointe spoke for all his teammates after the game when he said Osgood "knew he had to come up with a big game and he did. We all knew that. That's why he's our No. 1 goalie. He knows how to face adversity."

Center Sergei Fedorov concurred: "We all stand behind Ozzy and he didn't let us down."

The Stanley Cup final series against Washington was a mere formality, as the Wings captured their second straight championship by sweeping the Capitals behind Osgood's spectacular 30-save performance in Game 4.

But the story of the 1998 playoffs was Osgood and how he finally erased the memory of the fateful giveaway against San Jose in 1994, silencing his critics.

Osgood started all 22 Red Wing postseason games in the spring of '98, posting a 16-6 record along with a 2.15 GAA and .917 save percentage. Along the way, he outdueled future Hall of Fame net minders Grant Fuhr and Ed Belfour to capture his second Stanley Cup ring.

"There's no way we would have won the Stanley Cup if [Osgood] didn't play the way he played," said Holland. "All he did was rattle off wins. Other goaltenders are on teams where they need to be the first star to win games. Here, Chris just goes about his business."

Through his first seven seasons in the NHL, Osgood posted a 196-91-42 record. The vaunted 500-win mark at the end of his career is not out of the question. "I think I am one of the best goalies in the league," Chris said after the 1998 Cup win. "I think I can reach those numbers and I look forward to doing that. I just try to make a difference every time I play. I want to be the guy who gives our team a chance to win.

"I don't want to focus on [career numbers], but I want to be in that position. Everybody wants to be known as the best. I'm fortunate to be in this situation and I have to take advantage. I want to win as many games as possible. I've accomplished a lot, but I still have a long way to go."

Though Osgood did not win another Stanley Cup, he played adequately for Detroit through the 2000-01 season. But in the summer of 2001, the Red Wings obtained Dominik Hasek. Osgood was placed on waivers and claimed by the New York Islanders. He became New York's starting goalie and helped them to their first playoff berth since 1994.

45

GORDON "RED" BERENSON

BORN: Regina, Saskatchewan, December 8, 1939
POSITION: Center
NHL TEAMS: Montreal Canadiens, 1961-66; New York Rangers, 1966-67;
St. Louis Blues, 1967-71, 1974-78; Detroit Red Wings, 1971-74
AWARDS/HONORS: Team Canada, 1972

To contemporary Detroit fans, Gordon "Red" Berenson is best known as the successful coach of Michigan's varsity hockey team, incubator of many National Hockey League stars. But to hockey historians, Berenson occupies yet another niche. He was a big-leaguer whose career endured several ups and downs but was never uninteresting.

When Berenson, the scholarly center with the educated stick, was traded by the New York Rangers to the St. Louis Blues in November 1967, the deal was largely ignored. But when Berenson was dealt from St. Louis to the Red Wings early in February 1971, the news resounded with the impact of a thunderclap. In less than four years the anonymous redhead from Regina, Saskatchewan, emerged as the Babe Ruth of St. Louis hockey, the man who put the Blues on the ice map and into the Stanley Cup finals.

It was Berenson who once scored six goals in a single game against the Philadelphia Flyers and who became the first superstar of the NHL's expansion West Division. "The Red Baron" of the Blues, as he came to be known, had lifted himself up to a class with Bobby Hull, Gordie Howe, and Jean Beliveau.

Then, without warning, he was traded away by the very team which held him so dear. It was the shot heard round the hockey world. The precise reasons for the trade may never be known, but its repercussions

lasted for years. Berenson claimed the deal was simply a union-busting move on the part of the Blues' front office. "I think the Blues traded me because I was president of the NHL Players Association," said Berenson. "I don't know why the Blues should be uptight about the Association, but I'm convinced I was dealt because of that. Needless to say, I was shocked and disappointed."

So were the hockey fans in St. Louis. They were hardly ecstatic to learn that the Blues had obtained Garry Unger and Wayne Connolly in exchange for Berenson and Tim Ecclestone. Even the Blues' front office acknowledged the flak.

"I don't blame the fans," said Sid Salomon III, executive vice president of the Blues. "If I were on their side of the fence, I'd probably be writing or phoning my criticism. But we weren't trading for today, tomorrow, or the next NHL season. We were dealing for the next 10 years. We believed Unger was the kind of man we needed to build a Stanley Cup winner."

Red found himself at home in Detroit in more ways than one. He had earned B.A. and M.A. degrees from the University of Michigan and of course played much of his college hockey in that area.

When Berenson made All-American at Michigan, the late Jack Adams, Detroit's vitriolic manager, attempted to lure him to the Red Wings. But the Montreal

Berenson's departure from St. Louis caused an uproar among Blues fans.

Canadiens owned his rights at the time and had no intention of parting with them. Curiously, the Canadiens often seemed indifferent to Berenson once he moved up to the NHL in 1961-62.

Berenson's hockey smarts weren't always appreciated. Montreal's Toe Blake underplayed Red, and Berenson insists he never got a good chance to prove himself. "I was a different kind of player compared with the ones Blake was accustomed to. He knew I was a college man—not that I consider myself an intellectual, I don't—and I don't think he believed I could make it. When your coach is thinking that way, your chances are not too good."

But Berenson hardly saw more ice when he was traded to the Rangers. At first it seemed he'd be the No. 1 center, but an injury sidelined him and his place was taken by Orland Kurtenbach; every time he made a comeback, he'd suffer another injury, and the word—unfairly—made the rounds that he was brittle, maybe even that most dreaded of commodities, the "tissue-paper" athlete.

Then Red was traded to St. Louis by the Rangers in 1967, and the whole world seemed to come together: a young Scotty Bowman was coaching the new expansion club and the team desperately needed Berenson's skating and scoring touch. For several seasons it all worked. But by the 1970-71 season, the Blues needed to rebuild again and Berenson had worn out his welcome with St. Louis and the Salomon family owners— probably because of his deep involvement with the burgeoning players' association.

Traded to Detroit with Tim Ecclestone, Berenson came back to life and productivity. He played 24 games of the 1970-71 season, compiling 17 points (5-12) but blossomed a year later, finishing as Detroit's third lead-

Berenson's career was revived in Detroit.

ing scorer. Over 78 games, he tallied 28 goals and 41 assists for 69 points. As a Red Wing, he had become a complete player, offensively and defensively.

Unfortunately it was a brief respite, and a slumping team—plus injuries—caused a slumping Berenson. By January 1975, Red was back in St. Louis, where he played through the 1977-78 season. After retiring as a player, Berenson stayed on with the Blues as an assistant coach. Eventually, he migrated back to his alma mater—Michigan. There Berenson has coached so many championship and near-champ teams that his coaching prowess has become legend.

46

JOHN PAUL
"CHIEF" BUCYK

BORN: Edmonton, Alberta, May 12, 1935
POSITION: Left Wing
NHL TEAMS: Detroit Red Wings, 1955-57; Boston Bruins, 1957-78
AWARDS/HONORS: NHL Second All-Star Team, 1968; NHL First All-Star Team, 1971;
Lady Byng Trophy, 1971, 1974; Lester Patrick Trophy, 1977;
NHL All-Star Game, 1955, 1963-65, 1968, 1970-71; Hockey Hall of Fame, 1981

From time to time National Hockey League Hall of Famers split their careers between two teams but are only recognized for their exploits with one of the squads.

John Bucyk is just such an example, having cut his big-league puck teeth in Detroit but winning international acclaim years later as a Bruin. A left wing *par excellence*, Bucyk was a graduate of Detroit's vast farm system and originally gained notice in his hometown of Edmonton.

Bucyk played junior hockey for the Oil Kings and senior for the Flyers. Each was a Detroit farm club. He was finally promoted to the Red Wings for the 1955-56 season. In his autobiography, *Hockey in My Blood*, Bucyk recalled his rookie year.

"I remember my very first National Hockey League game," recalled the man they called "The Chief." "We played against Montreal and the first shift I was out on the ice, I got stuck with Rocket Richard. Of all people to be up against, I get the Rocket, who was one of the best hockey players of the day.

"I figured I'd enter my first game with a real bang. I did all right. I took a run at the Rocket the first time I got near him and I got a real good piece of him. Then the whistle blew. I got a penalty. We ended up winning that game, 4-3.

"The first goal I ever scored in the NHL was against New York. It was in New York and I beat Gump Worsley . . . I was on Cloud 9 when the puck went into the net.

"Making it with the NHL and in Detroit was a big thing for me . . . I'd get so excited and nervous before a game that I ended up in the back room throwing up. And when I came in as a rookie, and for my first three years in the NHL, I didn't say two words. You didn't talk then, you didn't say anything; you just listened and watched. Things have changed."

Bucyk was mishandled by the Detroit brass, however, and was dealt prematurely to the Boston Bruins on July 24, 1957, in a controversial deal for goalie Terry Sawchuk. Bucyk would go on to have a sensational career with the Bruins.

In Boston, Johnny was reunited with Edmonton buddies Bronco Horvath and feisty Vic Stasiuk, and the Uke Line (for Ukrainian) came into being. The world looked rosy that season, with the Bruins making the Stanley Cup finals in 1958. It was Horvath who dubbed Bucyk "The Chief" for his straight ebony hair, swarthy complexion, and stoic visage.

In 1958-59, Bucyk was so good at digging the puck out of the corners for linemate Horvath that Bronco came within two points of winning the scoring title, behind Bobby Hull.

"I always work the corners and get the puck out," Bucyk explained. "You can't score from the corners. If you pass off and the other guy scores, what's the difference? A goal is a goal."

But the goals of the Uke Line were to no avail, for Boston dropped to fifth place that year, and when Horvath was drafted by Chicago and Stasiuk traded to Detroit, the Uke Line became a thing of the past.

Bucyk continued his efficient ways, but the Bruins mopped up the basement for six years and were next to last another two. It wasn't until 1967-68 that Boston, with Bobby Orr, Phil Esposito, Ken Hodge, Wayne Cashman, net minder Gerry Cheevers and of course John Bucyk once again climbed to the top of the NHL.

Bucyk's life then became one of setting records while his more spectacular teammates, Orr and Esposito, broke bigger ones or more of them, leaving the Chief in the shadows, which he seemed to prefer.

Quietly Bucyk would become known as one of the best NHL finishers in The Game's history. His single best season came at the age of 35, when he scored a whopping 51 goals and an even more impressive 65 assists for his career-best 116 points. It was the only season in which Bucyk scored 50 goals or more and tallied 100 points or more.

The chief at the peak of his career.

What was even more remarkable about Bucyk's career than his longevity was his consistency. This was a player who never scored 30 goals in a season until the age of 32. Most impressive of all, Bucyk simply got better with age.

Bucyk's career accomplishments included playing in seven NHL All-Star Games in the years 1954-55, 1962-63, 1963-64, 1964-65, 1967-68, 1969-70 and 1970-71. He was also an NHL second team All-Star in 1967-68 and a first team NHL All-Star in 1970-71. What is even more amazing about that 1970-71 season was that Bucyk also won the Lady Byng Trophy for the most gentlemanly player. Pretty amazing stuff for a guy who found the net more than 50 times that year. Bucyk also took home a Lady Byng in 1973-74 and in 1976-77, he was awarded the Lester Patrick Trophy.

In 1978, after 23 seasons and 1,540 games, Bucyk retired with 556 goals and 813 assists for a total of 1,369 points credited to him. Granted, a majority of those points were tallied for Boston. But it was the Detroit organization which nurtured young John Bucyk, signed him to an NHL contract, then pointed him in the direction of stardom.

47

Bruce "The Redheaded Rocket" MacGregor

BORN: Edmonton, Alberta, April 26, 1941
POSITION: Center
NHL TEAMS: Detroit Red Wings, 1960-1971;
New York Rangers, 1971-74

Bruce MacGregor could have been forgiven had he thought he would be a Red Wing for life. After all, he was born in Edmonton, which for years had been home to Detroit's senior level farm team in the old Western League. He played junior hockey for Edmonton's Oil Kings, and as Red Wings property, he went on to skate for the Edmonton Flyers, his first pro team.

In 1960-61, the 5'10", 180-pound right wing played 54 games for Edmonton, scoring 20 goals and setting up 26 others. It was enough to convince the Detroit brain trust that MacGregor belonged in the bigs. He was promoted to the Red Wings for a dozen games and although he only registered one assist in the regular season, management had enough faith to use him in eight playoff games during which he scored a goal and had two assists. It was the last MacGregor would see of the minor leagues.

The 1961-62 season was his first full year as a Red Wing, and the skills that would make him a fixture at Olympia Stadium were evident in his rookie year. MacGregor was slick and speedy, a forward who could do just about anything required of him. While never an outstanding scorer, he did however emerge as a remarkably effective penalty-killer. The combination of rapid acceleration and excellent hockey sense enabled MacGregor to play 10 full seasons in Detroit.

The "Redheaded Rocket" came into his own dur-ing the mid-1960s, hitting the 28-goal mark—his personal high—in 1966-67.

He never played on a Stanley Cup winning team but in 1965-66, Bruce reached the Cup finals with Detroit at a time when he could almost taste the champagne. The Red Wings had won the first game of the finals at Montreal. In Game 2 at The Forum, the Habs scored first before Detroit tied it late in the opening period. The score remained tied at one into the third period when MacGregor finally broke the ice, giving Detroit a lead they never relinquished.

The 5-2 victory over Montreal catapulted the Wings to a two-games-to-none lead and the Cup was now tantalizingly close, especially with the next two contests in Detroit.

But for MacGregor and colleagues, it was as close as it would get. Montreal rebounded and won four straight and the Cup.

MacGregor's fortunes trailed off at the end of the decade of the 1960s. His last season in the red and white was the 1970-71 campaign in which he played 47 games, scoring six and creating 16 other goals.

By the time February 1971 rolled around, MacGregor's days in Detroit had become numbered and a trade became inevitable. The split finally came, and the Rangers traded Arnie Brown, Mike Robitaille and Tom Miller to Detroit for MacGregor and Larry Brown.

Bruce MacGregor played 10 full seasons in red and white.

The Broadway ambience proved a tonic for Bruce. He helped the Rangers to the Stanley Cup finals against Bobby Orr's Boston Bruins in 1971-72 after New York had toppled the Canadiens in the opening round and then followed with a triumph over Chicago in the semifinals before losing to Boston in a six-game final series.

His last year in New York was 1973-74, after which MacGregor took advantage of the fledgling World Hockey Association which then had a franchise in his native Edmonton. It was there that MacGregor finished his pro career in the 1975-76 season.

When Edmonton finally entered the NHL, Bruce's former teammate on the Rangers, Glen Sather, took command of the Oilers. MacGregor came aboard as one of Sather's top aides and remained with the organization until the summer of 2000 when Sather left Edmonton to run the New York Rangers.

But MacGregor is best remembered as a player for his excellence with the Red Wings for more than a decade and his overall gentlemanly play over 15 years of pro hockey.

"His goals were seldom spectacular," said Hall of Famer Emile Francis, who coached both for and against MacGregor. "But he was a hard-working, industrious type who rarely made a mistake on the ice."

As a diligent, productive Red Wing checking forward, MacGregor to this day stands out as a special Detroiter.

48

DARREN McCARTY

BORN: Burnaby, British Columbia, April 1, 1972
POSITION: Right Wing
NHL TEAMS: Detroit Red Wings, 1993-Present

Among the outstanding foot soldiers of Red Wings history—Glen Skov, Marty Pavelich, Bill Dineen—Darren McCarty ranks with the best in the modern National Hockey League era. A member of three Stanley Cup winning teams, the British Columbia native was drafted in 1992 by Detroit in the second round, 46th overall, after three seasons with Belleville in the Ontario Hockey League.

The Wings dispatched McCarty to their Adirondack farm club in the American League for seasoning during the 1992-93 season. Neither his goal scoring (17) nor playmaking (19 assists) arrested attention of the Detroit general staff. But McCarty totalled 278 penalty minutes, displaying the grit required by the big clubs.

Just one year out of junior hockey, Darren won his audition at the Red Wings 1993 training camp, and on October 21, 1993 he tallied his first big-league goal against the Winnipeg Jets.

While less than productive (9-17-26 in 67 games), McCarty's rookie NHL campaign was positive enough talent to the table to warrant further scrutiny.

Following the 1994-95 lockout of NHL players, McCarty returned to Detroit and has been a Red Wing fixture ever since. Combining size, strength and speed, McCarty gradually began improving his production, and in 1996-97 he reached a career-high 19 goals and 30 assists for 49 points in 68 games.

McCarty lifted his game a notch in the playoffs. In the 1998 postseason he scored three goals and eight assists for 11 points in 22 games, tying him for 18th among all playoff scorers.

But when it comes to Darren's game, the goals are gravy. More important are his physical game and his willingness to stand up for a teammate when required. This was most evident after teammate Kris Draper had been felled by Colorado Avalanche forward Claude Lemieux during a bitter 1996 Red Wings–Avalanche playoff series. Draper had been badly injured in the clash with Lemieux and it rankled the Red Wings.

McCarty wreaked revenge during a rematch with Colorado in October 1996. Darren challenged Lemieux and belabored the Avalanche disturber to such an extent that Detroit fans conceded it was "mission accomplished."

Precisely what effect the bout had on the Red Wings season is debatable, but there are some who believe that it set a tone for the gifted club to rollon to Detroit's first Stanley Cup triumph since 1955.

It was now clear that Darren's value was twofold. On the one hand, he was capable of producing meaningful, if not abundant, offense. And on the other, he

OPPOSITE: Darren McCarty winds up on top in this encounter.

McCarty tries to block Joe Nieuwendyk of Dallas from the puck.

gained acclaim as a well-rounded forward who often made life miserable for opposing goaltenders by parking his 6'1", 215-pound body directly in front of the crease. There have been few better "screens" among contemporary big-leaguers.

When the Motor City sextet repeated as Cup champions in 1997-98, McCarty achieved a career playoff high of three goals and eight assists for 11 points in 22 games. Likewise, he had perfected his forecheck enabling him to win many battles in the offensive corners.

Furthermore, his spirit infected teammates such as Draper, Martin Lapointe, Kirk Maltby and Tomas Holmstrom. Each came to play on a nightly basis and enabled the Red Wings to remain among the NHL elite through the late 1990s and into the new millennium.

But the goals inevitably bring the glory, and if one were to single out *the* most noteworthy McCarty score, it would be rooted in the 1997 finals against the Philadelphia Flyers. Detroit led the series three games to one on June 7, 1997 and led the match 1-0 midway in the third period.

Only one goal away from tying the score, the Flyers were stunned when McCarty skated from a group of checkers on a clean breakaway against goalie Ron Hextall. Darren went to his forehand and beat the Philadelphia goalie with surgical precision. To this day the goal is replayed as a playoff classic. And since Eric Lindros scored a last-minute goal for the Flyers, it was McCarty's tally which proved to be both the game-winner and Cup-winner all in one.

If Steve Yzerman has been regarded as the soul of the Red Wings for the past decade, one could say that Darren McCarty has been the heart.

McCarty moves the puck down the ice.

49

WILFRED KENNEDY "BUCKO" MCDONALD

BORN: Fergus, Ontario, October 31, 1914
DIED: July 21, 1991
POSITION: Defenseman
NHL TEAMS: Detroit Red Wings, 1934-39;
Toronto Maple Leafs, 1939-44; New York Rangers, 1944-45
AWARDS/HONORS: NHL Second All-Star Team, 1942

When it came to rock-hard bodychecking defensemen, Wilfred McDonald was among the sturdiest. Hence his nickname, "Bucko." Actually, McDonald launched his athletic career as an exceptionally fine lacrosse player who had a go with the 1932 professional indoor "box" lacrosse league. When the organization folded after only one year of operation, McDonald was beside himself. In a desperate move, he went to Frank Selke, an aide to Conn Smythe, boss of the Toronto Maple Leafs, to inquire about a career in pro hockey.

"Can you skate?" asked Selke, trying to sound sympathetic.

"Oh," replied Mac, trying his best to sound confident. "I can skate a little."

Selke advised Bucko to practice his skating, which he did faithfully for the next three years. After a stint with the Buffalo farm club, McDonald caught on with the 1935 Detroit Red Wings. The awkward McDonald became an instant favorite with the Olympia Stadium fans and led the Wings to two successive Stanley Cups. He later starred in Toronto and New York.

McDonald played five steady years with Detroit before being dealt to the Maple Leafs on December 19, 1938, for Bill Thoms and $10,000. In Toronto he became an even bigger star, but Detroit is where the

defenseman actually made a name for himself. After scoring one goal and two assists in his 15-game rookie year, 1934-35, McDonald would score four goals and six assists for a total of 10 points in 47 games played in his sophomore year in 1935-36. That same year, McDonald scored three goals in seven playoff games. For his career in Detroit, McDonald tallied 11 goals and 20 assists for 31 total points, which was not bad for a defensive defenseman of his era.

His playmaking skills would improve once he became a Maple Leaf. He reached double figures in assists three different times, including the 1941-42 season, when McDonald recorded 19 assists in only 48 games. That was the same year he made the NHL All-Star Team, clearly his best season. The irony is that McDonald was benched after Toronto lost the first three games of the 1942 finals to Detroit, before Toronto came back to win the next four in a row—and the Cup.

He remained with Toronto until 1944, when Selke, of all people, traded him to the New York Rangers.

McDonald's Rangers experience proved an inglorious end to a career made famous in Detroit. Following his NHL career, Bucko returned to his native Ontario, where he became a distinguished member of the Canadian Parliament.

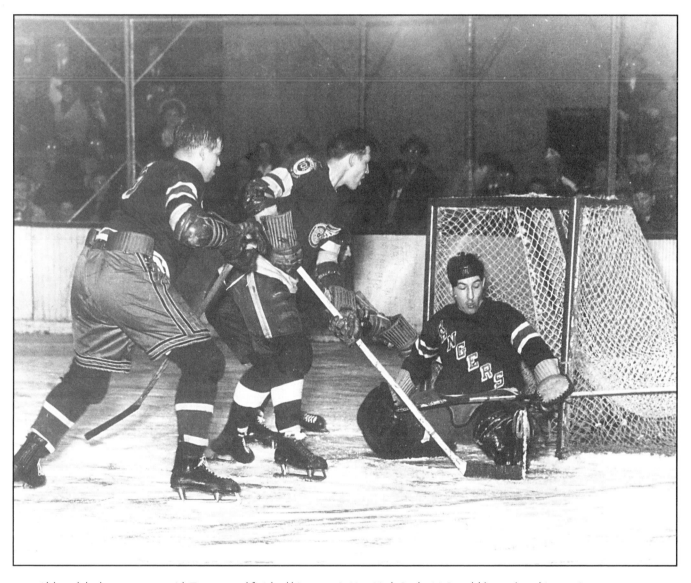

Although he became a star with Toronto and finished his career in New York, Bucko McDonald (center) got his start in Detroit.

50

KIRK MALTBY

BORN: Guelph, Ontario; December 22, 1972
POSITION: Right Wing
NHL TEAMS: Edmonton, 1993-1996; Detroit, 1996-present

Perhaps if the Red Wings had not won the Stanley Cup in the spring of 2002, Kirk Maltby would have gone unnoticed to most of the hockey world outside Detroit.

Overshadowed by the galaxy that included the likes of Sergei Federov. Brett Hull and Steve Yzerman—among other faces—Maltby merely went about the business of being an ace-without-portfolio.

The limelight was for others more talented; all that mattered to Maltby was the business of winning hockey games. And he took care of that business very well.

But when a team rides through four playoff rounds on the Stanley Cup highway even the lesser vehicles occasionally gain a headline.

Such was the case with this native of Guelph, Ontario. During the regular 2001-2002 campaign, Maltby unobtrusively performed Yzerman's duty with precious little fuss or fanfare. His numbers were quiet, 9-15-24, but five of those goals were of the game-winning variety, showing Kirk's knack for big goals.

However, the playoffs proved to be another story; one with a happy ending for Kirk and the Red Wings. Playing on a line with Darren McCarty and Kris Draper, Maltby helped energize a veteran team that occasionally needed its batteries restored.

Dubbed "the Grind Line," Maltby, McCarty and Draper redefined tenacity. And while coach Scott Bowman relied on them primarily for checking purposes, the trio developed a knack for scoring important goals at impromptus times.

Maltby played all 82 games of the regular season and appeared in all 23 post season games. In the playoffs, the bigger the games, the more noticeable Maltby was on the score sheet.

In the first two rounds of the playoffs vs. Vancouver and St. Louis, Kirk only tallied a lone assist. In the Western Conference Finals against Colorado, Maltby had a short-handed goal and two assists. And with the stakes at the ultimate high in the Stanley Cup Finals vs. the upstart Carolina Hurricanes he would register a goal in each of the first two games, the second of which was scored while killing a penalty.

OPPOSITE: Kirk Maltby hoists the Stanley Cup.

A CHRONOLOGY OF 50 MOMENTOUS EVENTS IN RED WINGS HISTORY

1. September 25, 1926—A Detroit syndicate purchases the Victoria (British Columbia) Cougars of the defunct Western Hockey League and moves the team to Detroit. The Cougars play their inaugural season in Canada at Windsor's Border Cities Arena.

2. November 18, 1926—The Cougars lose to the Boston Bruins 2-0, in their first NHL game.

3. November 27, 1926—The Cougars defeat the New York Americans by a score of 4-2 in their second game of the season, recording their first win in franchise history.

4. November 22, 1927—The Cougars lose the first game in their new home, Olympia Stadium on Grand River Avenue, 2-1 to the defending Stanley Cup champion Ottawa Senators.

5. November 15, 1927—After retiring as a player, Jack Adams replaces Art Duncan to begin a storied career with the Detroit franchise in which he would serve as the club's coach and later as general manager.

6. November 27, 1927—With Harry "Hap" Holmes in goal, the Cougars register their first home victory and shutout with a 2-0 win over the Montreal Canadiens.

7. September 29, 1929—Detroit changes team name from Cougars to Falcons at the urging of Detroit media, who believe a new symbol might bring some luck to a club that missed the playoffs the previous season.

8. December 11, 1932—Carl Voss is acquired from the New York Rangers for $5,500. He will go on to score six goals and 14 assists in 38 games to win the first-ever Rookie of the Year award.

9. September 30, 1933—At the NHL Board of Governors meeting, American industrialist James Norris is introduced as new owner of the franchise. Norris renames the club Red Wings, drawing inspiration from the Winged Wheelers of the Montreal Athletic Association for which he had played. The winged wheel logo is chosen to honor the industry that dominates the Motor City.

10. April 3, 1934—After winning their first division title, the Red Wings advance to the Stanley Cup finals for the first time. But Detroit loses to the Chicago Blackhawks three games to one in a best-of-five series.

11. March 24, 1936—In the first game of the playoffs, rookie Moderre "Mud" Bruneteau scores the game-winning goal against the Montreal Maroons four minutes and 46 seconds into the sixth overtime period. At 116 minutes and 30 seconds, the contest remains the longest game in NHL history. Final score: Detroit 1, Montreal 0.

12. April 11, 1936—After finishing the 1935-36 season as the regular season champs, the Red Wings defeat Toronto 3-2 in Game 4 of the Stanley Cup finals to win their first-ever championship.

13. April 6, 1937—Goalie Norm Smith is forced to retire during the first game of the Stanley Cup finals. He joins captain Doug Young, Orville Roulston, and leading scorer Larry Aurie on the sideline with injuries.

14. April 15, 1937—The Red Wings defeat the New York Rangers three games to two, becoming the first team to repeat as both regular season champs and Stanley Cup champs.

15. April 18, 1942—The Maple Leafs defeat the Red Wings 3-1 in Game 7 of the Stanley Cup finals—a series in which Detroit once held a three-games-to-none advantage. It remains one of the most stunning playoff collapses in NHL history.

16. April 8, 1943—The Red Wings finish first in the regular season, posting a 25-14-11 record en route to capturing their third Stanley Cup. The Red Wings swept the Boston Bruins four games to none.

17. January 23, 1944—In Detroit, the Red Wings establish a team record for most goals scored in a game, defeating the New York Rangers 15-0.

18. February 3, 1944—In Detroit, Syd Howe scores six goals against the New York Rangers and establishes a team record for the most goals scored in a game.

19. October 16, 1946—In the home opener against Toronto, 18-year-old Gordie Howe debuts at right wing alongside center Sid Abel and left wing Adam Brown. Howe scores the first of 801 regular season goals, but the game ends in a 3-3 tie.

20. November 11, 1947—Coach Jack Adams assembles a line of Gordie Howe, Sid Abel, and left wing Ted Lindsay. The high-scoring trio soon become known as the Production Line.

21. March 26, 1950—Members of the Production Line—Lindsay, Abel, and Howe—finish one-two-three in NHL scoring. Lindsay leads with 78 points. Abel finishes with 69, followed by Howe with 68.

22. March 28, 1950—Gordie Howe's career is almost ended in a playoff game against Toronto. Checked hard by the Maple Leafs' Ted Kennedy, Howe crashes headfirst into the boards and suffers a fractured skull. He is rushed to Harper Hospital in Detroit and misses the remainder of the playoffs.

23. April 23, 1950—In a Cup finals series that saw the New York Rangers play their "home" games at Maple Leaf Gardens in Toronto because Madison Square Garden was preempted by a circus, the Red Wings get an overtime goal from Pete Babando at 8:31 of the second overtime in Game 7, to give the Red Wings their fourth Stanley Cup.

24. October 29, 1950—In a 2-0 Detroit victory, rookie Terry Sawchuk blanks the Boston Bruins and records the first of his NHL-record 103 regular season shutouts.

25. March 23, 1951—Gordie Howe wins the first of six Art Ross Trophies as the league's leading point scorer, tallying 47 goals and 39 assists in 70 games. He would later receive the first of his six Hart Trophies as the league's Most Valuable Player.

26. April 15, 1952—During the playoffs, with the Red Wings enjoying a seven-game winning streak, diehard fans Pete Cusimano and brother Jerry decide to throw an octopus onto the ice of Olympia Stadium. "It had eight legs and that might be a good omen for eight straight wins," Pete is quoted as saying. Detroit goes on to win the Cup, and the Cusimano brothers hurl the slimy creatures onto the ice at every Detroit playoff game for the next fifteen years.

27. April 16, 1954—A then club record 15,791 fans watch as "Tough" Tony Leswick beats Montreal net minder Gerry McNeil on a screened shot at 4:29 of overtime in Game 7 of the Stanley Cup finals. The Wings defeat the Canadiens 2-1 and win their sixth Stanley Cup.

28. March 17, 1955—On St. Patrick's Day, a riot breaks out at Montreal's Forum after a fan tosses a tear gas bomb at ice level during a Montreal-Detroit game.

29. April 14, 1955—With Detroit again facing the Montreal Canadiens in the Stanley Cup finals, Alex Delvecchio scores two goals in a 3-1 Game 7 victory to give the Red Wings their second consecutive Cup.

30. February 1, 1959—During a regular season game against the New York Rangers, Gordie Howe and Lou Fontinato, then regarded as the NHL's best fighter, erupt into a brutal fight. Howe demolishes Fontinato, shattering the Ranger enforcer's nose as well as his fighting reputation.

31. April 25, 1963—After 35 seasons with the club, Jack Adams resigns as Red Wings general manager. Under Adams, the Red Wings won 12 regular season championships—including seven successive first-place finishes from 1949 to 1955—and seven Stanley Cups.

32. November 10, 1963—In his 1,132nd NHL game, Gordie Howe scores his 545th career goal in a 3-0 win over the Canadiens, breaking the all-time goal scoring record held by Maurice "Rocket" Richard. In the same game, Terry Sawchuk notches his 94th career shutout, tying George Hainsworth for the all-time record.

33. May 5, 1966—Despite losing to the Montreal Canadiens in six games in the Stanley Cup finals, Red Wings goaltender Roger Crozier becomes the first player from a losing team to win the Conn Smythe Trophy as playoff MVP.

34. September 9, 1971—After 25 seasons with the Red Wings, Gordie Howe announces his retirement. He departs holding team records for most games, goals, assists, and points.

35. November 9, 1973—After 22 seasons with the Red Wings and 1,549 NHL games, Alex Delvecchio retires.

36. December 27, 1979—The 19,000-seat Joe Louis Arena opens, becoming the Red Wings' new home.

37. June 22, 1982—Mike Ilitch purchases the Red Wings from Bruce Norris and takes over a team that had fallen on hard times.

38. July 12, 1982—Jim Devellano, who helped build the New York Islanders dynasty of the 1980s becomes Detroit's general manager. By the mid 1990s, Devellano transforms the Red Wings into a perennial Cup contender.

39. June 8, 1983—The Red Wings select Steve Yzerman in the first round (fourth overall) of the NHL entry draft.

40. October 1, 1984—Reed Larson surpasses Red Kelly to become the highest scoring defenseman in Red Wing history.

41. June 17, 1989—Detroit acquires Sergei Federov in the third round (fourth selection, seventy-fourth overall) of the NHL entry draft.

42. February 24, 1993—Steve Yzerman records his 1,000 career point, joining Gordie Howe and Alex Delvecchio as the only players to achieve such a feat in a Red Wings uniform.

43. June 15, 1993—Scott Bowman becomes the 22nd head coach in Detroit history.

44. June 17, 1994—Sergei Fedorov becomes the first Russian-born player to win the Hart Trophy, Frank Selke Trophy, and Lester B. Pearson Award.

45. June 24,1995—In Detroit's first Stanley Cup finals appearance since 1966, the Red Wings lose Game 4 against New Jersey, 3-2, as the Devils sweep the series.

46. December 29, 1995—At Dallas, Scott Bowman sets the NHL record for the most games coached with 1,607, surpassing Al Arbour.

47. January 17, 1996—Steve Yzerman captains Detroit to an NHL-record 62 wins and scores his 500th career goal on the power play against the Colorado Avalanche.

48. March 6, 1996—Goalie Chris Osgood scores a goal in his 100th career game—a 4-2 win over the Hartford Whalers.

49. June 13,1997—Vladimir Konstantinov, Slava Fetisov and trainer Sergei Mnatsakanov are injured in a serious car accident. Konstantinov's playing career is cut short when he suffers near-fatal head injuries.

50. June 7, 1997—After the second longest Stanley Cup drought since the New York Rangers' 54-year dearth, the Red Wings defeat Philadelphia 2-1 to secure their eighth Stanley Cup. Detroit wins the series 4-0.

51. June 16, 1998—For the third time in franchise history, the Red Wings win back-to-back Stanley Cup titles, this time with a four-game sweep over the Washington Capitals.

Best, Worst, and
Most Unusual

Best

Best Goaltender: Terry Sawchuk. Sawchuk backstopped the Red Wings to their five Stanley Cups between 1950 and 1955. He finished his career with 103 shutouts in the regular season, far and away the best mark for a goaltender, and a dozen more in the playoffs. Sawchuk picked up 12 shutouts in one regular season, still a Detroit record, three times in his career (1951-52, 1953-54, 1954-55).

His finest season might have been 1952, when the Red Wings won eight straight playoff games to win the Cup. In that playoff year, Detroit did not surrender a goal in any of their four home games and Sawchuk finished the playoffs with a microscopic 0.62 GAA.

Sawchuk was the first goaltender in the league to crouch in the goal, which allowed him to see pucks with traffic in front of the net. Sawchuk was one of the last goaltenders to use a face mask.

Best Cup-Winning Goals (Game 7 Overtime Winners): Pete Babando (1950), Tony Leswick (1954)

In another case of winning the battle before it is fought, center George Gee (who had five assists in the 1950 playoffs and was considered one of the shrewdest forwards of his era), set up this goal before the puck was dropped. Facing the New York Rangers in the Stanley Cup finals, Detroit found itself in Game 7 at Olympia. On Gee's left wing was Pete Babando, who had scored just one goal in his previous seven playoff games. With the faceoff inside the Rangers' zone, Gee stepped out of the faceoff circle and instructed Babando to move a few inches. Then, Gee won the faceoff cleanly and sent the puck right onto Babando's stick. Babando took the puck in stride and fired a 15-foot backhander that Rangers net minder Chuck Rayner never saw. The puck had eyes, finding its way through a labyrinth of legs and into the net at 8:31 of the second overtime, giving Detroit the first of five Cups in its 1950s dynasty.

Another unsung hero, Tony Leswick, got his moment of glory on April 16, 1954. In Game 7 of the 1954 Cup finals against Montreal, shortly after the four-minute mark of overtime, Leswick took a pass from linemate Glen Skov and fired a relatively weak shot towards Montreal net minder Gerry McNeil. It would have been a routine save for the Montreal goalie except that defenseman Doug Harvey was in the way. An expert baseball player, Harvey thrust his glove in the air to bat the puck out of danger, but only nicked a piece of it. He did manage to alter its trajectory enough to send the rubber over the astonished McNeil and into the net at 4:29 of overtime.

Most Goals in One Game: Six. Long before Gordie joined the club, another great Howe was skating for the Winged Wheels. Syd Howe, a Hall of Fame winger in his own right, started his NHL career with the first-generation Ottawa Senators in 1929. He stayed with the Senators until the team moved to St. Louis in 1934, playing 36 games in the 1934-35 season in the Gateway City. Howe was then sent to the Red Wings, and he wore the Winged Wheel for another 11 seasons. On February 3, 1944, Howe scored six goals in a game against the New York Rangers, leading Detroit to a 12-2 blowout victory. Even after the exploits of the other Howe, as well as many other prolific scorers in Red Wings history, Syd's record still stands today.

Best Playoff Impact By A Rookie: Detroit faced the Montreal Maroons in the opening round of the 1936 playoffs, and the first game, on March 24, 1936 at The Forum in Montreal, was an all-time classic. It stands today as the longest game in NHL history. The two teams combined for 116 minutes and 30 seconds of sudden-death overtime, or nine extra periods of play. The winning goal was scored by the unheralded Modere "Mud" Bruneteau.

Bruneteau was a rookie that year and the youngest man in the lineup for either team. As the game wore on, the players with the most stamina saw an increased amount of ice time. This gave Bruneteau the opportunity to make history.

Bruneteau and linemate Hec Kilrea skated towards the Montreal defense. Bruneteau passed to Kilrea. Kilrea faked a return pass, then slid the puck just over the Montreal blueline. Bruneteau sneaked behind the defense, retrieved the puck, and banged it past Maroons goalie Lorne Chabot for the winning goal.

"Thank God," said Bruneteau years later. "Chabot fell down as I drove it in the net. It was the funniest thing. The puck just stuck there in the twine and didn't fall on the ice."

The victory gave the Wings the momentum they needed to sweep the Maroons, 3-0, and advance to the Stanley Cup finals. Detroit went on to beat Toronto, three games to one, to capture the Stanley Cup. Bruneteau went on to play 10 more seasons with the Red Wings, finishing his NHL career in 1946.

Best Playoff Tradition: The Octopus. During the 1952 playoffs, the Red Wings won seven consecutive playoff games, leaving them just one win away from the Stanley Cup. Brothers Pete and Jerry Cusimano, both diehard Red Wings fans, wanted a symbolic finish to the Cup run.

"My dad was in the fish and poultry business," explained Pete. "Anyway, before the eighth game in '52, my brother suggested, 'Why don't we throw an octopus on the ice for good luck? It's got eight legs and that might be a good omen for eight straight wins.' "

On April 15, 1952, Pete threw his first octopus onto the ice at Olympia Stadium, and Detroit won their eighth straight playoff game to capture the Cup in 1952. Cusimano continued to sling a slimy creature in every Detroit playoff series for the next 15 years.

"You ever smelt a half-boiled octopus?" asked Pete. "It ain't exactly Chanel No. 5, ya know. You should see how the refs jumped!"

Best Goaltender Resurrection: In 1943, hoping to find their goaltender of the future, the Red Wings gave a two-game tryout to a 17-year-old, whose poor performance—13 goals against in the two games—earned him a one-way ticket to New York. But the Rangers, who were deep in goaltenders at the time, sent the kid back to Detroit after just one period on Broadway, thinking that they would never see him again.

That kid's name was Harry Lumley, and he made sure that the Rangers, as well as the rest of the NHL, would see him for a long time. Lumley made the most of his second trip to Detroit, backstopping the Wings for six seasons, sending them to the Cup finals four times, and sipping champagne from the silver chalice in 1950, his last year in Detroit. He finished his Red Wings career with a 163-103-56 record in 322 regular season games in Hockeytown.

After a couple of seasons in Chicago, Lumley played four seasons for the Maple Leafs, then finished his playing days in the Boston Bruins organization, finishing his NHL career with a 330-329-143 record in 804 games.

Worst

Worst Trade Made and Worst Trade Not Made: Jack Adams, 1955. Fresh off of another championship, the Big Red Machine seemed destined to dominate the league for another decade. But that did not come to pass, and many feel that Adams's meddling cost Detroit future titles.

With top goaltender Terry Sawchuk nearing the end of his career and Glenn Hall ready to step into the job, Adams knew he had to make a deal. On June 3, 1955, Adams traded Sawchuk, Vic Stasiuk, Marcel Bonin, and Lorne Davis to the Boston Bruins for Ed Sandford, Real Chevrefils, Norm Corcoran, Gilles Boisvert, and Warren Godfrey.

"Adams was a lousy hockey man," captain Ted Lindsay later told David Shoalts of the *Toronto Globe and Mail*. "He traded nine players from the 1955 team. I'm still mad at Adams because he cheated me out of five minimum and possibly seven or eight Stanley Cups."

Later in the summer, news that a better deal had been left on the table surfaced. Montreal manager Frank Selke Sr. was willing to trade defenseman Doug Harvey even up for Sawchuk, but Adams nixed the deal. "If we had Harvey," said Lindsay, "we would have seven or eight Stanley Cups. Adams didn't want to make the deal because he didn't want to make Montreal stronger. Geez, they won the next five Cups, so how much stronger could you have made them?"

Defenseman Johnny Wilson noted the biggest loss in the exchange that was made. "The players we got back in the trade were of equal ability, but Adams stripped away so many of the regulars that the chemistry that we had in winning the Cups was no longer there."

Worst Overtime Nemesis: Maurice "The Rocket" Richard, 1951. Montreal finished 36 points behind the vaunted Red Wings in the 1950-51 season, and few outside of Montreal expected the Canadiens to be more than a warm up for the defending champions. However, Richard had other ideas.

In Game 1 at Olympia Stadium, Montreal came back from 1-0 and 2-1 deficits to send the game into overtime, 2-2. It was not until the fourth overtime that Richard finally had had enough. He stole a careless Red Wing pass, went around the defense, and beat the legendary Terry Sawchuk upstairs to win the game at 1:09 of the fourth overtime, at 1:10 AM.

In Game 2, Sawchuk and his Habs counterpart Gerry McNeil fought to a scoreless duel at the end of regulation. In the third overtime, Montreal defenseman Bud MacPherson passed to Billy Reay, who faked a shot and sent a pass over to Richard. Sawchuk had no chance on Richard's shot at 2:20 of the third extra session.

Though the Red Wings tied the series with two wins at The Forum in Montreal, the Habs, with 10 rookies on their roster, took out the Red Wings in six thrilling games.

Worst Upset of a Red Wings team: 1994, San Jose Sharks. The Sharks were in their third season in the NHL, and made their first playoff appearance thanks to defensive-minded coach Kevin Constantine and unsung Latvian goaltender Arturs Irbe. As the eighth seed in the Western Conference, the upstart Sharks drew the heavily favored Red Wings, a consensus pick to come out of the West. The Sharks had beaten Detroit just once in their 11 previous meetings.

The Sharks took everyone by surprise by beating the Red Wings at Joe Louis Arena in Game 1, 5-4. But the Red Wings stormed back to take the next two games. In Game Four at San Jose, the Red Wings had a commanding 3-1 lead when the Sharks scored three unanswered goals and tied the series with a 4-3 win. San Jose put Detroit on the brink of elimination with a 3-2 win in Detroit, but the Red Wings pounded the Sharks in Game 6, 7-1, in San Jose. Game 7 was closely contested at The Joe, and with the game tied at 2-2 Wings goaltender Chris Osgood wandered too far to retrieve a puck. His clearing attempt up the left boards was picked off by Jamie Baker, who threw the puck into the goal with just 6:35 remaining in the third period, and the Sharks held on for the victory and the series.

Worst Injury: Gordie Howe, March 28, 1950. Toronto at Detroit, Olympia Stadium. With Toronto clearly in control and time winding down, Maple Leaf' captain Ted "Teeder" Kennedy carried the puck toward the Detroit blue line. The Toronto center was being pursued by two opponents. Defenseman Black Jack Stewart was coming up from behind Kennedy while Gordie Howe cut across at an angle to head him off at the pass. Peripherally, Kennedy spotted Howe an instant before contact and pulled up quickly enough to avoid his check.

Unable to stop his momentum, Howe plunged headfirst into the boards and lay there, unconscious, blood streaming from his nose and eye. "That he was badly injured was evident," said Toronto journalist Ed Fitkin, who wrote a biography of Howe, Ted Lindsay, and Sid Abel. "First reports were that he might lose sight of an eye."

Howe was immediately rushed to the hospital, where it was instantly apparent that his condition was extremely serious. In an era before television had yet taken hold, newspapers were the prime source of information. In this case the Detroit dailies—the *Times, Free Press,* and *News*—rushed "Howe Extras" into the streets. Among the reports were those that stated Howe had suffered a fractured skull, broken nose, and cheekbone.

A prominent brain surgeon was summoned and his examination determined that Howe had suffered an accidental injury similar to one that resulted in the death of a boxer not long before. That is, presuming it was an accident, and there was no presuming in Detroit. Making no bones about their position, the Red Wings accused

Kennedy of butt-ending Howe while attempting to elude him. This prompted even more charges and counter charges from the Toronto camp.

"What happened was that as Kennedy saw Howe coming at him he jumped out of the road and just then Howe lost his balance and went into the boards," explained Max McNab, then in his first full season with the Wings. "Of course in those days there was no such thing as television replay to check it out so everybody had his own version and, naturally, the Detroit people had it in for Kennedy. To hear some of them talk, Kennedy had given our guy a vicious backhander."

"A lot of people in Detroit thought that Kennedy had tried to injure Gordie, but I know Ted Kennedy personally and I can assure you he was not the type of player who would try to injure Gordie Howe," said Wings forward Johnny Wilson years later about the incident.

Meanwhile, Howe's life hung in the balance. His diagnosis included a brain concussion and a fractured nose and cheekbone. Surgery had already been performed to remove fluid causing pressure on the brain. Although his condition was still listed as "serious" some 24 hours after the collision, he was reportedly out of danger and the prognosis was for a recovery.

"We were a mighty sick bunch all the way to [Detroit's playoff base in Toledo, Ohio]," coach Tommy Ivan said. "I've never seen any of the boys that low before. There wasn't one of us who thought about going to bed until we found out that Gordie was okay."

"We were all keyed up anyway over the playoffs," said center Ted Lindsay, "and the injury to Gordie sort of set off the explosion. We blew our tops, but believe me, when there's so much at stake out there, you sometimes get out of control."

Early the next morning word was received in Toledo that Howe had sufficiently improved to allow the Red Wings to refocus on the Maple Leafs. An inspired Red Wings team dispatched Toronto in seven games, then beat the Rangers in overtime of the seventh game of the Stanley Cup Finals. When Pete Babando's goal ended the game, Olympia rocked as it never had before. The thunderous ovation remained at its highest decibel count ever as president Clarence Campbell stepped onto the ice and presented the Stanley Cup to team captain Sid Abel. Then came the *piece de resistance*. A bandage-swathed Howe stepped onto the ice, and the roar redoubled.

Most Tragic Off Season: Summer 1997. The Red Wings ended their 42-year-old Stanley Cup drought with a four-game sweep of the Philadelphia Flyers in the Stanley Cup finals. However, the Red Wings' celebrations were quickly marred by tragedy.

The Red Wings entered the 1996-97 season as the best team in the 1990s not to have won the Stanley Cup. After being upset in the first round by San Jose in 1994, the Wings were swept by New Jersey in the finals in 1995 and then were stunned by the eventual champs Colorado in 1996. Adding depth and toughness to the 1996-97 squad were winger Brendan Shanahan and defenseman Larry Murphy, and the Wings romped through the playoffs and swept the Flyers for their first Cup in 42 years.

However, euphoria turned to anguish just a week after the Cup was won. Defenseman Vladimir Konstantinov, whose superb defensive play and penchant for big hits kept the Flyers' big guns John LeClair and Eric Lindros at bay, and team trainer Sergei Mnatsakanov were badly injured in a limousine crash. Both suffered life-threatening head injuries, and there was concern that Konstantinov had lost all his motor skills, including the ability to speak and walk.

The following season, the Wings turned the tragedy into inspiration for another successful season, finishing the playoffs with a four-game sweep of the Washington Capitals to keep the Cup in Hockeytown. At the end of Game 4 in Washington, the Red Wings brought Konstantinov, wheelchair and all, onto the ice. Teammates took turns pushing the wheelchair around the rink while Konstantinov, with the Cup in his lap, smiled broadly, deeply touched by the gesture.

Worst Playoff Collapse: 1942, Stanley Cup Finals versus Toronto. The Red Wings shocked the hockey world by defeating Toronto in both Games 1 and 2 at Maple Leafs Gardens, then came home and defeated the Leafs, 5-2, at Detroit's Olympia Stadium. Down three games to none in the series, Billy "The Kid" Taylor vowed that his Leafs would win the next four games.

Leafs coach Hap Day shook up his lineup before Game 4, benching veterans Gordie Drillon and Bucko McDonald in favor of rookies. The inspired, desperate Leafs won Game 4, 4-3. Detroit's fiery manager Jack

Adams, displeased with the officiating, rushed onto the ice and tried to start a fight with referee Mel Harwood and was suspended indefinitely by NHL President Frank Calder.

In Game 5, the Leafs' rookies took charge. Don Metz scored a hat trick and two assists, and the Leafs routed the Wings 9-3 at Maple Leaf Gardens. The Red Wings were no better back home, dropping a 3-0 decision at Olympia in Game 6.

In Game 7, Detroit took the lead in the second on a Syd Howe tally, but Sweeney Schriner tied the game for the Leafs at 1-1 early in the third period. Just two minutes later, Pete Langelle gave the Maple Leafs the lead. The desperate Red Wings attacked the Leafs goal with abandon, but the Toronto defense held, and the Leafs scored the backbreaking third goal when none other than Billy Taylor set up Schriner for his second of the game. The Leafs went on to win 3-1 and capture the Stanley Cup.

To this day, this comeback remains an inspiration to all teams that a playoff series is not over until a team notches its fourth victory.

MOST UNUSUAL

Most Unusual Stanley Cup Championship: 1955, Detroit versus Montreal. Towards the end of the season, the Canadiens were ready to break Detroit's streak of six consecutive regular season championships, and Maurice "The Rocket" Richard seemed poised to win the scoring championship. However, with one week to go in the regular season, the Rocket got into a scrum and knocked over linesman Cliff Thompson. Already displeased with the Rocket's hot-tempered antics over the course of the season, NHL President Clarence Campbell suspended Richard for the remainder of the regular season and the entire playoffs. On St. Patrick's Day, March 17, 1955, the Red Wings were in Montreal for the first game of the suspension. As soon as Campbell found his seat at The Forum, a fan attacked him, another set off a tear gas bomb, and soon riots broke out all along St. Catherine's Street. The Red Wings were escorted out of the arena by police, the game was forfeited, and one week later, Detroit picked up its seventh consecutive regular season title. "Boom Boom" Geoffrion of the Habs overtook his teammate Richard for the scoring title. Detroit faced Montreal in the Stanley Cup finals and though they were without Richard, the Habs stretched the series to seven games before Detroit finished them in Game 7 at Olympia Stadium. Had it not been for Richard's temper, Detroit would have had a much tougher ordeal for the title.

Most Unusual Advertisement Deal: Herb Lewis and Camel Cigarettes. It's hard to imagine that a hockey player's career could be helped by cigarettes, but that's exactly the endorsement that Camel got from Herb Lewis in the 1930s. "Herb Lewis of the Detroit Red Wings says: I go for Camels in a big way!" The lightning-quick camera eye caught Herb Lewis before the goal, then in the next split second, he scores. After the game, Herb said: "You bet I enjoy eating. And I'll give Camels credit for helping me enjoy my food. Smoking Camels with my meals and afterwards eases tension. Camels set me right! Camel smokers enjoy smoking to the full. It's Camels for a 'lift.' It's Camels again 'for digestion's sake.' Thanks to Camel's aid, the flow of the important digestive fluids—alkaline digestive fluids—speeds up. A sense of well-being follows. So make it Camels—the livelong day!" Nobody knew whether Herb actually smoked the weeds!

STATISTICS

BEST

TEAM

Most points in a season: 131 points in 82 games in 1995-96. Lost in Western Conference Finals to Colorado. 62 wins, 13 losses, 7 ties.

Longest undefeated streak: 15, November 27 to December 28, 1952 (8 wins, 7 ties).
Home streak: 18, November 19, 1931 to February 28, 1932 (13 wins, 5 ties); December 26, 1954 to March 20, 1955 (13 wins, 5 ties).
Away streak: 15, October 18 to December 20, 1951 (10 wins, 5 ties).

Most goals in a season: 369, 1992-93, in 84 games.

Fewest losses in a season: 13, 1950-51 (in 70 games), 1995-96 (in 82 games).

Most goals in a game by team: 15, January 23, 1944. (New York Rangers 0, Detroit 15)

President's Trophy Winners: 1995, 1996. Runner-Up: 2000.

Fastest five goals in a Red Wings playoff game, both teams: 4 minutes. Los Angeles at Detroit, April 15, 2000. First Period. Scoring: Brendan Shanahan, Detroit, 0:55; Martin Lapointe, Detroit, 1:33; Luc Robitaille, Los Angeles, 2:04; Kris Draper, Detroit, 3:32; Zigmund Palffy, Los Angeles, 4:55. Detroit wins game 8-5 and first-round series 4-0.

Fastest three goals in a Red Wings playoff game, both teams: 27 seconds. Phoenix at Detroit, April 24, 1998. Second Period. Scoring: Jeremy Roenick, Phoenix, 13:24; Mathieu Dandenault, Detroit, 13:32; Keith Tkachuk, Phoenix, 13:51. Phoenix wins game 7-4, Detroit wins first-round series 4-2.

Fastest two goals by one team in a playoff game (NHL record): 5 seconds. Chicago at Detroit. April 11, 1965. Second Period. Scoring: Norm Ullman, 17:35 and 17:40. Detroit wins 4-2. Chicago wins best-of-seven semifinal round, 4-3.

Longest Overtime Win (NHL Record): 116 Minutes, 30 Seconds. Detroit at Montreal Maroons, 1936. Mud Bruneteau scored, assisted by Hec Kilrea, at 16:30 of the sixth overtime, or 176 minutes, 30 seconds after the start of the game. Game ended at 2:25 a.m.; Detroit won the best-of-five, 3-0.

Most shutouts, both teams, one series (NHL record): Toronto versus Detroit, 1945 and 1950. Toronto has three shutouts, Detroit two. Toronto wins 1945 series, 4-3, while Detroit wins 1950 series, 4-3.

Fewest Penalties, Seven-Game series, both teams (NHL Record): 19. Toronto versus Detroit, 1945. Toronto received nine minors, Detroit received 10 minors. Toronto wins series, 4-3.

INDIVIDUAL

Most goals in a game by one player: 6, Syd Howe, February 3, 1944.

Most assists in a game by one player: 7, Billy Taylor, March 16, 1947 (NHL Record).

Most points in a game by one player: 7, Carl Liscombe (November 5, 1942, 3G, 3A), Don Grosso (February 3, 1944, 1G, 6A), Billy Taylor (March 16, 1947, 7A)

Most powerplay goals in a game (NHL record): 3. Syd Howe, March 23, 1939, Montreal 3 at Detroit 7; Dino Ciccarelli, April 29, 1993, Detroit 7 at Toronto 3; Dino Ciccarelli, May 11, 1995, Detroit 5 at Dallas 1.

Moat shorthanded goals by a Red Wing in one regular season (80 game schedule): 10, Marcel Dionne, 1974-75

Most shorthanded goals by a Red Wing in a playoff series: 2. Sergei Fedorov, 1992, first round versus Minnesota. Detroit won series, 4-3.

Most three-or-more-goal games in one playoff year by a Red Wing rookie: 2. Petr Klima, 1988.

Most three-or-more-goal games in the playoffs by a Red Wing: Steve Yzerman has four.
April 6, 1989 3 goals against Alain Chevrier and Chicago (Chicago 5 at Detroit 4)
April 4, 1991 3 goals against V. Riendeau and St. Louis (Detroit 6 at St. Louis 3)
May 8, 1996 3 goals against Jon Casey and St. Louis (Detroit 4 at St. Louis 5)
April 21, 1999 3 goals against Anaheim (Hebert and Jablonski) (Detroit 5 at Anaheim 3)

Penalty Shots taken in a playoff game by a Red Wing: One. Petr Klima beat Allan Bester and Toronto as Detroit beat the Maple Leafs, 6-3, on April 9, 1988.

Fastest two goals by one player in a playoff game (NHL record): 5 seconds. Chicago at Detroit. April 11, 1965. Second Period. Scoring: Norm Ullman, 17:35 and 17:40. Detroit wins 4-2. Chicago wins best-of-seven semifinal round, 4-3.

Game 7 Overtime winners in the Stanley Cup Finals: Pete Babando (1950) and Tony Leswick (1954)

Most shutouts, one playoff year (ties NHL record): 4, by Terry Sawchuk in 1952, out of 8 games.

Most wins by a goaltender in one playoff year (ties NHL record): 16, by Mike Vernon in 1997 (out of 20 games) and Chris Osgood in 1998 (out of 22 games)

Most goals in a season by one player: 65, Steve Yzerman, 1988-89.

Most assists in a season by one player: 90, Steve Yzerman, 1988-89.

Most points in a season by one player: 155, Steve Yzerman, 1988-89.

Most PIM in a season by one player: 398, Bob Probert, 1987-88.

Most shutouts in a season by one player: 12, Terry Sawchuk (1951-52, 1953-54, 1954-55); Glenn Hall (1955-56)

Longest shutout sequence (NHL record): Normie Smith, 1936. In best-of-five series, Smith shut out Maroons 1-0, March 24, in 116:30 of overtime; shut out Maroons in second game, 3-0; was scored against at 12:02 of first period of game three by Gus Marker. Total shutout time: 248 minutes, 32 seconds.

Most seasons with the Wings: 25, Gordie Howe. Total games: 1687. Howe played in 20 playoff seasons with Detroit and Hartford.

Longest coaching tenure: Sid Abel, 1958-59 to 1967-68.

Longest captain tenure: Steve Yzerman, 1986-87 to date.

Most goals in a career: 786, Gordie Howe.
Most assists in a career: 1023, Gordie Howe.
Most points in a career: 1809, Gordie Howe.

Most points by a defenseman in one season: 77, Paul Coffey, 1993-94, 14G, 63A
Most points by a center in a season: 155, Steve Yzerman, 1988-89, 65A, 90A
Most points by a right wing in a season: 103, Gordie Howe, 1968-69, 44G, 59A
Most points by a left wing in a season: 105, John Ogrodnick, 1984-85, 55G, 50A
Most points by a rookie in a season: 87, Steve Yzerman, 1983-84, 39G, 48A

AWARD WINNERS

Art Ross Trophy: Gordie Howe (1951-54, 1957, 1963), Ted Lindsay (1950)
Hart Trophy: Gordie Howe (1952, 1953, 1957, 1958, 1960, 1963), Sid Abel (1949), Ebbie Goodfellow (1940)
Bill Masterton Trophy: Brad Park, 1984.
Lady Byng Trophy: Marty Barry (1937), Bill Quackenbush (1949), Red Kelly (1951, 1953, 1954), Alex Delvecchio (1959, 1966, 1969), Marcel Dionne (1975)
Vezina Trophy: Norman Smith (1937), Johnny Mowers (1943), Terry Sawchuk (1952, 1953, 1955)
Calder Trophy: Jim McFadden (1948), Glenn Hall (1956), Roger Crozier (1965),
Selke Trophy: Sergei Federov (1994), Steve Yzerman (2000)
Conn Smythe Trophy: Roger Crozier (1966), Mike Vernon (1997), Steve Yzerman (1998)
Norris Trophy: Red Kelly (1954), Paul Coffey (1995)
Adams Trophy: Bobby Kromm (1978), Jacques Demers (1987, 1988), Scotty Bowman (1996)

WORST

TEAM

Most losses in a season: 57, 1985-86, in 80 games.
Most goals against in a season: 415, 1985-86, in 80 games.
Fewest wins in a season: 16, 1976-77, in 80 games.
Longest Winless Streak: 19, February 26 to April 3, 1977 (18 losses, 1 tie).
Home streak: 10, December 11, 1985 to January 18, 1986 (9 losses, 1 tie).
Away streak: 26, December 15, 1976 to April 3, 1977 (23 losses, 3 ties).

Longest Losing Streak: 14, February 24 to March 25, 1982
Home streak: 7, February 20 to March 25, 1982
Away streak: 14, October 19 to December 21, 1966

Fewest Goals in playoff series by both teams: 7. Detroit versus Montreal Maroons, 1936. Detroit outscored Montreal 6-1 to win series 3-0.
Fewest Goals in seven-game series by one team: 9. Detroit versus Toronto, 1945. Toronto wins series 4-3. Teams tied for nine goals each in series.

Fewest Goals in seven-game series by both teams: 18. Detroit versus Toronto, 1945. Toronto wins series 4-3. Teams tied for nine goals each in series.

Most Penalties, both teams, one playoff game (NHL record): 66. Detroit at St. Louis Blues, April 12, 1991. Both teams received 33 penalties, an NHL record. The teams combined for 298 minutes, also an NHL record. Detroit received 152 minutes, St. Louis 146, setting individual NHL records for those marks. St. Louis won the game, 6-1.

Fastest goal surrendered from start of period other than the first in a playoff game: 9 seconds. Eric Vail of Atlanta scored against G Ron Low 9 seconds into the third period on April 11, 1978. Detroit won the game 5-3.

Longest overtime game lost in playoffs by Red Wings: 61:09 of extra time needed to decide Canadiens versus Detroit Stanley Cup finals on March 27, 1951, when Maurice Richard scored to give the Montreal the 3-2 win. The Habs went on to win the Cup.

Worst playoff drought: From 1967 to 1986, the Red Wings made the playoffs just four times, losing all four first round series (1970, 1978, 1984, 1985). "They just got rid of so much talent," said [Gordie] Howe. "They made bad trades, the people didn't come up through the system, and they made more bad trades trying to fill the holes." (*Total Hockey* P. 189)

MOST UNUSUAL

Most Unusual Playoff Records: Toronto and Montreal. Though the Red Wings have more aggregate wins than the Maple Leafs (59-58), Toronto has a 12-11 edge in series won. The opposite is true for Montreal, where the Red Wings lead 7-5 in playoff series versus the vaunted Canadiens, but are just 29-33 in aggregate.

Red Wings overtime record in the playoffs (fourth best in NHL) heading into 2001:
Aggregate: 64 games played, 31 wins, 33 losses, no ties.
Home: 39 games played, 16 wins, 23 losses
Road: 25 games played, 15 wins, 10 losses

Most Unusual Goal by a Red Wings rookie: Detroit at Montreal Maroons, 1936. Rookie Mud Bruneteau, recalled from minors just two weeks prior to this game, scored, assisted by Hec Kilrea, at 16:30 of the sixth overtime, or 176 minutes, 30 seconds after the start of the game. Game ended at 2:25 a.m., Detroit won the best-of-five, 3-0.

Detroit's Greatest Defensive Forward

One of the foremost hockey writers of the 20 Century was New Yorker Stan Saplin, who worked for the New York Journal-American. *Saplin wrote the following for* Sport *magazine for its March 1954 edition. The author gave permission for it to be reprinted before his death in March* 2002.

Have you heard of Marty Pavelich? He's a hockey player, a left wing who came up to the majors with the Detroit Red Wings six years ago and has been with them ever since.

We conducted a survey in the Madison Square Garden lobby recently to discover what hockey patrons knew about this young man.

A lady fan who has been attending every home game of the New York Rangers for "Oh, about six years," never heard of him. An equally ardent male customer knew him "very well." He said, "He's with the Blackhawks."

Two veteran New York sportswriters strolled in. One covers eight to ten games each year and sees another five or six as a spectator. "What is this, a gag?" he demanded. "Of course I know who Pavelich is." His first name? "Pete." His team? "Montreal." The other writer was more to the point. "I dunno," he answered.

Twenty people were asked to identify Pavelich. Seven placed him with the Red Wings, but two of these thought he was a defenseman rather than a forward. Only one of the seven was accurate all the way down to the line position, first name, etc. Five couldn't identify Pavelich at all. Three assigned him to the Chicago Blackhawks. Then there was the Montreal reply. Four others were "sure" they had seen him in action but couldn't recall the team he was with.

None of these was a casual visitor to hockey games. They were not necessarily fans who see every contest, but before any interview was permitted to pick up steam, it was established that the subject knew the difference between the crease and the blue line.

Prompt and correct replies to another set of questions verified this. Each was asked to identify three other Detroit players—Ted Lindsay, Gordie Howe and Len (Red) Kelly. These are the stars of the Red Wings, the skaters generally credited with being the reason Detroit holds an unprecedented string of five National League regular season championships. They'll receive additional acclaim if the Wings make it six this season. Everybody we asked knew Lindsay, Howe and Kelly and most people were able to tell us something about each of them.

Lindsay has been the league's All-Star left wing for four years and was the NHL's scoring champion in 1949-50. Howe has won the Hart Trophy as hockey's most valuable player for the past two seasons and has been All-League right wing for three. He took the scoring crown away from Lindsay three years ago and hasn't relinquished it. Kelly, top scoring defenseman in the league, has been on the All-Stars three years and has twice won the Lady Byng Trophy, which is awarded for sportsmanship plus effectiveness.

Only four men in the lineup this year have been members of every one of Detroit's five pennant winning teams. Kelly, Howe and Lindsay are three of them. Marty Pavelich, the man nobody seems to know, is the fourth.

Pavelich has never been up close in the scoring race. He's never been a contender for a league trophy. He's never figured in the voting for All-League selection. Why do they keep him? What has he got?

Jack Adams, general manager of the Detroit club, has often said, "I'm not married to any of my hockey

A case could be made for Marty Pavelich as the NHL's all-time best defensive forward. But Pavelich was also an offensive threat, and Chicago's Hank Bassen discovers.

players." In other words, he never hesitates to get rid of a player he doesn't want.

Since the Wings moved out front to become the Yankees of the ice world, he has disposed of plenty of top-drawer talent. Those sold or traded include Jack Stewart, Sid Abel and Bill Quackenbush, each an All-League performer; Harry Lumley, an excellent goalkeeper; and Leo Reise, a sound and outstanding defenseman.

Pavelich, who averages 11 goals a year in a league in which a player who scores 20 per season no longer

creates excitement, doesn't appear to be on a disposal list. Disposal? "Pavelich is one of the key men around whom we build our hockey club," says Adams.

Marty shares the fate of the blocking back in football, who's essential to the success of a team but who watches the headlines go to the fellow who scores the touchdowns. This comparison is intended to convey only the anonymity of the job, not its function. Pavelich's role as a wing, by title, calls for him to score the goals, not to clear the way for others.

But as the figures show, he doesn't score them.

However, Marty has two qualities which make him something of an indispensable man in the eyes of his bosses, even if those who cast ballots each year for awards and honors fail to recognize or reward him for these attributes.

His primary asset is his ability as a defensive or checking forward, and there is no one in the sport to-day who can match him in this department. Marty draws the assignment of checking the league's great right wings. He's the man who covers Maurice "The Rocket" Richard, hockey's all-time record goal scorer, when Detroit meets the Montreal Canadiens. He's "on" Wally Hergesheimer when they play the Rangers. Against the Blackhawks, Willie Mosienko is his man.

Detroit attained a peak of achievement in 1952 by winning eight straight playoff games. It was much more than coincidence that the forward line headed by Pavelich and containing Tony Leswick and Glen Skov did not permit a single goal to be scored against it throughout the playoffs. In the final round of four games with Montreal—the Toronto Maple Leafs were disposed of in the preliminary round—Marty com-pletely tamed the dangerous Richard, not permitting him so much as an assist, much less a goal.

This left wing's secondary value to his club sug-gests a storybook touch, for it is wrapped around the old rah-rah theme, a rare item these days, at least in professional sports. It is a fact, though, that Pavelich is like a tonic to his teammates. Spirit is an intangible commodity, but Marty clearly bubbles over with it, spreads it among his mates. How many games have been won by the Red Wings as a result of Marty's mo-rale boosting, hustle, and defensive work cannot be es-timated, but the figure must be considerable.

It was spirited labors of this youngster that earned him his big-league chance, shortly after he turned 20, in December of 1947. Marty—his teammates call him Sabu because his black hair and flashing white teeth make him look something like the little Hindu boy in the movies—had turned pro only two months before with Indianapolis of the American League, a Detroit farm. A need developed to plug some holes in the De-troit lineup, and Tommy Ivan, the dapper and quiet little fellow who coaches the champions, took advan-tage of an open date one night to watch the farmhands in a game.

Next morning back in Detroit, in Adams's office at Olympia Stadium, the general manager asked, "Is there anybody down there who can help us?"

"That Pavelich kid won't get us many goals," Ivan replied, "but how the boy works! He'll never stop try-ing." A day later Marty was summoned to the parent club.

Working, in the case of Sabu, means never letting up. A Wing should sail down the ice when his team is on the offense. But when a play is broken up and the opposition takes the puck and swings quickly to the attack, far too many forwards let their men get away. They rely on their defensemen to prevent a goal. Pavelich torments the man he's covering. He makes passing difficult, shots almost impossible, and as often as not he steals the puck. The mere presence of this 170-pounder on ice, players from other teams will tell you, makes it tough to get a goal.

When a Red Wing is sentenced to the penalty box and the team faces the hazardous job of playing five men against six for two minutes, Sabu's defensive skills pay off by preventing enemy scores and saving games.

"Why, it's a job to keep him off the ice even when he's injured," Adams says. "We practically have to put handcuffs on him to hold him down."

Hockey fans in Detroit and the Ontario cities of Sault Ste. Marie and Galt will probably react to our findings in the Pavelich survey with consternation and indignation. A native of Sault Ste. Marie and a per-former in junior amateur ranks at Galt, Marty is ex-tremely popular and very much a sports hero in both communities.

For the small kids playing shinny to the All-League stars on his team, Pavelich (you pronounce it "Pavelitch") has a smile, a word of encouragement and a pat on the back. On the bench or on the ice during a game, he is the Wings' holler guy. On train trips when the club is on the road, Marty plops into a vacant seat next to a player who has been in a slump and offers encouragement.

On the latter point, Red Kelly, Marty's roommate, explains, "Sab's had so much bad luck on scoring goals that a fellow with a little slump going gets to thinking: 'Marty's missed so many goals himself and he isn't down in the mouth. What right have I got to be that way.' At least, it goes something like that—and it works miracles."

Kelly recalled that he was having some trouble in mid-season last year. "I couldn't get my shots away fast enough. My timing or my judgment was bad and I was beginning to walk around with a long face. First thing I knew, Sab had started in on me. He heard my com-plaints and suggested that we work on my shooting after practice.

"That's what we did. Just the two of us in the

rink. He'd stand there with a hatful of pucks and pass them to me . . . to my right, to my left, off the boards and so on. I shook the slump in no time. Imagine the guy, giving up his own time, getting no benefit out of it himself. Just helping me."

Ivan too, offered an illustration of the value of the Pavelich spirit to the club. "I don't know how many times we've gone into the dressing room between the second and third periods a goal or two behind . . . and before I can open my mouth to say a word to the fellows, Marty starts in. Before he's through, he's got them all fired up, and as often as not we'll pull out of the game with a win," the coach said.

Pavelich did just that early this season. The Wings had played three ties in a row, and for the champs that's not good hockey. Their next game was with the Rangers, and they were trailing 1-0; going into the last period. Marty not only got results from others with a fight talk but he set up plays that resulted in a pair of goals to put the team out in front to stay.

Probably the first hockey pep talk ever delivered by Marty Pavelich was to his mother when he was six years old. He went through some soft ice in Sault Ste. Marie when he was indulging in shinny and almost drowned. A minister walking by rushed to his aid and took him home. When his mother got over the initial shock of the near tragedy, she ruled, "You'll never play hockey again!"

"I loved the game so much, even then," Marty recalls. "I talked her out of it, eventually."

After playing in midget hockey ranks, he moved up to the juvenile classification at Sault Technical School where he got his first formal coaching from a coach who had never skated in his life. His name was Ben Littner and Marty still remembers his teaching—endless chalk talks, shooting against mats over and over, penalty killing, passing. "I really got my grounding in the fundamentals under Mr. Littner," Pavelich says. "Joe Klukay, who's with the Boston Bruins, was one of his players, too. Tech won the city title about six times."

When Sabu was 15, a Red Wing scout, Fred Cox, saw him and offered him a berth with the Galt Red Wings, then a Detroit-sponsored junior team. He played three seasons there, two under Al Murray and one under Normie Himes, both former National Leaguers. One of his opponents in league games there was Red Kelly.

Detroit brought Marty in from Galt at the end of the 1946-47 season and the following fall sent him to Indianapolis. He played only 26 games before joining the Red Wings.

His NHL debut was marked by two unique developments. In his first game, Pavelich likely played a shorter time than any man before him. In the second, he undoubtedly registered the fastest goal ever scored.

In his first appearance in the league, against Toronto, Marty was on the bench when Ivan suddenly called for a change of lines while play was on and signaled for the rookie to go in. Pavelich climbed over the boards to replace a skater coming off, and as he hit the ice, a linesman detected a player offside and blew his whistle to stop play. During the pause, Ivan decided to send out a different line and Marty returned to the bench, where he remained for the rest of the game. He estimates he "played" a half-second that evening.

The next game was against Chicago three nights later. In the first period, Ivan sent him out, again on the fly, to replace Ted Lindsay. The action was heading for the Chicago net and Pavelich skated furiously in that direction. He reached his destination just as goalie Emile Francis was brushing aside a shot by Gordie Howe. The rookie got his stick on the puck instantly and poked it into the net before Francis could wheel around to defend against the rebound. Not more than five seconds had elapsed from the moment he left the bench until he scored his first major-league goal.

Pavelich, who is of Croatian descent, might have made his way in baseball had he not preferred hockey. A catcher and a hard-hitting left-handed batter, he played in both junior and senior company at Galt. In the summer of 1946, Dick Fisher, a scout for the Brooklyn Dodgers, invited him to Olean, New York, for a tryout. On the strength of his showing there, the Dodgers offered him a contract and wanted to send him to their club at Zanesville, Ohio. He declined, however.

In 1947, he accepted an invitation to a St. Louis Cardinals tryout camp at Hamilton, Ontario, and again was offered a contract. This was just before he entered pro hockey, and he refused once again. In '49, while he was in Boston with the Red Wings, Jeff Jones, a scout for the Braves, attempted to interest Marty in a baseball career, but again he elected to stay with hockey.

Marty's baseball activities these days are confined to summer ball in his hometown where as playing coach of the Lock City Beverages nine, he has led his team to the city senior title five years running.

Since last summer he has been an off-season sales representative for the Carling's brewery in the Soo. He did well in his first year at the job and he expects to stick with it, and perhaps make it a 12-month job after he is through with hockey. The Red Wings, however, don't plan to release this underrated hockey player to full-time beer selling for some time yet.

THE GREATEST DETROIT
RED WINGS TEAM OF ALL TIME

When discussions about hockey dynasties develop, experts invariably mention the Detroit club constructed by Jack Adams in the post-World War II years starting with the 1949-50 season.

Although Adams had already crafted a magnificent club in 1947-48 and again in 1948-49, the Toronto Maple Leafs won the Stanley Cup in both years.

But it wasn't until the maturation of right wing Gordie Howe—and his insertion on the Production Line with left wing Ted Lindsay and center Sid Abel—that the dynasty-to-be finally took shape.

During the 1949-50 season, Howe—along with Maurice Richard—became the predominant forward in the NHL.

Gordie scored 35 goals—matching his total for the previous three years—and added 33 assists for a point total of 68. For the second consecutive season he was voted to the second team of All-Stars, again finishing behind Rocket Richard in the voting for the right wing position. More important, Howe was the league's third highest scorer. Only his linemates, Lindsay and Abel, compiled higher point totals.

The Production Line had become one of the best in the history of professional hockey and Howe, more mature and confident, blended in perfectly. For hockey fans of that era, there were few greater thrills than watching this Motor City trio on a rush into enemy ice. The Production Line helped Detroit to a first-place finish that year, and the Wings were favored to win the Stanley Cup.

It was at that point, at the start of the semifinal round, that Howe was struck down, nearly for life.

There was an air of optimism around Detroit's Olympia Arena on March 28, 1950, as the Red Wings prepared for an opening round against the Maple Leafs. Detroit had finished the regular season schedule 14 points ahead of third-place Toronto. Jack Adams frankly told reporters: "There'll be no alibis if we don't take the Cup. Barring injuries, we have the team we think can take it."

But the Red Wings were confronted with two very significant obstacles, both mental. They realized that the Maple Leafs had won the Stanley Cup for three consecutive seasons, the last time with a fourth-place club. Furthermore, the Leafs had won 11 straight playoff games from Detroit and had knocked the Wings out of the running for three straight seasons.

On the eve of the opening game, headlines in the *Toronto Globe and Mail* pretty well summed up the feeling in the respective camps: "Leaf Boss Prescribes Hard, Honest Toil for Cup Retention . . . Wings Feel Leaf Jinx Has Run Its Course."

The bitterness that flamed among the players on the opposing teams was reflected best by Ted Lindsay. "This is our profession. It's a game you get paid for—but when it comes to the Leafs, we'd play them for nothing."

In the first period, Marty Pavelich and Fleming Mackell slugged it out. Red Wing Pavelich bloodied Mackell's nose, and both received major penalties. Later, Bill Juzda, the tank-like Leaf defenseman, and Howe swung freely at each other, and both were sent off the ice with major penalties.

Neither team scored in the first period, but after ten seconds of the second, Max Bentley of the Leafs outdrew Max McNab and got the puck to Bill Barilko. The huge defenseman saw Joe Klukay scooting to the right side. Klukay called for a pass, got it, and flipped a backhander past Detroit goalie Harry Lumley.

Additional goals by Barilko, Johnny McCormack, and Cal Gardner fortified Toronto with a 4-0 lead as the clock ticked away toward the middle of the third period. The Red Wings' cause appeared hopeless as Toronto captain Teeder Kennedy methodically lugged the puck out of his territory toward the Detroit goal.

Kennedy was six feet from the left boards as he reached center ice. Behind him in pursuit was defenseman Jack Stewart of the Wings. Sweeping in from the right side was Howe, who attempted to crash Kennedy amidships. Howe was a trifle too slow to hit Kennedy with full force, and it appeared that the best

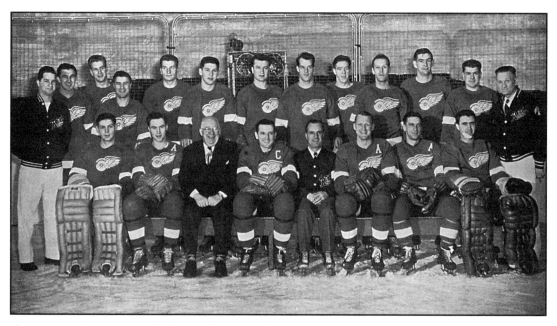

The greatest Red Wings team of all time—the 1951-52 edition—winners of eight straight playoff games including

he could do would be to graze the Leaf player and throw him off balance.

But Howe appeared to miss even that opportunity, and as Kennedy stopped short and then pressed forward, Howe tumbled, face first, into the thick wooden side boards.

"I don't know how he got it," said a worried-looking Kennedy in the noisy Leafs dressing room after the game. "I avoided his check along the boards and didn't feel anything hit me, although he may have struck my stick. It could have happened when he crashed into the boards."

Seconds after Howe rammed the boards, his face was a bloody pulp, and he lay unconscious on the ice. He had suffered a stiff concussion of the head, a bruised cheekbone, and a broken nose. As 13,659 fans sat awestruck by the scene, he was carried off the ice on a stretcher and removed to Harper Hospital. Doctors there described his condition as serious.

His head injuries were indeed so serious that the doctors ordered him into the operating room, where neurosurgeons probed for additional injuries. They decided to operate to relieve pressure on his brain. For several hours there was doubt that Howe would survive the ordeal. He did survive the first-night crisis, but he remained in critical condition.

The episode was hardly finished. What started out as a typical brushfire feud between the two rival teams, would soon erupt into one of the biggest conflagrations in the league's history. It was fed by verbal gasoline poured on by antagonists from both sides. The Red

Wings camp charged that Kennedy had purposely injured Howe.

By the time the opening face off approached for the second game of the semifinals, on Thursday, March 30, a pitch of bitterness of infinite intensity had been reached. In the Red Wings dressing room players were chanting, "Win this one for Gordie."

In the Maple Leafs dressing room there was a grim feeling that the Detroiters were going to try to "get" Kennedy.

They were right, but it is doubtful that the Toronto players had any idea of the extent of the brutality they would encounter.

"Somebody pulled an invisible trigger," said Jim Vipond, sports editor of the *Globe and Mail*, "and mayhem broke loose."

It started when Lee Fogolin sent Kennedy rolling to the ice with a stick trip. As play halted and referee Butch Keeling thumbed Fogolin to the penalty box, Ted Lindsay rushed up and cross checked Kennedy to the ice. Gus Mortson flew at Lindsay, and fights broke out all over the ice.

Veteran onlookers were stunned by the panoply of terror. "This writer," said Vipond, "has often avowed that no player would intentionally injure another player, but not after tonight. There could be nothing more brutal and deliberate than the Detroit players' attempt to even a trumped-up injustice to one of their mates."

The fighting finally subsided, but it erupted again in the final minutes of the third period, when several other battles kept the referee on a belt line to the penalty box. When the ice had cleared, the Wings had won the game. They trooped happily into their dressing room with Lindsay at the head of the march yelling, "We won it for Gordie."

Meanwhile, Howe was still in critical condition in Harper Hospital. Doctors had refused to permit him to hear the game or to be told the result until the following day.

Kennedy emerged from the fracas with more dignity than most. He had not backed away from any of his assailants, and he left the ice with a discolored eye and a cut above his lip. "He was supposed to be slowed up because of a charley horse, " said his boss, Conn Smythe. "He played a terrific game. His line scored our only goal and had no goals scored against it. He's still the greatest hockey player in the world."

Across the hall, Detroit's manager Jack Adams was saying, "The Red Wings are champions of the world... and don't forget we played without the greatest player in the world—Gordie Howe."

All Kennedy would say was, "The game's over. They won it."

Referee Bill Chadwick ruled the third game, played at Maple Leaf Gardens, with an iron hand. The Leafs scored twice in the second period on goals by Joe Klukay and Max Bentley and won the game, 2-0, to take a 2-1 lead in the series.

Detroit tied the series with a 2-1 victory in the fourth game; then the Leafs went ahead again, blanking the Wings 2-0, to skate to within a game of winning the bloody series. But Detroit still had some energy left, even though it now was apparent that their star, Gordie Howe, would be lost to them for the playoffs.

They defeated Toronto 4-0 in the sixth game, carrying the semifinal to a seventh and deciding game at Detroit.

The final game of the 1950 series is regarded as one of hockey's classics. The teams battled through three periods of regulation time without a goal. Checking remained close through the opening eight minutes of the sudden-death overtime. That night Olympia Stadium was not for the weak-hearted.

Coach Tommy Ivan sent out a line of George Gee, Steve Black, and Joe Carveth against Toronto's Max Bentley, Fleming Mackell, and Vic Lynn. The Leafs had Bill Juzda and Bill Barilko on defense, while Detroit's defenders were Jack Stewart and Leo Reise.

Gee, Black, and Carveth launched a dangerous rush for the Wings, backed by Stewart and Reise. Several times the puck bounced dangerously close to the

goal line, only to be cleared, but the Leafs couldn't quite get the disk out of their own zone. Finally, Gee captured the puck and slid it across the ice to Reise, who was standing near the blue line 60 feet from the goal.

Turk Broda appeared to have the short side blocked with his skate, pad, and stick. But the puck bounced over Broda's stick and hit the back of the net. Detroit won 1-0.

The final round against the New York Rangers might have been anti climactic except that it, too, was decided in sudden-death overtime in the seventh game. In fact, the Wings and Rangers went into the second overtime before Detroit's Pete Babando took a pass from George Gee and backhanded a 15-foot shot past goalie Chuck Rayner to give the Wings a 4-3 victory and the Stanley Cup.

Gordie Howe was in the arena that night, and when the ancient silver mug was pushed out to center ice, the 13,095 fans spontaneously chanted: "We want Howe! We want Howe!" As Gordie gingerly stepped on the ice, Lindsay grabbed his hat and sent it flying into the stands. Then he tapped the head of his star linemate and joked, "You big lucky stiff. You sit in the seats and watch us go out and make a couple of thousand dollars for you."

When the ceremony on the ice had ended, Howe was given the Cup, and he carried it through the milling, cheering crowd to the Detroit dressing room. He was well on his road to recovery, ready for even greater accomplishments than before.

Less than three months after his near-fatal injury, Howe was well enough to start playing baseball in the Northern Saskatchewan League. By the time he reported to the Red Wings training camp, he was in near-perfect-condition; as the 1950-51 season opened, Howe pronounced himself ready to go.

Still, Howe's teammates and opponents wondered if Gordie would play as aggressively as he had before the accident. Howe answered these doubts—and perhaps his own fears as well—in the best of possible ways. He scored 43 goals and added 43 assists, good enough to lead the league in both goals and total points.

The Wings again finished first, only to be upset by Montreal in the first round of the Stanley Cup playoffs. But the loss of the Cup was no fault of Howe's. He had four goals and three assists in the six-game series.

The embarrassing demise of the Red Wings from the Stanley Cup playoffs in April, 1951, stung the Detroiters to the core. They vowed to avenge the calamity, and in the following season they did so with a vengeance. Gordie led the league in scoring for the second straight year, and his colleagues finished atop the NHL, winning 44 games, precisely the number they had captured the previous year.

Haunting the Red Wings, however, was their hasty exit in 1951. More troubling was the fact that the Red Wings would go up against the Maple Leafs in the opening round. The Toronto sextet had enjoyed more success against the Wings than any other club, winning four and tying four in 14 games. "The breaks," said Jack Adams, "will be decisive in the series."

As events later indicated, Adams had uttered the understatement of the half-century. If breaks were needed, the mighty Red Wings would somehow manufacture them. Whatever Adams's club did, it did right.

The Wings opened the postseason with a four-game romp over Toronto, but neither Lindsay nor Abel would allow a letdown against the second-place Montreal Canadiens, who faced them in the 1952 Stanley Cup Finals. But if any Red Wing needed reassurance, it was 22-year-old goalie Terry Sawchuk, who was already being hailed as "Hockey's New Mister Zero."

Acclaimed as the best young goaltender in all of hockey, Sawchuk nevertheless had been in goal the previous year when Rocket Richard and the Canadiens knocked Detroit out of the playoffs. Coach Tommy Ivan was doing everything possible to perfect Sawchuk's near-flawless style for the Canadiens series.

The Canadiens knew that Sawchuk feared the Rocket, and they knew he had one soft spot in his goaltending repertoire. "His weakness," said Montreal coach Dick Irvin, "is a shoulder-high shot on the right side. Personally, I think we'll have the Stanley Cup by April 19th. Remember that."

Sawchuk was hardly the picture of overconfidence, especially when he discussed Richard. "No matter where the Rocket shoots from, said Sawchuk, "it's always on the net. His backhand is even tougher than his forehand, and he shoots a heavy puck. When you stop it, it feels like it's going through you."

But once the series started, the Rocket's best shots were blunted by Sawchuk, and Detroit won the opening game 3-1. There were just too many stars in the Red Wings galaxy for even the mighty Canadiens to handle. One of them was Red Kelly, who could score goals as handily as he could defend against them. Even Montreal's high command recognized that.

Montreal's managing director Frank Selke said: "Kelly is as good a player as I've seen in my long connection with hockey. More than that, he exemplifies everything that is desirable in a young man, and the Detroit club is fortunate to have a man of his integrity and character in its lineup."

By contrast, Lindsay was the hard-nosed type, and he thought nothing of shoving his stick across an enemy's face or ramming him from behind. As a result, Lindsay was a marked man throughout the league, especially in Montreal. "I take the boos right along with the cheers, if any," Lindsay said. "With the price a fan pays for his ticket, he gets the right to howl at me. I expect it."

It was Lindsay who bounced the puck off defenseman Butch Bouchard's chest in the second game of the finals, to give the Red Wings a 2-1 victory and a 2-0 series lead. When the teams moved on to Montreal, Howe took over and scored twice, leading Detroit to a 3-0 triumph. "The Red Wings," said the Canadian Press, "stand on the threshold of the greatest Stanley Cup sweep in the modern-day, big-league game."

An eight-game sweep was unthinkable in the Stanley Cup playoffs. Surely, a team, no matter how powerful, would suffer a letdown along the route, or the enemy would obtain a surplus of breaks, or the hometown crowd would provide a lift to the contenders and encourage them to win at least one game. At least this had always happened in the past.

But there never had been a player like Gordie Howe before. "They should use two pucks every time Detroit plays," said Hap Day, who had coached Toronto to three straight Stanley Cup wins from 1947 through 1949. "Give one to the other team and the second one to Howe. He's always got the puck anyway."

Curiously enough, Howe did not score a single goal in the fourth and final cup match. Metro Prystai scored twice, and Glen Skov scored once, to spearhead the Wings to another 3-0 triumph and the Stanley Cup in an astonishing eight-game sweep.

Clearly this team was one of the strongest collections of hockey players ever to skate in the NHL. At first Jack Adams was cautious. After the first round he had been asked whether the 1951-52 edition was the greatest Detroit hockey team of all time. Adams said that critics would have to wait until the Wings had finished the final round against the Canadiens. When that was over, he was emphatic about his club's niche in hockey history: "This is the best-balanced club I've had in 25 years in the NHL. I'll let the figures speak for themselves and let any other club try to match them."

The Detroit dynasty had been built, and as Adams pointed out, the figures spoke for themselves. Between 1949 and 1955 the Red Wings finished first seven consecutive times and won the Stanley Cup in 1950, 1952, 1954, and 1955.

THE LONGEST GAME

If one were trying to select *the* most notable game in Detroit Red Wings history there would be several choices.

One would certainly be the seventh game of the 1950 Stanley Cup finals which extended into two overtime periods before Detroit won on Pete Babando's screened shot.

Another would be the seventh game of the 1955 finals in which Alex Delvecchio single-handedly beat the Montreal Canadiens for the Cup.

But for totally unforgettable drama, one—and only one—game takes the top spot. That would be the longest game in big-league hockey history.

Here's how it happened:

In 1935-36 the National Hockey League was still divided into two sections; a Canadian Division including the Montreal Maroons, Toronto Maple Leafs, New York Americans and Montreal Canadiens, and an American Division including the Detroit Red Wings, Boston Bruins, Chicago Blackhawks and New York Rangers. The Maroons finished first in the Canadian Division and the Red Wings were the American Division champions. According to the system of the day, the two first-place teams would meet in the opening round of the Stanley Cup playoffs.

Judging by their respective records, which were almost identical, the Maroons and the Red Wings would be in for a difficult series with bookmakers at a loss as to whom to list as the favorites. The opening game of the series at the Montreal Forum on March 24, 1936, proved how evenly matched they were.

Led by Hooley Smith, Baldy Northcott and Jimmy Ward, the Maroons presented one of the most formidable attacks in the league. Detroit, however, was strong up front, too. The Red Wings' first line of Marty Barry, Herbie Lewis and Larry Aurie had an impressive season with Barry winning the scoring championship in the American Division.

Despite the notable scorers on both teams three periods of play elapsed without either club scoring a goal. This meant sudden-death overtime, the first team to score winning the game. Although the Forum crowd was excited about the prospect of sudden death, there was some reason to suspect this might be an exceptionally long one. For one thing both teams were getting excellent goaltending from Normie Smith in the Red Wings cage and from Lorne Chabot of the Maroons. For another, there was precedent for a marathon match. On April 4, 1932, the Toronto Maple Leafs and Boston Bruins played past 1 a.m. in what had been the longest NHL game on record.

By the time the Maroons and the Red Wings had played through the second overtime without a goal, the crowd began to get restless. The players, of course, were laboring on badly chopped ice that didn't have the benefit of modern resurfacing machines in vogue today. Nevertheless, they plodded on past midnight with no end in sight.

When the sixth period began, a cascade of cheers went up from the previously numbed crowd. Perhaps they hoped to inspire the Maroons to a spirited rush and a score, but this didn't happen. Neither team scored, and the teams moved into the seventh period as a handful of fans streamed to the exits.

Despite the hour, the majority of spectators remained in their seats. By now the monumental contest became an obsession with both players and fans and everyone seemed determined to see it through to a conclusion, no matter what happened. Nothing very much happened in the seventh period, but the eighth—or fifth-sudden death—period loomed as the decisive one.

Near the end of the period, Marty Barry, the Red Wings' accomplished center, was approaching collapse. With what energy he had at his command, Barry sent a pass to Herbie Lewis that catapulted his wing into the clear for a play on goal. He moved into striking distance and released a hard shot that obviously beat goalie Lorne Chabot. As Lewis prepared to raise his stick in the traditional victory salute he heard the puck clang off the goal post. It rebounded harmlessly to the corner where Hooley Smith retrieved it and began a counterattack with as much danger as Lewis's play.

Baldy Northcott accompanied Smith on his rush. There was a choice; either Smith could make the play himself, using Northcott as a decoy, or he could try the pass. At first, Smith cut sharply toward the net, giving the impression he would go it alone. But at this precise moment, he skimmed he puck to Northcott who shot hard at the Red Wing net. However, Normie Smith anticipated the play, caught the puck on his pad, and steered it to teammate Doug Young who reversed the field.

Now, it appeared that each team was bent on wild kamikaze attacks in the hopes of bringing the game to a sudden end. Young raced along the boards until he reached Maroon territory. Then he fired wildly, but the puck suddenly hit Maroon defenseman Lionel Conacher's skate and changed direction, sliding straight for an empty side of the net. It appeared to be equidistant between Young and goalie Chabot. The Red Wing skater lunged for it, but before he could get his stick on the rubber, Chabot smothered it with his glove. Shortly thereafter the period ended and the teams had completed eight scoreless periods of play.

Four minutes and 46 seconds after the ninth period began, the teams had broken the longest-game record set by Toronto and Boston, and still there was no end in sight. It was past 2 a.m. and many of the spectators were fighting to keep their eyes open, not wanting to miss the decisive goal if it ever was to be scored.

By this time the veterans of both teams were fatigued beyond recovery. It was essential to employ the players with the most stamina, and naturally, those with even a smidgen of energy remaining were the inexperienced young skaters. One of them was Modere "Mud" Bruneteau, a native of St. Boniface, Manitoba, who had just one season ago played for the Wings' minor-league team, the Detroit Olympics. He was the youngest man in the longest game, equipped, Jack Adams believed, with the strongest legs. Adams was the Detroit coach and he remembered, "The game settled into an endurance test, hour after hour. One o'clock came, and then 2 A.M., and by now the ice was a chipped, brutal mess. At 2:25 I looked along our bench for the strongest legs, and I scrambled the lines to send out Syd Howe, Hec Kilrea and Bruneteau.

As a rookie on a loaded first-place club, Bruneteau saw very little action during the season and scored only two goals while achieving no assists for a grand total of two points. But he was young, and at the 12-minute mark of the ninth period, young Mud Bruneteau was in a lot better shape than most of his teammates or opponents.

Adams's instructions were typically explicit. "Boys, let's get some sleep. It's now or never!"

Bruneteau surrounded the puck in the Detroit zone and passed it to Kilrea. They challenged the Montreal defense, Kilrea faking a return pass then sliding it across the blue line. Bruneteau cut behind the defense and retrieved the puck. "Thank God," he says, "Chabot fell down as I drove it in the net. It was the funniest thing. The puck just stuck there in the twine and didn't fall on the ice."

There was a dispute when the goal judge neglected to flash his red light, but referee Nels Stewart arbitrated. "You bloody right it's a goal!" Stewart announced, and he put up his hand as a signal. After 116 minutes and 30 seconds of overtime the Red Wings had defeated the Maroons 1-0.

There was a wild, capering anticlimax. Bruneteau's sweater was removed, not delicately, by his relieved associates. One fan thrust a $20 bill on Bruneteau as he left the ice. Other spectators reached for their wallets. "There I was, my stick under one arm and my gloves under another, and," laughing, "I grabbed money in every direction!"

When he reached the Detroit dressing room, Bruneteau tossed a bundle of bills on a rubbing table. "Count it," he told Honey Walker, the trainer, "and split it for the gang." The windfall was gratifying for professionals in a Depression year: $22 for each member of the Wings, including Adams, Walker and the stickboy.

Mud Bruneteau's shot went into the net at 16:30 of the sixth overtime or 2:25 a.m. Eastern Standard Time. Normie Smith, who was playing in his first Stanley Cup game, was limp when it was over. He had stopped 90 shots in all. "We were all pretty much all in," Smith recalled years later, "but very happy."

Meanwhile, Bruneteau sat on his bed in Montreal's genteel Windsor Hotel near 5 a.m. on March 25, 1936, still unwinding from a Stanley Cup playoff match that he had won for Detroit Red Wings less than three hours before. He was about to undress after a beer celebration when there was a knock on the door. He sat very still, not caring to be disturbed. The knocker persisted. Finally Bruneteau let his visitor in, somewhat startled to recognize the Montreal goalkeeper he had beaten to end the weary marathon. Lorne Chabot, dark eyes staring under a thicket of black brows, had come to call.

"Sorry to bother you, kid," Chabot said, "but you forgot something when you left the rink." Then, handing Bruneteau a puck, "Maybe you'd like to have this souvenir of the goal you scored."

Bruneteau once mused, "Can you imagine that

such a great man as he would do such a thing for a rookie? I remember him standing there in the door, big, handsome guy with a kind of fat-looking face. I felt, I guess, funny. He came in and we sat on the bed, and talked for a long time."

Bruneteau was a journeyman, mutely remote from stardom until one goal left him with reverberating notoriety. Afterward, apart from 35 goals scored in the wartime season of 1943-44, he was undistinguished.

"The publicity never ended," he said. "It could've happened to a lot of guys who were better players. I was just another guy named Joe."

Adams's gratification paused short of hoping prolonged games would become habitual. "Rotten ice produced rotten hockey that was torture for the players and boring for the fans. I knew the NHL had to do something."

Adams discovered what to do in the spring of 1938, when the Red Wings and Montreal Canadiens toured Europe. "I noticed one night at an ice show that attendants swept the surface with sheepskin brushes and then flooded it before the next show." He recommended ice-flooding between periods to the NHL governors, and in 1940-41 resurfacing became mandatory. "That legislation speeded up play, because it meant the players didn't have to skate through slush late in the game. It convinced me that there'll never be any approach to Bruneteau's overtime record. There are too many shots and too much wide-open play to permit long stretches with no goals."

The impetus gained from the Red Wings' marathon opening-game win was enough to lift the Red Wings to a three-straight playoff victory over the Maroons and a four-game win over the Toronto Maple Leafs for the Stanley Cup. Smith, the other hero of the marathon match, lost both trophies he had hoped to win as souvenirs.

His goalie stick was autographed by every member of the Red Wings but somehow wound up in the hands of a Judge John Scallen. "I also was supposed to get half the puck that was in play at the finish of the game," said Smith, "but I don't know what became of that."

Nor did he get his name inscribed in the record book that lists the longest game. That honor was bestowed on Modere (Mud) Bruneteau, the rookie who had scored only two goals all season.

WHY GORDIE HOWE—
AND NOT WAYNE GRETZKY—
IS THE GREATEST PLAYER
OF ALL-TIME

BY STAN FISCHLER

Who was the greatest hockey player of all-time?
Contemporary experts would have you believe that Wayne Gretzky holds that distinction. However, those experts would be wrong.

In making a serious comparison about the two many factors must be involved in the decision.

For starters, one must make a notable distinction between GREATEST and MOST PROLIFIC.

Gordie Howe, who launched his NHL career in 1946-47 and concluded it in 1979-80, is the greatest player of all time for a very simple reason: he could do more things better in a hockey game than anyone who ever laced on a pair of skates.

He shot better. He hit harder. He checked better and he could pass with Gretzky on the best playmaking day Wayne ever had.

Not to mention the intimidation factor. Take Mark Messier in his prime, multiply him by ten, and you begin to understand why Howe was so feared.

There were many ways to describe Howe's game because it was so multi-dimensional. But former New York Rangers right wing Aldo Guidolin once summed up the prevailing opinion on Gordie's stickhandling: "Howe plays the 'funny kind of game'—he doesn't let anyone touch the puck." One reason for that was Gordie's ambidextrous shooting ability. By switching hands, he could fire equally as well from either side. No other superstar could make that statement.

Oh, sure, there are dozens of "experts" out there in the uncivilized hockey world who swear by Gretzky but they are what is commonly known as Wayne-lov-ers-come-lately. How could they possibly judge Gordie Howe when they never saw him in his Detroit Red Wings prime, from the late 1940s through the late 1960s?

But talk to a deeply knowledgeable hockey person, such as Hall of Fame referee Red Storey, who watched both Gretzky and Howe in their respective primes, and you obtain an exquisitely accurate appraisal.

"If Gordie had played in the (watered-down) NHL the way it is today," said Storey, "he'd have had 1,000 goals, instead of 801, and Gretzky never would have caught him. Howe was a marvel playing after he was 50. He and (Canadiens defenseman) Doug Harvey were the best natural athletes I've known."

The Howe vs. Gretzky debate really isn't one because Gordie was the quintessential multi-dimensional player. Why, Gordie could even be a defenseman—which he was when the Red Wings were in need of backliners in the early 1960s—and no doubt would have been an excellent goaltender if ever put between the pipes.

Then, again, how would most of you know, if you hadn't had the luxury of seeing Howe in his prime. But legendary Canadian broadcaster, Foster Hewitt, did and succinctly observed:

"Everything you can think of in hockey, Howe is."

Beyond Howe's cache of talent was muscle on top of muscle. In the frontier-era during which he played—also known as "old-time hockey"—superstars were expected to fight their own battles and, remarkably, they did. Not only did they go toe-to-toe on a regular basis but they did so without the aid of henchmen to fight their battles. Like Dave Semenko, Marty McSorley and Jeff Beukeboom.

Like it or not, fighting has been part of hockey since the introduction of the rubber puck.

During that century of stickhandling, there never has been a superstar who could fight as well as Howe. During the 1958-59 season, for example, Gordie was challenged by the then alleged NHL heavyweight champion, Lou Fontinato of the New York Rangers.

"They were punching so hard," Hall of Fame defenseman Harry Howell remembered, "that not even the linesmen would dare break it up."

When the dust had cleared, Fontinato's face had been rearranged and his reputation destroyed. It was neither the first nor the last of Howe's TKOs. And can anyone remember when Gretzky had a fight?

Not that The Great One was compelled to put up his dukes. Why should he when he had a Dave Semenko as his permanent tail-gunner? Breathe hard on Gretzky and, chances are, some enforcer of some kind would do The Great One's bidding. In Edmonton, Semenko was the man although he wasn't always crazy about it.

In fact it was Semenko, himself, in his autobiography, Looking Out For Number One, who accused his teammate of faking injury to earn penalties, something Howe never would have dreamt of doing.

Semenko put it bluntly, that Gretzky didn't need acting lessons. He recalled the night when a Pittsburgh defenseman checked Gretzky "who immediately hit the ice as though he'd been shot." Trainers were summoned to the ice to see if The Great One was still alive. Turns out he was faking it. "I'm fine," Wayne whispered. "How's the crowd taking it?"

As we all know, the crowds took to Gretzky—and deservedly so. He was the first superstar to turn public relations into an art form. He conquered the media as

no hockey player ever has to a point where fair criticism directed at him was viewed by many in The Fourth Estate as heretic.

To obtain a fair judgement on the two, one also must consider the quality of competition; when the NHL was a six-team league it was at its height and diminished with the advent of expansion in 1967-68. Thus, Howe played 21 NHL years when quality was at its highest (six-team level). Gretzky's big-league debut was 1979-80 at a time when the NHL had diluted to 21 teams.

In terms of Stanley Cups conquered, each won four but bear in mind that the moment Wayne lost Mark Messier as a teammate, Gretzky never played on another Cup-winner. Significantly, Messier played on two more championship clubs. When Messier and Gretzky were New York Rangers teammates, the Blueshirts made the playoffs, reaching the Conference Finals. Then, Messier departed Manhattan and Gretzky's Rangers missed two straight playoffs.

Let it be said loud and clear, that we have the utmost respect and admiration for Gretzky as a performer, as a person, and as the best salesman The Game has ever had. But this is not about that, this is about ALL-TIME greatness. Not from 1946 to the present, but ALL-TIME.

That includes the decades preceding Howe. And with that in mind, we offer you a comment from Flash Hollett, who had been a record-breaking defenseman and broke into the NHL in 1933 and eventually watched Howe in his prime.

Hollett: "Gordie is the greatest player I ever saw and that includes all the greats including Howie Morenz, Rocket Richard and Bill Cook. Howe was the only man who could switch hands when he was right in on goal. And if they had put him back on defense, he could have been an All-Star."

We rest our case—and not behind the net!

JOHN J. "JACK" ADAMS

BORN: Fort William, Ontario, June 14, 1895
DIED: May 1, 1968
POSITION: Coach
NHL TEAMS: Toronto Maple Leafs, 1922-23; Detroit Red Wings, 1927-47
AWARDS/HONORS: Hockey Hall of Fame, 1959

Without Jack "Jovial Jawn" Adams there might never have been a Detroit Red Wings franchise today. A native of Fort William, Ontario, Adams played NHL hockey with the Toronto Arenas, the Toronto St. Patricks, and the Ottawa Senators, as manager-coach. An exceptionally galvanic personality, he would do anything to win and rarely concerned himself with the consequences.

NHL president Frank Calder must certainly have admired Adams when Jack walked into the NHL office prior to the 1927-28 season and asserted that he was the man for the vacant Detroit NHL coaching job. Calder agreed and telephoned club president Charlie Hughes to set up an appointment.

Adams then met Hughes and revealed the same brashness, a characteristic for which he was renowned. "I'd been involved in winning the Stanley Cup for Ottawa," said Adams, "so I told Hughes he needed me more than I needed him."

Hughes must have agreed, because he signed Adams to a contract and told him to get started building a winner. A year later Hughes knew he had taken the right course. From a dismal 12-28-4 record, the Detroiters climbed to the .500 mark, winning 19, losing 19, and tying 6 games. It wasn't a good enough record for a Stanley Cup berth, but there was no question that the road to the Cup had opened for Detroit's then Cougars. The following season, Detroit, with a new nickname, the Falcons, finished third in the American Division.

Adams soon discovered that building a winner requires more than mere enthusiasm. Money was necessary to buy and sign players, but the Depression had hit the motor industry and loose cash was as distant as the Stanley Cup.

The turning point toward better times for the team was reached in 1933, when the franchise was bought by James Norris, Sr., a grain millionaire with a fervent love of hockey. Norris had played hockey for the Montreal Amateur Athletic Association's famous Winged Wheelers. He suggested a new team name, the Red Wings, and an insignia symbolic of the industry which dominates the city.

A no-nonsense type, Norris was even brasher than Adams. He laid it on the line with the manager. "I'll give you a year on probation," Norris warned, "with no contract."

Adams may not have had a written pact with Norris, but he quickly gained the millionaire's confidence as well as access to his bankroll to sign superior players. He bought Syd Howe (no relation to Gordie) from the St. Louis Flyers for $35,000. Howe was soon playing the brand of hockey that eventually put him in the Hall of Fame. Hec Kilrea was purchased from Toronto for $17,000, and the Wings were off, flying toward two straight Stanley Cups.

By the 1935-36 season, the Adams-Norris combine was the best in hockey. The manager was not only off probation but had become so friendly with his awesome boss that he referred to Norris as "Pops."

By March 22, 1936, the final day of the 1935-36 season, Detroit was perched atop the American Division with a record of 24 wins, 16 losses, and 8 ties for 56 points, the best record in either division.

To win the Cup in 1936 first required that the Red Wings dispatch the strong Montreal Maroons in the opening playoff round that began March 24, 1936 at the Forum in Montreal. To this day, the game remains a classic among classics. It was the longest hockey match ever played in the NHL. Exactly 116 minutes and 30 seconds of sudden-death overtime was required, almost two additional full games. The winning goal was scored by Modere "Mud" Bruneteau of the Red Wings at 16:30 of the sixth overtime.

After winning their second straight Cup in 1937, the Red Wings plummeted in 1937-38. Not only did they fail to retain their hold on first place, but they didn't even gain a playoff berth. It took six years for Adams's Red Wings to win another Stanley Cup. That was accomplished in the 1942-43 season when they finished first.

Without any question, 1946 was the most important year in the history of Adams and his Detroit hockey club. It was then that a muscular youngster with a Saskatchewan drawl arrived in Detroit. His name was Gordie Howe. He was accompanied by another young player, Ted Lindsay, who had joined the Red Wings two years before. After juggling combinations of players, Adams eventually placed captain Sid Abel, the center, on a line with Howe on the right wing and the truculent Lindsay on left. No three forwards ever jelled more firmly, and as they began to pump goal after goal

into the enemy nets it was rather appropriate that the city which developed the motor production line should name the Abel, Lindsay, and Howe trio *the* Production Line.

However, they weren't the only stars. The defense was replete with talented skaters, such as "Black" Jack Stewart, Bill Quackenbush, and Leonard "Red" Kelly, who guarded rosy-cheeked Harry Lumley in goal.

To reach the top, however, they would have to cope with the dynastic Toronto Maple Leafs sextet, which from 1947 through 1949 was to win a then record three straight Stanley Cups. It wasn't until 1949-50 that the Red Wings were ready once again for a serious assault on the championship. After finishing first, for the second year in a row, the Wings' first objective was the Maple Leafs, whom they defeated in seven games, but only after Howe had sustained a near-fatal head injury in the opening match. That put Detroit in the finals against the New York Rangers, whom they beat in seven games.

Adams's clubs went on to win three more Stanley Cups and finish first six more times until Jack stepped down in 1962-63 to become president of the Central League.

Adams died in 1968, but his memory lingers on in the NHL. The Jack Adams Award was first presented by the NHL Broadcasters' Association in 1974 and serves as the preeminent honor for coaches in the league.

As long as there's a big-league hockey team in Detroit, the name Adams will always be synonymous with the Red Wings.

WILLIAM SCOTT "SCOTTY" BOWMAN

BORN: Montreal, Quebec, September 18, 1933
POSITION: Coach
NHL TEAMS: St. Louis Blues, 1967-71; Montreal Canadiens, 1971-79;
Buffalo Sabres, 1979-87; Pittsburgh Penguins, 1991-93;
Detroit Red Wings, 1993-Present
AWARDS: Jack Adams Award, 1977, 1996, Hockey Hall of Fame, 1991

Early in the year 2001, when Scott Bowman was presented with the Lester Patrick Trophy for "service to hockey in the United States," it surprised absolutely no one in the civilized ice world. Unquestionably, the Montreal native is regarded as *the* coach of the half-century, if not the greatest NHL bench boss of all time.

The accomplishments can neither be challenged nor matched by anyone. Yet with all his trophies and accolades, Bowman has remained an enigma and a paradox. At once he is both the most appreciated and misunderstood man in major-league hockey. He also is the winningest coach in NHL history.

Bowman is complicated yet simple, warm but distant. It all depends on the time of day and season of the year.

The Great Expansion of 1967-68, when the league ballooned from six to twelve teams, spawned Bowman's career. St.Louis Blues general manager Lynn Patrick signed Bowman, and he has been winning ever since.

During stints in St.Louis, Montreal, Buffalo, Pittsburgh and most recently, Detroit, he has perplexed both friend and foe alike. But there's no disputing his intensity. Bowman is what the trade calls "a hockey man's hockey man." He has been steeped in the game dating back to his Montreal youth and was a gifted Junior level player until a serious head injury ended his career.

Without missing a beat, he moved into amateur hockey as a coach, then scouted for the Montreal Canadiens, and finally got his big break, being named

first-year coach of the expansion St. Louis Blues in 1967. "At first the Blues weren't a factor in the race," recalled Larry Zeidel, a defensemen with rival Philadelphia Flyers at the time, "but later in the season Scotty took over as head coach, and St. Louis was primed by playoff time." In fact, the Blues upset Philadelphia in the playoffs and went all the way to the Stanley Cup finals before losing to the Canadiens in four straight. Bowman directed them to the finals again in 1969 (vs. Montreal) and 1970 (vs. Boston), and although St.Louis didn't win a game, Bowman was highly praised for his efficiency. Following a dispute with Blues ownership in 1971, Bowman became the Canadiens' head coach for the 1971-72 season and thereby launched one of the most impressive runs behind the bench the NHL has known. He won the Stanley Cup in his second year piloting the Habs, and starting in 1975-76, he ran off four consecutive championships, culminating with a Cup win in 1979.

At the time it was freely predicted that Bowman would ascend to the general managership in Montreal, succeeding Sam Pollock, but when it became apparent that Scott would be aced out of the job, he left the Habs to both manage and coach the Buffalo Sabres.

Although the Sabres finished first in 1979-80, Bowman could not win a Cup during his Buffalo stint, which became less successful than anticipated. He left the Sabres in 1987 to become a television analyst, and for all intents and purposes, his coaching career had come to a dead halt.

To everyone's surprise, the Pittsburgh Penguins

hired Bowman in June of 1990 to become director of player development and recruitment. But when Penguins coach Bob Johnson became ill shortly before the 1991-92 season, Bowman moved behind the bench once more and and directed Pittsburgh to its second consecutive Stanley Cup.

The Penguins were favored to make it three straight in 1993 but were upset by Al Arbour's New York Islanders in a Patrick Division final series. Bowman was criticized for being too aloof and hands-offish in his orchestration of the champions.

Whatever the case, Scott moved on to Detroit where he signed a lucrative contract with the Red Wings. Owner Mike Ilitch made it abundantly clear that he expected Bowman to do what he had done six times before: produce a Stanley Cup winner. He achieved that goal in 1997 and repeated in 1998. But it wasn't easy at the start.

Bowman led the Red Wings to a respectable (46-30-8) finish in the regular 1993-94 race. After a shaky start, Detroit moved into a contending position and emerged as one of the NHL's elite teams. Nevertheless, Bowman was unhappy with Tim Cheveldae's goaltending and finally prevailed upon general manager Bryan Murray to obtain Bob Essensa from Winnipeg. Essensa was less than superb upon settling in Detroit, but Bowman brought his club to the playoffs.

In the playoffs, Bowman failed where he was expected to succeed. The Red Wings opened against the little-respected San Jose Sharks and suddenly found themselves behind the eight-ball.

What was expected to be a breeze turned into a death struggle. Armed with such stars as Sergei Fedorov, Steve Yzerman and Paul Coffey, Bowman nevertheless could not firmly establish Detroit superiority. Ultimately, he gambled on rookie Chris Osgood in goal, and Osgood blew the deciding game.

Bowman and his favored Red Wings were humiliated by the first-round elimination which eventually resulted in the firing of Bryan Murray. As expected, Bowman accepted the defeat with equanimity, and slowly but relentlessly, he built two championship teams.

Away from the rink, Bowman is a homebody who loves to tinker with model electric trains, eat lobster and read books like *The Rise and Fall of the Third Reich*, see films like *Rain Man* and never tires of visiting Montreal which, as he puts it, "is my home town." He is an insatiable teacher, always willing to impart hockey knowledge to younger coaches.

"Scotty made me what I am today," said Florida Panthers coach Mike Keenan. "He got me started in the coaching business." Ditto for Pierre McGuire, who made his head coaching debut with the Hartford Whalers in 1993-94 and more recently has become a TV analyst. Bowman discovered McGuire at St. Lawrence University.

"If it weren't for Scotty taking a chance on a 28-year-old kid, I wouldn't be where I am right now," said McGuire. "I'm eternally grateful to him. Scotty doesn't talk about himself much. That's why I love to brag about him. I want people to know that as much of a champion he is as a coach, he's more of a champion as a father and a husband."

Like so many others who have worked with Bowman, McGuire was amazed at Scotty's mental activity when they were colleagues in Pittsburgh. Pierre spent two years with the Penguins as an assistant coach and now owns a pair of Stanley Cup rings for his efforts, although Pierre fully credits Scott for the jewelry.

"I've seen Bowman outcoach people, just eat them up," said McGuire. "They knew what he was going to do and still were defenseless. He knows how to get the star players on the ice at the right time, especially on the road and in the playoffs."

That's why Ilitch imported Bowman from Pittsburgh. And Bowman fully proved his worth.

The author huddled with Scott, an old friend, during one of Bowman's frequent visits to New York. The conversation follows.

SF: What surprised you the most about the Detroit situation?

SB: Hockey interest in Detroit. I didn't realize how intense it was. There are four major-league sports teams in Detroit, and frankly, I don't know where we stand on the list, but I know we're not number four.

SF: How have you changed your coaching style from 1968 to today?

SB: I've had to adapt to the new style of play, which is certainly more offensive-minded. Players are more individual nowadays. It's much more difficult to think as a team now. But the values haven't changed. You still need good self-discipline. You still need players to come to the rink and play, and come to the rink and practice.

SF: What has been the most dramatic change in hockey that you've seen since you came into the NHL as a coach?

SB: Certainly the goaltenders' equipment has changed an awful lot. We have cages and all kinds of headgear. Equipment becomes a part of a goalie's play now right up to them using the masks to stop shots. We didn't have that before. Also, the advent of the offensive defenseman is a change, the one who can pressure-forecheck. When I first started, if you couldn't go in and really forecheck, you stayed back.

SF: From a coaching viewpoint, which was your most satisfying Stanley Cup win?

SB: The first one is always the most cherished. Whether you're a player or a coach, you want to win at least one Stanley Cup. In another way the fourth Cup [in a row] we won in 1979 was very important to me. That was the season when we went to the finals against the Rangers after they had upset the Islanders in the previous round. There was a tremendous amount of hype involved in our series with New York because we were gunning for a fourth straight Cup and Freddie Shero had the Rangers sky-high. The first game was at the Forum and they beat us. Game 2 was also in Montreal and New York took a two-goal lead before we came back and won the game. The other thing that made it so special was that this was the only Stanley Cup of the five that the Canadiens had won for me that was won at the Forum. My family was able to enjoy it more and they were all a little bit older. There's nothing like a home-ice Cup victory, especially when it's the fourth consecutive Cup.

SF: Even though you won it four games to one, it was not an easy series for you because some weird things happened.

SB: One of the strangest things was the goal that was "stolen" from us in the second game at Madison Square Garden [fourth game of the series]. This was in overtime when Larry Robinson took a shot that beat John Davidson in the Rangers goal, but the light didn't go on and play didn't stop. That goal should've ended the game, and I had a hard time restraining my players and keeping them going, which was important because the Rangers had a counterattack going and moved into our end. We were fortunate enough to stop them, and then within a minute or two after we has scored the goal that was never counted, Serge Savard beat Davidson and this time the goal counted. But we had good fortune behind us in that series.

SF: What do you mean specifically by "good fortune"?

SB: The Rangers had us reeling after Game 1. We were concerned because Fred Shero had brought this team from really nowhere and he had them believing they could win. They had a strong goaltender in John Davidson who was at the top of his game. I had planned to make a goalie change for Game 2. I've always gone on the assumption that when things aren't going well you have to try something. So, I decided to remove Ken Dryden and insert Bunny Larocque, who was our second goalie. Talk about good fortune! In the pregame workout, Bunny got hit by a shot and had to leave the ice. He was injured enough that I had to start Dryden after all. Ken went back in and shut the door on the Rangers. In the end I was fortunate that I didn't have to experiment with Larocque because we went with Kenny all the way to the Cup.

SF: You've pulled yourself out of other desperate situations as a coach, haven't you?

SB: A lot of people remember the Bruins series when we were down by a goal in Game 7 against Don Cherry's club and Guy Lafleur saved us after they got penalized for too many men on the ice. It was quite a game. We had previously fought back to tie the game and then Boston went ahead again with a goal from behind the net. That's when I was experiencing that special coach's feeling that I could have stayed there all night and we weren't going to win the game. But they got called for the extra man and Guy did his thing. It was odd because we were going onto the power play and we weren't doing well with the power play up to that point. And even then, Lafleur's shot wasn't a result of setting up well. What happened was that Guy came down the right side and took a routine shot from just over the blue line—and scored!

SF: Jacques Lemaire had a lot of trouble coaching Lafleur. How difficult was he for you?

SB: I had no problem with Lafleur. At the beginning it was a bit of a challenge to make him realize how good he could be. We had been upset that fellows like Marcel Dionne and Richard Martin, who had been drafted after Guy, were putting up big numbers on the board while Guy wasn't, at first. Then, Guy finally realized he could be the best player and from that point on it wasn't really difficult. He was a very coachable player because he enjoyed coming to the rink. He enjoyed playing and he enjoyed practicing as well.

SF: The first Cup win of the string—in 1976—must have been especially satisfying since your Canadiens stopped the two-year Cup streak of the Philadelphia Flyers. It was your Good Guys against the Broad Street Bullies.

SB: That was a series we won in four straight and yet, strangely enough, it was a close series. Actually, it easily could have gone seven games. We won the first two games in Montreal by a goal, but we still were concerned because they were a strong home-ice team. That's when Dryden shut the door on them for the most part and we got key goals from our top players. But that was some challenge for us because Bobby Clarke was the premier centerman in the league and it took Jacques Lemaire's ability to play two-way hockey against him for us to win. Plus two other centermen came through for us: Doug Risebrough and his feistiness and Doug Jarvis's defensive ability. I wound up throwing three different players at Clarke because I remembered how we couldn't shut him down the other way during the regular season.

SF: What sort of emotion do you experience these days? People who watch you get the impression that you're emotionless.

SB: I try to control my emotion more than I try to let it out. I can be emotional at times, but what I try to do is structure it so that the team itself feels that the coach at least is in control. The Red Wings were not as emotional a team as they should have been. That's one of the points we discussed, the fact that we had to get more emotion into our game. It's hard to give it every night but they have to do it.

SF: How close are you with fellow longtime coach Al Arbour who retired after the 1993-1994 season?

SB: We talked a lot but more about things that were not involved in hockey. I thought nothing of picking up the phone and asking Al about a certain player. When I was coaching Pittsburgh, it was a little strained because then we were in the same division. But when I moved to another conference, we talked more. You see, our families grew up together in St. Louis when he played defense for me on the Blues. My wife, Suella, is very close to Al's wife Claire. We share a lot of the same interests. Al is a good friend to have outside of hockey, but when I was involved in the games themselves I didn't consider him as a friend because in hockey you have no friends [*laughs*].

SF: You went up against Al in the 1993 playoffs and he beat you. What went wrong?

SB: What happened was Mario Lemieux's problem of not playing in two or three of the games. That, plus the Islanders goaltending of Glenn Healy. Everybody dumped on our goaltender, Tom Barrasso, but the difficulty was that we ran into a hot goalie. It's been proven over and over again that a hot goalie in the playoffs can win a series. We couldn't put the puck in the net, and ironically, it was the seventh game when we felt we really got our offense going. But the Islanders got the goaltending you need to win. Also, it didn't help that Kevin Stevens got hurt early in Game 7. It had been said that Kevin needed Mario, but Stevens is also the one player who had been able to play constantly in the past few seasons without Mario. Remember, Mario was back in that game feeling pretty good so that when we lost Stevens we really never replaced him in that game. If you examine Mario's games in the playoffs, you'll see that this wasn't one of his vintage games.

SF: Who is your favorite player of all you've coached?

SB: I'll go back to my first coaching years when I was with St. Louis, but I won't limit myself to just one or two players. Red Berenson, who came into his own when he joined us in St. Louis, is one and Glenn Hall, who played goal for me with the Blues, is another. In Montreal I enjoyed Bob Gainey, Guy Lafleur and Ken Dryden. Lafleur was the best offensive player in the league and Gainey was the best defensive forward. We also had Larry Robinson, Serge Savard, and Guy Lapointe. I have a hard time distinguishing which of those three I enjoyed the most. Then, in Pittsburgh, I had Tom Barrasso, Mario Lemieux, Ron Francis, Joey Mullen and Kevin Stevens. I can't pick one player from among them.

SF: Pick one.

SB: The one player who contributed for me for a longer period of time than the others was Guy Lafleur.

SF: You've been a general manager and a coach. Which is more fun?

SB: Coaching. It's the job where when the season is over, you can totally focus on something else. Which is good. So, I had two or three months in there. If I'm a manager, there's always something to do, signing or negotiating of some kind. And you're at the mercy of both players and coaches.

SF: What aspect of coaching gives you the most satisfaction?

SB: The game gives me a sense of accomplishment. But there are many factors in coaching. Obviously the practice and the preparation—not only game preparation but the game itself. When the game is on and you're coaching, you're doing things, putting certain players together, experimenting.

SF: Name the player you coached against whom you would have wanted on your club.

SB: I would have to say Bobby Clarke. He was a special type of player for the Flyers. Looking further back than that, I'd pick Gordie Howe.

SF: Name the player who played for you and succeeded more on drive and motivation than he did on ability.

SB: Al Arbour, because he had to work for every inch of the ice. He played in an era when you had to do all of the little things right. It took total concentration for him to really be an effective defenseman. When I was in St. Louis, Al was at the end of his career, but he was still the glue for our team. Another player like that, whom I had in Montreal, was Doug Risebrough. Also Yvon Lambert. They were very underrated players who would come to the rink every day and put their work shoes on. When I was in Buffalo, Craig Ramsey was like that—a special player. When those guys were on the ice, you had the feeling that they were doing more for the team than people realized. Terry Crisp. Looking back, it's not hard to imagine why people like Arbour, Gainey and Crisp became coaches in the NHL.

SF: You got Mike Keenan his coaching break; how close are you with him?

SB: Mike and I have been pretty good friends from the time he came to Rochester in the American League. When he started as head coach in Philadelphia, we talked and we've stayed close. When I made the decision to leave Pittsburgh for Detroit, I talked to Mike quite a bit. He talked to me as well about his plans.

SF: Do you remember giving Keenan his first coaching opportunity?

SB: Actually, Mike would have been my choice to coach in Buffalo after he had been in Rochester. What happened was that Red Berenson had joined us the year before and Red and Mike became very good friends. Mike respected the fact that Red might come back. In late August of that year, Red changed his mind, which was a bit of a tragedy because we were scrambling and we never really replaced him. If we had known that June that Red was not coming back, Keenan would have been the coach.

SF: How intense was it to coach against Keenan in the 1992 Stanley Cup finals?

SB: It was not insane like some people might have thought. A coach doesn't get on his uniform against the other coach. At least I don't feel that I do. When we played against Chicago, both teams were on a roll. There was a fine line and the line was so fine that it set the stage for the rest of the series.

SF: Why did you leave Pittsburgh?

SB: In Pittsburgh I was sort of an interim coach and I didn't think I was going to be compensated for the experience that I had put into the game. Obviously, I wanted to keep coaching, but the contract that I had signed the year before with the Penguins was not the type of deal that I wanted to end my career with, and then came the chance to go to Detroit. I knew that the Red Wings had a young team and that they were one of the teams in the conference that had had a good season the year before. Besides, Detroit was the same distance from my home as Pittsburgh. It was also a good move for me because one of my children was trying to get into the University of Michigan and my son was probably going to go to the University of Dayton, the same school that Al Arbour's daughter went to.

SF: Your salary in Detroit was considered astronomical by previous coaching standards. You're getting more than some managers are making.

SB: Times have changed. Salaries have gone up and all you have to do is look at what has happened with players. Then you have to remember that the coaching business is very volatile. And in the end, you have to average it out just like they do on the stock market. They look at a stock and average what it has done for three, four, five years.

DAVE LEWIS

BORN: Kindersley, Saskatchewan; July 3, 1953
POSITION: Defense
NHL Teams: New York Islanders, 1973-1980; Los Angeles Kings, 1980-1983;
New Jersey Devils, 1983-1986; Detroit Red Wings, 1986-1988
Coaching: Assistant Coach, Detroit 1987-2002; Head Coach, Detroit 2002-present

*If ever there was a natural heir apparent to succeed the retired
Scott Bowman, Dave Lewis was that man.*

Talk about paying his dues, the former NHL defenseman did it in spades–both as a player and behind the bench.

Starting his career as a defenseman for the New York Islanders, Lewis also played for the Los Angeles Kings and New Jersey Devils before retiring on November 6, 1987, in Detroit as a teammate to Red Wing captain Steve Yzerman.

Who could claim more experience behind the bench with one team? The native of Kindersley, Saskatchewan was a Detroit assistant coach for no less than fourteen years. "I felt Dave was the man for our hockey club," General Manager Ken Holland said. "He knows our team. He knows our players."

Lewis beat out a number of candidates including Barry Smith who was retained as an associate coach. Joe Kocur was promoted from video coach to the other associate coach's position. "The players know these guys and they like these guys," Holland said.

The daunting task of succeeding Bowman was roughly equivalent to an unknown soloist in Las Vegas following Madonna's act. But Holland emphasized that a younger coach such as Lewis could be as effective in his own way as a veteran such as Bowman. "He brings real good communication," Holland said. "With today's coaches, you find that's a big factor. You have that fine line of when you're the boss, but the players respect you and your decision and they know they have the ability to come in and talk something out."

Known for his gentle disposition, Lewis was quick to point out that he will know when to crack the whip with the Detroit club. "Beware of the wrath of a patient man," said the 49-year-old Lewis. "I'm not afraid of that by any means. I'm looking forward to that opportunity and challenge. Sooner or later, Scotty was going to retire. Hopefully, the continuity we will have will be an easier transition than if somebody new was coming in, regardless of whether they were experienced or not."

The Red Wings gave a number of candidates consideration but in the end it turned out that Lewis was best qualified. "In the days after Scotty Bowman retired, I had some of the top players on our team recommend to me that the best thing we could do for our team was to hire a coach from within," said Holland. "We obviously had two great choices in Dave and in Barry Smith. It was a difficult decision, but I just felt in the end that Dave was the man for our hockey club. He's got a tremendous amount of respect in our locker room and in the league. He knows our team, he knows our players and he knows their roles."

Lewis understood that all the rhetoric would be meaningless if he did not deliver. But only time will tell whether he would be the right man at the right time with the right team.

Certainly the endorsement from veteran defenseman Chris Chelios said it all. "With this group of guys," Chelios said, "it would be tough to break in a new coach (from outside the Wings organization). "These guys (Lewis and Smith) have been here for nine years (under Bowman). They deserve a chance."

JIM DEVELLANO

BORN: Toronto, Ontario, January 18, 1943
POSITION: St. Louis Blues–Ontario scout, 1967-72;
New York Islanders–Eastern Conference scout, 1972-74;
Director of Scouting, 1974-80; Assistant GM, 1981-82;
Indianapolis Checkers (CHL) GM, 1980-82;
Detroit Red Wings, GM, 1982-90; Senior VP, 1990–Present
AWARDS/HONORS: Stanley Cup, 1980-82 (Islanders); 1997-98 (Red Wings)

If ever there was someone to write the primer on building a major-league hockey club, Jimmy Devellano is that man.

How many executives—in one form or another—have had a hand in creating championship teams in three different NHL cities?

Devellano did just that in St. Louis, Long Island and Detroit. He also was one of the architects of two Stanley Cup dynasties—first with the Islanders in the 1980s and then the Red Wings a decade later.

Working under general manager Lynn Patrick in St. Louis beginning in 1968, Devellano was a part of the expansion Blues organization whose club reached the Stanley Cup finals in all three of its first years.

After linking with Bill Torrey in 1972, Jimmy helped transform the infant expansion Islanders from a hapless hulk of a hockey club into a National Hockey League dreadnought. Not only did the Isles win four consecutive Stanley Cups, but they also annexed a league-record nineteen consecutive playoff series from 1980 through the Spring of 1984.

It was Devellano who redefined the term bird-dog into "super-scout," helping to unearth such draft gems as Bryan Trottier, Ken Morrow, Stefan Persson, Adam Graves, Steve Yzerman, Mike Bossy, Bob Probert, Dave Langevin and Randy McKay, to name just a few.

Devellano's most notable accomplishment of all was transforming the metropolis of Detroit from an NHL wasteland into Hockeytown USA.

"In Stevie Yzerman, I drafted the second greatest player in the history of the franchise," said Devellano. "The first one is Gordie Howe. Being second to Howe is not bad, because we're talking about a team that's been around a long time. Certainly, Yzerman is the best Red Wing of the modern era."

The Devellano Era in Detroit began on July 13, 1982 when the Red Wings' new owner Michael Ilitch made his first major move, hiring Jimmy as his general manager. Slowly but relentlessly, the affable Jimmy crafted a winner, and in 1987, the boss rewarded him with a contract extension.

"Jimmy was the engineer behind the Red Wings' revival," said Jim Lites, now president of the Dallas Stars but then the Red Wings' executive vice president..

Just three years later Lites promoted Devellano to senior vice president, a post he has held to this day. In that time, the Motor City sextet won a pair of Stanley Cups and has remained among the NHL's elite teams through the new milennium.

"With the additions of players like Steve Yzerman and Bob Probert, among many," said Ilitch, "Jim laid the foundation for our team."

More than that, Devellano was mentor to three aspiring hockey executives who made their marks in the big tent. Jimmy's first project was Neil Smith, whom

Jim Devellano

STAN FISCHLER: What led you to a hockey career?

JIM DEVELLANO: When I was a kid growing up in Toronto, my parents had season tickets at Maple Leaf Gardens. Starting in 1958, I never missed a Leafs game, which was a great time, because Punch Imlach had taken over as coach and general manager and Toronto would win three straight Stanley Cups, from 1962 through 1964. Plus another in 1967 under Punch.

SF: Who was your favorite Maple Leaf?

JD: It's funny, because most of my friends had idols like Tod Sloan, George Armstrong and Dick Duff—all player heroes—but mine was Imlach. Punch had quite an impact on me, partly because he was quite a colorful character; very outspoken and confident. I liked the way he operated his team. Punch was very demanding, and he got results. He also was very good at selling the franchise with the media and I liked the way he looked, always wearing a fedora while he coached behind the bench.

SF: What steered you to the executive side of hockey?

JD: First I tried playing, but I was a lousy skater and not that big, so I turned to coaching on the juvenile level in the Toronto Hockey League. I was a young fellow with this pipe dream of someday making it in the National Hockey League. But at that time there were only six teams in the NHL, and opportunities were limited.

SF: How did you get your break?

JD: For starters, the NHL expanded from six to twelve teams in 1967, which meant that a lot of opportunities were opening up, and one of them was in St. Louis where Lynn Patrick had taken over as general manager and coach. I was twenty-three at the time when I wrote a letter to Patrick, offering to scout for him. I wanted to prove to Lynn that I could find players. I wasn't interested in the money, just the opportunity, and Patrick gave me that chance. Before the 1967-68 season began, he named me the Blues' Toronto-area scout.

he lured from Long Island to become his aide in Detroit.

Smith eventually moved on to New York where he developed a Stanley Cup-winning team in 1994. Devellano's successor in Hockeytown, Ken Holland, is another of Jimmy's proteges, as is Atlanta Thrashers general manager Don Waddell.

"Jimmy had no problem hiring young people if he felt they had a passion for the game and a work ethic," said Holland. "Not only does he have a great eye for hockey players, but he's got a real keen eye for spotting and developing young coaches and managers."

Devellano, 57, was also instrumental in the NHL growth of such personalities as Scott Bowman, Jacques Demers, Barry Melrose and Colin Campbell. After more than three decades in the business, he remains one of the most insightful and effervescent NHL executives. Nor does he have any plans to leave the ice scene.

"I like the excitement and the terrific people in our business," Jimmy asserted. "I don't plan to walk away."

In an interview with the author, Devellano detailed his rise to the top of hockey's executive world:

SF: What was it like to break in with a brand-new expansion team?

JD: It was tremendous, because I was starting my big-league career alongside some others who were making their debut. Early that season, Patrick turned the coaching reins over to Scotty Bowman, and Bowman's career was off and running. Even then, you could see his drive, determination, his photographic mind at work. I could sense then and there that he would be something. Al Arbour was our captain, and Bowman brought Cliff Fletcher over to St. Louis as well. I stayed with St. Louis for five years, becoming the Blues' Ontario scout before my next big opportunity arrived on Long Island.

SF: How did that happen?

JD: In St. Louis I had built up a bit of a reputation as a hard worker, and when the league expanded again in 1972—the New York Islanders and Atlanta Flames were added—I contacted Bill Torrey, who had been named the general manager. He came to the rescue and named me the team's Eastern Canada scout. Within two years, I had become the chief scout and I had made my first big move for Torrey.

SF: What was that?

JD: When the team began operations, Bill had named Phil Goyette the head coach, but that didn't work, and then he brought in Earl Ingarfield to finish the first season on a temporary basis. Now Torrey was looking for a new head coach and was considering Johnny Wilson and John McLellan. Both were good candidates, but I said, "Bill, can I throw in another name—Al Arbour." I had known Al from St. Louis and Bill decided to interview him. Well, we know what happened after that!

SF: Which qualities convinced you that Arbour had the right stuff?

JD: In St. Louis he was the captain and a character guy. For the first three years of their existence, the Blues reached the Stanley Cup finals. After each one, the owner, Sid Salomon, would invite the team to a Florida resort he owned. I really got to know Arbour sitting around the pool and talking with him. I liked his manner; he was in no way braggy or pushy, but there was a solid strength and sense

of determination. He was very direct but good with people and had a wonderful family. On top of that he had been brought up as a player in the Detroit Red Wings system under [general manager] Jack Adams and played on Cup winners in Detroit, Chicago and Toronto. He worked hard and studied hard.

SF: What was it like working for Torrey?

JD: Bill is a great guy in that he lets you do your job. Right off the bat, he made it clear that I was totally responsible for the amateur draft and that he would rely on me to decide which direction we would take. You could say that Torrey put his career in Jim Devellano's hands, as he did with Al Arbour as coach. I realized then that with the autonomy Bill had given me, someday—down the road—I could become a big-league general manager. But first I had to prove myself.

SF: Name players with whom you were involved.

JD: One of the first—and most interesting—was Denis Potvin. Our first year (1972-73) had been dreadful, and now we were picking first in the draft. Potvin was the best player available—a no-brainer—but (general manager) Sam Pollock of the Canadiens was making us an offer he thought we couldn't refuse. He gave us a list of ten names from his big club and farm team and said we could have four or five for Potvin. There were some pretty good players in that group, including Murray Wilson and Tony Featherstone. Torrey sent me to Halifax to scout Montreal's prospects, and there were some good ones. But I told Bill that if we were to build the Islanders from the ground up, we needed a star, and Denis Potvin could be our star. Eventually, Torrey turned down Pollock and we got Potvin.

SF: What other picks helped put the Islanders on the map?

JD: The same year we drafted Potvin, I picked a third-rounder, defenseman Dave Lewis. We rounded out our defense, getting Bert Marshall on waivers from the Rangers, and (general manager) Keith Allen in Philadelphia did us a favor by letting us get Jean Potvin, Denis's older brother. Having Jean helped us bring Denis to our side rather than the World Hockey Association which was raiding the NHL of players at the time. In the first year of the underaged draft, we got Bryan Trottier, and we had taken Clark Gillies fourth overall that year [1974].

SF: How did you manage to get a Hall of Famer like Mike Bossy as the first pick in 1977?

JD: I had a part-time scout in Montreal named Henry Saraceno who had recommended Boss. The question for us was whether we should take Mike or Dwight Foster, who had led the Ontario Hockey League in scoring with Kitchener. Our group was divided when I told them that Bossy was a pure goal scorer but lacked the checking ability, and there also was a question about his toughness. Al Arbour broke the deadlock. He said, "We've got a pretty good grinding team, but it's hard to find natural goal-scorers. I can teach a guy to check, but I can't teach him to score. That's why we picked Bossy over Foster. But don't forget, in that same draft, I picked John Tonelli in the second round and Hector Marini in the third.

SF: You and Torrey had built a solid team but the Islanders were upset both in the 1978 and 1979 playoffs by the Maple Leafs and Rangers, respectively.

JD: We learned from both defeats. The Toronto series went seven games and it was mean. In the end the Leafs out-toughed us, so we knew we needed more strength. The answer was to trade Mike Kaszycki, a talented but soft forward, for Gord Lane, a tough defenseman. That was the end of us getting pushed around. The second challenge was finding a center to take the pressure off Bryan Trottier. To do that, I used one of my drafts, Ken Morrow. We brought him up right after the 1980 Olympics and he showed he had the goods, so that enabled us to trade Dave Lewis and right wing Billy Harris to L.A. for Butch Goring. Getting Butch allowed us to form a strong second line behind Trottier-Bossy-Gillies. That trade propelled the Islanders to their first Stanley Cup.

SF: How did these moves help your career?

JD: Torrey not only kept me as chief scout but also made me general manager of our Central League farm team in Indianapolis. I was doing two jobs and never worked harder in my life. I was named minor league executive of the year an award that

allowed me to get closer to my dream of becoming an NHL general manager In the meantime, I was developing a parade of goaltenders in Indy for Bill—Roland Melanson and Kelly Hrudey—in case he wanted to make any moves.

SF: How did you figure in maintaining the nucleus for the four straight Cup wins?

JD: We had traded for Bob Bourne back in 1974 and he had come into his own. Bill needed another point man on defense, so we unloaded [goalie] Chico Resch to Colorado for Mike McEwen who helped us to our second Cup. Melanson was an excellent back-up to Billy Smith when we won our third Cup.

SF: How did you get the general manager's job in Detroit?

JD: By 1982, I had been Torrey's right hand man for a decade. We had already won three straight Cups and had a good shot at a fourth. My name had been bandied about for a couple of years as a general manager prospect. I had had an approach from Colorado, but Billy MacMillan got that job, and now it was June 1982 and the fifty-year reign of the Norris family as owners of the Red Wings was coming to an end. Mike Ilitch, who had been in the pizza business, purchased the Detroit team and called people for leads on a general manager. Lou Nanne, who had been g.m. of the Minnesota North Stars and had reached the Finals in 1981, got a call from Ilitch and recommended me. Ironically, I was competing against my former idol, Punch Imlach, as well as Red Berenson, David Poile and Wren Blair. But Ilitch felt that I had a terrific draft track record and that I could build the foundation of a winner in Detroit. Mike called Torrey for permission to hire me, and although Bill would have liked me to stay, he gave his okay. At the age of thirty-eight, my dream of becoming an NHL general manager had come true.

SF: How difficult was it to rebuild the Red Wings?

JD: It was a mess. When I arrived in Detroit, I asked Marian Ilitch how many season ticket-holders they had. She said, "We were told 5,000 when we bought the club, but it's actually 2,100." The club had missed five straight playoffs and missed in sixteen out of the eighteen previous years so I had my work cut out for me. At that point in time Detroit was anything but Hockeytown USA.

SF: How did you rebuild the franchise?

JD: The trick was to have an exceptionally good draft so that we could set the foundation. That year [1983] we selected fourth overall. Brian Lawton was picked first by Minnesota, followed by Sylvain Turgeon [Hartford] and Pat LaFontaine [Islanders]. We selected Steve Yzerman as the guy we wanted to build around, but there were three others I picked farther down who would help us immensely. Bob Probert was 46th overall, Petr Klima was 88th and Joey Kocur was 91st. Probert and Kocur became the Bruise Brothers and helped us sell tickets because they beat the shit out of everybody. Then I made a deal with Ranger's g.m. Craig Patrick and got Ron Duguay, Ed Johnston and Eddie Mio which gave us a good line of John Ogrodnick, Duguay and Yzerman. That Summer, I "stole" Brad Park from Harry Sinden in Boston. Even though Park was playing on one leg, he was better than most on two. After six years out of the playoffs, we finally made it, and hockey was off and running again in Detroit.

SF: What about your coaching decisions?

JD: One of my best moves was getting Jacques Demers out of St. Louis after the 1985-86 season. Harry Ornest owned the Blues at the time, and Demers had done a terrific job getting them to the seventh game of the third round against Calgary before they bowed out. I needed a colorful guy behind the bench, one who could motivate the town and the media. Jacques was that guy, and as it happened, Ornest had been too slow in signing him to a new contract, and that turned off Jacques to the St. Louis ownership. Demers signed with me, and in his first year with us [1986-87] he led the Red Wings to a 38-point improvement and the Campbell Conference Finals. A year after that, we finished first for the first time since 1964-65! Our point total improved from 78 to 93 and we climbed from eleventh to fifth overall in the league.

SF: What made Demers tick?

JD: He had good motivational ability; he was always

on fire. Jacques had a good way of making an average player feel good about himself. The results were obvious; in his first two years we reached the conference finals against the great Edmonton Oilers and even though they beat us—with Wayne Gretzky, Mark Messier and that All-Star cast—we gave them a battle, and Detroit came alive again as a hockey town. Whereas there had been loads of empty seats when I had arrived, now the team was selling out. It was a combination of things: colorful coach, the Bruise Brothers, and of course, our young captain, Stevie Yzerman.

SF: Which qualities enabled Yzerman to become the franchise cornerstone?

JD: Actually, we had planned to send him back to the junior [Peterborough Petes] because we questioned Stevie's physical strength. He weighed only 160 pounds when he came to training camp in September 1983 but within five minutes, he showed us that he was the best player we had at camp. That year he was runner-up to Tom Barrasso as rookie of the year and averaged better than a point per game in the playoffs. But it was Demers who seized on his leadership qualities. When Jacques took over in 1986, we needed a new captain. My original suggestion was Dave Lewis, who was a veteran I had known since I drafted him to the Islanders. But Demers told me, "We should make our best player the captain, and Stevie is our best player." So at age twenty-one, Yzerman became the youngest captain in team history, and that certainly turned out to be a good move.

SF: What other elements went into building the championship teams?

JD: We had to have good scouts. I brought Neil Smith with me from the Islanders, Alex Davidson from Philadelphia, and Kenny Holland. Good drafts were the key—and not trading draft choices. Our owners were not scared to spend some money to sign a free agent or two in order to give us experience and depth. Players such as Harold Snepsts, Dave Lewis and Mel Bridgman were able to blend with the kids. In addition, from day one, ownership created a good atmosphere for players who came to Detroit. By being fair and treating the people right, the Ilitches showed that this franchise was a good one to be a part of, and the word got around the league and helped us attract players who might not want to go to a place where the atmosphere wasn't just right.

SF: Which elements enabled you to interact so well with your owners?

JD: I learned from watching Bill Torrey on the Island and saw how he dealt with the owners, first Roy Boe and later John Pickett. When people own the team, they *own* the team. My policy has always been to be up front and honest with Mike and Marian. I made sure that I communicated on a regular basis, and they appreciated that. I handled their money the way I would handle my own.

SF: How did you manage to groom Ken Holland to be your successor as general manager?

JD: I had originally signed him in 1983 to play for our farm team in Glens Falls. Kenny was a little minor-league goalie whose contract had expired two years later. I was about to release him when I got a call from Bill Dineen who suggested that I hire him as our Western Canada scout since we needed one at the time. Actually, I had wanted Darcy Regier for that job, but Darcy said he wanted to work as assistant to Al Arbour on the Island. So for $30,000 I hired Kenny, and in 1989, when Smith left, I promoted Holland to director of scouting. Eventually he became my assistant, and I told the Ilitches that I wanted to train Kenny for my job. I liked the fact that he paid his dues, worked his way up, and was willing to roll up his sleeves and do the job.

SF: What aspects of the business side do you like and dislike in terms of change?

JD: I like the fact that Detroit leads the league in season tickets [17,000] and that has been due to a good hockey team. I don't like the fact that we've had to raise ticket prices, and I can assure you that ownership feels pain in doing that. But the pain has been dulled by the fact that we've put an excel-

lent product on the ice—and won two Stanley Cups.

SF: What has expansion meant to your career?

JD: If the NHL had remained a six-team league, I wouldn't have been working, but the expansion created jobs in every category, from players, to coaches, to scouts, and managers.

SF: Pick your all-time Islanders and Red Wings teams which you helped mold.

JD: For New York, Bill Smith in goal; on defense Denis Potvin and Stefan Persson, while up front, Bryan Trottier with Mike Bossy on the right side and John Tonelli on the left. For Detroit, it would be Chris Osgood in goal, Nik Lidstrom and Vladimir Konstantinov on defense, and on attack, Stevie Yzerman, Brendan Shanahan and Sergei Fedorov.

SF: Which late-round draft picks have given you the most satisfaction?

JD: I drafted two college kids for the Islanders' defense. One was Dave Langevin, a hard-hitting, stay-at-home type who played on all four Cup-winners, and [the other was] Bob Lorimer, who was a quiet, solid type. After I came to Detroit, I drafted a little-known right wing out of Michigan Tech. He was 113th overall in 1985 and should have remained a Red Wing. That would be Randy McKay, who won two Stanley Cups with New Jersey and who we lost—against my wishes—in an arbitration case when Bryan Murray wanted us to get Troy Crowder. I was very disappointed that we lost him.

SF: What advice would you give NHL Commissioner Gary Bettman?

JD: Having thirty markets spread over the continent is a wonderful thing. Now is the time to make each one stronger while not adding any more. The NHL should not expand again. Thirty teams is enough!

KEN HOLLAND

The trail to the general manager's office of an NHL team takes many strange turns, depending on the GM in question.

Lou Lamoriello of the New Jersey Devils launched his career at Providence College.

David Poile of the Nashville Predators learned from his father, Bud, who had been a player and later GM of the Philadelphia Flyers.

As for Ken Holland, the road to the top began in Vernon, British Columbia, in a most curious way.

Holland was a goaltender for the Vernon Lakers, but his true passion was collecting souvenirs. He was particularly interested in a jersey from the Medicine Hat Tigers.

Since Vernon's Lakers happened to be the farm team of Medicine Hat, Ken arranged to go to the Tigers' training camp, not so much to make the varsity, but rather to return home with a uniform for his collection.

"That was my main purpose," Holland chuckled in retrospect. "But I managed to stick around long enough to play in an exhibition game."

Holland's goaltending impressed the powers that were enough for them to give him a jersey, because he was good enough to make the big club. And thus a professional goaltender's career was off and running.

Ken played two years for Medicine Hat and eventually was the Toronto Maple Leafs' 13th pick (188th overall) in the 1975 draft.

Never a Vezina Trophy-candidate, Holland bounced around the minors (Binghamton, Springfield, Glens Falls) and finally reached the NHL for a few cups of coffee.

His big-league debut was with Hartford's Whalers in 1980-81. He played one game for them and later three for the Red Wings in 1983-84. His first NHL game was at Madison Square Garden against the New York Rangers. "We lost," he said, "seven to three. In my last game (with Detroit), we tied 6-6 after being up 6-3 with eight minutes left. They scored three goals in the last eight minutes."

When it became obvious that he would never be another Bill Smith, Grant Fuhr or John Vanbiesbrouck,

Holland began looking for a day job.

As luck would have it, then Red Wings general manager Jimmy Devellano was on the lookout for a Western Canada scout. Well, Holland knew the Canadian West like he knew the palm of his hand.

Devellano has made many a solid move for the Detroit organization, but getting Holland aboard ranks among the best acquisitions ever made for the club's high command.

"One of Kenny's strengths," Devellano explained, "is that he worked his way up from level to level. Actually, my first choice was [Buffalo Sabres general manager] Darcy Regier, but he respectfully told me that he had other plans. That's when I went after Ken."

Holland took to bird-dogging and immediately impressed with his insights and loyalty. When Neil Smith left the Wings to become general manager of the Rangers, Jimmy D needed a chief scout. He didn't have a second thought; Holland was the man.

"He already showed that he wasn't afraid to get his hands dirty; he was willing to go into the trenches," added Devellano. "And he always had been smart. Once Bryan Murray and Doug MacLean left Detroit, I brought Kenny over as assistant general manager.

"That meant he had to oversee our farm teams, especially Adirondack, and get to know all our personnel. When I decided to move on, I recommended to [Red Wings owner] Mr. [Mike] Ilitch that Kenny be made our general manager." The date was July 18, 1997. He had already proven his ability to assess talent, having drafted such players as Keith Primeau, Martin Lapointe, Chris Osgood, Darren McCarty and Slava Kozlov. He was also on staff when Detroit signed Sergei Fedorov and Nicklas Lidstrom. In his rookie year as GM, Detroit won its second straight Stanley Cup. A year later, with Holland at the helm, the Wings acquired—within a 24-hour period—Chris Chelios, Ulf Samuelsson, Wendel Clark and Bill Ranford. One of his most arresting summers took place in 2001 when he obtained Frederic Olausson, Dominik Hasek, Luc Robitaille and Brett Hull. "To see where I came from and now realize where I am," noted Holland, "I sometimes have to pinch myself."

THE ILITCH FAMILY

It would not be a stretch to say that were it not for Mike and Marian Ilitch, there might not be a Detroit Red Wing franchise as robust and competent as it is today.

In 1982, the Red Wings were in the throes of a hockey depression and required an owner with vision and substance to right the floundering hockey club.

The start of the renaissance began when Ilitch purchased the Red Wings from Bruce Norris on June 22, 1982 and took over the team. Ilitch put together a solid organization and spared no expense in rebuilding the club and restoring pride in the franchise.

The son of Macedonian immigrants, Mike was raised in Detroit and eventually spent four years in the Marine Corps and three in the Detroit Tigers' farm system, but he always kept "thinking pizza." In 1959, he and wife Marian saved enough money to open their first Little Caesar's restaurant in the Detroit suburb of Garden City. Two years passed, and they opened another.

Marian and Mike developed an empire of Little Caesar's restaurants extending across the continent and into England and Puerto Rico. By 1991, there were more than 3,500 of their eateries. The success of the business enabled Mike to invest substantially in the sports field. In January 1983, he purchased Olympia Stadium Corp. from Bruce Norris and renamed it Olympia Arenas, Inc.—the management company for Joe Louis Arena, Cobo Arena and the Glens Falls [N.Y.] Civic Center. He also owned the Adirondack Red Wings of the American Hockey League before the franchise was moved.

The Ilitch family's commitment to excellence eventually paid off when the Red Wings won a pair of Stanley Cups and remained among the elite members of the National Hockey League.

Mike and Marian have raised seven children—Denise, Ron, Mike Jr., Lisa, Atanas, Christopher and Carole.

It is safe to say that Detroit's nickname, Hockeytown USA, did not exist before Mike Ilitch became owner of the Red Wings. That the Motor City is now synonymous with top level hockey is as much due to Mike and Marian Ilitch as it is to anyone connected with the ice game in Michigan.

EBBIE GOODFELLOW

BORN: Ottawa, Ontario, April 9, 1907
POSITION: Center/Defenseman
NHL TEAMS: Detroit Cougars, 1929-30;
Detroit Falcons, 1930-32; Detroit Red Wings, 1932-43
AWARDS/HONORS: NHL Second All-Star Team, 1936;
NHL First All-Star Team, 1937, 1940; Hart Trophy, 1940; NHL All-Star

Ebbie Goodfellow was conspicuously interested in reminiscing and even carried a sheet of notes to remind him of treasured memories. He spoke glowingly of his earlier days with the Red Wings, then with less relish about the twilight of his playing career, and he turned surprisingly and adamantly bitter when the subject reverted to his coaching career with the Chicago Blackhawks. Obviously, he felt betrayed by his players who lacked his competitive fire. A wistful look crossed his face as he stuffed the page of notes in his pocket and said goodbye. The following is the result of our conversation in Goodfellow's own words.

I can thank my father for getting me interested in hockey. He was a farmer in a small hamlet, and before I grew up he took a job on an experimental farm run by the government in Ottawa, and we moved there. He was the biggest hockey fan in the world, with my mother right behind. Consequently, there was no problem in my finding ice time, and in those days Ottawa was famous for its hockey players. Frank Boucher, King Clancy, and many other stars came from the area.

Around 1919 a big, new indoor arena was built called the Auditorium. Before that we had only one hockey building—Dey's Arena—but it had natural ice; the Auditorium was the first to have the artificial stuff. Still, I didn't really care, because I played on the outdoor rinks where we had ice from November to March.

And even if the park rinks were crowded we could always go out on the Rideau Canal and skate in the shadows of the Parliament buildings. Now the winters are a lot milder and all the kids play on artificial ice.

I started playing organized hockey when I was a teenager in school leagues and finally with a senior

league team called the Montagnards. I must have been pretty good, because the Detroit Red Wings scouted me and I wound up playing for their farm team, the Olympics, in the old International League.

Getting there wasn't easy, however. For one thing, I came from a poor family. Hockey equipment cost money, and to us, money was scarce. My first pair of skates cost twenty-five cents. They were called spring skates, the kind you put on right over your shoes, and they had heel clamps on the back and two clips on the side that you tightened with a key, something like roller skates.

When the snow fell it would get packed down hard on the sidewalks because nobody bothered to shovel them, and we could skate on them and play hockey after school. Those spring skates weren't very steady, but they were good enough to learn on and better than nothing. After that I graduated to tube skates and made my pucks out of hardwood.

I played whenever I could, sometimes three games in one day: morning, afternoon, and evening. When I was seventeen I played intermediate hockey, and I remember a game at an outdoor rink in -30 weather and riding home afterwards fifteen miles in a hay sleigh, pulled by a team of horses.

A year later we traveled to a neighboring town for a game in a blizzard. Drifts were twenty feet high in places, but this time we had cars. Unfortunately, we had to push them practically the whole distance and didn't arrive until midnight. We started the game at 1:00 a.m. and finished about three or so. But we won.

Then I played two years in the Ottawa senior league before I got my big break and signed with the Detroit Olympics. Jack Adams, an old Ottawa boy himself, who was coaching the Red Wings at the time, scouted me with the Olympics and decided to sign me for the big team. Before he did, though, I looked up my friend Pat Kilroy, who was playing for the Ottawa Senators, and got his advice on what to ask for. Adams came up with an offer of $6,800 for two years, which was a pretty good contract. In fact, it was a hell of a lot of money then.

That really set me up for the NHL because word gets around to the old pros about how much the rookies are getting. They all knew I was an all-star center in the IHL and had won the rookie award and stuff like that. Everybody expected me to be a hotshot. The write-ups all said I was a great prospect and claimed that Boston offered $50,000 for me, an unheard-of sum in 1929.

Naturally I arrived with a big chip on my shoulder. I remember my first night in the NHL; we were playing in Boston against a strong Bruin team that included such big fellows as Eddie Shore, Lionel Hitchman, and Dit Clapper. Right in succession Shore hit me, then Hitchman, then Clapper, and I came off the ice after the game a very cooled-off rookie. "Ebbie," I said to myself, "you'd better start picking your spots if you want to stay alive up here."

That made sense, and I wound up with 17 goals in 44 games, not bad at all considering I played with a lot of different wingers. Jack Adams's theory was to balance the team, have equal strength. So I never played with the best wingmen for long.

Some fellows objected to Adams's style; they figured he was too tough a guy. He was a hard competitor—all he thought about was winning, and I can't blame him for that. We'd say about Jack, "All he can ever do is win."

I don't mean we won big right off the bat. It wasn't easy at the start because our team was not that good, but each year Adams made it stronger, and in 1932-33, Jim Norris bought the team and Adams was able to bring in good players like Syd Howe, a forward, and Wilf Cude, a good goaltender. We made the playoffs that year and knocked Toronto, the favorites, out in the first round. Then when we went up against Chicago it was touch and go until I lost the whole thing for us.

The score was tied 1-1 in sudden death overtime and I was back on defense. Clint Smith of the Blackhawks came skating down at me and I jabbed my stick out for a pokecheck. I missed the puck, and he stepped on my stick and more or less fell down while I came up with the puck. Now anybody would say in

fairness that I didn't deliberately trip him, but I was still given a two-minute penalty.

So there I was, anxiously sitting in the penalty box, watching the clock tick away, hoping we could kill the penalty until I got out. But then just as I was about to leave the box one of the Chicago players got off a long shot from the blue line that our goaltender should have handled. He didn't, though, and there went the game and the playoff for us—all because of my penalty.

Still, that wasn't as memorable as another game I was involved in, the longest one in NHL history. It was on March 24, 1936, at the Forum in Montreal. We were up against the Montreal Maroons, a pretty good club with scorers like Hooley Smith and Jimmy Ward, and we had a big line then of Larry Aurie, Herbie Lewis, and Marty Barry. Neither team scored in regulation time, so it went into sudden death.

I know that game is considered a classic because of its length, but as for quality, it wasn't much after the first three periods. Both teams were very cautious, and in those days they didn't resurface the ice, just swept it with brooms after each period. By the time we got to sudden death the ice was full of cracks and sticky as hell; there just wasn't any possibility of spectacular play.

Nobody scored in the fourth and fifth period—but we nearly broke the tie in the sixth when Herbie Lewis worked his way through for a shot at Lorne Chabot, the Maroons' goalie. Herbie beat him and it looked like we had the game, but the shot bounced off the goalpost; no goal.

It went on and on into the evening, past midnight with still no goal. Montreal had a few good chances too, but Normie Smith, our goalie, played well and stopped them all. Meanwhile, it was past 2 a.m. and the guys were so tired they were just walking around out there; a lot of fans had left too. Finally, we got a break. Mud Bruneteau, our youngest player, got hold of the puck in our zone and passed it up to Hec Kilrea who moved past center and in on the Maroons. Hec carried the puck around their defense but was checked by one of the Montreal players as he circled in the corner. He managed to get the puck out in front of the net—and that's just where Bruneteau was standing. He stuck it in past Chabot at about 2:30 a.m., after more than nine periods of hockey.

Afterwards we all got cleaned up, and instead of going to sleep, we went to a night club to have a few beers. It wasn't unusual for us to go out drinking after a game because times were different then. We didn't play nearly as many games as they do now, and there was a lot more camaraderie. When we were home in Detroit, for instance, it was quite common to go across the border as a group to Windsor, Ontario, to someplace where we weren't known and just have a lot of fun. We might not have a game for three or four days, so we could let off a little steam this way, but today it seems that everything's out of bounds for the players.

The whole atmosphere was more conducive to laughs. Like when Harry Jacobson used to hang around our dressing room.

He was a coal dealer, and he'd come in before every game and say, "Well, you guys, I'm going to pay you $10 for every goal and $10 for every assist and $25 for a shutout."

Once, he came in on a night we were playing the Montreal Canadiens. That was when Montreal had its terrific line of Howie Morenz, Aurel Joliat, and Johnny "Black Cat" Gagnon. At the time, Gagnon was really hot, and he happened to be wearing Number 14 on his jersey, so Jacobson announced: "Fourteen dollars for every time Gagnon is knocked down." Of course everybody on the team liked that, especially our big defenseman Bucko McDonald, who really knew how to bodycheck.

Well, Bucko really did a job on the Black Cat that night, and when the game was over he came tromping into the dressing room over to Jacobson, who said, "Bucko, I think you got him four times!"

Bucko roared so loud he nearly blew Harry out the door. "Hell," he said, "I got him five times if I got him once!" So Jacobson coughed over 70 bucks together with about $300 more for goals, assists, and knockdowns.

Naturally, this got around to newspapermen as well as some others, and Harry started to worry because he was planning to go with us to Montreal and was afraid the French Canadian fans would try to get him for what we'd done to Gagnon to get Harry's bonuses. Harry had reason to worry about being noticed, since he was known as a health addict; he never wore a coat or hat in winter, and everybody in Olympia Stadium would recognize him. But he wanted very much to go with us to Montreal, so he put on a coat and a hat, bought a false mustache, and got away unnoticed.

If Bucko was our hardest hitter, I must have fit in somewhere right behind him, although my style of roughness was a bit different. Ching Johnson, the great old Ranger defenseman, once said I was the dirtiest player in hockey. He must have decided that because of the way I'd developed the knack of cutting him when I played center. I'd skate down the ice, see Ching coming at me with his two arms spread out, and know I had to protect myself.

At the last split second I'd bring my stick up, and down he'd go. Luckily for me, Ching was a lot like our Bucko McDonald; he was a nice guy, too nice to really give me the business. True, he hit hard, but he wasn't ever mean and wouldn't hurt a fly if he could help it.

A bit later we had a real tough cookie in Jimmy Orlando, a defenseman who came from Montreal. He was a lovable guy off-ice, but in a fight on skates he was the best puncher I've ever seen. Before him there was Lionel Conacher who was amateur champion of Canada. Lionel once fought an exhibition with Jack Dempsey; it was just a few rounds, but Lionel took a crack at Dempsey that almost floored him. Dempsey stared a good hard look at Conacher and said, "One more like that, kid, and you're gone!"

Remember, though, fighting wasn't everything. The name of the game is scoring goals and winning, and I think I did my share. I don't believe a really mean guy lasted in the league very long, because his reputation would get around and somebody would say, "That dirty sonofabitch gave me the stick," and the other guys would then lay for him and straighten him out.

Playing forward and defense, I saw both sides of the action. Forward seemed a better position because a man can make more mistakes there and not be criticized as much for it. When you're back on defense and somebody skates by you, then you're the goat. That happened to me one night in Madison Square Garden, and some guy yelled down from the balcony, "Goodfellow, you look like one of Jake Ruppert's brewery horses!"

Another time in Detroit, Charlie Conacher of the Maple Leafs, who weighed about 210 pounds and came down on you like a freight train, shifted around me and scored. "Hey, Adams," some guy shouts at our coach, "why don't you try Ebbie as a referee?"

You hear a lot about how much tougher the game was in the thirties—and it was—but there were also some funny things happening on the ice that you don't read about. There was a game one night with Toronto, and it was brutal. At one point both benches emptied into a terrific brawl.

We had a player, Connie Brown, who stood only about 5'5" and the Leafs had a fellow named Pat Kelly; they were good friends and didn't want to fight, but when they saw everybody else paired off and battling, Connie said, "Pat, you tackle me." Kelly obliged, and they went down and started throwing fake punches at each other, rolling all over the place until Connie wound up on top, looked around, and saw that all the action was at the other end of the ice. "I'll get up," Connie suggested, "and you chase me and tackle me down there where the action is." And that's what they did.

Off-ice we always had to be careful of Jack Adams. Once, we had some trouble with him on a trip to Montreal after we'd had a bad game at the Forum. He was good and mad and told us to be back at our hotel no later than 12:30. About six of us, including Eddie Wiseman, a rookie who was making his first trip to Montreal, went to a tavern where we got something to eat, then headed back to the hotel. In those days we stayed at the old Windsor Hotel which had two entrances, one for the main lobby and the other for the back. It was now about a half hour after our deadline, and we figured Adams would be waiting for us in the lobby.

At the last minute the other guys decided to duck around to the rear, but I was brave—I was a veteran—so I went in through the front door and saw Jack. "Where is everybody?" he asked. I told him, as innocently as I could, that I didn't know. All of a sudden he let out a howl. He had noticed some of the guys scooting towards the back entrance.

Jack jumped out of his chair and raced upstairs with me right behind him. When he got to our floor, he arrived just in time to hear one of the doors slam shut. He figured it must have been one of his players, so he dashed to the door and barged in. Eddie Wiseman, the rookie, was there lying peacefully in bed, snoring to beat the band with his blanket pulled up to his neck. Adams didn't care. He walked right up to him, pulled the blanket off, and there was Wiseman with all his clothes on, even an overcoat. Before Adams could say anything, Eddie looked up, rubbed his eyes, and said, "Geez, coach, it's awfully cold in here!"

Adams and I usually got along, but there was one night when he took a dim view of me. It occurred in the mid thirties—I can't remember the exact time, just that we all were wearing helmets—and I got in a mixup in front of our bench. All of a sudden my helmet slipped over my eyes and I couldn't see a thing. I was afraid of getting belted, so I yanked it off, and, in the same motion, heaved it over the boards in the direction of our bench. Naturally, it hit Adams right on the head, knocking his glasses off. Everyone on the bench thought it was a riot, and they sat there laughing their fool heads off, but Jack was furious.

Like everybody, Jack was at his best when he was winning, and he hit his peak in 1936 when Detroit won its first Stanley Cup. That was the first year I

switched to defense, and it was a memorable team with Aurie and Lewis and Barry, the Kilrea Brothers, Syd Howe, Johnny Sorrell, and Normie Smith. Beautiful. We beat the Maroons in three straight games—including the longest one on record—in the first round, then went up against Toronto in the finals. We took them easily in the first two games at Olympia but they beat us at Maple Leaf Gardens in the third one. At that time it was only a best-of-five series, so we still needed only one more win.

The final game was on April 11, 1936 at the Gardens, and we won it 3-2. Toronto had a marvelous team that season, but I remember Adams's explanation of how we took them: "We played aces against aces," he said, "and our aces topped theirs. It was decided when the Lewis-Aurie-Barry Line held their Kid Line of Joe Primeau, Busher Jackson, and Charlie Conacher to one shot in two games."

When we got back to Detroit after the game, the town had gone wild. There seemed to be thousands of people at the railway station, and we were driven in a procession to Olympia, where another celebration took place. It was thrilling, but we had just as good a time the following year when we beat the Canadiens in the first round three games to two—the final game went into sudden death—and then faced the Rangers in a best-of-five final.

They called that "The Broken Leg Series" because our captain, Doug Young, and Aurie had broken legs, I had a bad knee, and our goalie, Norm Smith, had an arm injury. The opening game was at Madison Square Garden and the Rangers beat us 5-1, but then we got a break. The Ringling Bros. Barnum and Bailey Circus came into the Garden, so New York had to play the rest of their games with us at Olympia. We split the next two, but Normie Smith wasn't available for the fourth so we went with sub goalie Earl Robertson. He shut out the Rangers 1-0 in the fourth game, and we won the Cup when he shut them out again, this time 3-0.

Age didn't seem to bother me; in fact when I was thirty-five-in 1941 I won the Hart Trophy, probably because I led all defensemen in scoring. I don't know how much longer I could have played if I hadn't been hit with a knee injury then. It required an operation, and afterward I played only 12 or 13 games. Adams got some mileage out of me, using me as his assistant coach when we were losing; when we were winning, however, he was the coach.

One time, though, Adams had no choice. It was during the 1942 Cup finals with the Maple Leafs—

that notorious series where the Red Wings won the first three games and Toronto took the next four. Never before had a team made such a comeback.

If I'm not mistaken, we got beat in the fifth game and Jack thought we took a lot of lousy penalties from referee Mel Harwood. At the end of the game he charged across the ice and took a swing at the ref. There was quite a scene, and when the dust cleared, NHL President Frank Calder suspended Adams for the rest of the playoffs. That's when I was made coach.

But Jack even got around that by managing to seat himself right behind the bench where he could call all the plays. I was on the bench itself, more or less in charge of changing the lines.

We should have taken the series with the lead we had, but Toronto was really up once they'd won the fourth game, and their coach, Hap Day, did some interesting things. For instance, Bucko McDonald was playing for the Leafs then and since we knew his style, and that he'd gotten slow, we took advantage of him in the first three wins. Then Day benched Bucko and stuck a rookie named Ernie Dickens in the lineup; he also benched his leading scorer, Gordie Drillon, which really was a surprise, and put in another unknown named Don Metz.

Well, those two Toronto kids just went like hell. In the end, though, the difference was that the Leafs had more depth than we did, because when they benched four veterans and came back with the kind of hockey they did, that's remarkable.

I tried one more season after the series with Toronto, played twelve games, and decided I'd had it. Management had something to say about it too, I'll admit. They wanted me to go down to the minors and be a playing coach for Indianapolis in the American League. Except by then Adams and I weren't getting along too well, and I think he had something to do with that suggestion. One of Jack's failings was that if you started slipping over the hill you immediately fell out of favor. And I wasn't the only one who suffered. Of course, my knee had been giving me trouble, and I couldn't play a game without having it swell up for three or four days. So playing in the minors was out.

At that point I could have done a lot of things. A friend of mine was in the tool and die business, and I tried that for a few years, but somehow I had hockey on my mind. Coaching still looked glamorous to me and when Jim Norris, who owned the St. Louis Arena, asked me to try it with his team in the American League I said I would.

I spent three years learning the trade in St. Louis and then Norris asked me to coach the Chicago Blackhawks in 1950-51. That sure was a dismal period for them. Jack Stewart, who had been my teammate in Detroit, was with Chicago, but he needed a spinal operation; Doug Bentley was at the tail end of his career; and there was a guy named Ralph Nattrass on defense who was one of the worst hockey players I ever had.

It was a tough hockey team to coach because the players weren't good, and on top of that, they liked to "go." I remember one time when we checked into Montreal for a game the next night and I gave them orders not to stay out late.

"Have a beer or a sandwich or something," I told them, "and be back at the hotel by midnight."

Bill Tobin was the club's manager then, and the next day I got a call from him telling me that a lot of our guys had spent the night at Jimmy Orlando's club. I told him I didn't know a thing about it.

"Well," he said, "[the NHL President] Clarence Campbell just called me and said somebody had reported it to him."

All I could do was tell Tobin that we had checked the players into the hotel but that they must have sneaked out afterwards. That kind of stuff just tore my heart out. However, there were a couple of guys I liked on the club. One was Bill "Mosie" Mosienko , a real pro, and a terrific little hockey player; he gave me a great thrill before I finally quit.

It was the last night of the 1951-52 season— March 23, 1952—and we were playing the Rangers at Madison Square Garden. I'll admit our opposition was no bargain. New York had finished just ahead of us in fifth place and they had a kid named Lorne Anderson in goal that night who was up from their farm team in the Eastern League.

It was in the third period, when the Rangers were leading 6-2, that Mosie got going. He was playing on a line with Gus Bodnar and George Gee, two pretty good hockey players, and there were about six minutes gone in the period when he got his first goal.

Then they came back to center ice for the faceoff. Bodnar won the draw and sent it to Mosie. You have to go pretty straight to score that fast, and he did. He scored his second goal only 11 seconds after his first.

It's funny. I was thinking of pulling Mosie off the ice but decided to let him stay on for another minute. This time Bodnar took the faceoff and gave the puck to Gee. He relayed to Mosie who got around Hy Buller, the Rangers' defenseman, and beat Anderson for the third time in 21 seconds. It's a record that's never going to be broken as I see it. I left him out there, and Mosie damned near scored a fourth goal, but he shot wide and finally came back to the bench. "Get off the ice," I shouted at him, "you're in a slump!"

That was the last game for me. I just couldn't take that Chicago club any more, and I prefer to win, so I quit and felt really good about it. I came back to Detroit, lived a normal life, and began to watch hockey simply as a spectator and to look at it a little differently.

I still like seeing a good hockey game, but given a choice, I'd much rather watch one the way we played it in the thirties or early forties. They have too much scrambling now; we had set plays. In our day the defense would more or less stand back at their blue line while we'd get organized and our three forwards would go down and pass the puck back and forth much more than they do now. Fellows like Bill Cook and Charlie Conacher could stick handle through a whole team, throw fancy shifts, and score a beautiful goal. You seldom see that type of play now.

We had a hell of a lot more beautiful goals, nice passing, and good stick handling.

I've got to admit that the players today are bigger, stronger, and skate and shoot faster; I also think they're in better condition. Personally, I wouldn't want to play today because hockey is all a big business, whereas we seemed to have more fun.

This doesn't mean I don't enjoy watching some of today's players. Bobby Orr is the best I've ever seen on defense. My all-time favorite is Gordie Howe—I thought he was the greatest. It's just amazing what he could do and the stamina he had. He could shoot, he was tough, he could skate, stick handle, and pass. I don't think he had a failing.

Times change, though, and so does the game. If I had to do it all over again, I wouldn't have gone to St. Louis or coached Chicago; I would have stayed where I was. Chicago was a bad setup. We had no players, and since Jim Norris owned the Red Wings and the Blackhawks, we only got the old castoffs.

Otherwise I enjoyed every minute of it.

MAX MCNAB

BORN: Watson, Saskatchewan, June 21, 1924
POSITION: Center; Detroit Red Wings, 1947-50

I
t's anyone's guess just how brilliant Max McNab's career might have been had he not suffered a crippling injury that curtailed what loomed as a bright major-league future.

A product of the bitterly cold outdoor rinks of his native Saskatchewan, McNab was scouted by the Red Wings in 1945-46 and signed to their American Hockey League team in Indianapolis in 1946-47.

McNab never became a superstar but he did play on the Red Wings' 1949-50 Stanley Cup champion teams.

In an oral history taped by the author for the book Motor City Muscle, *McNab, now living in Las Vegas, offered the following insights on his life with the Red Wings starting in the 1948-49 season.*

"I went to camp and impressed them enough to have them ask me to join the big club once the regular season began. I started in Detroit, played a dozen games, had two goals and two assists and two penalty minutes, and then we played the Rangers. One of New York's defensemen was a fellow named Pat Egan, nicknamed "Boxcar." He really earned that one, because he was built like one—not that tall, but filled with muscle on a fireplug frame. When he hit you, it hurt.

And, brother, did he ever hit me. It was a body check that first made contact at my elbow and drove it back until I separated my shoulder. I was out two or three weeks, and I remember Jack Adams driving me to the Detroit airport after I recovered so that I could get back into condition with Omaha.

"We'll pick you up in two weeks," said Adams.

So I returned to Omaha and two things happened: the Red Wings started winning, and the Knights started winning. Detroit didn't need me, and Omaha was tickled to have a player who finished with 44 goals in 44 games.

Anyhow, I played in three playoff games for Detroit, and that earned me an invite to training camp for the 1948-49 season. This time I stayed in 'the show,' but it wasn't easy. Even though they hadn't won the Stanley Cup in a while, the Red Wings were building a very strong team. They had an excellent goalie in Harry Lumley, a fine defense with fellows like Black Jack Stewart, Red Kelly and Bob Goldham and terrific forwards—Ted Lindsay, Gordie Howe and Sid Abel, as well as second-liners such as Jimmy McFadden, who had won the Calder Trophy in 1947-48.

Of all the group, Lumley was one of the more interesting, because he joined the club during the World War II years, and he was just a boy when he broke in and the youngest goalie ever to become a regular in the NHL. Harry was a big, robust guy who would whack you if you happened to be around his net. He was also very superstitious and funny about his use of time.

Another fascinating character was our left wing ace, Ted Lindsay. The first time I had been at the Red Wings' training camp, I had heard stories about Teddy. He was a little guy, and when he had first come to Detroit, the betting was that he wouldn't last a full season; he'd be out of hockey. They figured that he was such a troublemaker that somebody was surely going to get him. But he was a tough, cocky guy, and for his size, he could fight.

According to Jack Adams's plan I was supposed to center Lindsay and Howe while Sid Abel would kill penalties. But after I got hurt, Abel was moved in there, and the Production Line was formed and became the best line for the next several years. Sid was reborn because he had the two great young kids doing all the work. That's not to take anything away from Sid; he was excellent in front of the net, a terrific playmaker and a good faceoff man. He could do all the things, and besides that, he was the team captain. He was the guy who got everyone together for the team meetings. I might add that Abel was also an awfully nice guy.

Even though Sid was thriving with Howe and Lindsay, he was up in years and he'd get tired when they had long shifts. So what Ivan did was have Abel go for 40 or 50 seconds and then send me in to mop up for the remainder of their shift. My job was to do defensive work and let them take care of the offense.

Since I quickly understood that our club had oceans of talent, I knew that I had to find a role for myself if I was going to stick in the NHL. What I realized most of all was that I had to learn how to check, and I worked hard at that. After a while, I got better and better as a checking center.

My favorite of all time was Black Jack. He had unbelievable strength and would take on anybody and never lost. Naturally, he was not a favorite among out-of-town fans. When we would go play in Toronto, Montreal, New York, Boston or Chicago, Jack would be the last one to step on the ice for us. At the very last minute this unbelievable booing would start. I would look up into the stands think, "What the hell is that all about?" Then I'd realize that the booing was because Black Jack had just stepped on the ice for us. He just skated around like a prince, but that booing from the enemy fans was actually the greatest form of respect that a visiting player could get.

There was Bill Quackenbush who actually won the Lady Byng Trophy, which was really unusual for a defenseman. I'll never forget the first scrimmage I had with Bill. He put three passes on my stick that were so perfect, I couldn't believe them. In fact, I missed every one of them because I never thought Quackenbush could find the space to put them through such a maze of players. I had never seen anybody who could pass the puck like that. Bill also was a great pokechecker and also was magnificent on the power play alongside Red Kelly.

In 51 games I scored 10 goals and 13 assists for 23 points, but the important thing was that I did what I was supposed to do for the club, and that was really all that mattered to management.

When the 1949-50 season began I was put on a defensive line with Marty Pavelich and Gerry "Doc"

Couture. Marty was a terrific little hockey player who usually was given the unpleasant assignment of checking the great Rocket Richard, which, by the way, he did pretty well.

Detroit had finished in first place a year earlier, and now we were on top again. This was when the NHL had only six teams, so when the playoffs started, the first-place club played the third and second played fourth. Our first assignment was the Maple Leafs, who had wound up third but already had won three consecutive Stanley Cups starting in 1947.

It really rankled Jack Adams that we couldn't beat Toronto in the playoffs; I mean it really bothered him. Plus, Jack had such a terrible temper. If we were losing a game, he would come into the locker room and all of a sudden, every single player would lean down and pretend to tighten his skate laces. Jack would walk up and down by the training table where we had oranges cut up in quarters for the players to eat between periods. If he didn't like the way you were playing, he'd throw oranges at you to get your attention. But it was only because he wanted to win so badly.

We opened the 1950 playoffs at the Olympia, and that first game has since become quite famous—or maybe infamous is the better word—because of what happened to Gordie Howe. After Rocket Richard, Gordie was the best right wing in the league and he was fast becoming the best player. Period!

Gordie could do everything, and I mean everything; he had a terrific physique with sloped shoulders and a powerful skating stride. He could shoot from either side—which was very unusual—he could fight, and, well, he could do just about everything but play goal. And I'm sure that had he put his mind to it, he would do that well too.

So now it's the big first game; Toronto had beaten Detroit in eight straight playoff games, and we had something to prove, right.

Well, before the game is over we've lost Gordie Howe, and we also lost the game by a big score. Naturally, everyone was talking about Howe because he was pretty near death.

Gordie was trying to hit Teeder Kennedy of Toronto and wound up sliding into the boards where he hit his head against the dasher. Everybody in Detroit said that Kennedy had illegally used the butt end of his stick on Gordie, but I was sitting at the end of the bench watching the action take place, and what I saw made Kennedy innocent.

What happened was that as Kennedy saw Howe coming at him he jumped out of the road, and just then Howe lost his balance and went into the boards. Of course in those days there was no such thing as television replay to check it out so everybody had his own version, and naturally the Detroit people had it in for Kennedy. To hear some of them talk, Kennedy had given our guy a vicious backhander.

I can't begin to tell you how devastated Jack Adams was. Here was a guy whom I had only seen with one emotion: "Go get 'em, gang!" But after Gordie's injury, Adams came into the room and I saw him cry.

This episode taught me a lesson, and that was that I never thought there was a weakness in anyone who shed a tear.

Personally, I didn't have any vindictive feelings toward Kennedy, but some of my teammates who had been in the NHL a lot longer than me and had played against Teeder had an axe to grind with him. Obviously, they saw things differently, and when we played Toronto in Game 2, all hell broke loose with fights all over the place.

Me, I was a skinny kid and not one of the heavyweight champions of the NHL. But we had a lot of tough guys, so I didn't feel that I had to get involved in a big way. But after a while it got to the point where everybody was on the ice and each player was taking a man from the other team.

One of the most surprising aspects of the brawl was the role of our defenseman Red Kelly. Normally, Red was one of the most peaceful guys you'll ever meet, a true gentleman who never cursed or screamed. But on this night he was right in the midst of it, and that didn't help the Leafs, because among other things, Kelly was as physically strong a player as you'll ever meet in the league.

More importantly, we bounced back to win Game 2 and that set the stage for one fantastically exciting series, which we finally won in overtime of the seventh game. The winning goal came in sudden-death overtime, and what was strange about that was the Cup-winning score came off the stick of one of our lowest-scoring defensemen. Leo Reise was a big, tough defensive defenseman who scored only four goals in 70 games that season, but he already had one sudden-death goal in the Toronto series and now he got his second one. I can still see the faceoff in the Leaf end. The puck swung around and came back to Leo and he banged one that went past Turk Broda. That we did it without Howe in the lineup was quite a feather in the cap of our management team, GM Jack Adams and coach Tommy Ivan.

We had managed against the Leafs, but the Rang-

ers were a whole other story, and here's where good management came into the picture. Adams and Ivan made sure that we all were in the proper frame of mind, and when I say all, I mean all of us.

Especially Ivan. He had the knack of making a fourth-line guy think he was as important to the team as Lindsay, Abel and Howe. What Tommy did was take Joe Carveth, a veteran right wing at the tail end of his career, and put him in Gordie's spot with Sid and Ted. It was the most difficult transition anyone could ask of a player, but Joe came through like the trooper he was.

One reason why was that Tommy Ivan made Joe feel his contribution was as significant as anyone else's. So when he went alongside Abel and Lindsay, he did so with a lot of pride. Tommy knew how fragile the confidence factor was and how players were scared this might be their last year, especially with the strength of our farm teams.

Anyhow, Joe came off the bench, and by the time we came up against New York, he was a regular fixture on the first line. Still, we missed Howe and we were still far from the Cup. Before the finals started, Black Jack called a team meeting in my room and said to the younger guys like myself, "You fellows are going to be around for another 10 to 12 years. Me and Sid have to win it this year, so I don't want to see you guys screwing around. And if anybody has a bad night because he isn't ready or isn't working, just remember one thing, when the game is over and you come into the dressing room, I'll be the first guy you'll meet. And I don't care what Mister Adams says tomorrow or what Mister Ivan says tomorrow; that doesn't mean anything. Just listen to what I'm saying, or you'll meet me after the game."

That was the strongest pep talk I ever heard in all my years in hockey. And let me tell you something: Black Jack Stewart was the last guy in the world you would want to mess around with—the last!

Nevertheless, as hard as we tried, we missed Gordie, big-time, and the Rangers had us down three games to two and actually had us down 3-1 in Game 6. But that's when Joe Carveth came through and set up our second goal and then set up Abel for the game winner midway through the third period. That tied the series, but we still had our work cut out for us.

In Game 7, we were down 3-1 but tied it up on two power-play goals, and the game went into double overtime before we finally got the winner.

Talk about planning a big play, this was a classic. The faceoff was deep in the Rangers' zone, and we had a fellow named George Gee out there to take the faceoff. His linemate was Pete Babando. They were lining up to the right of Chuck Rayner, and just before the linesman dropped the puck, Gee yelled, "Wait a minute!"

He skated back to Babando and moved him about 18 inches from the original spot where he had been lining up for the faceoff. This was like right out of a Hollywood script—like in a big football game where the quarterback designs a play—when everything works just picture perfectly. I mean it had everything, including Gordie Howe being there, watching from the stands. So George, God bless him, seemed to know who he was going up against and exactly what he had to do. Then George went back for the draw, and on the faceoff, he won it perfectly and slipped it right back to Babando. Pete slapped at it one time and fortunately, he had a little bit of a screen in front of Rayner, and he fired it past the goalie.

Every once in a while I stop and wonder what would have happened if Babando had stayed where he had been originally; the puck would have been won by Gee but it would have come right back to Pete's skates and he wouldn't have been able to get the shot off. We might have lost the game and the chance to win the Cup.

How does it feel to win your first Stanley Cup?

Good question. Start with one word—euphoria. Or another—unbelievable. I mean without Howe, we were really underdogs when you think about it, which is why winning was so terribly sweet. It was a dreamy sort of experience and never in a million years did I think I was going to get a chance to be on a Cup winner.

Tommy Ivan was also good to me. When I played for him I was just a hard-working defensive kind of player. Sure, I had scored big in the minors but Tommy had enough goal scorers, so I knew my place. And when Alex Delvecchio made the big club at center, it didn't surprise me that I was traded to Chicago.

Then I hurt my back in the Blackhawks' training camp, and they put me in a Chicago hospital for two months. The doctors there couldn't find the problem, so I came back to Detroit to pick up a car and drive out to Vancouver where we were living. I happened to bump into Jack Adams at a hockey game, and he said, "Jesus Christ, kid, what's the matter?"

I said, "I've got a bad back, and I'm going back to Vancouver because the Chicago doctors can't find the problem."

He said, "Why don't you come and see our doctors?"

So I saw the Red Wings' doctors even though I was now with Chicago, and they checked me all over and suggested I return the next day. Sure enough, they sent me to an orthopedic hospital where the doctors ran some tests and said I needed back surgery.

The operation was done, but the amazing thing was that during my stay in the hospital my Chicago boss, Bill Tobin, never once came to see me. But Tommy Ivan and Jack Adams visited me three or four times a week.

As I said, I was around for only the 1950 Stanley Cup. Detroit missed it next year, then won it in 1952, missed in 1953 and won two in a row in 1954 and 1955. Some people have wondered why they didn't win more Stanley Cups, considering the talent they had. The answer is simple; the competition in the NHL was so close in those days that any team had a good chance in any given year.

Me, I only wish I could have played longer in Detroit, because they had a terrific bunch of guys. We used to travel by train all the time in those days and we didn't have such electronic magic as video replay, but we knew how to compensate. After a road game, we'd be sitting in the parlor car of the train, discussing the game. Somebody would fetch a bar of soap and draw a picture of the rink, with the red and blue lines and goals. They then would diagram the goals that were scored and the mistakes that led to them. Then, everybody would sit and argue.

But when I look back at those years with the Red Wings, I consider it a great run. And to think, my mother thought I should get into something with more security!

JOHN EDWARD
"JOHNNY" WILSON

BBorn: Kincardine, Ontario, June 14, 1929
Position: Left Wing
NHL TEAMS: Detroit Red Wings, 1949-55, 1957-59; Chicago Blackhawks, 1955-57;
Toronto Maple Leafs, 1959-61; New York Rangers, 1961-62
AWARDS/HONORS: NHL All-Star Game, 1954, 1956

Johnny Wilson's 11-year NHL career included a string of 580 consecutive regular season games, a record he set in 1960 while playing for the Toronto Maple Leafs, broken by Andy Hebenton of the Rangers in 1964.

Johnny broke into hockey with his brother Larry and played alongside him for several campaigns with Detroit and Chicago.

Although never a big scorer, Wilson nonetheless collected 23 goals in 1953-53 and 24 in 1955-56 for the best seasons of his career. He also played in the NHL All-Star Game in 1953-54 and 1955-56.

Wilson was not in the class of Gordie Howe or Steve Yzerman, yet he performed nobly during the dynastic years when the Red Wings won Stanley Cups in 1950, 1952, 1954, and 1955.

In an interview which originally appeared in Mo-tor City Muscle, Wilson told the author what it was like to play on those great Red Wing teams.

The best way to understand the Red Wings is to know about the man who made them tick. That would be Jack Adams, who managed our club and had been the coach for many years before Tommy Ivan took over in 1947-48.

One reason why our team was so successful was Adams's personality. Jack was a perfectionist, and because of that, a tough man to play for. You had to give

him a maximum effort or you heard about it. By the same token, if you played well he would be the first to acknowledge your efforts.

Jack's moods were easy to read. One day I walked out of the dressing room after a practice and Adams was walking in the other direction. Normally, he would wish me "Good morning!" but this time there was not a word. He walked past me as if I didn't exist, and that was the message for me: Jack didn't like the way Johnny Wilson was playing.

That was okay with me, because I knew Adams was fair. He didn't favor one player over another. On any night he would walk into the dressing room and pick on the stars as much as the scrubs. Gordie Howe, Ted Lindsay, Alex Delvecchio and Terry Sawchuk—our best players—would be picked on by Jack as much as anyone.

If Adams had a favorite, it was Terry Sawchuk, because he always had a tender spot for goaltenders. When somebody scored on Sawchuk, Adams said that the goal developed in the offensive zone. If I missed my check or a defenseman like Marcel Pronovost missed his check or didn't grab the rebound, that would be the problem, not the goaltending.

The greatest player in the game was Gordie Howe, but Adams—as much as he loved the big guy—was unsparing in his criticism. One night Jack was in his favorite spot, sitting in the back of the dressing room, when he suddenly got to his feet and walked over to Gordie. "You know, Gordie," Adams said, "you were terrible out there tonight. You were so bad, you should have paid to get to the rink."

After that, Adams walked out, but the guys were feeling bad for Gordie. One of us said, "Don't worry, Gordie, a bad game for you is a great game for everyone else." That's how much better he was than the rest of us.

After Adams retired as a coach, he still kept his nose in the coaching side of the business. He would sit right behind our coach Tommy Ivan, and when we did something wrong, we would hear a big clang behind the bench, like the clash of metal. That was Jack's gate, and when you heard that around the building, you knew Adams was unhappy.

On this particular night, I was playing on a line with Alex Delvecchio, who would go on to be one of the best centers in history, and Metro Prystai, a pretty darn good forward. Our problem was getting out of our own end; it seemed like we were going one way and the puck was going another. Sure enough, we heard Adams's clang, which meant trouble for us.

After the period ended, he came into the dressing room. The three of us were sitting next to each other with our heads bent over, which was a customary stance when you know you're going to get hell from your manager or coach. I could see Jack's big feet right under my nose. His fists were clenched as he started screaming, "I don't know what kind of game you guys are playing out there tonight, but it sure isn't hockey!" In case we hadn't gotten the message, Jack warned us that unless we shaped up, we'd be shipping out to either Indianapolis or Omaha.

Needless to say, the minute the second period began, we played as if we had been shot out of a cannon. I mean we never stopped, because of the fear Adams had instilled in us.

Not that I'm complaining about it; far from it. I believe that today's hockey players should have a little more fear. Now they have three-year contracts and can't be sent to the minors, not even to overcome an injury to get back in shape. If we made a mistake or got hurt, we could have been sent to the minors in a second— and might never have come back.

Another thing about Adams which was important to the Red Wings' philosophy was his refusal to let complacency grow in the dressing room. We would win Stanley Cups, but to Adams that meant nothing. For example, we beat New York for the Cup in 1950, but when we came to camp that fall every single player on the Detroit roster had to fight for his job all over again.

That was the way Adams handled his players. Nobody was secure, with the possible exception of Gordie Howe and Ted Lindsay, our best players. The rest had to fight all over again, and of course, each veteran lived in fear that a rookie would come along and take his spot. I mean it was a constant war, and a player like myself had to give himself a pep talk or he might not be around the next season.

That's why we were so tickled to be in the NHL and why it was relatively easy for Jack to trick us into signing contracts. Adams had what we called "Three-Way Contracts."

He would get a player in the room with him and then say, "Son, where do you want to play—Detroit, Indianapolis (AHL), or Omaha (USHL)?" Now everyone knew that there was about a three to four thousand dollar difference between Detroit and Indianapolis and another difference between Indianapolis and Omaha. As a result, the natural reaction of just about everybody was, "Mister Adams, where's the pen?"

One notable exception was Billy Dineen, who came to the big club in 1953 and wanted a raise the next year. Jack was sitting there waiting and made his offer, which Billy rejected. Adams said to Dineen, "You know, son, you were so bad last year, people around here are accusing me of being a relative of yours!" P.S.— Billy wound up signing on Jack's terms.

Adams's contract ritual began after a week of training camp, once everyone had worked the kinks out of his body. Then, the word would go out that Jack was starting to sign players. Mind you, he had about 110 players in the entire organization to deal with but he'd wipe them out in a week's time.

What Jack would do was take 10 to 15 a day. He would sit each fellow down and say, "Did you have a nice summer? You look like you're having a pretty good camp, and we're looking for a great year from you." Then he would pull out the contract and say, "Son, this is what you're getting; this is for Detroit."

Then he'd throw in a few bonuses, hand you the pencil and wait for you to sign. If you said, "Yeah, but..." he'd shoot back, "But what? Son, where do you want to play—Omaha or Detroit?" That did it; you'd say, "Detroit, Mister Adams," and sign right up. Then, you'd send in another guy, and before he went in you'd tell him, "Boy, I got a big raise—I scored 20 goals and Jack gave me a $250 raise." Today that's postage stamp money.

Mind you, I'm not knocking Jack Adams. He was a tough son of a gun, but he was also a great guy and a great coach and manager.

Of course, he had some pretty good talent on his

clubs, and that made life a little easier for him. I mean, how many managers can boast that they have a Gordie Howe in their lineup?

I've watched a lot of hockey players over the years—and I'm talking about a half-century—and I've seen them all. Rocket Richard was my idol when I was a kid. I watched Bobby Orr, Jean Beliveau, Phil Esposito, Wayne Gretzky, and Steve Yzerman—the best.

And if an NHL club owner came up to me and said, "Johnny, of all the great players you've seen, which one would you pick to start a team?" I'd say Gordie Howe.

The reason why I pick Gordie over the rest of them is that he could do anything. He could stick handle, he could shoot, he could get into the toughest battles, and he would fight. He would do anything asked of him, and brother, could he backcheck. When Gordie Howe was on the ice, it was like having a third defenseman playing for your team.

In any battle, nine times out of ten Howe would come up with the puck, open up the play and move it up the ice. He was always around the puck and the opposition had an expression, "Howe plays 'the funny game;' he doesn't let anyone else touch the puck."

He could score more goals than anyone during an era when it was a lot tougher to score than it is nowadays. He could throw the most vicious checks you would ever see and always come out on top. In today's hockey you couldn't find a coach who could tell a Wayne Gretzky or a Sergei Fedorov or a Steve Yzerman or other great players, "Listen, we've got to go out and slap this guy around." But you could do that with Gordie because he'd be the first guy there. The others I mentioned would back off because they're finesse players.

Gordie Howe was the most well-rounded player there was. For a while, his competitor was Rocket Richard. But the Rocket was only great from the blue line in or on the perimeter of the crease. And Bobby Orr, Gretzky, and Bobby Hull all had their specific talents, but Gordie was the most complete.

He also was incredibly team-oriented. Gordie would do whatever was necessary for the Red Wings to win even if he was injured. One year in particular comes to mind. This was the semifinal playoff round in 1953 after we had swept the 1952 playoffs in eight straight games. We had Boston in the opening round in '53 and beat them 7-0 at Olympia in Game 1. Then they came back and surprised us 5-3 in the second game at Detroit and went on to win the series four games to two. That was quit an upset, them beating us at that time, and a lot of people were wondering how it happened. Well, the Bruins had a big, smart veteran left-

winger named Woody Dumart who was assigned to check Gordie, and Dumart got a lot of credit for stopping our big guy. But it wasn't so much that he contained Gordie, it was that Howe was playing the entire series with cracked ribs and an injured wrist.

The thing was, Gordie never complained; he went out there and played, and because of the injuries, he was missing chances he ordinarily might have put away. They got a couple of fluke goals and beat us. Meanwhile, Gordie accepted all the blame; put it all on his shoulders and had tears in his eyes after the series was over. He was saying, more or less, "I let you guys down." That was the type of player he was.

His sidekick was Ted Lindsay, one of the best left wingers of all time and, after Sid Abel left Detroit, a great captain. I enjoyed playing alongside Teddy because he could get you up for a game better than most. He hated the opposition more than just about anybody I ever knew, but he hated the Canadiens more than any team.

As a leader, there was none better. When a rookie broke into the lineup, he would take the kid aside and spend time giving him an education about life in the NHL. And he always made a point of telling the kid that he, Ted Lindsay, would be there to back him up. "Just go out there and play your game," he would tell the kid, "and we'll support you."

The thing about Teddy is that he not only motivated the kids, but he could do it for the older players as well—including Gordie Howe. He was constantly inflating Gordie's ego, telling Howe that he was the toughest, the best and that he could outskate anyone. Another thing about Lindsay was his size. He wasn't very big, but pound for pound he was about the meanest I've ever encountered.

Here's a good example. I had been traded to Chicago for the 1955-56, season and we had a game against Detroit. Now I'm skating on a line with a brash kid named Hector Lalonde against Lindsay. Before we took the ice, I warned Lalonde, "When you go into the corner with Lindsay, get your stick up, because he'll rub your nose in it if you're not alert."

Hector said, "Don't worry about me, Johnny, I'll straighten out that little guy."

No sooner are we on the ice than there's an altercation in the corner between Lindsay and Lalonde. They've got their sticks up and it's getting worse. Being as I had been a pal and teammate of Lindsay's for several years, I skated in between them in an attempt to separate the pair. I turned to Lindsay and said, "Teddy, leave the kid alone!"

Lindsay looked up at me as if I was some foreigner and said, "Get that head of yours out of the way before I cut it off." Obviously, there were no friends on the ice with Ted Lindsay.

As good and tough as our scorers were, we wouldn't have nearly been the great team we were without special goaltending, which is where Terry Sawchuk comes into the picture. In plain English, Sawchuk was the greatest goaltender I have ever seen. That includes old-timers to the present. He finished his career with a total of 103 shutouts in his career over regular season games. One hundred and three; think about that. And a dozen more shutouts in the playoffs. How many goaltenders can make that statement?

Sawchuk was a moody guy and people would complain about that aspect of his personality, but I would be moody, too, if I had guys taking pot-shots at me in the morning during practice and then again at night during the games.

The bottom line is that Sawchuk did his thing and did it well. As good a team as we had, it also was necessary to get the big save at the right time to turn a game around.

Here's a good example of how Sawchuk made a difference. In the 1953-54 Stanley Cup finals we played against a terrific Montreal Canadiens' team with Rocket Richard, Boom Boom Geoffrion, Dickie Moore and Jean Beliveau. They had Gerry McNeil in goal and we had Sawchuk and the series came down to the seventh game at Olympia. Floyd Curry scored for them in the first period and Red Kelly tied it for us in the second. It was 1-1 late in the third period when Kenny Mosdell, one of Montreal's best forwards, somehow worked his way through our defense. If he had scored it would have been all over, but Terry came up with the big save, and we went into the dressing room still tied.

Early in the first overtime, Tony Leswick fired a blooper for us that hit off their defenseman Doug Harvey's glove and bounced over McNeil, and that's how we won the Cup. But if Sawchuk hadn't come up with that save, we wouldn't have won anything. He made the spectacular save when it counted.

When Terry came into the league, his style was different from others. He didn't stray too far from the net, basically staying around the crease. But this was a time when screened shots had become more prevalent, and to stop them, Sawchuk developed this crouch which enabled him to peer through the legs and see the puck. He would go down, look through his defensemen or the opposition, and see the shot coming.

As great players go, Terry was unusually modest and tried to evade stardom. He was like a blue-collar guy who preferred the background. He was also one of

the last goaltenders to use the face mask. He played most of his career without one and got hit in the face more than a few times. With the blood dripping down his head, he would go into the dressing room for ten minutes or so, get sewn up, and then come right back in the net. He was a gamer.

One thing I learned when I joined the Detroit organization was that this was a team of rich tradition. It had won two straight Stanley Cups in the 1930s and already had a long list of great players in the alumni. When I came to Detroit in 1949-50 one of their top defensemen, Black Jack Stewart, was finishing his career with the Red Wings, but he still was a big help to a kid like me.

I recall one incident when I wound up with the puck at training camp behind the net and tried one of those spectacular end-to-end rushes. Anyhow, I picked up the puck and took about four strides when I found myself skating right at this big hulk, Jack Stewart. He looked me right in the eyes and said, "Son, you'd better keep your head up, or the next time it will be curtains."

I learned something valuable right then and there from Black Jack.

Not that I didn't already know about him. One of the old-time Red Wings, Carl Liscombe, played on the 1943 Cup winners when they beat Boston in four straight, and he said that Stewart and Jimmy Orlando would team up to be one of the toughest defense combinations in NHL history. He told me, "They would chew up the opposition and spit them out in little pieces." After watching Black Jack in action, I knew what he meant.

But my most memorable moment with Black Jack happened during the 1950 finals against New York. The series was tied at three games apiece with the last game at Olympia. During the series, Jack Adams had us staying at a place in Toledo, Ohio, so that players could be shielded from the media and their families. It was then that Stewart announced that we were going to have a team meeting in his room; no manager, no coach. Just the players gathering in Black Jack's room.

Sure enough, he got us all together—I'm talking about our captain Sid Abel, Ted Lindsay, and the rest—and Black Jack stood up before all of them. "You guys are a bunch of patsies. You're letting the Rangers skate all over you. I'll tell you one thing, you'd better get your asses in gear for the next game. If you've got to hit every damn guy on the ice, hit him!"

Black Jack turned the whole team around, and we went out and won the game and the Stanley Cup. The thing was, you never wanted to disappoint Jack because he would look you in the eye and scare you to death. You either did what he said or you didn't belong on the team. When I saw a guy like Stewart, almost ready to kill to win, I said to myself, "Hey, I'd better do something about this to help the guy along."

After Stewart left the club, Red Kelly soon became the best defenseman on the team although he had a totally different style and disposition from Black Jack. Red was tough, to be sure, but he didn't display his toughness as obviously as Stewart. Even though he was a defenseman, Kelly liked to rush the puck and he was a splendid enough skater to be able to do that.

One of Kelly's assets was his use of the skates to move the puck. He was one of the few players ever to be able to use his feet as well as his hands. This technique was particularly effective along the boards. While most guys were trying hard to get their stick on the ice to get the puck, Red wouldn't even worry about that. He would just drag his foot and kick the puck up to his stick and get it out of our zone.

Red was a great skater who could shoot as well as make the pass. In one 70-game season he scored 19 goals, which was amazing for the team. Another time he got 50 points in 70 games.

To top it all off, he was a very nice guy and always in first-class shape. During the off season he worked on a tobacco farm his family operated in Ontario, and he would always ask Jack Adams for permission to miss the first four or five days of training camp so he could harvest the tobacco. Jack, who normally wasn't into granting such special favors, did so with Red because he knew that the first day Kelly jumped on the ice, he would be flying.

Since Kelly was one of those Ontario boys, he could very well have been playing for the Maple Leafs, but he was with us along with another Ontario boy named Ted Lindsay, not to mention myself. The fact that any one of us could have been a Leaf probably helped make our rivalry a bit stronger; not that it wasn't strong enough.

In those days of the early 1950s, when the NHL was only a six-team league, the intensity of play in each game was unbelievably high, and part of it had to do with the fact that you played each other so many times. It was not unusual for us to play a club like the Rangers on Saturday night at Olympia and then return to Madison Square Garden for a Sunday night game in New York. When you have back-to-back games as often as we did then, the games reach a fever pitch.

Every team had its share of tough guys. Toronto had Bill Barilko, Gus Mortson, Jim Thomson and Bill Ezinicki. Montreal had Butch Bouchard and Doug Harvey and so on. But the rivalry between Detroit and Toronto seemed to be the most intense of all because of an incident that took place during the 1950 playoffs. This was in the first game of the semifinals between the Wings and Toronto. Howe tried to check their captain Ted Kennedy and wound up hitting the boards. A lot of people in Detroit thought that Kennedy had tried to injure Gordie, but I know Ted Kennedy personally and I can assure you he was not the type of player who would try to injure Gordie Howe.

Nevertheless, there was a lot of bad blood as a result of Gordie getting seriously hurt and it stimulated an intense battle between the Wings and Leafs. It was a natural reaction.

Naturally, I'm very proud to have been a part of those championship clubs in Detroit, especially the 1952 winner when we swept Toronto in four and then Montreal in four. I finished the series with four goals—tied with Rocket Richard and Floyd Curry of Montreal—only one less than Ted Lindsay, who led everybody.

I got all four of my goals in the opening round against Toronto. We won the first game 3-0, but Toronto played strong in Game 2. Old Turk Broda was in goal for them and he played the game of his life, but I managed to get one past him and we took the game 1-0, which put us in great shape to take the next two games at Maple Leaf Gardens, which we did.

My only assist in the series was a big one, too, because it was on the Stanley Cup-winning goal in Game 4 of the finals. Alex Delvecchio and myself helped set up Metro Prystai who beat Gerry McNeil at 6:50 of the first period. We got two more goals later, but ours was the winner. I finished the playoffs with four goals and an assist. My five points left me only two behind Howe, Lindsay, and Prystai, who led our team with seven each.

Prystai was an important name on our championship club, because he represented the second-liners behind the stars. And we had plenty of solid backup players. They included Glen Skov, Marty Pavelich, and Tony Leswick who all were hard-working guys overshadowed by the greatness of Howe, Linsday and Delvecchio. But if it hadn't been for the contributions of these guys, I don't know if we ever would have won a Stanley Cup.

I played on championship teams in 1950, 1952, 1954, and 1955, but the first one is always the most memorable. This was 1949-50, the year that Gordie suffered that serious injury in the collision with Ted Kennedy. Howe was lost to us for the remainder of the playoffs, so when we went up against New York in the finals, we had to play without our best player.

As things developed, the Rangers had their problems as well. In those days, the Ringling Brothers' Circus took over Madison Square Garden, their home ice, in the spring, and there was no provision for the circus and hockey to coexist. So what happened was that when the Rangers got to the 1950 finals against us, they were allowed to play two "home" games at Maple Leafs Gardens in Toronto.

New York played a terrific series, and it came down to three wins apiece with the seventh game on our ice. But we had the game tied at 3-3 by the time the second period was over and went a full sudden-death period without a goal. Then in the second overtime, Pete Babando beat Chuck Rayner and we had the Cup.

The weird thing was that a year later the Rangers didn't even make the playoffs and we went out in the first round. That was the year that Rocket Richard was hotter than a pistol. We went up against him and the Canadiens in the first round and lost the first two games in sudden death to them at Olympia. Then, we beat them twice at The Forum, but they came back and won the next two and the series.

Rocket was one of the fiercest hockey players I ever faced. I would try to check him in our zone and he'd shoot the puck right through me. He'd play against an opponent like me as if he didn't even see me, like I was a shadow. I mean his eyes were glued on that puck. It was unbelievable. And he was powerful. The interesting thing about Richard was that his backhand shot was as good as his forehand; it didn't make a difference, the shot was always on goal.

Richard wasn't much at handling the puck coming out of his own end, but his centerman would set him up and from the blue line in, if you so much as blinked your eyes or turned your head, he was gone. He also had a knack of sticking out his left leg as he cut left towards the net. He would sort of slip that leg out and spin in toward the net. He would lock in with the puck on his backhand. To stop him, you had to stay to the inside of him, because if he got to the inside, he had you beat.

My first Stanley Cup win in 1950 was terrific because it was the first and because we won it with Gordie on the sidelines. But the second championship in 1952 was the greatest thrill, because we won it in eight straight games and had a shutout in every one of the four games we played at home. That was when Terry Sawchuk was at his absolute best; every game was up and down and the intensity was fierce. You just didn't want to make a mistake for feat it would cost the team, and of course, I wanted to be a hero just like the next guy on the bench. Once we started putting the wins together, people in

the press began to talk about an eight-game sweep, but all we would think about in the dressing room was winning that night's game; that's how focused we were.

That year we worked hard, created our own breaks and won, but as I said, Sawchuk was phenomenal; four shutouts and a 0.62 goals-against average. To this day I maintain that that was the greatest Detroit team ever.

I say that for several reasons. First of all, we had tremendous confidence in our ability. We always seemed to know—or feel—that we were gong to win no matter who we played.

In the 1952 playoffs Jack Adams had us holed up in Toledo as he had in other years, and then we would take a bus to Detroit for games. When we got on that bus in Toledo you could hear a pin drop all the way to our destination. We'd get out, walk into the dressing room and you still could hear the pin drop! Coach Tommy Ivan would come into the room and Teddy Lindsay would say his little speech, and we all went out on the ice knowing we would win. It became routine.

While all of this was going on, Adams would be playing his little games with us. He always knew when to pull some psychological ploy on an individual or the entire team.

Once, before the playoffs began, he got us in the room and said, "I got a very disturbing phone call." Naturally, everybody in the room started looking around at each other trying to figure out what this was all about. Adams never identified anyone, but then he went on, "A good friend of mine called me and said he saw several of you guys walking out of a bar and you'd had more than one drink."

Meantime, we were thinking, "Jack, let us know which bar," but he would never say. So after he left the room all the guys would get together and say, "What the heck was that . . . what bar . . . who went?"

Of course, we would find out later there was no such thing. Jack had invented the whole story just to make sure we didn't go into bars during the playoffs.

Because of Adams's powerful personality, our coach Tommy Ivan was in the shadows, so to speak. Yet Tommy was a great coach for our team. He knew he had the talent and he never interfered. He knew how to change lines and he would go with whoever his best players were on any given night. Those were the days when teams only used three forward lines, and Ivan saw to it that everybody played a lot.

Tommy didn't say much, but then again, he didn't have to because we had such a great team. We didn't need reprimanding, because in a sense, we coached ourselves and disciplined ourselves. Ivan just guided us along.

When things were going a little bad, Adams would be sure to stir things up, because he didn't believe in sitting back and letting the coach run the team. Jack wanted to be a part of it. Despite that, Ivan and Adams got along, but eventually Tommy jumped to Chicago where he became manager of the Blackhawks. Jack was disappointed in that Tommy didn't tell him about it; he found out by reading it in the newspaper.

Adams wasn't alone when it came to managerial interference. In those days the managers were very powerful—Adams in Detroit, Conn Smythe in Toronto—so it wasn't unusual for them to get involved in the operation of the club.

One time when Metro Prystai was in a slump and we were having a practice, Adams came down to the sideboards and called Metro over right in front of the entire team. "Let me see your stick," Adams said. Prystai liked to doctor his stick with more and more tape so it wouldn't break.

Jack alluded to Aurel Joliat, a little guy who had starred for the Canadiens in the late 1920s and early 1930s. "That looks like one of Aurel Joliat's sticks that's been out in the rain all summer," said Jack. With that, he took the stick and threw it across the rink. "Go in there and get yourself a new stick."

He did something like that to Gordie Howe who used a short stick even though Adams wanted him to use a longer one. One year we had a rookie named Billy McNeil who also was using a short stick. Jack called Billy over because he wasn't scoring any goals and said, "Let me see that stick. I want you to use a long stick like Gordie's." So Billy went over and got one of Gordie's sticks and it was even shorter than his!

My last Stanley Cup win was in 1954-55, a season that had one of the wildest endings in NHL history. That was the year that we were neck and neck with the Canadiens for first place, but they were leading down the stretch and Rocket Richard was sitting on top of the scoring race.

As we hit the last week of the season, it looked like Rocket was going to win the Art Ross Trophy and that Montreal would sew up first place. But Richard had an incredible temper and had been in hot water with the league over problems he had had with referees all season. On the next to last Sunday night of the season, he got into a battle in Boston and floored a linesman named Cliff Thompson. League president Clarence Campbell ordered a hearing on the following Tuesday and then stunned everyone by suspending Richard, not only for the remaining games of the season, but for the entire playoffs as well!

It so happened that the schedule called for us to play a game at The Forum on St. Patrick's Day night, March 17, 1955, which was right after Campbell had announced his suspension of Richard. You can imagine that Montreal was in an uproar. The Rocket was the biggest hero in the entire city, if not the entire Province of Quebec, and the fans—especially the French Canadians—were furious about the decision.

We knew all about this by the time we got into our dressing room for the start of the game. Richard was sitting in the stands near the ice, and later, Campbell would come to his seat—up higher—with his secretary.

The game started, and when Campbell arrived, late, a fan ran up and attacked him. Then somebody threw a tear gas bomb and the smoke went up all over the arena. Adams got us all together and said we had better get dressed and get out of the arena as fast as we could. He said the people outside on St. Catherine Street were rioting. Suddenly, a couple of policemen came down and we followed them out of the building. The riot went on into the night, but we escaped unscathed.

As a result, the game was forfeited to us and we went on to win the regular season championship again. That was our seventh first place in a row. Rocket Richard lost the scoring title to his teammate Bernie Geoffrion and we wound up playing Montreal in the finals. They didn't have the Rocket, but they took us to seven games before we beat them at Olympia.

HOW DETROIT WON
THE 2002 STANLEY CUP

It was not easy; be sure of that.

Winning the Stanley Cup in the Spring of 2002 was one of the most demanding challenges that ever confronted a National Hockey League club.

That the Red Wings were able to surmount the obstacles—starting with a difficult Vancouver Canucks uprising—is a tribute to the patience, fortitude, perserverance and determination of coach Scott Bowman's club.

More than anything, it is a testment to the unabashed greatness of a roster that encompassed captain Steve Yzerman, goalie Dominik Hasek, defenseman Nicklas Lidstrom, forward Brendan Shanahan and senior citizen, Igor Larionov, among the sterling cast.

The hallmark of a champion team is its ability to handle adversity and come from behind to win. On more than one occasion—starting with the first playoff round in Vancouver—Detroit demonstrated that admirable ability.

Let's examine the trail to the 2002 Stanley Cup, round by round.

DETROIT VS. VANCOUVER

Although the Red Wings finished with the best record during the regular season (116 points), they received the scare of their lives from the Vancouver Canucks.

Coach Marc Crawford had his Canucks in excellent position for an upset. Vancouver had just completed a superb homestretch run, annexing a playoff berth at the tail end of the season.

A sizzling hot club, the Canucks merely continued their heads-up play at Joe Louis Arena where they stunned the home crowd with successive victories; first, 4-3 in overtime and then, 5-2.

Facing such a confident club at their home rink in British Columbia was a daunting prospect for Bowman and his assistant coaches, Dave Lewis and Barry Smith.

Once again, the Canucks played hard and well. The scored was tied 1-1 late in the second period when defenseman Lidstrom launched a seemingly innocent slap shot at Vancouver goalie Dan Cloutier.

The odds of a 90-foot blast going in—especially during the playoffs—are slim, particularly when a netminder such as Cloutier had been playing the best goal of his life.

But the shot beat him and the goal stunned the Canucks to the very core. Meanwhile Hasek stopped Todd Bertuzzi, Vancouver's best forward, on a penalty shot. Cloutier never recovered after the puck fluttered under his catching mitt and allowed nine goals on the next 32 shots he faced.

"If I don't let that in," Cloutier later said in reflection, "it might have been a different game."

And a different series.

But he did blow it. Detroit won the game, 3-1, and returned to Vancouver for Game Four, which the Wings won, 4-2. Yzerman, playing despite a severely sore knee, scored the game-winner early in the third period.

Suddenly, the series was tied and reverted to The Joe where Hasek blanked the

Canucks, 4-0. Sergei Fedorov picked up the scoring slack with two goals and an assist.

With a three games to two lead, the Red Wings

Nearly one million fans attended the Detroit Red Wings' Stanley Cup winning parade on June 17, 2002 in Detroit.

jetted back to British Columbia and wrapped up the opening round with a 6-4 triumph. Brett Hull scored a pair of power play goals and a shorthander while Larionov and defenseman Chris Chelios each tallied four points.

Despite the come-from-behind series triumph, the Red Wings were uncertain of their ability to stay on track. Although Hasek recorded a key shutout, his play was erratic and left critics wondering whether he had enough solid play left to take Detroit to the Finals.

Round Two would provide a good criteria.

DETROIT VS. ST.LOUIS

One of the keenest rivalries in major league hockey would be rekindled as the suddenly-revived Red Wings took on the Blues of St.Louis.

Like Detroit, St.Louis boasted a high-priced squad of talents imported to deliver the first hockey championship to the Mound City. But unlike the Red Wings, the Blues would attempt to do with with an inexperienced playoff netminder, Brent Johnson.

This time the faithful at Joe Louis was not traumatized in the opening two games as they had been in

the first round. Hasek pitched a 2-0 shutout in Game One and was good enough to beat the Blues, 3-2, in the follow-up.

Yzerman continued to defy medical science by performing nobly on his gimpy wheels and Hull, a former St.Louis star, had his scoring gun on target.

What was so amazing about Hull was his defense-offense ability. With 56 seconds left in the second period of Game One, he scored his second shorthanded goal of the playoffs.

Carrying the puck from deep in his own end, Hull blasted a wrist shot which dribbled off Johnson's leg. The Golden Brett then grabbed his own rebound and beat the goalie.

An even more pleasant surprise was the play of rookie Pavel Datsyuk, who scored his first playoff goal in the first period and look every bit a veteran with dazzling moves.

With each game, the media questioned Yzerman's ability to go on and the captain responded by simply leading—and scoring. With only 2:46 gone in Game Two, he brought The Joe's crowd to its feet by scoring on the game's first shot. Hull and Luc Robitaille followed with power play goals while Hasek totaled 35 saves to put Detroit ahead, two games to none.

Even more important The Dominator seemed to have found his groove although Game Three—this time at St.Louis—would be a major test.

As it happened, Hasek failed, miserably. After allowing five goals on 16 shots, he was lifted by Bowman while the Wings were humbled, 6-1. Keith Tkachuk, the Blues most potent forward, enjoyed his first career playoff hat trick and Pavol Demitra added four points.

St.Louis now was in position to tie the series at home. The Blues got on track early in the first period when Scott Young beat Hasek on a power play goal.

Then, it happened.

As in the Vancouver series, the Red Wings got a break when they needed it most only this time the break was literal as well as figurative.

At 10:20 of the first period, the Blues captain and balance wheel, Chris Pronger collided with Yzerman, fell over the Detroiter, landing awkwardly on his right knee. Diagnosed with badly torn knee ligaments, Pronger would be lost to St.Louis for the rest of the series.

A tactical blunder by Johnson—he cleared the puck on to Yzerman's stick—led to the game-winning goal at 3:03 of the third period. The power play score was the gamed-winner and a fitting result on Yzerman's 37th birthday. Shanahan, Tomas Holmstrom and Jiri Fischer also tallied in the 4-3 decision.

Once again, a young talent emerged as a force for the Winged Wheelers. This time it was Fischer on the blue line. Working alongside veteran Chelios, Fischer looked more and more like a future all-star.

St.Louis never recovered from the Pronger debacle. Returning to The Joe, the Blues were simply demoralized by the loss of their leader and Hasek's goaltending. The series mercifully ended with a 4-0 victory.

Fischer and Holmstrom scored second period goals while Shanahan sealed the elimination game with a pair in the third. His two earlier assists gave Brendan 100 career playoff points.

The confidence gained by Detroit's improved play was vital because the opponent in Round Three would be the defending champion Colorado Avalanche.

DETROIT VS. COLORADO

This was a playoff marriage made in Heaven— or Hollywood.

The Defending Champions against the Aspiring Champions.

Patrick Roy vs. Dominik Hasek.

Steve Yzerman vs. Joe Sakic.

For the fifth time in seven years the rivals were on collision course and Game One in Hockeytown hardly disappointed.

If anything it demonstrated that the Red Wings depth would make a difference. Grind Liner Darren McCarty paced the victory with a natural hat trick in the third period that broke a tight game and enabled Detroit to skate off with a 5-3 decision.

It marked the first time McCarty had scored three in a playoff game and he was not exaggerating when he opined, "I'll cherish this for a couple of days." After all, there several more games to play.

Sure enough, the defending champs showed their mettle in the return engagement at The Joe. They led Detroit, 3-2, when Roy blundered with 6:35 left in the third period, kicking Lidstrom's richochet off the boards into his own net. It would not be the last time St.Patrick betrayed such flaws.

Despite the psychological advantage, the Wings couldn't put the Avalanche away in overtime. Just past the two minute mark Chris Drury beat Hasek to win the game for the visitors, 4-3.

With the series resuming with two games in Denver, it was difficult to get a line on the eventual outcome. Colorado's recovery was impressive although Roy was not. Detroit was opportunistic yet failed in the clutch.

If nothing else, Game Three underlined the point that the teams were evenly matched. Once again they headed into sudden-death overtime and once again an unlikely hero surfaced.

At about 12:35 of overtime, Hasek cleared a loose puck to Yzerman at center ice. The captain then threaded a pass to a streaking Frederik Olausson. The defenseman released a shot from just inside the blue line. Its trajectory was less than true as it appeared to glance off Avalanche defenseman Martin Skoula's leg and then past Roy. The time was 12:44.

For the Swedish backliner, it was his first playoff goal since April 18, 1992 when he played for the Winnipeg Jets against the Canucks.

Undaunted, the defending champions came right back and tied the series at two, 3-2, without having to go into overtime—although it was close. The game was tied, 2-2, with just under five minutes remaining when Drury scored his second game-winner of the series.

Game Five in Detroit had all the makings of a fatal torpedo to the hull of the good ship Red Wing. While the hometown fans thirsted for the victory that would put their heroes on the threshold of the Finals, Peter Forsberg spoiled the show, scoring 6:24 into overtime, sending the series back to Colorado for what many

Nicklas Lidstrom holds up the Conn Smythe Trophy for playoff MVP after defeating the Carolina Hurricanes, 3-1, in game five of the NHL Stanley Cup Finals on June 13, 2002 at the Joe Louis Arena in Detroit.

in Michigan assumed would be the coup de grace for Bowman & Co.

Each goalie was flawless for most of the first period as the clock wound down for the buzzer to sound. But with just a bit more than a half-minute remaining, a play took place which, ultimately, would be the turning point of the series.

Roy had made a save and assumed that the puck was well-ensconced in his mitt.

As had been his want as a showboat-type goaltender, St.Patrick then lifted his catching glove as if to show all witnesses that he had made yet another stop.

Yes, the glove was there but not the puck. To many, it seemed as if he was doing a magician's "now-you-see-it-now-you-don't" routine. The problem for Patrick was that the puck still was sitting on the paint of the crease, not in his mitt. Shanahan rushed the net and easily tipped his rebound past the embattled goaltender.

It proved to be the winning goal. McCarty added another with 6:33 left in the second period.

A second Colorado gaffe involved coach Bob Hartley. The Avalanche bench boss believed that Hasek was playing with an illegal stick and hoped to capitalize on it during his team's power play. He summoned the referees who then measured The Dominator's blade. Had Hartley been right, Colorado would have had a two-man advantage. However, he erred and the Avalanche was left with no power play at all.

Detroit left a capacity crowd in a state of shock, exiting with a precious, 2-0, win, a Game Seven at home and a Patrick Roy the goat of all goats.

In previous years, Roy had been able to shake off such faux pas and return with a brilliant performance. It was part of his legend.

"We thought it would be a 1-0 game or go into overtime," said Yzerman. "Or be a 2-0 game."

Instead, it was an unequivocal rout.

Holmstrom scored at 1:57 of the first period on Detroit's first shot. By 6:28 of the second period, the score was 6-0 for Detroit and Roy had been yanked.

Hasek delivered his second consecutive shutout after making 19 saves. The Dominator also set an NHL record with his fifth whitewash in one post-season.

The Champions were dead. Now the pretenders had only one more obstacle to The Stanley Cup, a team called the Carolina Hurricanes.

DETROIT VS. CAROLINA

It was supposed to be a snap.

At least that's what several seasoned hockey critics thought about the 2002 Stanley Cup Finals between the Red Wings and the Carolina Hurricanes.

Only two months earlier, teams were evaluating the Raleigh-based sextet as a pushover. The prevailing thought was that if a club could meet the Hurricanes in the first round, it was destined to, at least, reach the second round and possibly head for the Finals.

As it happened, the Hurricanes fooled a lot of observers; not the least of which were the RedWings— especially in Game One at Joe Louis Arena.

The rout-that-was-supposed-to-be was rooted in several theories. One of them was Carolina's inability to win at The Joe. Over the previous dozen games played by the Hurricanes in Detroit, not one was a victory for the Southern club.

Furthermore, the Wings had come off a stirring triumph over Colorado and were super-motivated to bring another Cup to the Motor City.

For a time it appeared that Game One was in the bag; nice and early.

Detroit opened 1-0 and 2-1 leads but late in the second period, Jeff O'Neill wrested a shot past Hasek and the score was tied at two. It remained that way through the third period, necessitating sudden-death overtime.

Already, the Hurricanes had outfoxed the experts. Next, they would outplay the Wings.

Not a full minute had gone by in the extra session when Ron Francis knocked in O'Neill's short pass and Detroit already was down by one game!

Francis' tally—at 58 seconds of overtime—left the capacity crowd speechless although the Detroit skaters had a few things to say, particularly Robitaille.

"We knew all along that they were a great team," said Lucky Luc. "We knew it wasn't going to be easy."

He was right.

Once again, Carolina played Detroit tight; real tight. The score was tied, 1-1, late in the third period and Arturs Irbe was starring once again in goal for the

visitors. With six power plays to that point, the Red Wings still didn't have an extra-man goal but another opportunity was in the making.

This time, Bowman's troops did not fail.

Lidstrom, who would play 34 minutes and 38 seconds over the entire match, one-timed Sergei Fedorov's pass over Irbe's glove and under the crossbar at 14:52 on the power play.

"I felt energized," Lidstrom later explained. "I tried to get the shot up high and it went in."

Before the Hurricanes could regain their composure, Kris Draper whizzed along the left boards and beat Irbe at 15:05 for his first goal in 16 games. It was, however, the second goal of the game by the Red Wings' checking line of Maltby, Draper and McCarty.

"There's not a lot of room out there and they play such a trapping style, that it benefited our line," said Maltby. "The bottom line is that we had to win this game and we did."

The Stanley Cup Finals moved to Carolina for the first time ever and Game Three developed into a competition few hockey historians ever will forget.

A sellout crowd of 18,982 at Raleigh's Entertainment and Sports complex was "college-like in its enthusiasm," as one reporter noted. When Josef Vasicek put the Canes ahead, 1-0, at 14:49 of the first, the place went berserk. It remained loud for most of two periods with the home club nursing a one goal lead. But 41-year-old Igor Larionov muted the noise ever so slightly with the tying goal.

Carolina went ahead again midway in the third period on O'Neill's score and appeared capable of guarding its 2-1 lead through the end of the third period and take a two games to one series lead.

But Detroit would not be denied. With only 1:14 remaining in the third, Lidstrom shot toward the crease where Bret Hull was hoping to do damage.

He did.

As the rubber sailed toward Irbe, The Golden Brett lifted his stick and deflected it past the goaltender. It was Hull's 99th career playoff goal and sent the teams into overtime once again.

Only this time it was over-overtime!

According to most witnesses, the Red Wings took command in the first two extra-sessions by employing four lines to Carolina's three. In the second overtime, each team had a power play but could not score. Irbe robbed Yzerman by extending his stick and glove to just barely deflect the captain's shot at an open net.

In the third overtime, Carolina coach Paul Maurice chose to use his fourth line and it was effective, but not good enough to score.

Back and forth the teams battled, clearly weary as the third extra session moved past its half-way point but neither Irbe nor Hasek gave an inch.

As the clock ticked toward the 15-minute mark, the Hurricanes launched yet another offensive but it was thwarted by the red-and-white defense. Almost instantly, the Red Wings counterattacked, developing a three-on-two break.

Holmstrom nursed the puck in the home team zone, looking for an open man. He spotted Larionov and skimmed him a pass. The slick Russian cut across the slot as backchecking Hurricanes' forward Bates Battaglia desperately slid across the ice to intercept the puck.

Battaglia failed in his mission and Larionov—seemingly relaxed beyond belief—fired a backhand shot that eluded Irbe.

The tie-breaker c ame at 54 minutes, 47 seconds of overtime, or only four seconds shorter than the second longest overtime in the Finals. Dallas' Stanley Cup-winning win over Buffalo. Ironically, that one had been decided by a Brett Hull goal in 1999.

"It's the biggest goal of my career," said Larionov. "Holmstrom made a great play, and I decided to wait a little bit. Battaglia committed to me, and he slid on the ice, so I took my time and put it in."

The victory put Detroit up, two games to one. "It's their team that's sagging," said Hull, and he was right.

Home ice no longer was an advantage to Carolina although the Hurricanes' crowd did everything it could, decibel-count-wise—to help its heroes in Game Four.

If any game of the series could be considered anticlimactic, the fourth contest was the one.

For one thing, Raleigh fans were clamoring for a victory; just one home win would have been just fine for them. For another, each game, so far, had been pulsatingly close and Game Four figured to be a one-goaler as well.

But, happily for Detroit, it was not to be.

Hasek was unbeatable while Irbe proved mortal.

Once again Hull and Larionov delivered the key goals and the final score, 3-0, was reflective of the play.

Perhaps the most astonishing aspect of the victory was the fact that Detroit's senior citizens were performing like colts. "Age," said Hull, "in today's game, has zero to do with anything."

The experience, of course, had a lot to do with the victory. Hull scored his 100th career playoff goal at 6:32 of the opening period. It was his tenth of the 2002 playoffs. His shot rang off the post and into the net in the second period. Larionov posted the second goal early in the third.

Carolina enjoyed an excellent scoring chance late in the first period when rookie Eric Cole skated around Chris Chelios and appeared ready to fake Hasek. But the goaltender anticipated the move and pokechecked the puck harmlessly to the side before the attacker could finish his play.

"Dominik saw the guy was skating with his head down," said Lidstrom, "so he came out and made a great play."

Most importantly, it kept Carolina off the score sheet at a critical point in the game's development. "The break we got," explained Bowman, "was scoring the first goal. In a game like that it was big."

Hull's goal proved to be the winner, making it his 23d game-winning goal in the playoffs and his fourth game-winning goal in the Finals in four years.

It also enabled the Red Wings to return to Hockeytown with only one more victory needed to win The Stanley Cup.

Those who expected a final game blowout in the manner of Detroit's rout of Colorado in the previous round were sadly mistaken.

Once again, the Hurricanes battled hard and well, holding the Red Wings scoreless in the first period. But Detroit's relentless attack finally dented Irbe's armor and at 4:07 of the second period, Larionov passed to Holmstrom who stuck out his stick with his right hand and deflected the rubber through the goalie's pads.

The Joe erupted in a cacophony of joy which was re-doubled nearly ten minutes later when Brendan Shanahan powered in a drive from the right circle at 14:04 with the home club enjoying a man advantage.

Those who expected Carolina to cave in were disappointed. With a shutout streak at 166 minutes and three seconds, Hasek finally was beaten at 18:50 of the second period by O'Neill's power play goal.

The gap was narrowed to one goal and when the third period began, the Hurricanes made a final, desperate effort to tie the count. Time after time they attempted to bisect the Detroit backline but they were repulsed on almost every foray.

Finally, as victory faded away, coach Paul Maurice lifted Irbe for an extra skater. It was a worthwhile gamble—but it failed. With 45 seconds left, Shanahan slid the puck into the unguarded goal and, thus, the game ended in a 3-1 decision for Detroit.

Once the red light flashed, Bowman grabbed his own pair of skates which he had stashed nearby just for the occasion. He laced them on while the crowd roared down the remaining seconds and was fully prepared to skate on the ice when the ultimate celebration began.

"I enjoy being with the guys," said Bowman.

In a matter of minutes, the coach then made the announcement that stunned the hockey world. "It's my last game as a coach," he revealed before NHL Commissioner Gary Bettman even presented the Stanley Cup. "It's time to go. I'm not an old man, but it's time to go. I never knew before, but I felt this year that this was it. I'm so happy that I was able to go out with a winning team."

They won fair and square, no doubt about that.

General manager Ken Holland spent heavily for veterans and they came through. Hasek, who later would announce his retirement, was 37-years-old; Luc Robitaille, 36; Steve Duchesne, 36; not to mention other seniors such as 33-year-old Brendan Shanahan, Chris Chelios, 40, the captain Steve Yzerman and, the dean of them all, Larionov.

Sprinkled throughout the veteran lineup were "middle-aged" hockey types and some very promising youngsters. It was the perfect balance, in this case, because the franchise did what the $65 million payroll was supposed to do—win.

"Detroit has surpassed its status as a mere hockey powerhouse," commented Sports Illustrated, "and become the pin-striped dynasty of the ice."

The comparison to baseball's New York Yankees sat well with the Red Wings. "We are like the Yankees," observed Hull. "Year in and year out this team will be there. They'll always be at the top."

A good part of the success formula had to do with leadership. Yzerman, wounded in the first round and apparently skating on his last legs, appeared to get better as the playoffs progressed. That, in and of itself, was astonishing. If ever there was a captain worthy of his title, Yzerman—originally drafted by Jimmy Devellano—was that man.

"We try to have not only good players but also good role models," said general manager Ken Holland. "Jiri Fischer progressed during the season because he was teamed with Chelios."

Holland was building a young nucleus to complement Sergei Fedorov, Nicklas Lidstrom and Yzerman. "Those three guys had to do it almost on their own through the early and mid-1990s," added Holland, "which is why we lost so many times in the playoffs. I hope that our young players will learn from Chelios and Larionov."

Perhaps they will, but this much is certain; with their third Stanley Cup in six years, critics were labeling the Red Wings as a dynasty. And why not?

Enjoying the accolades in the background were the club owners, Marian and Mike Ilitch.

"They weren't afraid to spend," said Jacques Demers, a former Detroit coach who more recently turned to hockey commentary. "Their goal at the start of 2001-2002 was to win the Stanley Cup for themselves and the fans.

"They—from ownership to management to players and to fans—deserve what they got—a winner!".

PHOTO CREDITS

Page 2	Stan Fischler Collection
Page 3	Stan Fischler Collection
Page 4	Stan Fischler Collection
Page 5	Stan Fischler Collection
Page 7	AP/Wide World Photos
Page 8	AP/Wide World Photos
Page 10	AP/Wide World Photos
Page 13	Stan Fischler Collection
Page 14	Tom Sarro Collection
Page 17	Tom Sarro Collection
Page 18	Tom Sarro Collection
Page 19	Tom Sarro Collection
Page 20	Tom Sarro Collection
Page 23	Tom Sarro Collection
Page 26	Tom Sarro Collection
Page 27	Tom Sarro Collection
Page 29	Tom Sarro Collection
Page 31	AP/Wide World Photos
Page 32	AP/Wide World Photos
Page 34	AP/Wide World Photos
Page 37	AP/Wide World Photos
Page 39	Tom Sarro Collection
Page 41	Tom Sarro Collection
Page 43	Tom Sarro Collection
Page 47	Tom Sarro Collection
Page 49	AP/Wide World Photos
Page 51	Tom Sarro Collection
Page 53	AP/Wide World Photos
Page 54	AP/Wide World Photos
Page 59	AP/Wide World Photos
Page 60	Tom Sarro Collection
Page 62	AP/Wide World Photos
Page 67	Tom Sarro Collection
Page 69	AP/Wide World Photos
Page 71	AP/Wide World Photos
Page 75	Tom Sarro Collection
Page 77	Stan Fischler Collection
Page 79	Stan Fischler Collection
Page 83	Tom Sarro Collection
Page 85	Tom Sarro Collection
Page 88	Stan Fischler Collection
Page 91	Bruce Bennett Studio Archive Photo
Page 92	Bruce Bennett Studio Archive Photo
Page 95	Tom Sarro Collection
Page 97	AP/Wide World Photos
Page 98	AP/Wide World Photos
Page 100	AP/Wide World Photos
Page 102	AP/Wide World Photos
Page 105	Tom Sarro Collection
Page 108	Tom Sarro Collection
Page 109	Stan Fischler Collection
Page 111	Stan Fischler Collection
Page 112	Stan Fischler Collection
Page 115	Stan Fischler Collection
Page 117	Stan Fischler Collection
Page 118	Stan Fischler Collection
Page 120	Tom Sarro Collection
Page 123	AP/Wide World Photos
Page 127	AP/Wide World Photos
Page 128	AP/Wide World Photos
Page 131	Tom Sarro Collection
Page 133	AP/Wide World Photos
Page 135	AP/Wide World Photos
Page 137	AP/Wide World Photos
Page 139	AP/Wide World Photos
Page 141	AP/Wide World Photos
Page 143	AP/Wide World Photos
Page 145	AP/Wide World Photos
Page 146	AP/Wide World Photos
Page 149	Bruce Bennett Studio Archive Photo
Page 152	AP/Wide World Photos
Page 154	AP/Wide World Photos
Page 156	AP/Wide World Photos
Page 158	AP/Wide World Photos
Page 161	Bruce Bennett Studio Archive Photo
Page 163	AP/Wide World Photos
Page 164	AP/Wide World Photos
Page 167	AP/Wide World Photos
Page 168	AP/Wide World Photos
Page 170	AP/Wide World Photos
Page 174	AP/Wide World Photos
Page 175	Bruce Bennett Studio Archive Photo
Page 177	Steve Babineau
Page 179	Tom Sarro Collection
Page 181	AP/Wide World Photos
Page 182	AP/Wide World Photos
Page 183	AP/Wide World Photos
Page 185	Tom Sarro Collection
Page 187	AP/Wide World Photos
Page 202	Tom Sarro Collection
Page 206	Tom Sarro Collection
page 223	Detroit Red Wings
Page 248	AP/Wide World Photos
Page 250	AP/Wide World Photos